Introduction to Animal Behavior

Introduction to Animal Behavior

Roland J. Siiter
Montclair State University

Brooks/Cole Publishing Company

I(T)P® **An International Thomson Publishing Company**

Pacific Grove • Albany • Belmont • Bonn • Boston • Cincinnati • Detroit • Johannesburg • London
Madrid • Melbourne • Mexico City • New York • Paris • Singapore • Tokyo • Toronto • Washington

Sponsoring Editor: *Jim Brace-Thompson*
Marketing Team: *Lauren Harp, Aaron Eden*
Signing Sales Representative: *Ed Yarnell*
Editorial Assistant: *Bryon Granmo*
Advertising Communications: *Kyrrha Sevco*
Production Editors: *Karen Ralling, Janet Hill*
Manuscript Editor: *Jennifer McClain*
Permissions Editor: *Catherine Gingras*
Design Coordinator: *Roy R. Neuhaus*

Interior and Cover Design: *Detta Penna*
Cover Photo: *Jim Brandenburg/Minden Pictures*
Art Coordinator: *Lisa Torri*
Interior Illustration: *Precision Graphics*
Photo Researcher: *Sue C. Howard*
Typesetting: *Carlisle Communications*
Cover Printing: *R. R. Donnelley & Sons Company*
Printing and Binding: *R. R. Donnelley & Sons Company*

For more information, contact:

BROOKS/COLE PUBLISHING COMPANY
511 Forest Lodge Road
Pacific Grove, CA 93950
USA

International Thomson Publishing Europe
Berkshire House 168-173
High Holborn
London WC1V 7AA
England

Thomas Nelson Australia
102 Dodds Street
South Melbourne, 3205
Victoria, Australia

Nelson Canada
1120 Birchmount Road
Scarborough, Ontario
Canada M1K 5G4

International Thomson Editores
Seneca 53
Col. Polanco
11560 México, D. F., México

International Thomson Publishing GmbH
Königswinterer Strasse 418
53227 Bonn
Germany

International Thomson Publishing Asia
60 Albert Street
#15-01 Albert Complex
Singapore 189969

International Thomson Publishing Japan
Hirakawacho Kyowa Building, 3F
2-2-1 Hirakawacho
Chiyoda-ku, Tokyo 102
Japan

Printed in the United States of America

10 9 8 7 6 5 4 3 2 1

Library of Congress Cataloging-in-Publication Data

Siiter, Roland J., [date]
    Introduction to animal behavior/Roland J. Siiter.
        p. cm.
    Includes bibliographical references (p. 368) and indexes.
    ISBN 0-534-34405-4 (casebound)
    1. Animal behavior. 2. Primates—Behavior. I. Title.
QL751.S588 1998
591.5—DC21   98-18907
                                                   CIP

To Katherine W. Ellison
without whom many good things would not be

Brief Contents

Contents

Part Two   Making a Living in the Wild   109

Part Three Mating and Parenting   **193**

Preface

This book was born out of years of frustration in teaching an animal behavior course in a department of psychology. Although there are several very good textbooks that cover animal behavior primarily from a biological point of view, I could find no text that was really suitable specifically for undergraduate students majoring in psychology. The available texts typically presume extensive knowledge of biological facts and principles with which psychology majors are not acquainted and often provide only minimal treatment of material more relevant to psychological issues. Biologically-oriented texts typically treat all species as equal in importance, with an emphasis on process rather than on the behavior of particular species. For me, psychological questions lead naturally to having a closer look at those species most closely related to humans—monkeys, apes, and other primates. For this reason, the last four chapters of this book sample the behavior of representative primate species and make explicit comparisons between human behavior and the behavior of other living primates.

Approach

The general approach to animal behavior I have taken in this book is evolutionary and ecological. Modern scientists understand that animal behavior results from millions of years of evolution, as well as from immediate genetic and environmental forces. A complete account thus requires us to understand not only *how* animals behave currently in their natural habitats but also *why* these behaviors occur rather than other behaviors.

Psychologists traditionally have been concerned primarily with studying animal behavior in the laboratory under controlled conditions to discover causal relationships among variables. While this approach is an essential part of testing theoretical predictions, modern psychologists have become more aware of the importance of comprehending behavior in the wild. Thus, psychologists nowadays are more open-minded about using a variety of methods, including those in the field. I believe this trend will continue as scientists from several disciplines—psychology, biology, neurophysiology, and anthropology—find that they need one another to achieve true understanding.

Although I developed this textbook specifically for an animal behavior course in a psychology curriculum, those teaching similar courses in other departments will find it useful. The biological and ethological approaches to animal behavior are by no means ignored in this text. In fact, my goal was to provide a more balanced approach than those presented in other texts. By balanced, I mean drawing on knowledge from all the disciplines that study animal behavior, presenting a greater range of example species than just those studied the most frequently, decreasing technical jargon and terminology in favor of student readability, and responding to students' interests and curiosity as well as instructors' concerns.

Content

This book is organized into four parts, preceded by an introductory chapter briefly reviewing animal taxonomy and history. Part 1 deals with basic concepts in the study of animal behavior—methods, evolution, genetics, and learning. Part 2 deals with how animals survive by obtaining food, avoiding predators, and living in groups. Part 3 deals with courtship, reproduction, and parenting. Part 4—the truly unique part of this text—focuses on the behavior of our closest relatives, monkeys and apes, and relationships of their behavior to human evolution and behavior.

This text features a balance of the most current research findings with the results of important, classic work on animal behavior. Relative to other texts, the writing style is more informal and down-to-earth, with examples drawn from a great variety of species, many that students want to learn more about, as opposed to examples responding primarily to the concerns of researchers. Although research on animal behavior has been dominated by such small, easily studied species as insects, small birds, and small fish, students respond more enthusiastically to receiving information and examples about species that are exotic, misunderstood, and dangerous, as well as those that are popular, whatever their size and accessibility.

Learning Aids and Supplementary Materials

My textbook is accompanied by an instructor's manual prepared by Anne Bizub, Chris Randall, and myself. Each section of the manual contains a list of terms from that chapter, suggestions for teaching the material in that chapter, as well as supplementary teaching materials, 30 multiple-choice questions, and 15 essay questions. I have attempted to produce a manual that really helps in teaching and testing the material, not just a cursory manual with a minimal number of test items.

Instructors who use this book also can make use of the website associated with the textbook. The website offers a large number of locations that present further information on animal laboratories, current research developments, endangered species, and many reference sources that instructors and students can use, especially for writing papers or doing projects.

Acknowledgments

I could not have written this book without the assistance of many other people, a few of whom I am pleased to mention here. Katherine Ellison, Alberta Handelman, and Suzanne Page read and reacted to the initial versions of the first chapters. They set me on the right track. Anne Bizub read the first draft of the entire manuscript and provided extensive comments and revisions, all of which were valid. Carlos Pratt and George Rotter gave me many helpful suggestions.

A number of people reviewed the first and second drafts, providing corrections and comments, all helpful, and some led to extensive revisions. These individuals included Elaine Baker, Marshall University; Richard Braaten, Colgate University; David Chiszar, University of Colorado; Jean-Louis Gariépy, University of North Carolina, Chapel Hill; William Hodos, University of Maryland; Roger Jennings, Portland State University; James King, University of Arizona; Fred Leavitt, California State University, Hayward; Donald Lysle, University of North Carolina at Chapel Hill; Martha Mann, University of Texas at Arlington; Denis Mitchell, University of Southern California; Chris Randall, Troy State University; Mary Lou Zanich, Indiana University of Pennsylvania.

Considerable thanks are also due to my editors at Brooks/Cole, beginning with Jim Brace-Thompson, whose encouragement and assistance carried me through to the completion of this project.

Finally, I could not have completed the book without the continuous constructive suggestions, encouragement, patience, and understanding of my wife, Diane Delaney.

The input of all these individuals made the final manuscript for this book a much better product.

R. Siiter

CHAPTER 1

Introduction

Although animals have always been with us, the scientific study of animal behavior is a young discipline that has come to fruition only in the 20th century. The fact that animal behavior is relevant to many different disciplines— psychology, biology, genetics, and anthropology, for example—is to some degree the result of historical accident; yet it also reflects how animal behavior is the product of many different forces: environmental, evolutionary, genetic, physiological, and so on.

The purpose of this chapter is to place the modern study of animal behavior in a historical context. While new discoveries about animals are being made all the time, many of today's fundamental questions about animal behavior are the same questions that scientists began to ask 150 years ago when Charles Darwin wrote down his theory of evolution. How did living species of animals evolve from earlier forms? What factors caused specific behaviors and survival strategies to develop? What is the place of humans in relation to other animal species?

Over the past few centuries, we have witnessed the emergence of a system for classifying and naming animal species that is now used by scientific communities across the world. The basics of this system reflect our understanding of the animal's place in nature.

The latter part of this chapter discusses the distinction between functional and prox-imate causal factors in behavior. Because behavior is determined by many factors, any account of behavior involves a multiplicity of explanations.

A songbird, silent most of the year, bursts out in a song unique to its species in the spring. A honeybee zooms back to the beehive and, somehow, communicates to the other bees the location of flowers containing the nectar the bees require in order to live. The giant panda of China appears to be a bear but, unlike most bears, eats only plants. Your pet cat greets your arrival home by rubbing itself against your legs after you come through the door.

These examples of animal behavior represent typical kinds of phenomena that pose important questions for the animal researcher: Why do animals behave the way they do? What kinds of abilities and skills must they have in order to survive? How have an animal's behavior and abilities evolved from its ancestors? Are an animal's behaviors largely built in, or must it learn what to do from experience?

Our modern understanding of animal behavior began in the 19th century with the work of Charles Darwin and his student George Romanes in England. Darwin's theory of evolution inspired biologists and psychologists not only to study animal behavior but also to gain new insights about human nature from animal behavior and evolution. Historically, biologists and psychologists have focused on somewhat different questions and problems and have employed different methods in their approaches to animal behavior. Biologists have put greater emphasis on understanding internal and physiological processes in animals and have tended to study many different animals in their natural habitats while emphasizing built-in behaviors, genes, hormones, and the evolution of behavior. In contrast, psychologists have focused more on how the behavior of individual animals is modified by experience and learning; they have traditionally been identified more with conducting highly controlled laboratory experiments employing only a few species. Recently, these and other differences have become less distinct as the study of animal behavior has come to be more multidisciplinary, combining the scientific efforts of biologists and psychologists with geneticists, neurophysiologists, paleontologists, anthropologists, ecologists, and so on.

The area of psychology concerned with animal behavior has traditionally been called **comparative psychology. Zoology** is the branch of biology that focuses on the classification and physical aspects of animals, whereas **ethology** (from the Greek *ethos* for behavior) is the branch of biology concerned specifically with animal behavior and its causes.

The most recent development in the study of animals, **behavioral ecology,** is inherently interdisciplinary (*eco* from the Greek *oikos,* meaning house). It deals with the interactions of animals with one another and with their physical surroundings, especially in complex, interdependent systems. Ecologists emphasize groups and populations, adaptation and evolution of behavior, and the costs and benefits of particular behaviors to the individual animal.

What this Book Is about

From the point of view of any of these disciplines, the theory of evolution provides the most important set of organizing principles in the study of animal behavior. Scientists want to understand how behaviors have evolved over long periods of time to the way animals behave in the wild today. Consequently, this book focuses on the principles of genetics, the current theories of animal evolution, the principles governing adaptation, and the effects of the environment on the development of behavior.

While some human attributes and abilities are certainly unique in nature, human beings also have much in common with other animals—especially chimpanzees, gorillas, and monkeys. By comparing human behavior with the behavior of other animals, we can often gain insights that may elude us when we focus only on our own species. It is my hope that the reader will gain from this book a better understanding of animal and human behavior and its relationship to both the present and historical natural world.

The survival of endangered species and the protection of the rights of animals in moral societies are—and should be—of great concern to scientists as well as to the general public. Hopefully, this book will also give the reader a greater awareness of the enormity and importance of these problems.

History of the Study of Animal Behavior

Prior to the 19th century, animals were studied almost exclusively in biological terms, or, more specifically, in the language of anatomy and physiology. The behavior of animals was studied only by those who needed information for practical purposes—individuals such as breeders and trainers of hunting dogs and hunting birds, carrier pigeons, and horses. New information was also acquired by farmers and those employing beasts of burden. Much of our knowledge about the practical care, breeding, and training of animals has come to us in haphazard ways from many ancient sources.

The first systematic study of animals is attributed to the ancient Greek philosopher and naturalist Aristotle (384–322 B.C.). Aristotle is considered to be the father of biology and psychology because he performed the first serious empirical studies in these areas and was the first individual whose writings on these topics have survived to the present. His most important works on animals are the *Parva Naturalia* and *Historia Animalium.*

Aristotle believed that all living things could be ordered in complexity on a "ladder of nature" (in Latin, *scala naturae*). Simple creatures were placed on the bottom rungs of the ladder, with human beings on the top rung and other creatures on the rungs in between, depending on their complexity. Many thinkers accepted this idea up to the 19th century. Aristotle also devised the system for classifying animals that we still use today: **genus** for the kind or group to which an animal belongs and **species** for its unique properties. Aristotle was the first thinker to observe animals carefully and then attempt to fathom what those observations meant. For example, after observing fish and whales, he concluded that whales were air-breathing mammals long before many Europeans later insisted on calling them fish.

After Aristotle, the domination of the ancient world by the Roman empire did not produce much new information on animals; the Romans were supreme soldiers, builders, and organizers, but they were not scientists nor systematic observers. The Roman writer Pliny the Elder (A.D. 23–79), for example, does give us detailed descriptions of the natural world of his time, but much of his accounts are mixed with legends, rumors, and stories.

The culture of the medieval period (roughly A.D. 500 to 1500) did not encourage the gathering of any new information on animal behavior. During this time, the religious authorities and guardians of knowledge in Europe regarded Aristotle and other ancient thinkers as having the last word on these matters. For European medieval people, curiosity was at best irrelevant to life and at worst a sin because their destiny (heaven or hell) did not depend on it. The doctrine of *mind-body dualism* dominated thinking about animals and human nature. Dualism held that the body and the soul are made of different substances. While both animals and humans have physical bodies, it was presumed that only human beings had immortal, incorporeal souls. It was further presumed that the human essence was contained in the soul, whereas the human body was less important and temporary. Thus, the medievals did not believe they could learn anything significant about human nature by studying animals. Humans and animals were viewed as distinctly different creatures; animals were regarded as lower beings created for the use of human beings. Such an attitude made comparisons between animals and humans inconceivable and irrelevant.

Medieval scholars did produce illustrated books of animals called bestiaries, but these were generally a jumble of myths, rumors, misinformation, and a few facts about actual animals. (Figure 1.1 shows an example.) These were the acceptable fantasies of their day, and they illustrate how medieval thinkers tried to summarize the wisdom of ancient writers and thinkers. Medievals made little attempt to gain new knowledge by making their own observations of animals.

Until the 19th century, perhaps the single most reliable factual source on animal behavior was *The Art of Hunting with Birds* by the Holy Roman Emperor Frederick II (1194–1250). This book detailed the breeding and care of hawks and falcons, including instructions for training these birds of prey to hunt game, and it contained valuable information on their history, anatomy, and biology. Unfortunately, because this book was written before 1451 when the printing press was invented, it had little impact on the science of the time.

Modern science began with many important events in the 16th and 17th centuries. For example, Andreas Vesalius (1514–1564), a Belgian anatomist and physician, helped rejuvenate anatomy and physiology by performing dissections on the bodies of both dead animals and humans rather than just citing the conclusions of ancient authorities. He concluded that the mind and personality were located in the brain and nervous system, thereby contradicting Aristotle who had maintained that the mind was located in the heart. Still, the animal biology of these times was almost totally descriptive, dominated by attempts to catalog and classify animals as well as plants.

The French philosopher, mathematician, and scientist René Descartes (1596–1650) still accepted mind-body dualism but encouraged others to think of animals as biological machines whose behavior could

Figure 1.1   "The gryphon is at once feathered and four-footed. It lives in the south and in mountains. The hinder part of its body is like a lion; its wings and face are like an eagle. It hates the horse bitterly and if it comes face to face with a man, it will attack him." (*Bestiary* 1992, pp. 38–39)

be explained by mechanical principles. Although this proposal ignited new studies on animal behavior, we no longer think so highly of Descartes's theory that animals, especially our pets, are merely unfeeling machines. Nonetheless, Descartes's work was important in convincing people that animal behavior was governed by laws and principles that could be understood.

A Swedish biologist, Carl Linné, known as Linnaeus (1707–1778), founded modern botany and consolidated the classification work initiated by many of his predecessors. Linnaeus created the system of classifying and naming animal species that we use today, beginning with *System of Nature* (1735). Like his contemporaries, Linnaeus thought each species of animal was eternally fixed in form, each animal being the descendant of an original pair of animals created at the beginning of the world, just as humans were thought to be descended from Adam and Eve.

The first systematic theory of animal evolution was offered by Lamarck (1744–1829). In 1801, he proposed that all living species are descended from older species; specifically, more complex animals developed from earlier, simpler forms. He explained this process by proposing that the more recent organisms inherit the characteristics that their parents had acquired with experiences during their lifetimes, an idea now known as the doctrine of the inheritance of acquired characteristics. One of Lamarck's favorite illustrations of his doctrine was his suggestion that giraffes have acquired long necks because their ancestors stretched their necks upward to reach the highest leaves on trees. Though the doctrine of the inheritance of acquired characteristics has been discredited by modern geneticists, Lamarck was instrumental in popularizing interest in animal and plant evolution in Europe.

The Darwinian Revolution

The modern study of animal behavior and biology is primarily a product of the 19th century, especially of events in the period from 1830 to 1870. The work of Charles Darwin (1809–1882, pictured in Figure 1.2) revolutionized the biological sciences and at last placed human beings in the animal kingdom. Previous thinkers were **anthropocentric,** situating human beings at the center of the universe and considering them to be in charge of everything and to be intrinsically superior to animals. In *The Descent of Man* (1871), his most controversial book, Darwin argued that human beings and all other living animals evolved, over time, from earlier forms of life.

In *The Origin of Species through Natural Selection* (1859), Darwin sought to clarify the principles that could explain evolution. Because he knew his ideas were controversial and would be met with scorn, Darwin was very cautious and spent over 20 years gathering evidence in support

Figure 1.2 English naturalist Charles Darwin, painted in 1840.

of his conclusions, refraining from publishing his ideas. He was finally persuaded to present his work to other scientists when Alfred Russel Wallace (1823–1913) independently discovered the same evolutionary principles on which Darwin had been working. The theory of evolution has been associated primarily with Darwin because of the enormous amount of evidence he had presented to support the theory.

In the early 19th century, ideas about animal evolution were popular in Europe. They were mixed with notions about the gradual ascendance and "natural" or predestined dominance of human beings over nature and animals. However, Darwin not only succeeded in establishing animals and humans in the same causal universe, he maintained that all animals are ultimately related to each other by being descendants of common ancestors. To him, the differences that exist between humans and animals are quantitative, not qualitative. Therefore, he reasoned, by studying animals and their evolution, we might learn some things about human beings since all animal evolution is from a common origin and is governed by one set of principles. The main difference between Darwin and his predecessors is that Darwin sought to describe the actual causal mechanisms that produce evolutionary changes rather than just to describe the changes. The most important evolutionary mechanism to Darwin and Wallace was natural selection. The issues of evolution and natural selection and their implications will be examined more closely in Chapters 3 and 10. In its time, Darwin's theory was initially controversial and hotly debated, but because he had provided in his books so much evidence in support of this theory, it was not very long before serious scientific thinkers accepted Darwin's fundamental ideas as fact.

Darwin is considered to have begun the modern scientific study of animal behavior with his book *The Expression of Emotion in Men and Animals* (1873). In this book, Darwin demonstrated how facial expressions in humans are related in their evolution to similar expressions in other species. For example, the human expression of baring teeth when angry may have evolved from the same origins of this expression in wolves. Darwin's book was the first important work to explain a significant aspect of human behavior in terms of its evolution in other animals. It also described the behavior of animals in words that humans use to describe their own feelings and experiences and encouraged other thinkers and scientists to do likewise.

Darwin's student, George Romanes (1848–1894), author of *Animal Intelligence* (1882) and *Mental Evolution in Animals* (1884), is credited with the idea that animal behavior should be studied for the purpose of understanding the behavior of human beings. Romanes tried to demonstrate that mental differences among animals are simply a matter of degree of complexity rather than any difference in quality. Romanes used the **anecdotal method** whereby, after obtaining the facts, stories, and descriptions of specific animal behavior, he tried to infer what sort of mind would be necessary to produce that behavior. He assumed that the same mental processes occurring in his mind would be occurring in the minds of animals, and any similarity between the behavior of humans and other animals implied a possible similarity in mental states, thinking, and consciousness. According to Romanes, for example, if we present an animal with a novel stimulus and the animal runs away, we may infer that it is experiencing fear because that is what we experience when we run from perceived danger.

Anecdotal methods in the study of animal behavior are now regarded as invalid because they tend to be subjective, they overestimate animal abilities, and they attribute to animals traits and experiences they may not have. Modern scientists believe that Romanes too readily attributed to animals complex processes that occur in human minds. Although modern researchers object to this unrestricted **anthropomorphizing** (attributing human characteristics to animals) to account for animal behavior, Romanes is nevertheless recognized as important for stimulating the development of comparative psychology and encouraging scientists to investigate the workings of the minds and consciousness of animals in addition to examining their overt behavior and utility to humans.

The discovery of the basic principles of modern genetics was made by Gregor Mendel in 1866, but these principles were not generally accepted by the scientific community until around 1900. At this time Darwin's theory of evolution had gained widespread acceptance, and Mendel's genetics further reinforced the theory. Currently, Darwin's theory is formulated in terms of our knowledge of genetics, which will be discussed in Chapter 4.

Another development that helped to increase interest in animal behavior was the publication of the *Principles of Psychology* (1892) by the American psychologist William James. The most widely read and influential work in psychology of its time, this book did much to transport Darwin's theory to America and to encourage the study of animal behavior. James accepted Darwin's theory and encouraged others to apply it to the study of the adaptive functions of human consciousness. Like Darwin and Romanes before him, James assumed that animal and human minds differed only in degree, not in kind. Therefore, he assumed, it should be possible to discover those aspects of the human mind that give humans their unique abilities. He believed the study of animal behavior and consciousness would contribute to this understanding.

Objectivity and Behaviorism

In 1894, C. Lloyd Morgan (1852–1936), a British psychologist, published *Introduction to Comparative Psychology,* one of the earliest textbooks to summarize the new discipline of animal behavior. Morgan became famous for "Morgan's canon"—or rule—which is as follows:

> In no case may we interpret an action as the outcome of the exercise of a higher psychical faculty, if it can be interpreted as the outcome of the exercise of one which stands lower in the psychological scale.

In other words, we should not look for more complex or sophisticated explanations for animal behavior if simpler ones are available. In general, this is an old idea in science, but Morgan was the first to state the idea explicitly for the study of animals. This marked the beginning of greater objectivity in the science of animal behavior.

In 1913, John B. Watson (1878–1958) founded the school of *behaviorism* in America, which advocated complete objectivity in psychology. Watson insisted on studying humans and animals with the same methods and resisted any speculation on "the mind" or the nature of consciousness. He rejected the use of any subjective process to explain observable behavior. These ideas ushered in the dominance of behaviorism in American psychology, which lasted until the 1950s.

Behaviorism marked the beginning of the preoccupation of American psychologists with rigorous control in performing laboratory experiments for the study of conditioning and learning processes in a few species—mainly the white rat, *Rattus norvegicus*. Since the emphasis was on controlled laboratory studies, psychologists did not learn a great deal about the behavior of wild animals in their natural habitats. The study of animal behavior became somewhat narrow in its focus and concentrated on a few methods and specific questions about the nature of learning and conditioning in only a few animal species. It was assumed that learning processes took place relatively independently of the species and its environment and that comprehending learning in a few key species would reveal the nature of learning in all species. This assumption, we now know, is not always true.

In a classic article, Beach (1949) implored comparative psychologists of his time to examine species other than the rat and processes other than learning and conditioning, noting that "excessive concentration upon a single species has precluded the development of a comparative psychology worthy of the name" (p. 6). Further, he stated that "they appear to believe that in studying the rat they are studying all or nearly all that is important in behavior" (p. 8).

Ethology

While comparative psychology was developing in America, a movement arose in Europe in biology, called **ethology.** Konrad Lorenz (1981) traced the beginnings of this movement back to the work of Charles Otis Whitman at the University of Chicago and Oskar Heinroth of the Berlin Aquarium in Germany.

Both Whitman and Heinroth studied birds and noted that the behavioral displays in many species of birds appeared to be extremely constant or stereotyped. For example, the courtship rituals of waterbirds such as ducks and geese typically involve a series of behaviors exchanged by the male and female bird before mating (see Figure 1.3). Later Lorenz called these constant behaviors **fixed action patterns** or FAPs. A FAP is a complex behavior that is typically initiated by a stimulus but continues until it is finished. Ethologists have also often considered FAPs to be unlearned (innate) and present in all members of a species. The gaping response of a young bird when a parent lands on the nest to feed it is a FAP, whereas the parent bird's placing the food in the bright red mouths of the young is also a FAP.

The specific environmental stimulus that triggers a FAP is generally called a **sign stimulus;** such stimuli are called **releasers** when the stimulus is a member of the same species. Ethologists determine what the precise releaser stimulus is by constructing artificial stimulus models and testing the models on the animals. For example, during the breeding season of the three-spined stickleback, a small fish inhabiting streams in Europe, the male stickleback will display a bright red un-

Figure 1.3   A pair of wandering albatrosses (*Diomedea exulans*) in a courtship dance before mating.

derside as it tries to establish a small nesting territory for itself at the side of a stream (see Figure 1.4). This red color is a releaser for aggression in other male sticklebacks since the breeding males compete with each other for the territories. By constructing models of sticklebacks and varying their size, color, and shape, researchers have found that it is the color red alone that stimulates aggression in other males. Following Lorenz's work on birds in the 1930s, Niko Tinbergen's classic studies of releasers in the stickleback fish (1951) helped establish ethology as a separate branch of biology.

After World War II, the study of ethology was led in Europe by Lorenz, Tinbergen, and Karl von Frisch, among others. These men were not behaviorists but, rather, trained biologists who did field studies on animal behavior in their natural habitats. They used evolutionary principles and made comparisons between closely related species. The ethologists succeeded in focusing the study of animal behavior on naturally occurring behaviors in the wild rather than on experimentally controlled behaviors in the laboratory. While the American behaviorists were more concerned with specific mechanisms and the development of behavior in the animal's youth, the ethologists were concerned with the purposes that behavior serves and how those behaviors evolved.

Figure 1.4   The appearance of the male three-spined stickleback (left) during the breeding season includes a red underside, a releaser of aggression in other breeding males.

Behavioral Ecology

The most recent development in the study of animal behavior, behavioral ecology, is inherently interdisciplinary, with greater emphasis than earlier approaches on the evolutionary principle of adaptation. Sometimes behavioral ecologists are labeled as "adaptationists" in the study of animal behavior. Behavioral ecologists regard the earth as a complex whole of interacting systems of organisms, environments, processes, and other factors. They are often trained zoologists who have focused on the natural history and adaptation of a species to its environment. This approach will be explained in more detail in the next chapter, with many detailed examples appearing throughout this book.

A movement related to ecology is **sociobiology,** which began in the 1970s. Biologists, including E. O. Wilson of Harvard University, refocused the interest of scientists in the biological sciences on the roots of social behaviors in animals. How much of our social behavior is determined by biology and how much by culture? In some species, especially in social insects such as ants and termites, social behavior appears to be completely controlled by biological factors. The behavior of the entire ant or termite colony is under the control of pheromones (chemical scents) emitted by the queen ant or termite. And while human social behavior is certainly more influenced by culture and learned experiences than is ant behavior, sociobiologists have succeeded in creating new interest in the potential biological origins of social behaviors in many species. Some of the research and theory on the biological origins of human social behavior will be reviewed in the last chapter of this book.

What have we learned from this brief historical sketch of studying animal behavior? First, like most of psychology and other life sciences, this is a young discipline that is continuing to grow. Second, we have learned that Darwin's theory of evolution and our modern understanding of genetics contain principles at the heart of the discipline. In this book, we ask, What are the origins of specific behaviors? How did these behaviors arise through geologic time? What does a behavior accomplish for an animal? Third, we have learned that different scientists with different backgrounds approach the study of animal behavior in various ways and that all the methods are needed and useful. This book is concerned with explaining animal behavior primarily in the natural world, not in the laboratory; for while the laboratory is useful for clarifying causal relationships among variables and for testing specific theories, ultimately we want to explain what happens in the world in which animals ordinarily live.

Animal Classification

In the last 200 years, scientists across the world have settled on a system, called **taxonomy,** for classifying and naming animals (as well as other living things) in such a way that the name indicates the relationship of that animal to other animals. Some of the basic facts about taxonomy, with some examples, appear in Table 1.1. The scientific name for an animal is given in Latin or in a Latinized form that often has no resemblance to its common name. All animals belong to the *kingdom* Animalia. Plants, fungi, bacteria, and other single-celled organisms make up other kingdoms. The same classification and naming rules apply in each kingdom.

Within the kingdom of animals are major subdivisions based on crucial differences in anatomy and physiology. These subdivisions are summarized, from most inclusive to most specific, in Table 1.1. The table shows that the grasshopper is an animal, but, unlike us, it is not in phylum Chordata since it does not have a spinal cord. Insects, spiders, crabs, and lobsters belong to phylum Arthropoda, which includes many animals that have external skeletons. Within kingdom Animalia, there are about 33 *phyla* of living animals. Each phylum contains divisions called *classes;* in phylum Chordata, one of these is Mammalia, the mammals. Within the classification Mammalia, human beings, gorillas, chimpanzees, and the many species of monkeys belong to the *order* Primates.

Each of these, in turn, belongs to a different *family*. Our closest living animal relatives are other primates. The human family is Hominidae, of which living human beings (*Homo sapiens*) are the only surviving representative. Elsewhere on the table, the family Canidae comprises dog-like animals, including the domestic dog, whose scientific name is *Canis familiaris*.

Taxonomists have tried to assign names that identify the most important characteristics of each group. For example, the Mammalia have mammary glands to nurse their young. Some of these names have made their way into English; for example, mammals are Mammalia and carnivores (meat-eating mammals) are Carnivora.

Genus is the nearest, most specific group or category to which an animal belongs. Animals of the same genus, such as the wolf and the coyote, are usually closely related genetically and in terms of evolution. Species that differ greatly from each other in size and behaviors may

TABLE 1.1 **Some Examples of Animal Taxonomy**
Zoologists classify animals into categories according to their genetic/evolutionary relationships to related species as far as can be determined. Taxonomic categories are given Latinized names, a sample of which follows:

Category	Human	Dog	Lab rat	Bald eagle	Grasshopper
Kingdom	Animalia	Animalia	Animalia	Animalia	Animalia
Phylum	Chordata	Chordata	Chordata	Chordata	Arthropoda
Class	Mammalia	Mammalia	Mammalia	Aves	Insecta
Order	Primates	Carnivora	Rodentia	Falconiformes	Orthoptera
Family	Hominidae	Canidae	Muridae	Accipitridae	Acridiidae
Genus	*Homo*	*Canis*	*Rattus*	*Haliaeetus*	*Schistocerca*
Species	*sapiens*	*familiaris*	*norvegicus*	*leucocephalus*	*americana*
Variety	"races"	"breeds"	"strains"	"subspecies"	"subspecies"

(Mnemonic device for remembering main classification categories: <u>K</u>ing <u>P</u>eter <u>C</u>ame <u>O</u>ver <u>F</u>rom <u>G</u>ermany <u>S</u>eeking <u>V</u>ariety.)

Other categories are also sometimes used. For example, *Homo sapiens* also belongs to the suborder Anthropoidea and the superfamily Hominoidea in some classification schemes.

Some Members of Family Canidae—Doglike Animals

Common name	African wild dog	grey wolf	coyote	red fox	black-backed jackal
Genus	*Lycaon*	*Canis*	*Canis*	*Vulpes*	*Canis*
Species	*pictus*	*lupus*	*latrans*	*vulpes*	*mesomelos*

nevertheless be closely related genetically, as are the mountain lion or cougar (*Felis concolor*) and the domestic cat (*Felis catus*).

Today the term **species** denotes a particular group or population of animals that not only can but do naturally interbreed with each other. Before this century, however, the definition of a species was not so precise. For example, lions and leopards are of different species not because they can't breed with each other—they can—but because in the wild they do not. Thus, the modern definition of a species depends partly on biology (reproductive compatibility) but also on behavior (preferring to breed with each other).

Of course, there are also differences between animals within a species. When these differences are consistently related to differences in the animals' habitats, the various categories within a species may be called "subspecies," "races" (e.g., gorillas), "strains" (e.g., rats), or "varieties." If the subspecies group also has a name, it is listed in small italicized letters after the species name (e.g., *Gorilla gorilla serengeti* vs. *Gorilla gorilla beringei*). The scientific name of a species always consists of two italicized words: the genus name (capitalized) followed by a modifier (not capitalized). Humans are *Homo sapiens,* "man the wise" or "the smart human."

As science gathers new information and makes new discoveries, taxonomic classifications may be changed or remain unsettled. For example, it has been debated for years how to classify the giant panda of China, *Ailuropoda melanoleuca*. At different times, it has been classified with bears (family Ursidae), with raccoons (family Procyonidae), or in a family of its own, Ailuripodidae. Despite the fact that the giant panda is primarily a vegetarian and eats bamboo plants, there is no question that it belongs in the order Carnivora; probably sometime in its evolutionary past it was forced by circumstances to switch to a plant diet. The smaller red panda (*Ailurus fulgens;* tree-dwelling, red-brown and white) is more often classified with raccoons, though its common name appears to relate it more closely to the giant panda (see Figure 1.5).

You should not get the impression that scientists have succeeded in finding, naming, and classifying every animal in the world. It has been estimated that less than 10% of all arthropods (mainly insects) have been discovered and named; the percentage of microorganisms discovered and named is even smaller. One study (Erwin 1983) that attempted to quantify the insects in a single tree in a South American jungle found about 100 species of beetles alone in the top branches of the tree, and most of these were new discoveries and thus unclassified. On a single day, the *New York Times* (Dec. 12, 1995) described the discovery of 33 new species of small organisms in a cave in Romania, a species of Tibetan red deer (*Cervus elaphus wallachi*) thought to be extinct, and a

Figure 1.5 The giant panda and the red panda are not closely related, though they resemble each other in appearance and share a common label.

new species (*Symbion pandora*) so unique that it may belong to an entirely new and undiscovered phylum of animals! The extinction of many species before scientists ever study them can result in the permanent loss to the world not only of potential lifesaving chemicals and drugs but also of many creatures beautiful and interesting in their own right.

Throughout this book, animal species will be referred to by their common names. In addition, the scientific name of each species will be presented either when the species is first mentioned in the text or when the species is dealt with in some detail.

Questions about Animal Behavior

Why does your cat rub against your leg when you come home?
How do honeybees tell other honeybees where the flowers are?
Why do songbirds sing in the spring but not at other times?

The answers to questions like these are not only of interest to the average individual but also to scientists. Modern scientists are interested in the how and why of behavior, not just in describing and classifying it. When we ask why with respect to animal behavior, there are several different ways of answering the question. Niko Tinbergen (1963a) clarified this issue in an influential paper many years ago.

Functional/Survival Value

One meaning of the question why focuses on what the behavior accomplishes for the organism, what it gets for its efforts. When the cat rubs your leg, what advantage does this give it? What does such behavior provide to the cat that it otherwise might not receive? Scientists always assume that behavior has a function for the organism, though what that function is may not always be obvious.

In animal research, *functional* causes are often referred to as *ultimate* causes, and it is important not to confuse the terms "ultimate" and "functional" with the term "purposeful." *Purpose* tends to imply a degree of future planning or consciousness that scientists are reluctant to attribute to animals. Our everyday, nonscientific language is saturated with terms that imply purposefulness; this is seen vividly in how we talk about our pets. For example, we might describe the cat as meowing in order to get food, or the dog as begging in order to go out, or the parrot as squawking for attention. We inevitably apply our subjective knowledge of human purposes to describe and explain our pets' behaviors: we anthropomorphize.

If purposefulness refers to behavior that is oriented toward the future, it is not what scientists mean by ultimate or functional causes. Causes lie in the evolutionary and developmental past of the individual species, especially in those factors that affect survival and reproduction. Beginning with classic studies in the 1930s, Lorenz (1935) showed that, immediately after ducklings hatch from their eggs, they will follow their mother as soon as they are able. An anthropomorphic or purposeful interpretation of this situation might go as follows: the ducklings follow their mother in order to find food, get her protection, or obey their mother's wishes. But other studies have shown that newly hatched ducklings will follow any moving object after hatching, as long as that object moves in the ducklings' visual field and is large enough (Hess 1973). (See Figure 1.6.) The ducklings will follow a human being or a block of wood! The tendency of the ducklings in the wild to attach themselves to a moving object (called **imprinting**) certainly has a function: it normally enables the ducklings to follow their mother quickly after hatching without further experience. But there is no assumption that ducklings are consciously aware of what imprinting accomplishes for them.

Functional causes are the product of the evolutionary development of the species. Thus, in the evolutionary past of ducks, ducklings that failed to follow their mother had little chance of survival. Those that did follow, and did survive to reproduce as adults, passed their genes on to their offspring, including genes that influenced their offspring to follow after hatching. But the behavior of following is not purposeful in the sense that the ducklings are planning or anticipating their own future.

Figure 1.6   In the laboratory, a duckling will imprint on the first large, moving object it sees after hatching.

Similarly, to continue the example with cats, the behavior of rubbing against people's legs may have gradually evolved from other behaviors with their own functions in evolutionary history.

Evolutionary questions are often difficult to answer because of the remoteness of the evolutionary events. Sometimes comparisons with other closely related species yield clues to the behavior's evolution. So, to get at this question, we might look at other feline species and attempt to determine what functions rubbing behaviors appear to serve in those species.

Proximate/Mechanical Causes

Another response to why a behavior occurs focuses on the immediate or *proximate* stimuli that provoke a behavior at the time it occurs. This response to why also may include what is really the how of behavior—namely, the internal, physiological processes that go on inside the organism when it performs a behavior. For example, we would want to find out why the cat rubs against your leg and not everyone else's, and what events or cues set off the rubbing. Does it rub your leg at some times but not others? And what physiological events take place inside the cat when it behaves this way?

Thus, the search for proximate causes of behavior typically begins with environmental stimuli but eventually leads to an examination of exactly what happens inside the organism—inside its body and nervous system—when the behavior occurs. For example, experiments have shown that some birds migrate successfully from one place to another by using information provided by the earth's magnetic field. To use this information, there must be some physiological mechanism inside the bird's body or brain that can detect the field and its characteristics. Scientists are not satisfied until they can find the exact location of the detector in the animal's body and until they can describe exactly how the detector works.

With proximate causes, we can also include those developmental events and experiences the animal has had during its entire lifetime that may have brought about a given behavior. Do domestic cats have to learn to rub your leg while they grow up? If the behavior is learned, how or from whom do they learn it? Behaviors may also emerge because genetic factors "turn on" certain physical changes and behaviors at certain times during the animal's development (processes sometimes subsumed under the term **maturation**). Animal researchers attempt to determine the necessary and sufficient conditions during growth and development that must transpire for a particular behavior to occur.

In the history of comparative psychology, psychologists have been more concerned with developmental causes and learning than any other kind. The countless number of studies done on learning and conditioning processes in the rat and in human beings have accumulated a great deal of information on the details of learning and memory, although learning has not been studied in very many species.

Thus, the answer to why is not simple. The key here is to keep in mind that any behavior always has both functional and proximate explanations. Often, determining the function of behavior is not so difficult, but we need to conduct careful research to discover the mechanisms underlying the behavior. For example, consider honeybees. In their social order, some bees function as scouts: they leave the hive to search for the nectar of flowers, which is the chief food source for honeybees. Karl von Frisch observed that, shortly after a scout bee returned to the hive, a bunch of bees would fly out together and go directly to the nectar, even when the scout bee stayed back at the hive! We know the function here: honeybees need nectar for food, and, in order for the flowers to reproduce, they need bees to carry pollen from flower to flower. But what is the mechanism?

Most scientists prior to von Frisch were baffled as to how communication among bees occurred. (Bee sounds, perhaps?) Through careful observation and experiments in the 1940s, von Frisch was able to demonstrate that the scout performs a kind of "waggle dance," which the other bees interpret by touch. The direction of the dancing bee's body indicates the angle of the nectar source with respect to the sun, and the speed of the dance indicates the distance away, that is, the faster the dance, the closer the flowers (von Frisch 1967).

Recent research by Kirchner and Towne (1994) has shown that honeybees also use sound as part of their communication (see Figure 1.7). Low-pitched sounds emitted by the dancer help her followers determine where she is and how she is moving in the dark hive.

The process of evolution, therefore, selects those *mechanisms* in the organism which best fulfill the *functions* of keeping the individual animal alive and reproducing. We cannot completely understand the causes of behavior until we understand both the functions and the mechanisms governing behavior and how those behaviors developed during the animal's lifetime and in the evolution of the species.

Figure 1.7 Experimental studies using an artificial dancing bee have shown that the dancer uses sound as well as motion to communicate the location of nectar to the other bees (Kirchner and Towne 1994).

Summary

The modern study of animal behavior is inherently interdisciplinary, drawing on research from psychology, biology, genetics, ecology, and other disciplines. Prior to the 19th century, knowledge about animals was primarily descriptive and for practical purposes. Darwin's theory of evolution provided scientists with a set of organizing principles for understanding animals and human beings, their relationships to one another, and how their traits and behaviors have evolved over geologic time.

The study of animal behavior by psychologists has focused on the role of learning and the environment in the development of behavior, with an emphasis on laboratory studies of a few species. In contrast, biologists have tended to focus more on internal processes, the role of genes, and behavior in natural habitats in a great many species. A more recent development, ecology, is a more middle-of-the-road approach, emphasizing the role of adaptation to the environment.

Animals are classified into a set of hierarchical categories based on their genetic and evolutionary relationships. A particular species of animal has a scientific name consisting of two parts—its genus (the immediate group to which it belongs) and a modifier (identifying its uniqueness). The particular classifications to which an animal belongs can change when new information about its evolution and relationships to other animals is discovered.

The question as to why an animal behaves as it does can be answered in several different ways. Functional/ultimate explanations focus on how behaviors have evolved to assist an animal in its survival and reproduction. Proximate/mechanical explanations include the immediate circumstances that evoke a behavior and the internal processes that accompany it. Proximate explanations also include developmental processes, such as maturation and learning. A complete understanding of behavior requires an account of all of these factors.

Part 1

Scientific Approaches

Most of us have experienced occasions when we have thought of or believed in explanations for animal behavior. Someone may have suggested that the violent behavior of a pit bull dog is born in the breed; or your cat brings home a dead mouse and proudly plops it on your doorstep, displaying its hunting prowess. Explaining the behavior of our pets in human terms is irresistible. Yet scientists must be skeptical about these assumptions, as they insist on discovering the proximal and functional causes of behavior by using methods that are objective and reliable. The next four chapters of this book survey the methods and fundamental operating assumptions underlying the modern study of animal behavior. The fundamental concepts of genetics, adaptation, and learning are joined in the modern, "synthetic" theory of evolution, which synthesizes our understanding of animal behavior under one set of organizing principles. Only through evolutionary principles can we understand how proximate mechanisms in behavior have evolved to serve functional ends.

CHAPTER 2

Research Methods

The scientific approach to the study of animal behavior employs the same methods used by other sciences—observation, experimentation, correlation, theory development, and hypothesis testing. In addition, studying animals has some methods unique to the discipline. The comparative method is used because comparisons within and between species yield valuable clues about the origins of behavior and relationships among species. Another method, cost-benefit analysis, reveals information about how individual animals adapt to their habitats. In this chapter, we will review all of these methods and others. Finally, we will examine a detailed account of attempts by researchers to find out why songbirds sing. The way this question has been researched demonstrates how all methods are needed to investigate a complex question for which the answer differs from species to species.

The latter part of this chapter is a discussion of issues relevant to animal welfare and research with animal subjects. Though animals continue to be a mainstay of medical and biological research, the concern of scientists and the general public for the welfare of animals has led scientists to develop many new, alternative methods that avoid killing or even using live animal subjects.

The study of animal behavior draws on scientific methods developed in many disciplines. This chapter reviews some of the principal methods used and some of those that are unique to the study of animals. Genetic methods will be discussed in Chapter 4 and conditioning methods in Chapter 5.

In general, scientific methods build on observations, hypotheses, predictions, and tests of those predictions, with the eventual goal of developing a comprehensive explanation for the phenomenon studied. However, serendipity—the fortuitous discovery of some phenomenon while scientists are looking for something else—or luck may also play a role. One of the most notable instances of serendipity in the history of psychology was Pavlov's "discovery" of classical conditioning while he was studying digestive processes in dogs. To Pavlov's credit, he recognized his discovery as being more important than what he had been studying and changed the focus of his entire laboratory to the investigation of this new phenomenon.

In the study of animal behavior, we are mainly concerned with what animals do—how they live and behave—in the natural habitats in which they have evolved and typically live. The initial stages of research involve gathering a great deal of factual information, using a variety of methods, that describes how individual members of a species develop, survive, and reproduce. Once this has been accomplished, findings can be tied together into some kind of theory or set of principles. In fact, these steps were followed by Darwin, who laid a solid foundation of observations, facts, and conclusions as the basis for his theory of evolution during many years prior to the publication of *The Origin of Species*. One reason why the theory was so successful from the beginning was that he provided an overwhelming amount of evidence for the fact of evolution and for the mechanisms he hypothesized were responsible for it.

The Beginning: Observational Methods

The study of animal behavior begins with the observation of typical behaviors that animals exhibit in their everyday habitats. Using this method doesn't mean just watching and listening; it includes the systematic recording (videotaping, filming, photographing, drawing, and making a written account) of what is observed. It also requires observing different individuals at different times (e.g., varying seasons, day vs. night, etc.) so that the record samples the behavior of a species and not just the peculiarities unique to an individual. Finally, the observations of different observers must be collected and compared so that observer biases can be taken into account.

Sometimes the only way to observe animal behavior is to place an observer in among the animals in the wild. For example, some of the most famous studies of the great apes were done by Jane Goodall with chimpanzees and Dian Fossey with the mountain gorilla in Africa. To find out how these animals live, both of these women spent great amounts of time with the animals in their environments. They stayed near the animals for years and took great care to do nothing threatening so that the animals would get used to their presence (see Figure 2.1). Gradually, the an-

Figure 2.1   Jane Goodall with a group of chimpanzees in Gombe, Tanzania.

imals learned to accept these observers as harmless fellow creatures. This acclimation process eventually allowed Goodall and Fossey to closely observe behaviors in the wild in a way that no one had ever done previously. The fruits of their effort yielded a host of new discoveries.

Sometimes scientists want their observations to be as free as possible from any intervention or effect of the observer. If observers wish to be relatively close to the animal to be observed, they may choose to remain hidden behind a blind, a shield, or a hut that prevents the animal from detecting them. If a blind is not desirable or practical, the observer may simply make observations from a distance through binoculars.

Often it is important to identify individual animals from a distance, including their sex and perhaps their status within a group of animals. This is a typical problem when studying the behavior of animals that live in large groups or herds. Some animals make this task easy by virtue of their unique characteristics, such as the pattern of stripes on a zebra or antler patterns on many deer species.

Following and observing a wild animal directly in its natural habitat is not always possible, as with, for example, many marine animals or nocturnal predators such as leopards. But modern technology has allowed researchers to solve these problems in other ways. Researchers can safely and harmlessly capture an animal and attach a radio transmitter to it. Armed with a tracking device, the researcher can trace the animal's path. Today there are satellites circling the earth that can receive the signals broadcast by an individual animal and relay the signal to a computer, allowing researchers to track the whereabouts of the animal very precisely over a period of weeks or months. Using these methods, scientists have been able to determine the sizes of the territories that many species range over, including deer species, antelopes, and large predators like bears.

With larger animals, researchers may have to use trucks, boats, or diving gear to actually follow an individual animal. Smaller, nocturnal animals can be followed by first dousing them with a fluorescent dye and later following the dye trail on the ground with a black light. This may be done for as long as eight hours before the dye has completely worn off. In other cases, it may be possible to follow an animal by the signs it leaves, such as tracks, feces, eggshells, the remains of food it ate, or, eventually, the animal's own remains.

Observational methods are criticized most often for their inability to yield causal conclusions and their lack of experimental control. However, observations form the factual base of any science, and naturalistic observations must always be done to answer the essential question, "How does the animal behave?" Ethologists call such a description an **ethogram**—a list of the typical behaviors performed by a species under investigation. After many observations have been made and facts gathered, then other methods that maintain experimental control and establish causality are needed to test theories about why the behavior occurs. In other words, it's appropriate to regard observational methods as most valuable and necessary for the early stages of studying animal behavior.

Ethologists typically begin with observations in the natural setting and try to generate hypotheses about the evolutionary and functional causes of behavior and the underlying biological mechanisms. Then the hypotheses are subjected to testing when possible, sometimes in the laboratory. Although testing hypotheses about the possible functions and mechanisms of behavior is often possible, devising theories about the evolution of behavior often involves guesswork because we cannot go back to distant points in time and see what actually happened.

Experimental Methods

Experiments in the laboratory have often been the preferred method for psychologists. The **experimental method** involves manipulating something (the independent variable) and measuring its effect on something else (the dependent variable) while trying to hold other factors constant. In the study of animal behavior, independent variables typically are conditions in the environment that may have an impact on an animal, whereas dependent variables are measures of the animal's behavior or performance. The laboratory provides a setting where manipulation and control can be maximized because the researchers determine everything that happens to an animal. On the other hand, highly controlled experiments are difficult to do in the wild or in natural habitats where it is simply impossible to control the effects of so many variables.

Despite their ability to provide the researcher with a good deal of control, there are disadvantages to laboratory experiments. Since highly controlled experiments always introduce some artificiality, it sometimes may be difficult to generalize conclusions drawn from lab studies to natural habitats. Animals may simply not behave in their natural habitats as they do in the lab. For example, laboratory rats are semidomesticated animals bred by humans specifically for research purposes. They are typically kept in an environment that is relatively simple when compared to the wild conditions confronted by other rodents.

In order to illustrate more clearly what an experimental study of animal behavior entails, let's examine an experiment by Metzgar (1967). He randomly assigned white-footed deer mice (*Peromyscus leucopus*) to two groups. Mice in the experimental group explored and lived in a room containing logs and trees. Control group mice remained in their laboratory cages. After these experiences, each mouse was placed in the same room with a screech owl (*Otus asio*), which eats mice. The owl caught 11 of the 20 mice that had no prior experience in the room but only 2 of the 20 that were familiar with the room. These results demonstrate that, for the mouse, experience and familiarity with its habitat are important for avoiding predation by owls. The study also illustrates the use of the classic **method of isolation** (or deprivation), in which one group of animals is deprived of some experience while another receives it. With such an experiment, differences in behavior between groups are then interpreted in terms of the effects of differences in experience. (The use of this method to study the effects of early experience on the social development of monkeys is discussed in Chapter 16.)

Since the 1960s, animal behavior researchers have often tried to reap the advantages of both the ethological and psychological approaches. The animal is studied in the field in order to maximize realism and generalizability, but manipulations are also employed to test specific hypotheses about causal relationships. This kind of **field experiment** inevitably yields less control than in the laboratory (a disadvantage), but the loss of control is balanced by the considerable advantage of keeping the situation as natural as possible for the animals studied.

For example, the female digger wasp (*Philanthus triangulum*) digs a nest on open ground in which to lay its eggs. Understandably, the wasp must periodically leave the nest to forage for food. The question is, how does it find its way back to the nest for which the entrance is simply a small hole in the ground? One possible explanation is that the wasp uses landmarks near the nest to locate it. Tinbergen (1958) reported a field experiment to test this hypothesis. While a wasp was in its nest, the researchers placed a ring of pine cones around the opening (see Figure 2.2). When the wasp left the nest, she flew around the area before flying off, possibly looking at the landmarks. While she was gone, the researchers moved the entire ring of cones only one foot away. This was done a number of times after she went foraging. After each of her 13 excursions, she searched for the nest each time but failed to find it. She was finally able to find the nest opening only when the researchers returned the pine cones to their original position. This field experiment provided clear evidence that the wasp does use her memory of local landmarks to relocate her nest.

Figure 2.2   A female digger wasp will memorize local landmarks so that she can return to her nest, which is a small hole she has dug in the ground.

Correlational Methods

When correlational methods are used, we look for measurable changes in animal behavior that are predictable from some other variable we can measure, like some state inside the organism or some factor in the environment. Unlike an experiment, nothing is manipulated by the researcher. For example, many animals that live in colder climates become more active when the weather is warmer. Therefore, a positive correlation exists between animal activity and air temperature: as temperature rises, activity increases. Does this mean the rise in temperature "causes" this greater activity? The problem in drawing a causal conclusion from the consistent relationship between activity and temperature is that animal activity may be provoked by many other uncontrolled factors that also vary with temperature—greater food availability, greater sunlight, higher humidity, the animal's internal clock, and so on. To arrive at a causal conclusion, an experiment must be conducted in which the possible causal factor is manipulated (e.g., temperature), behavior is measured (e.g., animal activity), and the other factors are held constant (e.g, humidity or amount of sunlight). A correlation can suggest a possible causal connection, but only experiments can verify that causation actually occurs.

Correlational methods have been used much more often by psychologists in the study of human behavior than in the study of animals. This has occurred because it is neither ethically permissible nor desirable to manipulate many kinds of variables when studying humans. For example, psychologists are very interested in the differences in intelligence and personality among individual human beings, including their possible causes and effects. However, it is neither practically nor ethically desirable to experimentally manipulate human personality or intelligence nor to manipulate environmental variables that might affect intelligence or personality. The best that can be done is to develop sophisticated methods to measure many aspects of intelligence and personality and to correlate these measures with other factors.

On the other hand, laboratory animals often enable psychologists and other scientists to manipulate experiential and individual factors that could not be manipulated with humans. Animals, for example, can be deprived of many early experiences for considerable lengths of time in order to ascertain the effects of these experiences. In addition, differences in intelligence among groups of animals can be created by selectively breeding for those differences, as described in Chaper 4.

The Comparative Method

The **comparative method** of research involves comparisons of behavior within species or comparisons among different but often related species. It can also involve comparisons between ancient and modern species for the purpose of drawing inferences about the behavior of extinct species from our knowledge of living animals. The comparative method attempts to answer questions such as, Are individuals of one species less successful in surviving alone than those who live in groups? Is a difference in behavior between closely related species due primarily to environmental differences or genetic differences? What forces caused ancient species to evolve into their modern descendants? By employing this method, we see how natural selection itself has "experimented" over evolutionary time to produce animals that are optimally adapted to their environments.

Comparisons among Living Species

Comparisons of individuals within a species may reveal the different strategies or lifestyles that existing individual animals use in different habitats to optimally survive and reproduce under different conditions. On the other hand, comparisons of different species in similar environments may reveal how these different animals have evolved different (or similar) solutions to the same environmental challenges.

Comparisons among related species may reveal the factors that have caused different species to evolve their differences in behavior as well as in physical traits. For example, **ungulates** are four-legged, hoofed mammals, many species of which can be found in Africa. Some familiar species include wildebeests, zebras, giraffes, warthogs, gazelles, impalas, and many antelopes. These animals vary greatly in size, diet, habitat, and lifestyles. One of the smallest antelope species is the dik-dik (*Madoqua guentheri*). It is only 14 inches tall, weighs about 13 pounds, and is a forest dweller. One of the largest ungulates is the common eland (*Taurotragus oryx*). It lives on the plains and may stand 6 feet tall at the shoulder and weigh up to a ton. Many other species range in size between these extremes. For example, the gerenuk (*Litocranius walleri*), another antelope species, stands about 3 feet tall, weighs about 110 pounds, and browses its meals from bushes and the leaves of trees but not grass. The dik-dik, gerenuk, and eland are pictured in Figure 2.3. African ungulates also vary in their lifestyles, some living in herds, some in small groups, and others solitarily.

Jarman (1974) tried to sort out all these factors by identifying the major environmental variables related to the different lifestyles of 74 African ungulate species. Initially, he classified these species into five categories by their body sizes because body size imposes severe limitations on where individual animals can live. Smaller antelopes like the dik-dik, for example, cannot survive on the open plains because of the

Figure 2.3   Three African antelope species: (clockwise from top left) the tiny dik-dik, the moderate-sized gerenuk, and the gigantic eland.

predators that hunt there (e.g., wild dogs, hyenas, and lions). So dik-diks live in the forest where there are few large predators and where they can hide effectively. Larger ungulates like the eland live on the open plains because large adult animals can either repel predators or outrun them. Those ungulates in the middle range of size, like the gerenuk, tend to live in habitats between the forest and plains extremes, unless, like some swift species of gazelles and impalas, they can run extremely fast and elude most predators.

In terms of nutrition and food, smaller antelopes have faster metabolisms. Thus, the dik-dik can satisfy its needs for higher-quality food by eating berries and shoots in the forest. On the other hand, the larger ungulates that live on the plains eat plants of poorer quality and must spend many hours a day bulking up on it. Plains antelopes must wander over a large home range, often in herds, to keep up their food intake. Some herds are dominated by one breeding male that tries to keep other breeding males away from his harem of females. Dik-diks live alone or in mating pairs and defend small territories where food resources tend to be concentrated. The middle-sized antelopes like the gerenuk tend to have lifestyles in between, living in smaller mobile groups and grazing or browsing in the bush or at the edges of forests.

In conclusion, the different lifestyles of African ungulates appear to be related to their body size, dietary requirements, and predation pressures. Body size heavily influences where the animal can live because of the presence of predators, but once the animal lives in a given habitat, the ecology of the habitat influences social organization and lifestyle. It can be argued further that small ungulates do not herd because groups of small animals get the attention of predators. Thus, animals like the dik-dik avoid predation by being solitary and by hiding. Large ungulates wander in herds for group defense (e.g., greater vigilance or watchfulness) and because dominant males try to keep many females for themselves.

Comparisons Across Time

Comparisons with closely related species may also give us clues about an animal's evolutionary history. Fossils of many long-dead species of animals may not always survive, especially when those animals had mainly soft tissues without bones. Under these circumstances, however, we may be able to make some tentative conclusions by examining several living representatives of the group to which the extinct animal belonged. Researchers often assume that traits that are widespread among closely related species have been inherited from some single, common ancestor that had that trait. Even bizarre, difficult-to-comprehend traits and behaviors are assumed to have evolved through steps, with each step having some adaptive advantage. More will be said about this in Chapter 3.

Like correlational methods, the comparative method yields tentative conclusions that must be tested further to establish certainty. However, the comparative method is one of the few ways for scientists to begin to understand how so many species of ungulates, for example, have evolved in Africa, all presumably having evolved long ago from one ancestor species. As the ancestor species spread into different African habitats, new species evolved in response to the varying pressures presented by each new environment. The comparative method helps us identify which of these environmental factors were likely most important in the development of present-day species.

Paleontologists collect and examine the fossils of long-dead animals and their ancient habitats and try to determine the circumstances under which they lived. The comparative analysis of such relics of the past has contributed immensely to our understanding of how living animals evolved from ancestors that were very different from their living descendants. Of course, drawing inferences about behavior from fossils is a difficult task, filled with speculation and educated guesses, but paleontologists have developed their skills to a high degree in the 20th century with the aid of technology and highly sensitive instruments. For example, with the electron microscope, tiny tooth marks on fossil bones may reveal what sort of animal preyed upon the fossilized victim. Careful measurements of the depth of footprints in fossilized mud, and the distance between them, can yield inferences about how large the animal was, how long its stride was, and how it walked and ran.

Cost-Benefit Analysis

Behavioral ecologists focus on the role of the entire environmental context as it affects behavior and try to find the adaptive strategies that promote species survival. Ecologists emphasize the importance of ecological validity, that is, finding out information that describes how animals actually behave in the natural world. One of the methods they use is **cost-benefit analysis,** in which the behavior of an animal is examined in terms of what a given behavior costs the animal versus what it gains. It is presumed that animals will often behave in such a manner as to maximize gains and minimize costs.

Cost-benefit analysis originates in some of Tinbergen's classic work (1953) on black-headed gulls (*Larus ribidundus*), a bird of north England pictured in Figure 2.4. These gulls remove their chicks' eggshells from the nest after the chicks hatch. Whereas the outside of the eggs and the chicks themselves are effectively camouflaged by their brownish, mottled color, which blends in with their backgrounds, the insides of the shells are bright white and stand out visually. Tinbergen hypothesized

Figure 2.4   Black-headed gull parents do not remove the bright white eggshells until nearly an hour after a chick hatches. Why?

that the white shells attract predators such as crows and other gulls that will eat gull chicks and any unhatched eggs. Thus, according to Tinbergen, the parent gulls remove the shells to gain the benefit of less predation on their offspring.

Avoiding the Pitfall of Storytelling

Any approach that is used to study animal behavior has its problems. Krebs and Davies (1993) call one of these problems "storytelling." Storytelling occurs when researchers devise a highly attractive, plausible-sounding theory for behavior (like Tinbergen's theory for the eggshell removal) that seems to tie everything together in a neat package. The trouble is, if the researcher doesn't bother to independently confirm the hypothesis with some new information or in a new setting, he or she may just be telling a nice story. Storytelling is often very tempting when we examine animal behavior—and it is irresistible when we talk about our pets—but a good explanation should be general enough that it goes beyond the immediate situation and applies to new situations, to other species, and to other times and places. Otherwise, we may just be "telling a story" that sounds good to us at the moment but carries no long-term value. Science is a process that must involve a constant interchange between theory and actual data.

Let's return to the Tinbergen example. Tinbergen (1963b) supported his conclusion further by testing how crows, which are quite fond of eggs, would react to empty eggshells in a field experiment. Tinbergen scattered intact gull eggs through a sand location often visited by crows. Next to some of the unhatched eggs he placed some white, broken eggshells, while he placed other eggshells further away from the intact eggs. The crows that visited the site ate more of the eggs that had the shells close to them. In a related example, Cullen (1957) showed that another seabird, the kittiwake (*Rissa tridactyla*), which has no nest predators, completely ignores its white eggshells after the chicks hatch.

Thus, Tinbergen was not content merely to assume that his hypothesis was correct: he tested his conclusion with a new study. In this endeavor, he showed that what might be regarded as a minor behavior may be important for the animal's reproductive success. But this was not the end of the story. The mother gull does not remove the bright shells right after the egg hatches: she waits for as long as an hour, taking a chance that a predator might see it. Why do they wait? Here the idea of costs and benefits is helpful. If the parent flies away with the shell at once, it has to leave the helpless newborn chick alone with the predators. Because its plumage is wet, the chick is easily swallowed by larger predators. Even a nearby adult of the same species may attempt to eat it! However, once the chick's down has dried out and becomes fluffy, it is much harder to swallow, and so its neighbors won't bother it. According to Tinbergen, the parent's delay reflects a balance or compromise between the benefits of maintaining camouflage and the benefits of waiting a while before removing the shells.

Is Tinbergen right or is this just storytelling? Tinbergen supported his hypothesis by showing that, when another species of chick (the oystercatcher, *Haematopus ostralegus*) is not in danger from its neighbors, the parents remove the bright eggshell immediately. Thus, comparing the black-headed gull with the kittiwake and the oystercatcher (as well as other species) helped to clarify the function of the gull's delaying in disposing of the eggshells. Tinbergen's use of the comparative method in testing his hypothesis and cost-benefit analysis in understanding the black-headed gull clearly illustrates how naturalists can avoid storytelling.

While many years ago researchers often put themselves in one methodological camp or another, modern researchers have come to realize the need for all kinds of methods: no method is perfect or ideal by itself, and each has disadvantages. When a variety of methods are used in a variety of places by different researchers and the same results are found repeatedly, then scientists begin to have confidence that they're building explanations and theories that will withstand the challenges of time and further testing.

Recently, the study of comparative animal behavior has become much more sophisticated than just making observations and guessing about the underlying causes of behavior (what was largely the anecdotal method in the 19th century). Researchers now want to apply quantitative methods whenever possible, and cost-benefit models are particularly receptive to quantification, as will be demonstrated in other chapters in this book.

A Detailed Example: Why Do Songbirds Sing?

The ways in which scientists have studied the songs that songbirds sing provides an illustration of how all the methods previously described have been needed for understanding this behavior. Songbirds are a group of bird species from the order Passeriformes, called passerines or perching birds. Some common songbirds native to North America include sparrows, finches, warblers, and wrens. The simpler vocalizations made by almost every species of bird are referred to as **calls** and may be used to announce the presence of a predator or to summon young birds to the parents. A **song** is a more complex series of sounds whose pattern is unique to a species and occurs only under certain circumstances.

As discussed in Chapter 1, a complete explanation of birdsong would involve an account of its functional/ultimate causes, including how and why birdsong evolved, as well as an account of its proximate/mechanical causes, including developmental as well as stimulus factors.

Functional Causes

What do passerine songbirds gain by singing? What is singing for? We presume that birdsong must have some survival and/or reproductive value for any species that sings. The research of Marler and his associates (e.g., Marler and Tamura 1964; Marler 1970a,b; Marler and Mundinger 1971; Marler and Peters 1988) on several species of sparrows has used a variety of methods to understand the causal factors involved in the birds' singing. Two of the most commonly used species, the song sparrow and the white-crowned sparrow, are pictured in Figure 2.5. Observational methods in the birds' natural habitat reveal that only the male sparrow sings and only in the spring or breeding season. All the males of one species sing the same basic song. Observations of the interactions between male and female sparrows in the spring indicate that one purpose of birdsong is to attract the female as a potential mate. In addition, many species of sparrows resemble each other highly. The

Figure 2.5   A male song sparrow and a male white-crowned sparrow, two of the species most frequently used in the study of the causal factors in birdsongs.

unique song that each species sings allows the male sparrow to identify himself as an appropriate potential mate for the female. In some species, males also apparently use songs to claim a territory and discourage other males of the same species from entering that territory. Thus, we can summarize the main functions of birdsong in sparrows as reproduction (attracting a mate), identification, and territorial defense. Furthermore, it has been found that songs may have different functions in other species and may have more than one function in one species (Slater 1989).

How did singing come about and evolve in the birds' ancestors? How did more complex songs evolve from simpler ones? Determining the evolutionary causes of birdsong is a difficult and highly speculative enterprise. We cannot hear the songs that ancient birds sang. The only physical evidence that survives from the ancient evolution of birds is their bones or fossil imprints in rocks or in fossilized clay. The only clues here are provided mainly by applying the comparative method to living species that sing different songs.

For example, one of the main questions researchers are concerned with is, why do species like sparrows have to learn their songs while other species (e.g., chickens, doves, cranes, cowbirds) have songs that are largely unlearned and built in? In these species, the final, adult song is relatively unaffected by isolation or unusual experiences. Why, then, have sparrows evolved all the complications and trouble of learning their songs when having the song preprogrammed or "built in" is so much simpler?

One theory is that in some species the song that is most attractive to the female may vary somewhat with the habitat in which the birds live. Marler and Tamura (1964), for example, found that different populations of one species of sparrow in Marin, Berkeley, and Sunset Beach, California, had somewhat different songs. This finding suggests that song learning might function as a population recognition mechanism, ensuring that the young male sparrow will learn the details of the song that is most useful for him to attract potential mates in a particular location. Thus, learning mechanisms in sparrows may have evolved to give male sparrows some flexibility in searching for a mate.

Proximate/Mechanical Causes

What makes the bird sing at some times and not others? How does the bird know to sing in the spring (usually) and not at other times?

The mechanical cause of birdsong refers to the stimulus conditions and the internal, biological events that tell each male sparrow to sing at the appropriate time, for the appropriate reason. Wingfield (1984) conducted a study on song sparrows (*Melospiza medodia*) and found a correlation between high male aggressive behavior and maximum levels of the hormone testosterone in the bloodstream of sparrows. Male song sparrows are most aggressive when they are establishing their territory and when their mates are laying eggs. These were precisely the times when the male's testosterone levels were highest and when singing was at its peak. This was a correlational study and a field study done in the song sparrow's natural habitat. Thus, the evidence suggests that it is testosterone that is regulating aggression in this species, and testosterone levels are high only in the spring. Other studies confirmed that males sing in the spring because it is at this time of year that (1) testosterone levels (and aggression) are high, (2) the male is competing for territory, and (3) males are trying to attract a mate.

Female sparrows do not normally sing. However, if in a controlled experiment young females are given testosterone injections and are made to have the same experiences as males during development, the female sparrows will learn to sing just like the males! (Of course, the normal sex difference in singing between males and females is originally created by differences in genes.)

How does singing develop? Do birds learn the song from other birds or is singing built in? What experiences must the bird have during development for appropriate singing to occur in adulthood? The study of the developmental causes of sparrow birdsong provides more challenges for the researcher. To achieve an understanding of how a bird comes to sing, the bird's experiences over months and even years must be monitored and controlled. Fortunately, tape recordings and electronic devices measuring sound waves enable researchers to reproduce bird sounds accurately and to manipulate virtually every aspect of the sounds of birdsong. Again, though, the use of this equipment requires close supervision of the animal. This is where the psychologist's classic method of isolation comes into play. In this situation, a control group of laboratory animals lives as close to a natural existence as possible while experimental groups are deprived of some experience. The purpose of this method is to find out what role the missing experience plays in either the animal's later development as a whole or the performance of some task.

Returning to our example, in the studies of Marler and colleagues, the eggs of wild sparrows were removed from their nests, hatched under laboratory conditions, and reared by hand in soundproof rooms in order to deprive young sparrows of hearing the songs sung by other birds. In other studies, young sparrows were prevented from hearing their own vocalizations, or the birds were exposed to songs from other species. In all of these studies, the researchers experimentally varied the times at which the isolation occurred and how long it endured.

If a sparrow's song is built in and largely unaffected by experience and learning, then social isolation should not affect its song much, and we would expect to hear the full-blown adult form of the song in isolated birds when they reach maturity. On the other hand, if the sparrow's song is primarily a matter of learning and experience, isolation should have severe effects on the adult bird's ability to sing appropriately.

Around 150 to 200 days after hatching, young male white-crowned sparrows (*Zonotrichia leucophrys*) will sing a **subsong,** a highly variable series of sounds, something like a human infant babbling. After many studies (as reported by Slater 1989), Marler (1970a) concluded there was a **critical period** in development during which the young bird "records" the songs of other birds of its species (usually its father and any other adult males around), forming a memory template or model of the song. In the white-crowned sparrow, this critical period apparently occurs during 10 to 50 days of age (Marler 1970b). Later the young male will vocalize parts of the song, and those parts will gradually blend into a song resembling the template. This matching of behavior to the template occurs only if the bird has the opportunity to rehearse until the song becomes complete. During this rehearsal process, it is vital for the bird to hear its own singing in order to compare it with the template. Once complete, the song is fixed in the bird for good.

Isolation research by Marler and associates demonstrated that, if the young bird is deprived of the opportunity of hearing any song from the start, it will develop and fixate its own individual song. If the bird hears a song that is different from its species' own song, the bird will copy that song if it doesn't differ too much from its normal song—it won't, however, copy just any song. For example, Marler (1970b) showed that male white-crowned sparrows will only copy other white-crowned adult models, not the song of other sparrow species.

More recent evidence by Baptista and Petrinovich (1984) has challenged the rigidity of templates and critical periods. These researchers placed young white-crowns next to a different species, adult strawberry finches (*Amandava amandava*), which sing their own song. Unlike the isolated white-crowns in Marler's studies, these white-crowns had a singing teacher! What is significant here is that the white-crowns learned the finch's song even after 50 days of isolation after hatching, though Marler and colleagues concluded the critical period was 10 to 50 days. Moreover, they learned their tutor's song even when they could hear other white-crowns (though they couldn't see them). The white-crown is apparently sufficiently flexible to be influenced by social experiences. Marler's important early studies show us the limitations of total laboratory control with artificially produced song stimuli.

Baptista and Petrinovich (1984) show us that social experiences, not just sound experiences, can play a major role in the development of birdsong. The so-called critical period is a period of greatest sensitivity, but some kinds of later experiences (such as having a singing teacher) can also affect the song of the white-crowned sparrow. To some extent, the recognition of this flexibility in species is reflected in the recent trend to reserve the term "critical period" exclusively for the most sensitive part of a longer **sensitive period.**

So, to some extent, the song in sparrows is built in, but the studies show that experiences are crucial for the bird to develop the final song.

Research Ethics and Animal Welfare

Just 50 years ago, researchers could do almost anything to animals in the name of research without any repercussions. All responsibility for animal care and treatment was left to individual researchers. Since the 1960s, the welfare of animals used in research—as well as those used in zoos and circuses and for sport hunting, furs, and food and cosmetics testing—has come under greater legal restrictions and has been of increasing concern to both scientists and the general public. We will limit our discussion here to animals used in education and research.

Animal Welfare

First we should make a distinction between animal welfare and animal rights. Animal welfare reflects an interest in minimizing the pain and suffering of animals and a concern for their care by researchers in terms of caging, lighting, food, water, exercise, and general health and well-being. On the other hand, animal rights involve the idea that animals have rights similar to human rights, and therefore animals should have protection under the law. Although there are no data on the matter, it is assumed that most people agree that the welfare of animals used in research and education should be maximized and pain and suffering minimized; however, far fewer people believe that animals should enjoy rights similar to those given to human beings. How animals should be cared for and treated by professional researchers is now defined in a number of documents, such as the National Institutes of Health "Guidelines for the Care and Use of Animals in Research" and similar publications by the American Psychological Association. These documents developed in response to the Animal Welfare Act of 1966 and subsequent amendments in 1970 and 1991.

Perhaps the main consequence of the increasing concern for the welfare of research animals has been to increase the accountability of researchers in the work they do with animals. Researchers are now expected to be able to justify their use of animals and the number of animals to be used. Most institutions or universities that do research with animals now have institutional research boards (IRBs), which are committees of scientists, laypeople, and animal experts who must approve research proposals using animals (as well as humans) before the research can proceed. Such IRBs evaluate the usefulness of a proposed study in terms of the potential benefits to be gained from the results of the study and the costs to the animals and the institution itself. The IRB might suggest revisions to a proposed study to make it conform more closely to published guidelines and accepted standards, or it might forbid a study for which the value is not clear, or the procedures are questionable.

This greater accountability has led some researchers to more seriously explore alternatives to using animals. For example, researchers investigating the behavior of fish may be able to use plastic models of other fish as stimuli rather than real fish. Other researchers are exploring the possibility of using computer simulations to study many aspects of the relations between animals and environments, thereby eliminating the necessity of always using live animals. Rollin (1981) recommended that researchers pay closer attention to the three R's—replacement (replacing animals with other methods), reduction (using as few animals as possible), and refinement (using methods that lessen the stress and discomfort that animals are subjected to in research).

The development of the principles and procedures that should govern our use of animals in research and education is ongoing and by no means settled. There are no universally prescribed rules about what kinds of animal research are acceptable. The many sources of input to developing guidelines include traditional moral attitudes and laws, religious principles, cultural differences, and individual values. To the scientist, many of these inputs may appear irrational or arbitrary in light of the potential benefits to be gained for humans from their research. It also should be noted that animal research often benefits animals as well as humans. For example, research on Lyme disease has led to a vaccination against the disease for dogs while there still is no such vaccine for humans.

On the other hand, the greater awareness and accountability about animal welfare in research in recent decades has helped greatly to prevent and discourage the occasional abuses of animals that do occur. More detailed discussions of animal welfare and research ethics are presented by Rollin (1981), Dodds and Orlans (1982), and Grier and Burk (1992).

Animal Rights

A concern for the welfare and humane treatment of animals has existed since the middle of the 19th century. However, according to Dewsbury (1990), the modern animal rights (AR) movement developed as a result of Vietnam War protests, the civil rights movement, and concerns about the environment that emerged in the 1960s. While individuals may have varying feelings about AR, the most extreme form of this position embodies the idea that all animal species, and especially those that experience pain, have the same right to live and prosper as humans do. This leads to the conclusion that, since animals cannot voice their permission to participate in research, all research involving animals should end. Consequently, the activities of AR activists have often centered on the pain animals might experience, especially in research laboratories.

Although animal researchers are certainly concerned with the welfare and humane treatment of their animals, they generally view animal research as desirable when the potential benefits to human (and animal) society appear to outweigh the costs. In response to the claims of AR activists about the abuse of animals by researchers, the following information is often cited:

1. Humans and animals have benefited greatly from animal research, as summarized, for example, by Miller (1985).
2. Many important phenomena in physiology, medicine, biochemistry, genetics, and other sciences can be studied and researched only by using live animal models.
3. The evidence does not support AR claims that scientists abuse research animals as often and as extremely as they claim (see (Coile and Miller 1984) for a review of this evidence).
4. The evidence is overwhelming that abuses, neglect, and mistreatment of animals take place much more often with pets, sport hunting and trapping, and habitat destruction than they do in research laboratories.

Animal researchers often regard the AR movement as not only inappropriate and misinformed but also misdirected from the real occurrences of animal abuse.

Summary

Understanding animal behavior involves many methods from several disciplines. Observational methods are primarily descriptive and factual, leading to a detailed record of how an animal species behaves in its natural habitat. Experimental methods and the laboratory are often used to test specific hypotheses for explaining animal behavior. Such methods also have been extended to field experiments that strive to combine the advantages of control and manipulation of variables with natural settings.

Correlational methods attempt to ascertain how variables are related without manipulation and control. The comparative method, unique to the study of animal behavior, involves comparisons of animal behavior within and between species. This approach attempts to find which environmental factors have led to the evolution of different species and the factors that have caused different species to evolve from common ancestors. For example, by comparing many living species of African ungulates and their different habitats, researchers better understand how all these species have evolved and diversified to fill all the available habitats in Africa. Behavioral ecologists use cost-benefit analysis to comprehend how animals adapt to and use the resources available to them in their habitats.

All of the methods for studying animal behavior can be seen in action in the study of how songbirds acquire their songs. Using the method of isolation, researchers have discovered that part of the sparrow's song is innate and part is acquired through experience, especially during a sensitive period early in the bird's development.

Concern for the welfare and humane treatment of research animals and the ethics problems generated by such concerns are very prominent today, leading to the development of written ethical guidelines for researchers and IRBs for overseeing animal research at many institutions. While animal researchers will likely never agree with the goals of the AR movement to end all research using live animals, the movement has led to greater accountability and caution in the use of animals in research and to the search for alternative research procedures.

CHAPTER 3

Evolution

Over long periods of time, animal species change and evolve into new species; but we, as individuals, never see these changes because the length of one human life is but a moment in geologic time. Thus, the concept of animal evolution always seems somewhat abstract to us—something conceptual rather than actual. To modern biologists, however, animal evolution is a fact, and Darwin's theory is the only set of principles that adequately explains evolutionary facts as we know them. From the beginning, Darwin's theory created controversy because it required humans to alter their view of themselves. We could no longer look at ourselves as intrinsically separate from the rest of the natural world. We could no longer regard the various forms of living creatures as permanent and unchanging. With evolution, the earth and its living inhabitants all become parts of a process for which the beginning and end are no longer certain.

In this chapter, the basic facts and principles of evolution are presented and explained, with a variety of examples from many species. We will also deal with the frequent misconceptions of what evolution is and how it works. Using the theory of evolution to explain the ultimate causes for how animal forms and functions arose in the past, modern biologists also examine the adaptive behaviors of living animals in order to understand the value of these behaviors to individual animals. Our modern understanding of evolution also depends on an account of genes and heredity, topics to be reviewed in the next chapter.

For modern biologists, Darwin's theory of evolution is vital to understanding animal behavior. Not only does his theory give us the basis for explaining how animal appearance, physiology, and behavior have evolved over immense periods of geologic time, it also explains how different species of animals have arisen from common ancestors. Sometimes the word *theory* causes individuals to believe that Darwin's ideas are tentative and unproven. In science, however, a theory is not a tentative belief but a highly developed and organized explanatory system. In the minds of modern biologists, evolution is a fact, and Darwin's theory organizes the facts in the only way that makes sense. While biologists and geneticists do argue about the details of evolutionary theory, the overarching set of principles as described by Darwin in *The Origin of Species* (1859) is well accepted.

The Theory of Evolution

For our intents and purposes, let us boil down Darwin's basic theory of evolution to the following general concepts:

1. *Variation within species.*   Darwin recognized that individual differences among animals are important for understanding how species change over time. Members of each species of animal vary in their physical and behavioral traits. Some are larger, some smaller; some are more aggressive, some less; some are more active, some less; and so on.

2. *Heritability.*   To some extent, these variations are a part of the species' genetic heritage and are, therefore, inherited. In other words, the variations can be passed on to the next generation by the parents because many of these variations come from differences in the genes (heredity) that the parent animals have. Actually, Darwin didn't know about genes, but the modern form of the theory states what happens in terms of our current knowledge about genes, chromosomes, and heritability. (Genetics will be covered in more detail in the next chapter.)

3. *Adaptation.*   For their survival, individual animals must adjust or adapt their behavior to the environmental conditions with which they are confronted, and they must compete with members of their own species for both food resources and mates. In this struggle to compete and adapt, the variations within a species confer on some individuals advantages and on others disadvantages, depending on the conditions they confront. For example, snakes, which generally thrive in warmer temperatures, might suddenly be confronted with a change in weather that drastically reduces the temperature. Those individual snakes that can better tolerate the cold will survive under these conditions.

4. *Natural selection.*   All sexually reproducing species have the potential for producing an unlimited number of descendants, but, of course, how many individuals actually survive and reproduce is small in comparison to the total number of individuals produced. Each animal in the wild must compete with members of its own species and with other species for space, food, water, and access to mates. **Natural selection** means that the conditions of nature will tend to select for survival those animals that cope best with whatever situations confront them. These survivors will be the ones that will be most well adapted to their environments and that reproduce and pass on their physical and behavioral traits to subsequent generations. Those individuals that cannot adapt and reproduce not only will die (every individual dies) but will also fail to pass on their inherited traits to subsequent generations. In the end, only those individuals of a species that most successfully compete with other individuals for food, shelter, security, and mates will produce the following generations of the same species. Inherited favorable traits and behaviors tend to become more common in each succeeding generation because they are precisely those characteristics that promote successful survival and reproduction.

Isolation and Speciation

Darwin's theory gives us the basic mechanisms to explain not only how organisms change and develop over time but also how new species and new kinds of organisms are created—a process called **speciation.** The most important factor usually implicated in speciation is geographic isolation (also called allopatric isolation). Typically, one species begins to diverge into two or more separate populations when members become isolated by environmental circumstances (e.g., earthquakes, storms, new lakes or rivers, continents separating, etc.). When groups of animals are separated so that they can no longer mate with each other, any differences in their environments will gradually select different traits as optimal for survival. Over long periods of times, when the two groups develop traits that are very different, the groups evolve into different species that can no longer interbreed even if they had the opportunity to do so. As the great geneticist Theodosius Dobzhansky stated over 40 years ago,

> Diverging geographic races become incipient species when they begin to develop reproductive isolation. The speciation becomes consummated and irreversible when the reproductive isolation is complete. (1955, p. 181)

For example, on the isolated continent of Australia, almost all the native mammals belong to one order, Marsupialia, the marsupials or "pouched" animals. All of these animals—kangaroos, wallabies, koalas, wombats, Tasmanian devils, and so on—employ a method of reproduction that is somewhat different from mammals on other continents. Marsupials have very short gestation periods and give birth to live young that are barely out of the embryonic stage of development. The newborn animal, usually no larger than a worm, must make its way to the mother's pouch without any assistance. The young marsupial attaches itself to the mother's nipple, grows, and develops to maturity inside the mother's pouch.

Millions of years ago, the ancestors of the marsupials originally evolved on one land mass composed of what is now South America and Australia. As the continents separated and Australia traveled east, so to speak, the Australian marsupials became isolated from the rest of the continents and continued to evolve without interacting with the rest of the world. The marsupials left on South America died out and were re-placed by mammals of other orders except for the opossum species, the only marsupials to survive in the Americas in modern times. The mar-supials gradually evolved many diverse species to fill every different habitat in Australia and its surrounding islands. The marsupials are per-haps the most dramatic demonstration nature has given us of how a long period of isolation can produce unique species and how eventually the offspring of one group of animals will spread or radiate into all the avail-able habitats. Similarly, many species of lemurs (monkeylike prosimi-ans) evolved originally in Africa but now exist only on the island of Madagascar where they have been isolated from African forces of ex-tinction.

When it appears that an animal's physical characteristics and be-havior are well adapted to the environment it lives in, it is described as occupying an **ecological niche.** A niche is simply a shorthand term for all the adaptive roles the animal must play in relation to its habitat and the other animals that live in it. In Australia, the marsupials gradually came to occupy all ecological niches, evolving different species appro-priate for each one. Because of this, many of these animals more closely resemble nonmarsupial (placental) mammals than other marsupials. However, modern marsupial species are still more closely related to each other than they are to other mammals, despite the fact that individual marsupial species may resemble each other very little (see Figure 3.1).

When a species spreads to new habitats and its offspring evolve into different species in response to habitat differences, this process is called **adaptive radiation.** Often a more generalized ancestor species will di-verge into a more specialized species as animals take advantage of the new resources each habitat has to offer. So, for example, the polar bear (*Ursus maritimus*) evolved from an earlier stock of bears in response to the extreme environmental conditions of the Arctic—freezing cold and open seas. As a result, the modern polar bear developed a thicker coat of

Jackrabbit

Red kangaroo

Prairie dog

Wombat

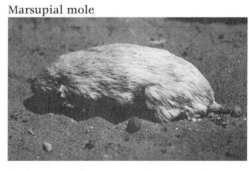

Pocket gopher

Marsupial mole

Southern flying squirrel

Sugar glider

blubber for warmth, webbed feet for swimming, and a white coat to blend in with the polar ice.

Individual Competition

The modern form of Darwin's theory refers to individuals that compete, not to groups. That is, the theory assumes that individuals will selfishly promote their own welfare and their own reproduction (i.e., genes). They do not restrain their own reproduction "for the good of the group" or for their species, a point clarified in some detail by Dawkins (1989). Individuals breed as fast as they can.

The phrase "survival of the fittest" is often associated with Darwin's theory, though he himself never used this phrase. In fact, it was first used by Herbert Spencer, who was a great popularizer of Darwin's theory in 19th-century America. We should be clear, however, about what "fittest" means and what it does not mean in the context of Darwin's theory. It does not necessarily mean the biggest and strongest species members. Rather, **fitness** pertains to the combination of physical traits and behaviors that help organisms survive to adulthood *and reproduce* in their environments. An individual has reproductive success when its genes are represented in the next generation's genetic makeup. Its reproductive success will therefore be maximized when it produces as many offspring as possible. But before an individual can reproduce, it must survive to an age when it can mate. Thus, fitness includes all the traits of the animal that enhance reproductive success, including those that promote survival to the age of reproduction. By definition, the fittest are those animals that produce the greatest number of offspring. Reproductive fitness is a narrower definition of fitness that we usually do not think about in ordinary experience. In Darwin's theory, however, fitness has no meaning unless the animal reaches adulthood and survives long enough to mate and pass its genes on to the next generation.

In many species, size, strength, and aggression may be important for survival and for fitness, but this is not the case for all species. With savanna baboons, for example, larger and stronger males are often at the top of the dominance hierarchy, giving them priority of access to females ready to mate. Even so, smaller, less dominant males are often nearly as successful as the dominant males in finding mates. They accomplish this by being sneaky, that is, by avoiding the dominant males and mating with females whenever the opportunity arises.

Figure 3.1 Australian marsupials (right column) have evolved to live successfully in many ecological niches in Australia. Consequently, many physically resemble North American nonmarsupial mammals (left column) that have evolved in similar environments.

Sexual Selection

Why do the males and females of many (but not all) species have such different appearances? For example, the male black widow spider (*Latrodectus mactans*) is miniscule when compared to the female (see Figure 3.2). Even with human beings, males are, on the average, taller, heavier, and more muscular than females. Darwin's concepts of fitness and natural selection specify that individuals will attempt to maximize their own reproductive success. Even in a mated pair of animals, two separate individuals are involved, and each is trying to maximize its number of offspring. **Sexual selection** refers to the process whereby nature selects different traits and behaviors in males and females because different characteristics maximize reproductive success for each sex. In some species (e.g., deer and large cats), males are larger and more aggressive because the males compete fiercely with each other for females, and a few of the largest and most aggressive males are, on the average, more successful in producing offspring.

More will be said about sexual selection and the potential conflicts it creates between the sexes in Chapter 10. For now, the reader should realize that an account of sexual selection is critical for a complete explanation of the evolution of different traits and behaviors in male and female animals.

Slow or Fast Evolution?

The theory of evolution provides us with the governing principles of the evolutionary process, and the foremost principle is natural selection. No serious scientist argues against this premise. But scientists do debate about many of the details of evolution. One of these details, for example,

Figure 3.2 The female black widow spider of the United States is much larger than the male.

is the speed at which evolution occurs. Darwin implied that evolutionary changes and speciation generally develop very slowly, over millions of years, with only tiny gradual changes occurring over shorter periods of time. However, several modern biologists have proposed that evolutionary changes can and do occur much more quickly and suddenly than Darwin originally thought. One of the most well-known formulations of these new ideas was originated by Gould and Eldredge (1977), which they called the punctuated equilibrium theory. (Stephen J. Gould is the author of many popular books on natural history, such as *The Panda's Thumb* and *The Flamingo's Smile.*) Gould and Eldredge (1977) suggested that a species may remain stable for hundreds or thousands of generations (the equilibrium) but may then change noticeably in relatively few generations (say, 10,000 years) in response to sudden environmental changes. In his works, Darwin presented a great deal of evidence to show that evolution was gradual, but what evidence supports a faster kind of evolution?

When we use the historical approach to carefully examine the fossils of many species, we often don't see steady, gradual change, as Darwin implied. Instead, we see the stability of species over long periods of time (the equilibrium) "punctuated" by dramatic changes over relatively short periods of time. In other words, for many species, the fossil record is filled with discontinuities where long periods of stability are followed by sudden changes that sweep through the entire population in relatively few generations. This implies that species evolution can take place quickly when a new, successful adaptation permits a population to survive and thrive.

Case in point: Darwin's finches. The Galápagos Islands lie off the coast of South America about 600 miles west of Ecuador. As a young man, Charles Darwin traveled there on the HMS *Beagle* and observed a number of species of birds—now referred to as Darwin's finches. It is believed that all 14 species of these finches evolved from one original species of bird and possibly even from a single pair of birds. Though scientists don't know for sure how the ancestors got to the Galápagos Islands, they surmise that the birds probably were blown there from the South American mainland by a large storm.

The Galápagos Islands present finches with a diverse set of habitats, which, in turn, provide wide foraging. Over a span of no less than 10,000 years, the 14 species of finches have evolved to take maximum advantage of all the food resources, which include seeds, prickly pears, cactus plants, buds, fruit, and insects. Six of the finches are primarily ground-feeding seed eaters while others live in trees and eat mainly insects. All of these birds resemble each other. One species, the warbler finch, looks more like a warbler than a finch but is judged to be a finch species from the anatomical characteristics it has in common with the other finches.

The most obvious feature distinguishing the different species of finches is their beaks, which vary in size, shape, length and thickness (see Figure 3.3). So, for example, among the seed eaters, those with larger beaks eat larger seeds. Those that eat the prickly pear have longer and more

Figure 3.3   The beaks of some of Darwin's finches, illustrating how natural selection evolves a species to adapt to the habitat requirements it confronts.

pointed beaks. Similarly, the insect eaters have beaks adapted to the size of the insects they catch. Perhaps the most unusual of the insect eaters is the woodpecker finch, which is a tool user. It typically feeds on grubs that it digs out of cracks in trees with its chisel-like beak. When it cannot reach the grub, the woodpecker finch obtains a twig or a cactus spine to reach the grub and pull it out. Despite the many similarities among these birds, Darwin's finches interbreed only with members of their own species. Each species mainly uses the beak characteristics to identify potential mates.

Scientists have found Darwin's finches so fascinating because, on a small scale, they illustrate most of the principles of Darwin's theory. The 14 species fill all the ecological niches present in the islands. The beaks of the finches are maximally efficient in obtaining each species' food source.

Since 1973, Peter and Rosemary Grant and their assistants have banded and tracked all the fortis finches—nearly 20,000 birds—on one of the Galápagos Islands, Daphne Major (reported by Weiner (1994). In some years of drought and other years of flooding, the Grants observed and measured changes in the finches' beaks, which quickly evolved in response to the available food supply: After the 1977 drought, only old, hard nuts were available, favoring the evolution of bigger, stronger beaks. After a flood in 1983, the next generation of fortis finches was smaller, better adapted to a large supply of tiny new seeds on the island. Thus, changes in these birds can evolve in only a few generations, and it is likely that Darwin's finches have all evolved in the last 10 to 20,000 years.

In their original article, Gould and Eldredge (1977) proposed that speciation, the generation of new species, is not typically gradual. But most evolutionary theorists still see the evolution of most species as a slow and gradual process, with faster evolution the exception rather than the rule. Thus, while these matters have by no means been settled, most scientists now accept the idea that different species have evolved at different rates—some faster, some more slowly. Arguments occur about how frequent or common such periods of fast evolution are.

Convergent Versus Divergent Evolution

Convergent (or parallel) **evolution** is the accidental process whereby different species of animals independently evolve similar solutions to adaptive and environmental problems and therefore come to resemble each other structurally. Structures in organisms that are similar in appearance and function but have different origins in evolutionary time are described as **analogous.** For example, consider the wings of butterflies, birds, and bats. They all look similar and all serve the function of flying. However, butterflies have nonliving membranes stretched over solid supports, whereas birds' wings are composed of feathers, muscles, and bone. Bats' wings, on the other hand, are living membranes stretched between fingers. Each organism has achieved flight by developing wings, but the wings originated independently in evolutionary time from different original structures.

Similarly, dolphins and whales are mammals that have evolved fins and tails, which allow them to swim like sharks and other large fish. This kind of parallel evolution often occurs because different organisms are exposed to the same environmental pressures over long periods of times. As Figure 3.1 illustrated earlier in this chapter, marsupial evolution in Australia has paralleled the evolution of mammals elsewhere, and each marsupial species tends to resemble another nonmarsupial that lives in a similar environment on another continent.

Divergent evolution is the process where species with a common ancestor evolve different bodily structures from the same original structures, like the polar bear evolving from earlier bears. A population becomes isolated from the rest of the species and begins to follow a different evolutionary course. Over long periods of evolutionary time, **homologous** body structures develop, which serve different functions in different species but which have the same origins (the opposite of analogous). For example, let's take bat wings, dog front feet, whale fins, and the human hand. In evolution, they are homologous because they all come originally from a handlike organ on a small mammal that bats, dogs, whales, and humans all have as a common ancestor.

Homologous and analogous structures create difficulties for scientists because they must try to determine whether similarities in body structure are due to common origins (homology and divergent evolution in related animals) or whether they were developed independently to solve similar problems (analogy and convergent evolution between unrelated animals). Sometimes scientists are greatly helped along by looking at animals' vestigial organs, or parts of the body that have no apparent function at all. For example, we don't think of pythons and other snakes as having legs or feet, but pythons actually have tiny, useless bones in their bodies exactly where we would expect to see legs if they had them. These bones have no function at all for the pythons but are definite homologous evidence that pythons are, in fact, descended from four-legged, crawling animals: the lizards.

Human beings also have vestigial organs: muscles in our ears, tail bones at the base of our spine, and the appendix in our large intestines. None of these have any present function for us; in fact, they may serve to hinder us. Our appendix, for example, not only is useless but often creates medical problems that result in its having to be surgically removed. The koala of Australia, however, has a large, functioning appendix (distantly homologous to ours) that helps it digest the tough eucalyptus leaves it eats. Thus, scientists have concluded that somewhere in our evolutionary past our ancestors probably ate mostly plant material.

Evolution as Fact

The evidence for the evolution of species as a fact is so overwhelming that biologists and other scientists no longer question "the fact" of evolution. We do not have space here to go over all of this overwhelming evidence in detail (that's what Darwin did, in part), but we can summarize the principal kinds of evidence that establish evolution as a fact.

The Fossil Record

Direct evidence exists for large-scale evolutionary changes based on sequences in the fossil record. Of course, scientists assume that biological processes and natural selection have operated consistently or uniformly over time, an assumption called the principle of **uniformitarianism.** When we look at the bones of animals that lived thousands and millions of years ago, we see systematic changes in their forms (anatomy) as we trace time to the present era. For example, all modern warm-blooded, fur-bearing mammals—from the smallest mouse to human beings to the largest whale—are traceable back in time to ancestors that existed about 65 million years ago. These ancestors of all mammals were probably small, shrewlike animals akin to the modern tree shrew, pictured in Figure 3.4. Prior to 65 million years ago, the dinosaurs ruled the earth. Mammals blossomed into many different forms in many different habitats across the world when the dinosaurs, dominant for so long, were largely

Figure 3.4 A modern smooth-tailed tree shrew (*Dendrogale murina*), a small, insect-eating animal believed to be the living animal most like the early mammals from which all modern mammals, including humans, are evolved.

wiped out by some cataclysmic event. Many scientists now believe this event to have been the impact of a giant meteor, six to ten miles in diameter, which struck the earth. Large-scale, unpredictable events such as this are assumed to have played major roles in the evolution of many species and in the extinction of many others through geologic time.

Biogeography

There is currently an amazing diversity of animals and plants on earth—literally millions of different species. Even today, new species are still being discovered all the time. But particular kinds of organisms occur in particular geographic areas and not in others. This implies that the environment plays a role in selecting which species can live in a given place. Moreover, systematic gradations in the environment, such as the weather being colder as you travel north, are directly related to the adaptive traits that animals possess. Thus, the match between animal attributes and properties of the environment implies that animals have evolved traits and behaviors that enable them to survive in just those environments.

Homologous Structures

All vertebrate animals have four limbs and two eyes. Why not three or six or twenty? The similarities among different species of animals in their anatomy, physiology, and behavior lend support to the contention that many of these similarities exist because these species have common ancestors in their evolutionary past. We see this most clearly in closely related living species that are not even genetically distinct, such as wolves and coyotes, or lions and leopards, or red and gray squirrels. Homology is less obvious in more distantly related species, but overall commonalities of structure and physiology usually lead to the conclusion that there was a common ancestor. Thus, while ants, bees, beetles, and butterflies have different external appearances, they are all insects because they have six legs, hard exoskeletons, and wings (though some forms are wingless).

Imperfections

There is direct evidence in current organisms of their evolutionary history, as indicated by their embryological traits and their anatomical imperfections. Why do pigs walk on only two toes while two other vestigial toes exist on each leg well above the ground? Why do human beings and other mammals in the embryonic stage have gills like fish? Only the theory of evolution can make sense out of these "useless" organs by assuming that animals are related and share a common ancestry. To some extent, current organisms retain in their development and physique what has happened to their species in their evolutionary past. Many of these historical characteristics are the same as, or similar to, those in other species, implying a common ancestry.

Questions about Evolution

Understanding the basic principles of evolution leads not only to many questions about the theory itself but also to questions about the place of the theory in our greater attempts to understand ourselves and our place in the universe. In the past, serious misunderstanding of the theory has led to accusations and assumptions of which the theory itself is not guilty. We can examine only a few of these questions here, but it is important to comprehend what the theory actually says and what it does not say.

Why So Many Variations?

If certain traits promote the reproductive success of individuals that possess those traits, why is there still so much physical and behavioral variation within species? Why aren't the less fit animals simply wiped out? Why are there so many species competing with each other? There are many reasons why considerable variation is a part of living species of animals. For one thing, while the most fit individuals experience greater average reproductive success than less fit animals, many less fit animals still succeed in mating and passing their genes on to the next generation. In the wild, chance and random opportunity play their roles so that sometimes less aggressive and smaller, less fit individuals are successful.

Another reason for within-species variation is that some traits may increase their reproductive advantage when they become rare, a process explained in some detail by Ayala and Campbell (1974) and called **frequency-dependent selection.** For example, a predator may prefer to prey upon a certain animal when that prey animal is plentiful. When the prey animal becomes more scarce, the predator may switch its preference to some other species, thereby giving the scarcer prey animal a chance to recover its numbers.

Selection may also be frequency dependent when it comes to reproduction within the species. For example, when the population of large and aggressive males of a species increases, the males may spend a great deal of time fighting and competing with each other for females. While these males are preoccupied with each other, the smaller and less aggressive males may enjoy greater reproductive success, keeping their genes for less aggression present in the population.

Variations in the population also occur because genetic mutations (random changes in the individual's genes) occasionally take place. This factor is discussed in more detail in the next chapter.

In contrast, some modern species appear to have little genetic diversity. A notable example is the cheetah (*Acinonyx jubata*) of the

African plains, the fastest land animal on earth. Genetic studies have shown that cheetahs have very little genetic diversity; individual cheetahs are almost clones of each other. This development is believed to have occurred because all modern cheetahs are descended from only a few surviving cheetahs thousands of years ago; nonetheless, how cheetahs have survived with so little diversity is not well understood.

Biological variation and diversity are not minor matters. Without diversity, evolution would not be possible. As Edward O. Wilson, one of America's most prominent biologists, has put it,

> Biological diversity . . . is the key to the maintenance of the world as we know it. Life in local sites struck down by a passing storm spring back quickly because enough diversity still exists. Opportunistic species evolved for just such an occasion rush in to fill the spaces. . . . This is the assembly of life that took a billion years to evolve. It has eaten the storm—folded them in its genes—and created the world that created us. (Wilson 1992, p. 15)

What Does Evolution Mean?

Misunderstandings about the theory of evolution have abounded since the theory became well known. Many of these misunderstandings arose from people assuming that the theory was saying things that Darwin never said nor intended to say.

Progressivism Fallacy.   Perhaps the greatest fallacy associated with the theory of evolution that still pervades the thinking of many people is **progressivism.** This is the idea that evolution is a kind of ladder of progress (like Aristotle's *scala naturae*) on which simpler organisms correspond to the rungs at the bottom of the ladder and humans are the rung at the top. To progressivist thinkers, evolution is a process that can only lead to improvements, human beings being the most perfected of all species. However, from a scientific point of view, natural selection does not inevitably lead to improvements or to the human species; it simply selects whatever works at a particular time and in a particular locality for that individual, whether the animal's physique or behavior is ugly or pretty, brutal or kind, simple or complex. Stephen J. Gould tells us that "Natural selection is . . . a principle of local adaptation, not of general advance or progress" (1994, p. 85).

When we look at the fossil record of evolution, what we see is an enormous number of dead ends and extinctions, failed lines, starts and stops, and lucky survivals. Unforeseen events in the environment (storms, earthquakes, ice ages, volcanic explosions, floods, etc.) led to mass extinctions of living species. About 99% of all past species of animals that have existed are now extinct, and, as far as scientists have been able to determine, these developments are clearly related to the environmental conditions in which these animals lived. Evolution is not a ladder of progress. Rather, it's a branching bush, with chance playing a large role in which branches emerge and how long they last.

Part of the progressivism fallacy is the common observation that life on earth appears to proceed from simpler to more complex forms, with living human beings being the epitome of advancement and complexity. But this misleading observation does not square with other facts about the history of life on earth. Millions of years ago, when life began, the majority of species on earth were one-celled organisms; this was the normal state of affairs for the first five-sixths of the earth's history. It is still true today. Many of the simplest forms of life have not disappeared and been replaced by complex forms—they're still here with us. For example, each of us carries within our digestive systems billions of bacteria, which are living organisms, that aid us in digestion. Without them, absorbing nutrients from food would be difficult. Like simple bacteria, insects, fish, and reptiles developed earlier than mammals because they were and still are less complex life forms. But mammals did not evolve to replace them. The offspring of fish and reptile species that successfully evolved and continued to adapt to the environments they encountered are still with us today as significant members of the world's ecosystems. The many species of sharks in the world are potent evidence for how the biology, design, and behavioral adaptations of these fish have been able to evolve long before us, to survive many of the earth's geographic catastrophes, and still dominate the world's oceans as great predators today (see Figure 3.5).

The relatively late appearance of more complex organisms does not mean that evolution equals progress; it only means that it takes more time, and perhaps more luck, to evolve complexity rather than simplicity. Thus, simpler organisms are going to appear first. "Our impression that life evolves toward greater complexity is probably only bias inspired by parochial focus on ourselves" (Gould 1994, p. 87). It's true that the more complex is more rare and develops later than the simpler, but it does not replace it.

Purposivism Fallacy.   Another fallacy related to progressivism is teleology or **purposivism.** This is the idea that the purpose of evolution and nature is to produce humankind, that all of nature exists for our benefit and is like a stage on which we are the principal actors. This is as anthropocentric a view (humans at the center) as we can have!

We cannot find purpose or "a reason for life" from the theory of evolution. Generally, we look toward religious or philosophical principles to reveal life's purpose. Science can only give us the mechanisms and principles that govern change, not the ultimate metaphysical reasons why changes might occur.

Figure 3.5 Sharks and their kind have been on earth since before the dinosaurs ever arrived, and they are still here today, in many forms and habitats.

Does Behavior Evolve?

The evolution of physical characteristics, or **morphology,** of animals and the evolution of animal behaviors are not independent of one another. In fact, biologists now believe that changes in morphology are often preceded by behavioral changes. Wilson (1975) refers to behavior as an evolutionary "pacemaker" because behavioral change leads the way for other changes. For example, large antlers on deer species have evolved as the result of larger, more powerful male deer winning more fights during the mating season and subsequently mating with more females. Therefore, they put more of their genes into the next generation than smaller males. But the behaviors of fighting and competing had to evolve before the antlers had a reason to grow larger. Similarly, the spectacularly long and elaborate feathers of the male peacock gradually evolved after males developed the behavior of displaying their feathers to attract females.

The study of behavior is difficult because, whereas physical characteristics are always visible, behaviors only appear occasionally and may not last long. Therefore, merely observing an organism's full repertoire of behaviors may require a great deal of time and patience. These problems are compounded considerably when scientists try to make conclusions about particular behaviors of a species and their evolution millions of years ago.

We will discuss two general approaches to answering questions about behavioral evolution. One approach involves using whatever evidence can be gleaned from the fossil record itself. Of course, fossils often reveal many details about the morphology of the animal: its size and weight, gender, diet, and means of locomotion. But fossils also reveal other signs of animal behavior: teeth marks on the bones may inform us it was a prey animal; fossilized tracks or footprints may tell us about its habitat and walking speed; fossilized nest materials and bones or tools near the nest may tell us something about the animal's feeding and parenting activities. Moreover, several fossils from the same species may give us more information about the animal's social behavior. For example, in many species, the heavier the male is relative to the female, the greater the number of female mates the male will have.

Different species that appear to be very similar physically may still behave differently. This is why the second approach to the evolution of behavior, the comparative method, is so important. With this method, we try to make inferences about the behavior of an extinct animal by comparing it to a living species of animal that has similar characteristics. So, for example, if we should wonder what the function was for head ornaments of dinosaurs—were they used to attract mates, or to intimidate competitors, or to cool off the blood, or for something else?—we may gain insight by looking at similar head ornaments in living deer and beetle species (Molnar 1977).

Ecology and Evolution

Some of the more recent insights about animal behavior and evolution have come from ecologists who have used cost-benefit analysis and quantification to develop Darwin's concept of adaptation further than their predecessors. To understand these ideas better, let's examine one study in some detail.

Clutch Size

The great tit (*Parus major*) is a bird that lives in the woods in England. Typically, the female tit will lay eight or nine eggs in a **clutch** (a bunch of eggs; see Figure 3.6). A traditional ethologist might focus on the unlearned or instinctive patterns of behavior involved in courtship, mating, and guarding the eggs. An animal psychologist might focus on the environmental cues the birds respond to and how much of their behavior is learned from experience. A neurophysiologist would be interested in the brain events, neural pathways, and hormones involved in reproduction.

Behavioral ecologists have asked a much more pointed question: Why do tits lay this particular number of eggs (eight or nine) and not four or fifteen? In behavioral ecology, it is assumed that there is a good reason for this number of eggs because current animals, in their natural habitats, will behave efficiently in surviving and reproducing. Behavioral ecologists try to find the reasons why fewer or more eggs would not work as well. The optimal clutch size should be the number that maximizes the animal's lifetime breeding success.

Figure 3.6   A clutch of great tit eggs.

Ordinarily, the great tit does not suffer from a lot of predation where it lives. Therefore, it can afford to have a fairly large clutch size and take care of its young for some time. Tits can afford to have more eggs than three or four, but more than eight or nine offspring starts creating problems; specifically, the parents cannot manage to feed so many offspring, so some of the young die (Lack 1966).

The circumstances are different for birds that experience greater predation in their habitats. In this situation, other animals typically try to eat them, especially when they're young and defenseless. Under these conditions, it's desirable for offspring to grow to adulthood as rapidly as possible because the longer young birds are helpless, the more likely predators will attack and kill them. So the parent bird must devote more time to feeding and protecting fewer young (four or five), which, in turn, develop at a faster rate. As a result, the young grow large enough to be on their own much sooner. Therefore, the clutch size will be correspondingly smaller.

In summary, the greater the predation on the animal, the smaller the clutch size, the more rapid the growth, and the sooner the young will leave the nest. The less predation there is, the larger the clutch size, the slower the growth of the young birds, and the later they leave the nest. The same quantity of food can be used to raise a few offspring quickly or a greater number more slowly. Similarly, it has been found that birds that nest in the holes of trees tend to have more offspring than those that nest in the open. Holes provide greater security from predators, enabling the parent birds to spend more time feeding them.

This kind of cost-benefit analysis assumes that the animal is capable of maximizing its environmental benefits while minimizing its costs. It is an intrinsic part of the ecological approach. Different ecological circumstances (e.g., variations in predation pressure) may lead to different life history strategies that will optimize survival and reproductive success. The word *strategy* is not meant to imply that animals consciously plan or think about what they do. It simply describes one way of behaving (e.g., having eight or nine eggs) rather than another (having four or five eggs).

Adaptation and Optimality

Thus, according to modern ecologists, natural selection favors individuals that adopt life history strategies or ways of living that maximize or make optimal their gene contribution to future offspring—in other words, those that adapt best to their circumstances. Stating it in reverse, those individuals in the past that adopted other kinds of strategies are no longer with us and neither are their offspring. How survival and reproduction succeeds in the animal's life history in turn depends on ecology: how the individual interacts with its environment, competitors, potential mates, predators, food sources, and so on.

Because living animals are the end products of millions of years of evolution at work, natural selection has designed current, living animals to be rather efficient in dealing with their environments, in foraging for food, in avoiding predators, in finding a mate, and in parenting. Living animals are good at what they do! Whether individuals can in fact achieve the highest possible reproductive outcome (optimality) is a question that must be tested or verified empirically. Therefore, examining the adaptive efficiency of individual animals on an everyday basis is one way to study the adaptiveness of the species.

The study of behavioral ecology is, in a sense, where evolution (genes and natural selection), behavior (animal activities), and ecology (environmental interactions) meet in examining the behavior of living individual animals. Ecologists try to answer such questions as, Why do different species behave in so many different ways? Why are there individual differences within species other than random genetic variations? What is it about an animal's behavior that makes it efficient and successful in its own habitat? What do more efficient individuals do that less efficient ones do not? Ecologists often ask questions that traditional ethologists and comparative psychologists have not inquired about in the past.

Thus, the new perspective that ecologists have brought to the study of animal behavior is to look at each animal's everyday, typical foraging, antipredator, courtship, mating, and parenting behaviors and to try to understand them in terms of their costs and benefits to the individual. The examination of the individual animal struggling to survive in its natural habitat reveals which factors in the animal's environment impinge most on the animal's survival behaviors.

During the first hundred years after Darwin's theory was published, scientists tended to emphasize the role that genetic processes played in evolution and speciation. The idea that individual animal behavior is efficient—maximizing benefits while minimizing costs to the individual—has deepened the modern evolutionary approach to understanding animal behavior by giving us a better understanding of the adaptation part of the theory. Answering the question of exactly how living species on earth adapt, cope, survive, and adjust to their environmental difficulties is the least developed and most challenging part of understanding animal behavior. The behavioral ecologist's adaptive approach, using cost-benefit analysis, will be returned to many times in this book.

Summary

Darwin's theory of evolution contributes the most important set of organizing concepts for understanding animal behavior. At the heart of the theory is the principle of natural selection, the idea that nature selects for survival those individual animals that cope best with the environmental problems with which they are confronted. These animals are the ones that most often survive and through reproduction pass their genes on to subsequent generations.

Natural selection is the predominant mechanism in the evolution of new species of animals. Also implicated in speciation is geographic isolation, the division of breeding populations into groups that can no longer breed with each other because they are separated. Sexual selection refers to the fact that natural selection will favor those individuals of one sex that compete better for reproductive success, resulting in the gradual development of different physical and behavioral traits for each sex. While Darwin's basic theory is well accepted, scientists do argue about the details, such as whether new species evolve slowly and gradually or sometimes quickly and suddenly.

The accumulation of evidence for Darwin's theory as fact includes many events in the fossil record, information from the biogeographical distribution of animal species, homologous traits in the anatomy and behavior of animals, and clues provided by imperfections in living animals.

Darwin's theory is often portrayed inaccurately because of assumptions about the theory that are not true. One fallacy, progressivism, assumes that the long history of evolution is the story of inevitable progress toward modern animals and humans. Another fallacy, purposivism, assumes that the purpose of evolution is to produce and support the human dominance of nature. Neither of these fallacies is a part of Darwin's theory, which seeks only to describe the mechanisms of evolutionary change, not the reasons for life or nature. In addition, the theory applies not only to animal anatomy and physiology but also to behavior, which is often regarded as preceding physical changes.

Modern ecologists have developed the concept of adaptation in evolutionary theory more fully than their predecessors. Ecologists examine and quantify the environmental variables impacting on individual animals. They try to understand how individuals are capable of making maximum use of their environmental resources while minimizing the costs of predation and energy.

CHAPTER 4

Genes and Heredity

Perhaps the single greatest achievement of the life sciences in the 20th century is the determination of the details of genes and heredity. The discovery that complex DNA molecules lay at the heart of heredity in all living things on earth reinforced Darwin's theory because it implied that all living things are ultimately related and have evolved from the same sources.

In this chapter, we will review the basic concepts of modern genetics and their consequences for understanding animal behavior. There is not room enough here to discuss the biological details of genetic mechanisms, but, for our purposes, these details are not necessary. What is important to understand is how our knowledge of genetics supports our understanding of how animal species and behaviors have evolved. Although our knowledge about the genetic basis for many physical traits is already extensive, determining the genetic basis for animal behavior is extremely complex because genes can affect behavior only indirectly through body structures. Modern scientists have had to exercise considerable inventiveness and skill to devise methods for getting at genetic influences on behavior. Some of these methods will be discussed in the latter part of this chapter.

Nowadays the theory of evolution is conceptualized in terms of our current knowledge of genes and heredity. Thus, if we are to fully understand animal evolution and behavior, we must begin with a basic understanding of genetic principles. Modern genetics began over a century ago with the studies of Gregor Mendel (1822–1884), an Austrian scientist and monk. He quietly discovered the basic laws of heredity by experimenting with varieties of garden peas. Although he published his results in 1866, they were initially ignored because his ideas were contrary to the popular belief that heredity resulted from a "blending" of parental traits. Some even suggested it came from directly blending the blood of the parents in the offspring. The influence of this fallacious theory can still be seen today in our everyday language in such phrases as "of royal blood," "bloodlines," "related by blood," and so on (even though heredity does not involve parental blood).

It wasn't until 16 years after Mendel's death that his work was recognized as revolutionary. By 1900, a botanist, Hugo de Vries, and two other European scientists, Erich von Tschermak and Carl Correns, had independently confirmed Mendel's findings, giving him full credit for discovering the basic "laws" of heredity. In 1909, Wilhelm Johansen coined the term *gene* to represent the basic unit of heredity. However, the underlying biochemical nature of genes was not understood at that time. In the early 1900s, T. H. Morgan at Columbia University began work on the genetics of the common fruit fly (*Drosophila melanogaster*) by interbreeding flies with differing characteristics. This small insect became the most frequently used animal in genetic studies because of four basic factors: (1) its size, (2) its two-week period of maturation, (3) the fact that the female lays hundreds of eggs, and (4) ease of care (hundreds can be kept in small bottles).

Basic Genetics

Mendel crossbred varieties of garden peas (*Pisum sativum*) to get new varieties, or hybrids, and examined their individual traits such as size, seed color, presence or absence of wrinkles, pod color, seed shape, and so on. The same fundamental laws he discovered to be true of plants apply to both animal and human heredity. Granted, our genes are more complex and more detailed, and we have more of them than a pea does, but the general rules for how genes combine are the same across nature.

We can summarize Mendel's work as follows:

1. The factors that control heredity are individual units known as **genes.** Genes are found as matched pairs, one gene of each pair coming from each biological parent. Each member of the pair is called an **allele** (pronounced a-*leel*).

2. The two alleles may not be functionally identical in determining a bodily trait, that is, each may convey different information. Some alleles may be dominant (for human eye color, brown is dominant) and others may be recessive (i.e., blue eye color for humans). When a dominant and a recessive allele are paired in offspring, the dominant allele is expressed (its effect is what we see), whereas the recessive allele is not expressed (though it's still present in the organism and can be passed on to future offspring).

3. The two forms or alleles of each gene are segregated or separated during the formation of reproductive cells. In other words, a parent's reproductive cell receives only one form or allele of a gene.

4. The different genes for different traits are said to "assort independently" of each other during the reproductive process. This means that the particular combination of different genes an individual receives from its parents is random and unpredictable. As we shall see, modern genetics has qualified this principle.

The **genotype** of an organism is its genetic makeup; **phenotype** refers to the physical appearance of the organism. Although genotype partly determines phenotype, we cannot always tell from looking at an individual's phenotype what the genotype exactly is. For example, if a person has brown eyes, the two alleles for eye color may both be for brown, or one may be for brown while the other is for blue. Both genotypes (brown-brown or brown-blue) will be expressed as a brown-eyed individual (the phenotype).

One of the revolutionary ideas in Mendel's original work was the notion that you could apply the mathematics of probability to heredity to discover what the genotypes probably are. For example, let's imagine that two brown-eyed people get married and have many children. For argument's sake, let's say the couple has exactly eight children: what can we say if one-fourth (exactly two) of the children have blue eyes, though both parents have brown eyes? Since alleles for brown dominate over those for blue, the only way an individual can have blue eyes is for that individual to have both eye-color alleles for blue, since each individual gets one allele from each parent. Both parents, therefore, must each have a recessive allele for blue eyes. Those children with brown eyes received at least one allele, or possibly both, for brown eyes from the parents. On the other hand, if all eight of the children had brown eyes, it is likely that at least one parent has alleles only for brown eyes, causing all of the children to have brown eyes.

Unlike Mendel's peas, which, like eye color, have only two alleles for each trait, many animal traits have more than two alleles. Consequently, they have more than two possible forms. Three, four, and five alleles are not uncommon; twenty alleles of one gene are not unheard of. Although many alleles might exist, we must remember that a specific individual can have only two alleles at each gene locus, one obtained from each parent.

The number of possible combinations of all traits from all gene combinations is an astronomical number—a number not only greater than the number of living people but greater than the number who will ever live! You needn't worry about meeting someone identical to yourself. Except for identical twins, who have the same genes, an individual is genetically unique.

Eye color is not the only human trait that appears to be determined by simple dominance-recessiveness properties. It has also been found that head hairiness dominates over baldness, color vision dominates over color blindness, and the ability to curl one's tongue lengthwise dominates over the inability to do so! But most physical and behavioral traits typically come from the combined effect of several or many genes, called **polygenic** traits; for example, the shape of an individual's nose or the markings on an animal's coat.

The fairly simple concepts we have discussed so far opened the door to the modern era of 20th-century genetics. They explained how units called genes combine in simple ways to produce observable phenotypes. But what is a gene? Where is it? How does it work? To approach these questions, more sophisticated, microscopic methods had to be invented for investigating what goes on within a cell in the body.

Chromosomes and DNA

As it turns out, genetic material is stored within the nucleus of every cell in the body in strings of molecules called **chromosomes.** Human beings have 46 chromosomes in 23 pairs. One chromosome of each pair comes from each parent. Together these chromosomes contain a total (for humans) of perhaps 80,000 or more genes. Each gene occupies a specific place or locus on only one of the chromosomes. The number of chromosomes (strings) varies from organism to organism. For example, some intestinal worms have 2, mosquitoes have 6, a fruit fly has 8, peas have 14, a cabbage has 18, a tomato and a grasshopper have 24, a frog 26, cats 34, rats 42, humans 46, a potato 48, a dog 78, a goldfish 94, a crayfish 200, and some ferns have nearly 500! Clearly, the diploid number (total number of chromosomes) is related neither to the size of the organism, nor to the size of the cell itself, nor to its place in the phylogenetic spectrum.

Genes reside in chromosomes, and the two alleles of a given gene (one from each parent) lie at the same site or locus on the chromosome pairs. Genes that reside close to one another on a chromosome ordinarily do not undergo independent assortment during reproduction. For example, in human beings, the bleeding disorder hemophilia is called **sex linked** because the recessive gene for this disorder is stored in the same chromosome that determines the individual's sex. Consequently, hemophilia is much more common in males than females. To be a hemophiliac female, you must get a recessive gene from both parents.

Let's look at this in detail. Female humans have two chromosomes for sex, one from each parent, called XX. Male humans also have two chromosomes for sex, called XY. The mother always gives her children an X chromosome during reproduction, but the father can give a child an X or a Y; it is this X or Y that determines the sex of the child. The gene for hemophilia is always carried on an X chromosome, not on a Y. If a male has the gene for hemophilia on the X chromosome, he will be a hemophiliac because the X dominates over the Y. But a female will be a hemophiliac only if both of her X's carry the defective gene because the healthy X will dominate over the defective X. Thus, a female needs two deficient X chromosomes to have a phenotype for hemophilia, that is, to actually have the disease. Though a woman might carry one deficient X and still be healthy, she may pass the defective gene on to her offspring. Therefore, if she carries the recessive gene for hemophilia, the chances are 50-50 that each of her offspring will inherit the defective gene.

As indicated by our example, the sex of the individual is determined genetically in mammals and birds but not in every organism. (In birds, the females are XY and the males are XX.) In the American alligator and some other reptiles, for example, sex is determined by the temperature the egg is exposed to in the nest. Higher temperatures produce male offspring whereas lower ones create female alligators. Some animals can even change sex during their lifetime, as will be discussed in Chapter 10.

As hemophilia demonstrates, for many physical traits, the dominant allele is typically "what works" to produce a normal or healthy effect. This dominance serves to protect the animal from succumbing to defective recessive alleles. This is also why most maladaptive but heritable traits are usually recessive. In addition, in some species, both alleles can be codominant; that is, they don't blend to produce their effect. For example, in chickens, black and white feathers are codominant. If a chicken is found to have both alleles, it won't have gray feathers. It will appear gray because it will have some black and some white feathers. Likewise, in some flowering plants, crossbreeding a white with a red flower will produce what looks like a pink flower. Yet, if you look closely, what you find is pure red strands mixed with white ones. Both genes have had equal effect.

What are genes themselves composed of? Scientists began to find answers to this question starting in the 1930s. In the 1940s, new intracellular analytical techniques in chemistry led to significant advances in research on the structure of chemicals known to be in the chromosomes—the nucleic acids. The definitive answers culminated in the 1950s with the work of a British scientist, Francis Crick, who worked with an American biologist, James Watson. On the basis of a great deal of information accumulated before them, they were able to figure out the structure of the chemical that carries the genetic code.

The "program" of a cell, or its genetic code, stores the instructions for how the cell can make other chemicals, the proteins, which serve as the building blocks for the body. The genetic code is contained in a complex chemical called DNA (deoxyribonucleic acid). This chemical stores and transmits genetic information from one generation of an organism to the next in all living things. Although Watson and Crick did not discover DNA, they figured out its structure, which enabled others to begin to break it down into its constituents. Though the biochemical details of how genetic information is encoded in the DNA molecule is now well understood, there is not space here to review the chemical details. Suffice it to say that, when these details were finally understood, they confirmed all of the general principles that Mendel and others had discovered without knowing anything about the underlying biochemistry.

Whereas human body cells have 46 chromosomes, the reproductive cells are *haploid* (meaning half), with 23. Mendel's principle of independent assortment implied that genes on different chromosomes would assort or be assigned to sex cells independently of each other, whereas genes on the same chromosome would all stay together. As it turns out, things are more complicated than that. When reproductive cells are formed, some gene segments can actually cross over between matched pairs of chromosomes, putting new alleles in combination with the alleles already on the chromosome (see Figure 4.1). These gene exchanges, while random and exceptional, make the number of possible gene combinations in an individual's offspring even larger than the already astronomical number of possibilities.

The number of strings of DNA in one chromosome varies from 500 to 5,000. It has been estimated that there are between 50,000 and 100,000 total DNA molecules in all the 46 human chromosomes, but these molecules contain perhaps three billion bits of information that can differ among individuals (Plomin, DeFries, and McClearn 1990).

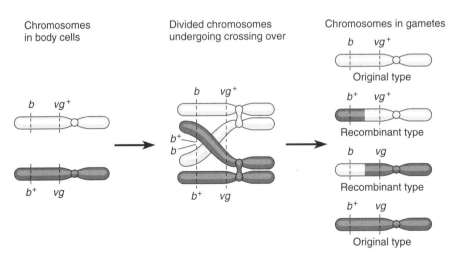

Figure 4.1   A simplified illustration of "crossing over" of gene segments between chromosomes during reproduction.

What Genes Do

Genes instruct the body in how to make molecules that control many bodily processes, but, of course, they aren't doing this all the time. Rather, they complete this task only when needed. When the product of a gene (a specific protein) is produced by a cell, we say the gene is being *expressed*. Within a single organism, some genes are rarely expressed, others are expressed constantly, and still others are expressed for a time, then turned off. For example, at puberty, the genes turn on chemicals (hormones) that produce the secondary sexual characteristics that emerge in the human body, namely, body hair, breast growth in females, muscle growth in males, and so on. On the other hand, certain other proteins involved in food digestion and metabolism must be produced by the body all the time, and, in a sense, the production of these proteins represents genetic influences being constantly expressed.

Let's return to hemophilia, the bleeder's disease. There is a protein normally found in the bloodstream called the "clotting factor," or vitamin K. When an individual is cut or wounded in some way, it is this protein that causes blood to clot and close the wound. A hemophiliac's cells lack the ability to manufacture vitamin K because the genes—the genetic instructions—are not there to tell the cells how to manufacture the substance. Thus, hemophiliacs may be perfectly normal in every way except they lack the gene that enables the body to make the clotting factor.

Heritability

Animal behavior is always the joint product of genetic and environmental influences. It makes no sense to regard behavior as exclusively the product of one or the other. But geneticists are interested in the extent to which differences in behavior in a given population of animals may be due relatively more to genetic or to environmental influences. Consequently, geneticists have devised ways to measure or estimate the relative importance of these two sets of factors. **Heritability (*H*)** refers to what proportion (0 to 1) of variability in a population phenotype is accounted for by variability in a genotype. *H* is a numerical answer to the question, How much (what proportion) of variability in a given population trait is attributable to genes? If we abbreviate the total variability in a population as *Vpop* and the variability attributable to genes as *Vgen*, then *H* is equal to *Vgen/Vpop*. Vpop−Vgen yields the amount of variability attributable to the environment, *Venv*.

Note that *H* is a term that applies only to a specific population, not to individuals. Measuring *H* for two groups that live in different environments is likely to yield different results. Thus, *H* is estimated for a given population under given environmental conditions.

Measuring the total variation (Vpop) of a phenotype in a population is often not difficult. So, for example, psychologists have devised tests for measuring many human psychological traits, such as intelligence, motivation, memory, and personality characteristics. Once a sample is assessed on any of these traits, we can obtain the average difference of scores from the mean score—a measure of total variability in the trait. However, it is not easy to estimate H most of the time because quantifying Vgen is much more problematic. To estimate Vgen, we must first get a sample where variability either in genetic differences or in environmental differences is held constant. For example, we can reduce Vgen virtually to zero by using identical human twins or inbreeding or cloning animals to obtain genetically identical animals. Once we get the variability in the sample attributable to the environment (Venv), then Vpop − Venv = Vgen, and we can estimate H. Similarly, in studies where environmental effects are held constant, we may be able to estimate Vgen. Because of these difficulties, estimates of H for human traits vary considerably. For example, using a variety of methods, experts have estimated H for differences in intelligence to be as high as .80 or as low as .50, though the estimates average around .60 (Snyderman and Rothman 1987).

Most research on estimating H for the genetics of behavior has been performed on fruit flies, rodents, and farm animals because these animals are easy to breed and monitor under controlled conditions. Some values of H for traits that have been well researched are reported in Table 4.1 (from (Ayala 1982)). As the table shows, some animal traits are relatively high in H, implying that differences in those traits are largely caused by heredity (e.g., white spots on cattle), whereas other traits are low in H, implying that differences in those traits are largely attributable to environmental factors (e.g., litter size in mice). Because of the many difficulties inherent in the effort to track breeding and genetic factors in larger organisms, the heritability of many of the traits and be-

TABLE 4.1   **Sample Heritability Ratios for Some Animals**

Trait	Value of H
White spotting in Frisian cattle	.95
Slaughter weight in cattle	.85
Egg weight in poultry	.60
Fleece weight in sheep	.40
Milk production in cattle	.30
Litter size in mice	.15
Conception rate in cattle	.05

haviors of large animals has not been researched and can only be guessed at.

Genetic Change and Evolution

The synthesis of Darwin's theory of evolution with modern principles of genetics is now called the synthetic theory of evolution, the word *synthetic* emphasizing the joining together of the two sets of ideas. Since World War II, the synthetic theory has been the dominant view of scientific thought concerning evolution. This synthesis created a new thrust in biology—the study of population genetics. This form of science involves surveying the total range of genetic variation within a population of organisms ("gene pool") in order to answer several questions: What genetic variations exist within a species? How do gene pools change over time? What are the factors that cause these changes? What roles do these changes play in the evolution of species?

As was discussed in the previous chapter, natural selection is regarded as the major force that determines and changes the frequencies of genes (alleles) in a population. Natural selection does not change the genes themselves but, rather, determines which genes survive to be passed on to offspring and which genes do not. However, the frequency of genes in a population of animals can also change because of other factors—namely, mutations, gene flow, genetic drift, and nonrandom mating.

Mutations

One of the key concepts in genetics that is important for evolution is that of **mutations,** the random, unpredictable changes that can occur in genes, sometimes due to radiation, chemicals, or other unknown factors. When genes from each parent are combined into new combinations in offspring, random mistakes or "copying errors" occasionally happen. Mutations can involve whole chromosomes, segments or sets of chromosomes (called chromosomal mutations), or just individual genes (gene mutations). Mutations do not refer to the normal variations among alleles in the gene pool; they refer to new, unusual changes in alleles that lead to new physical structures in the body and perhaps in behavior as well.

Most mutations occur spontaneously and, although they are caused, we often cannot identify the specific causal factor in each case. The rate of spontaneous mutations is rather slow. It has been estimated that each new human being, with as many as 100,000 genes, may carry as few as two new mutations on the average (others have estimated the rate as somewhat higher). Thus, whereas mutations may have some effect, it is assumed they are not the major mechanism of evolutionary change since random, spontaneous mutations are thought to be rare (Wilson and Bossert 1971).

Because they are random and unpredictable, most mutations are either meaningless, harmless, or simply result in the death of the organism. But mutations do provide raw material for evolutionary change. Mutations are a factor that may help evolution to progress faster, as in sudden spurts resulting in species changing over only a few generations; moreover, they provide variations that other evolutionary forces can act upon. They do not, however, determine the direction of evolution—the environment and natural selection do that. Once in a while, over the long haul, we should expect to see mutations that will occasionally produce changes that are advantageous to the animal. Thus, if there is a sudden dry spell that kills many frogs, those frogs that have some mutation that allows them to better withstand the drought will be more likely to survive.

Gene Flow

Specific genetic alleles may move into or out of a population simply because of the movement of breeding individuals from one geographic area to another. This kind of **gene flow** can introduce new alleles into a population or change the frequencies of specific alleles. A great deal of gene flow tends to decrease differences between populations, counteracting isolation and natural selection for new species. As discussed in Chapter 3, new species are often formed when geography creates barriers that prevent gene flow.

Genetic Drift

The composition of a population's gene pool can change largely as the result of chance, especially in small populations. In a small population, an allele can disappear permanently if the small number of individuals that possess the allele fail to reproduce. Similarly, in a large population, a particular allele may become more common simply because those individuals possessing that allele, just by chance, produce more offspring. Changes in the gene pool that are largely attributable to chance factors are called **genetic drift.**

The effects of genetic drift have been studied chiefly in small populations. For example, a small part of a population can be separated from the main body; subsequently, the members of the smaller, isolated population may reproduce exclusively by interbreeding among themselves. Only the genes that the isolated population possesses will be passed on to offspring, and any other alleles found in the original population will be lost, gradually resulting in a new gene pool. This form of genetic drift is called the **founder effect**—when it is mainly events of chance, rather than forces of natural selection, that determine the genes in a new population.

A similar phenomenon, known as the **bottleneck effect,** occurs when a population of animals loses many of its numbers by forces other than natural selection—frequently from human intervention such as hunting or fishing. For example, in the mid-1800s, the northern elephant seal living off California shores was hunted almost to extinction. Only approximately 20 individual seals were left alive when the Mexican and U.S. governments put the elephant seal under protection in 1884. Now the population of the elephant seal is over 30,000. All of these animals are descendants of the original 20; therefore, much of the genetic variability in the original population of the early 1800s has been lost (see Chapter 10 for more discussion on this seal). Sometime in the distant past, the same thing may have happened to the cheetah since individual cheetahs have been found to be extremely similar to one another genetically.

Nonrandom Mating

Genetic change can also occur because individual animals may have mating preferences that have nothing to do with the fitness of their mates. For example, snow geese (*Chen caerulescens*) come in two varieties, white and a blue-brown color called blue (see Figure 4.2). White geese tend to mate preferentially with other white geese and blue with blue. These preferences help keep the geese in the two distinct phenotypes (blue-white matings occur rarely). Although the blue color is dominant and the white recessive, the white geese are just as common in the population because they tend to mate only with each other. Of course,

Figure 4.2   The two forms, white and blue, of the snow goose.

nonrandom mating preferences also occur in human beings, with, on the average, taller males pairing with taller females and shorter ones with shorter females.

Genes and Behavior

How do genes influence behavior? This is a question for which the answers are highly complex and not well understood. In some species, behaviors may be largely genetically programmed, as, for example, in the web-weaving abilities of spiders. Spiders appear to weave their webs largely independent of learning experiences, even when the web appears to us to be very complex. However, this does not mean that a gene simply "produces" the web-weaving behavior. Instead, the genes enable the behavior to be performed through a long chain of biological processes. The direct function of a gene is to tell the cells of the body to make proteins and chains of chemicals, called amino acids, that are the building blocks of proteins. These substances, in turn, determine the biological constitution of the organism and influence how the organism ultimately behaves. A difference in genes between individuals will change the structure of the proteins, resulting in changes in anatomy and physiology, which may thereby alter behavior.

Thus, all traits of animals are ultimately physiological at their basis. During development, particular genes within a cell lead to specialization of that cell into skin, hair, muscle, neurons, internal organs, and so on. At the same time, other genes in other cells produce proteins and hormones, which influence the activities of yet other cells. Primary gene action may lead to several intervening steps before actual gene-influenced behavior is observed. The complexity of these steps and gene interactions, which may occur only at certain times during development as determined by yet other genes, make it very difficult for scientists to study the genetic bases of behavior. In addition, a given behavior may be influenced by several genes acting in combination.

The aspect of gene regulation that is perhaps most familiar to us is the way genes command cells to produce hormones that influence human growth and development. During puberty, human beings undergo changes in their bodies. Along with maturation of the gonads comes the development of secondary sexual characteristics: bodily hair in both sexes, muscle growth in males, breast development in females, and so on. At the same time, changes take place in sexual interest and behavior. Physiological changes responding to genetic control underlie all of these changes.

The possession of a gene that influences a given behavior does not guarantee the behavior will occur. The gene underlying a behavior may be "turned off" by other genes, or a particular behavior may require certain environmental events to occur before it can surface.

Studying Genes and Behavior

The experimental method of studying the relative effects of genes and environment on animal behavior takes one of two roads. The first is to manipulate genetic differences while holding environmental effects constant; the second is to manipulate environmental variables while maintaining constant genetic structure. Though gene manipulation is neither permissible nor ethically desirable with human beings, methods have been devised for manipulating the genes of animals and plants in order to study genetic effects.

In 1927, H. J. Muller discovered that exposing fruit fly genes to X rays greatly increased the rate at which mutations occurred, causing the flies to have missing or extra organs. Soon thereafter, others discovered that ultraviolet light as well as certain chemicals could also produce mutations. Using these agents to produce structural changes yields genetic mutants. Once the structure has changed, scientists could then observe changes in behavior. Most of the work done with genetic mutations has been done with simple insects such as fruit flies because specific genes can be affected. However, it is not a very practical method when used with more complex animals.

Another way to manipulate genes is to mate brothers with sisters, or offspring with parents, over several generations, a process called **inbreeding.** This is commonly done with rats or mice. When this is done repeatedly with the same group of animals, the result is that all the individual animals have identical genes. According to Fuller and Wimer (1973), when inbreeding is continued for 30 generations or more, the offspring in the final generation become as similar genetically as identical twins. This allows for the clarification of environmental effects on behavior: keeping genes constant while manipulating aspects of the environment. For example, we can have genetically identical animals raised by different parents to see what differences in maternal care might contribute to development.

On the other hand, we can also hold the maternal-rearing environment constant to see whether there are differences in behavior due to genes. In these studies, animals of the same species but different varieties or *strains* are often compared. For example, Lynch and Hegmann (1972) compared the nest-building behaviors of house mice (*Mus domesticus*) from five different inbred strains that had been raised in the same environment. The researchers measured the amount of cotton that each mouse used to make its nest in its cage, and the results indicated definite differences between strains in the amount of nest material used. These differences can be explained only by differences in genes.

Cross-Fostering

If genetically similar animals are raised under different conditions but still elicit similar behavior, then the genetic control of that behavior appears to be substantial. However, if behavior under these conditions is different, then the environment is playing a role. In typical cross-fostering studies, newborn animals are not raised by their mother but, rather, by a different female of the same or related species. Therefore, cross-fostering can only be done when the host species will accept offspring other than its own. This is possible with many species of rats and mice. For example, Reading (1966) performed a cross-fostering study of two strains of mice, using the open field test as a measure of mouse activity. An open field consists of a brightly lit enclosure such as that pictured in Figure 4.3. This kind of test was originally devised by Hall (1934) to measure "emotionality" in rats. When placed in this enclosure, a rodent's behavior may range from apparent stress and fear (i.e., the animal stays in one place and defecates) to active curiosity (i.e., low defecation and apparent unstressful exploration of the space). Modern electronics allows the researcher to record the animal's movements and activities automatically.

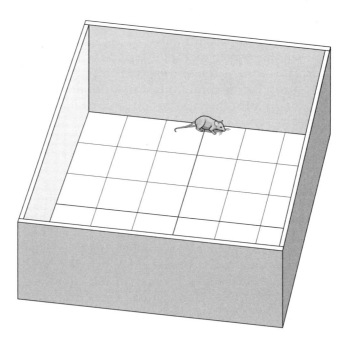

Figure 4.3   An open field apparatus used to measure activity or emotionality in rodent species.

Reading (1966) cross-fostered two strains of mice called B and C. The results of this study are portrayed in Figure 4.4. The figure shows that strain C (fourth column) was more active than strain B (first column) when mice were raised by their natural mothers, indicating a genetic difference in activity between the strains or a difference between B and C mothers' behavior. The two middle columns show the performance of cross-fostered groups, in which strain B pups were raised by strain C mothers (second column) and strain C pups were raised by strain B mothers (third column). These two middle columns indicate that strain B mice were more active when cross-fostered to the strain C mothers. This effect is attributable to the mothering behavior of strain C mothers, not to strain B genes.

We can also study existing populations with genetic differences and see how these differences might predict dissimilarities in behavior. This is the least intrusive method and the one used most often; with it, we can easily compare behaviors across species or within species, as was done with the ungulates in Chapter 2. Of course, since this method does not involve experimental manipulation, causal conclusions can only be tentative. We will see how this method is used in a variety of settings, with a number of species, in upcoming chapters.

Biochemical Analysis

Technological advances in recent decades have enabled scientists to determine with greater precision the genetic relationships between individual animals and between species. These microbiological techniques, which cannot be described in detail here, involve the actual measurement of proteins or DNA in the cells of animals and the examination of

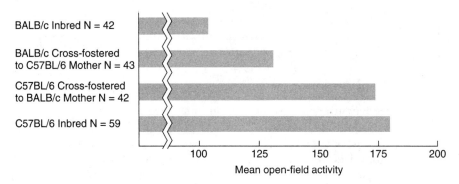

Figure 4.4 The results of the open field test for inbred and cross-fostered rats (Reading 1966).

specific gene loci in chromosomes. These advances have enabled researchers to answer questions that were previously educated guesses at best, such as, Does a female mate with more than one male during the breeding period, and if so, do her offspring have more than one father? Birdsall and Nash (1973) studied deer mice (*Peromyscus maniculatus*) by trapping pregnant females in the wild and taking blood samples from them and their offspring later. Using sophisticated biochemical techniques, they found that about 10% of the litters had mouse pups inseminated by more than one father.

More recently, DNA "fingerprinting" techniques have enabled scientists to find out the genetic relationship between particular individuals, with a high degree of accuracy. Using this procedure, scientists can try to answer questions such as, Can a male animal tell which of a female's offspring are his when the offspring were fathered by several males? Burke, Davies, Bruford, and Hatchwell (1989) observed hedge sparrows (*Prunella molularis*) and determined which males had mated with particular females to produce offspring. They then collected tissue samples from all the birds for DNA fingerprinting analysis to determine exactly which offspring had which particular males as fathers. They found that the male parents did not discriminate between their own and other males' offspring in groups of young birds with several male parents; that is, the males could not tell which offspring birds were their own, so they treated all the young birds the same.

Unfortunately, these methods of biochemical analysis are not likely to be available for extensive use in studying animals in the near future because they are so expensive.

Artificial Selection (Selective Breeding)

One of the oldest methods for studying genes and behavior is through the **artificial selection** (or selective breeding) of specific behavioral-psychological traits. Using this method, we can demonstrate whether a trait or behavior is under some genetic control and whether the genetic control is simple or polygenic.

Dog Personalities

For centuries, human beings have been breeding dogs for appearance characteristics and for behavioral-psychological traits, such as aggressiveness, sociability, and obedience. By crossbreeding relatively pure and long-isolated strains (breeds) of dogs, scientists have begun to find out which traits might be due to a single gene and which traits are polygenic.

Two breeds that have been used in such experiments are the cocker spaniel, long limited to Europe, and the basenji, a breed that doesn't bark and that originates in Africa. These dogs are about the same size, 20 to 25 pounds, but are very different behaviorally (see Figure 4.5). As you probably already know, cocker spaniels are generally nonaggressive, sociable, docile (trainable), and friendly. Basenjis, on the other hand, are more aggressive, aloof, independent (less trainable), and not as friendly to strangers.

Some interesting findings are obtained from breeding cocker spaniels with basenjis and looking at the hybrid offspring's physical characteristics and behavior. The hybrids can show us, for example, which dog traits might be dominant or recessive. Studies showed that the boldness-timidity and friendliness-unfriendliness dimensions are separate traits affected by separate genes, and different breeds of dogs reflect all possible combinations of these traits. A timid, unfriendly dog is one that avoids you but growls and bares its teeth when cornered (typical of chihuahuas and some other smaller breeds). Purebred cocker spaniels tend to be bold and friendly. Basenjis (and dobermans) tend to be bold but less friendly. Greyhounds are timid but friendly. Of course, these behaviors are also influenced by training and human treatment, but breeds do differ significantly in innate traits (Scott and Fuller 1965). In similar work, Pfaffenberger, Fuller, Ginsberg, and Bielfelt (1976) showed that German shepherds used as guide dogs for the blind could be selectively bred for slower walking speed, friendlier temperament, and greater trainability by interbreeding only those shepherds that tended to have those traits.

Figure 4.5   The basenji and the cocker spaniel, two dog breeds similar in size but very different in physical and behavioral traits.

Maze-Brightness in Rats

One classic study of both inbreeding and artificial selection for a behavioral trait is that of Cooper and Zubek (1958) on maze-brightness in rats (based on an earlier study by Tryon [1940]). The researchers first tested a population of rats for the speed at which they could learn to run a complex maze. By counting the number of errors (wrong turns) each rat made in a maze, the researchers determined which rats were faster learners and which were slower learners. Those who learned faster or were "maze-bright" were bred with each other and those who were slower or "maze-dull" were bred with each other, each group for several generations. Using this method, the researchers were able to create two distinctive "strains" of rats that differed in their learning ability. Thus, they demonstrated that maze-brightness in rats has a genetic component.

But this was not the end of the study. Some rats of each strain were raised in two environments, each different from the normal laboratory situation. Some were in an enriched environment where rats could play together with movable toys, while other rats experienced an impoverished environment consisting of gray walls, no movable objects, and no rat companions. The results are summarized in Figure 4.6. The two bars in the middle of the graph show the results of inbreeding for the two strains in the normal lab environment.

Such inbreeding creates two groups of rats for which maze-brightness differs considerably when the rats are tested in adulthood. The bars on the left show the results of the impoverished environment: the maze-bright rats made about as many errors as the maze-dull rats! On the right

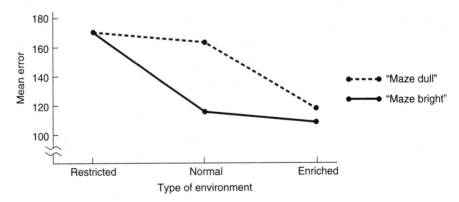

Figure 4.6   The results of the study by Cooper and Zubek (1958) on breeding maze-bright and maze-dull rats and raising them in three different environments.

of the graph (the enriched environment), the maze-dull rats did almost as well as the maze-bright ones.

These results are a vivid illustration of the principle of heredity-environment interaction: The expression of genetic potential depends on (is modified by) the environment in which the organism develops and lives. The environment does not change the genes themselves—the genes an animal is born with are permanent and unchanging. But the environment can change the genes' potential for expression. The enriched environment enabled the maze-dull rats to do about as well as the so-called maze-bright animals. The improverished environment caused the maze-bright rats to do no better than their maze-dull counterparts. We see a real difference in learning potential attributable to differences in genes only when the environment is the same middling lab environment for both strains (the two middle bars on the graph).

It is important to note that the rats were not bred for "general intelligence" but for a specific kind of intelligence (maze-brightness), in a specific maze setting. Years after Tryon's original study (1940) on breeding for maze-brightness, Searle (1949) retested the descendants of Tryon's rats in the same maze used by Tryon and confirmed that the descendants of the bright rats performed better in the maze than the descendants of the dull rats. However, when a different maze was used, the two populations did equally well!

We cannot understand to what extent behaviors of a particular species are genetically determined until we do studies (like the Cooper and Zubek study) for each behavior in each species. Similar behaviors in different species may have different evolutionary histories and developmental causes. For example, we know that the songs that birds sing (often male birds singing to attract a mate) are largely a fixed pattern and are not easily modifiable by experience in some species (e.g., the ring dove), are partly genetic in other species (a basic pattern modified by experience, as in sparrows), and are mostly learned by hearing other birds in yet other species (e.g., the mynah bird).

The Instinct Concept

In the history of the life sciences, few terms have had more meanings and more misunderstanding than the term *instinct*. Older definitions of instinct seemed to imply that, for an instinctive behavior, the environment is irrelevant and the behavior is completely built in the organism or innate or genetically determined. As we have seen in this chapter, any behavior is always the joint product of both genetic and environmental factors. Behavior cannot occur in either a genetic or environmental vacuum.

Thus, it only makes sense to regard as instinctive those behaviors that have strong innate determinants relative to the environment. In addition, modern biologists usually regard instinctive behaviors as having several other properties: they are typical of all members of the species, are difficult to modify during development, occur in complete form the first time they are performed, and are typically elicited by some simple environmental cue.

In some species, some behavior patterns are so built in that modification is almost impossible. For example, you cannot get rid of rooting in pigs, aggression in minks, or curiosity in cats. Thus, **instinctive drift** occurs when behavior tends to gravitate toward a strong instinctive pattern, even when learning or training contradicts the instinct. Generally, strongly instinctive behavior patterns are highly adaptive and useful for the animal in its natural environment, but such patterns may not be useful for human purposes. A pig in the wild that naturally roots in the soil for tubers and roots would be a nuisance to anyone proud of a finely terraced garden.

As explained earlier, genes alone never produce phenotypes or behavior by themselves. Behavior is always the joint product of what is inside the organism (genes, hormones, physiology), the environment the organism is in, and the organism's past experiences. It is simpler to think about this by using examples of extremes. Try to imagine a genetic organism that is not in an environment, that is, not anywhere. An organism in a vacuum would be dead! Obviously, some environment must always be there having some effect on the organism. By the same token, try to think of an organism in an environment but without any genes. Nothing would happen! There would be no living organisms without DNA. Clearly, a behavior is always the product of hereditary and environmental factors acting together. But a difference in behavior (or in any phenotypical trait) between two individuals may be due to a difference in *one* gene! Just as the difference in eye color between two individuals may be due to a difference in one allele, the differences between genes may determine differences in behavior in very simple ways.

Summary

Our modern understanding of heredity begins with the work of Mendel in the 19th century. Individual organisms that reproduce sexually inherit half of their genes from each parent. Mendel specified how the units of heredity, now called genes, combine with each other in ways that result in the outer appearance of the organism, its phenotype. With the development of more sophisticated microscopic methods in the 20th century, biochemists have been able to locate genes within the DNA molecules that reside in chromosomes in the nuclei of the cells of every living organism. These genes direct the cells in the manufacture of proteins that determine bodily functions, including growth and development.

Within a population of animals, variations in appearance and behavior are due partly to genetic differences and partly to differences in experience. Heritability (*H*) represents the proportion of total variation in a specific trait that is attributable to genetic influences.

Over time and during evolution, the genetic makeup of populations of animals changes because of several factors in addition to natural selection. Mutations are infrequent, random, and unpredictable genetic changes. Gene flow occurs when animals with new genes move to a different geographic area. Genetic drift occurs when certain genes spread or disappear because of mating accidents or human interference rather than natural selection. The frequency of genes in a population may also be affected by nonrandom factors, such as mating preferences, that are not related to species fitness.

The influence of genes on behavior is difficult to study, especially in highly complex organisms. Whereas genes and their effects can be understood through methods such as inbreeding and cross-fostering in small organisms like fruit flies and mice, such methods are generally impractical for large animals that breed slowly. Modern technology has opened new doors to understanding genetic factors by enabling scientists to examine genetic material through procedures such as DNA fingerprinting.

The selective breeding of specific physical or behavioral traits has been used for centuries in developing farm animals and dog breeds. This technique is useful for determining whether or not a trait has a genetic component and whether a trait is influenced by one gene or several in combination. Classic selective breeding studies have been performed on several species, including personality in dogs and maze-brightness in rats.

In modern biology, an instinct refers to a behavior for which innate, genetic determinants are very strong relative to environmental influences. Since all behaviors are always the joint product of both genes and experience, the conception of instincts as behaviors that have only genetic determinants is not tenable. Some behaviors, such as rooting in pigs, are so strongly programmed by innate factors that the behavior may drift toward the instinctive pattern even when minimal environmental stimuli are present.

CHAPTER 5

Learning and Adaptation

Experience changes us. If we're fortunate, the changes are good for us. They lead to growth, understanding, and, perhaps, an improvement in our social or occupational skills. It's no different for nonhuman animals. Those that are good at learning from experience may reap rewards when they can change their behavior to adapt better to their circumstances. Other animals may be forced to rely largely on their instinctive abilities to cope with their problems.

This chapter reviews the main types of learning processes in the context of adaptation to the environment. Although psychologists have spent many decades studying learning processes in the laboratory, we shall focus more on how learning abilities assist animals in survival in their wild habitats. The different types of learning perform somewhat distinct functions for the learner; they also differ in their complexity. More sophisticated forms of learning require animal nervous systems that can exhibit that complexity. Thus, whereas what an animal learns depends on its individual experiences, how an animal learns depends upon how its species has evolved over millennia.

Perhaps the greatest and most long-standing contribution made by psychologists to the understanding of animal behavior is their study of learning and conditioning processes. Beginning with the American E. L. Thorndike and the Russian Ivan Pavlov around the turn of the century, psychologists spent many years discovering and experimenting on the basic principles of learning. This enterprise was greatly promoted by John Watson's founding of behaviorism in 1913. Indeed, historians and writers now refer to the period from roughly 1920 to 1955 as the "golden age of behaviorism" because American psychology was very devoted to the experimental study of learning and conditioning phenomena. The reader is likely to be familiar with some of the great names here—Clark Hull, B. F. Skinner, Lashley, Tolman, Guthrie, and so on.

During this period, the study of learning by psychologists was dominated by laboratory studies using relatively few species, mainly rats and mice. For many historical reasons, some of which will be discussed later in this chapter, psychologists and biologists in the 1950s and 1960s turned their interests toward learning by a greater range of species in their natural habitats.

Learning takes many different forms, so it may be helpful here to provide a general definition of what learning encompasses and what it does not. **Learning** can be defined as a process by which long-lasting changes in behavior are acquired as a result of experience. Because learning is a process taking place in the nervous system of the organism, we cannot directly observe it. Rather, we must infer its existence from observing overt changes in behavior or performance of tasks—changes we often label as "improvements" when it involves something we want to learn. Learning must be defined as relatively long lasting in order to distinguish it from short-term changes that result from fatigue, motivation, or other momentary factors. However, learning is not necessarily permanent; what is learned can be forgotten. Finally, learning occurs because of experience, something that happens to the animal. All experiences the animal has may not lead to learning, but all learning comes from experience, by definition.

Learning as an Adaptive Mechanism

Scientists who study animal behavior are especially interested in those learning experiences from which an animal derives benefits not only for its immediate survival but also for its more general adaptation to its surroundings. For example, young predators often must learn what, where, and how to hunt prey from their parents and from practice. In general, it is assumed that the ability to learn must be the product of natural selection and that it is adaptive. Thus, superior learning abilities have evolved because of the advantages such abilities have for the individual's survival.

The process of evolution changes organisms slowly over many generations so that the offspring in succeeding generations gradually have more adaptive traits. But individuals are also confronted with environments that change quickly and are often unpredictable. Those animals that can learn may be able to change their behavior to cope with these changing circumstances. When changes are highly predictable, such as the day-night cycle or seasonal temperature changes, the organism may evolve cycled changes in its physiology or behavior that cope with these predictable environmental changes. But environmental changes that are random or unpredictable in the animal's lifetime cannot be anticipated by preprogrammed mechanisms. The ability to learn represents the ability to cope with these more chaotic changes. Thus, an ecological perspective regards the fundamental function of learning to be coping with environmental circumstances or changes that cannot be anticipated by the animal.

An individual cannot predict, for example, exactly how its habitat will look, where the best foraging will be located, or where a supply of water might be. To be successful, the individual must learn and remember such details from its experience. Learning and memory are definite adaptive advantages in species that live a long time. Information that was learned and retained long ago can prove very useful to an animal whose current food or water resources suddenly become unavailable. Using learned information, the animal can travel to a new location where there are alternate sources if it remembers what it has learned. On the other hand, many insect species have very short life spans, which largely make well-developed learning abilities costly and unnecessary. One insect or larval form of an insect may find all its lifetime needs in one tree trunk or in the roots of one tree. Consequently, many insects rely primarily on innate behavior patterns that give them all the adaptive benefits they need.

In the next part of this chapter, we will first discuss the different varieties of learning and their apparent adaptive functions for animals in their natural habitats. In the latter part of the chapter, we will examine how the learning process is affected and constrained by characteristics of the species.

Types of Learning and Their Functions

Habituation

The simplest form of learning, **habituation,** is a decrease or disappearance of a built-in, natural response to a stimulus that occurs when the animal repeatedly encounters the stimulus. It is considered to be the simplest form of learning because it occurs in many of the most primitive organisms, like worms and snails, and one-celled organisms such as protozoa. The adaptive value of habituation is that the organism learns not to waste time and energy reacting to an unimportant or harmless stimulus. In essence, habituation gradually removes attention from nonessential information so the animal can respond to the important events with which it is confronted. For example, young animals and children typically overreact to novel stimuli, such as new faces and unfamiliar places, with fright or flight. As they become more familiar with these new stimuli, the fear reaction habituates. Thus, a scarecrow may be effective initially in keeping birds out of your garden, but after a while the birds learn to ignore the scarecrow.

Gradually, an animal learns which stimuli are important to react to and which are not. All of us have largely learned to ignore or disregard many stimuli that continually surround us (sounds, lighting, our familiar surroundings). On the other hand, we would not want to habituate to fire alarms and police sirens. Generally, animals must have experience to learn which stimuli they can afford to ignore. For example, whereas a leopard learns to habituate to many sounds in the jungle, recognizing a few as threatening and others as alluring, our own house pets learn to ignore the sounds of cars and television sets.

Even a response as strong as aggression can become habituated because these kinds of responses require a great expenditure of energy. Moreover, such responses involve risk. Clayton and Hinde (1968) showed a Siamese fighting fish (*Betta spendens*) its mirror image at the side of a fish tank. The fish immediately made an aggressive display, but when the mirror was left in place and was not followed by an attack, the fish soon learned to ignore its own image. Clearly, familiarity and repetition lead to habituation even though, under other circumstances, aggression in this fish has the important survival function of keeping competitors out of its territory.

Habituation helps to explain why many animals can live in close proximity to each other as neighbors. On the African plains, many species of grazing animals, including zebras, gazelles, and wildebeests, graze together while largely ignoring each other. A more dramatic example of this neutral coexistence is found in Emperor penguins (*Aptenodytes forsteri*). During the breeding season, these flightless birds congregate in the thousands on the coasts of Antarctica. A monogamous male and female pair take turns caring for their one egg, standing only a few feet from another breeding pair (see Figure 5.1). It is important for the breeding pair to reserve all their energy for keeping the egg warm and, later, caring for the young penguin. Consequently, squabbles among the adult penguins are rare. When they do occur, they are short lived.

Classical Conditioning

Classical conditioning takes advantage of the fact that an animal already exhibits a certain built-in response (called an unconditioned response, or UCR) when a certain stimulus (called the unconditioned stimulus, or UCS) is presented. For example, a dog will salivate (UCR) when a bit of tasty food is put on its tongue (UCS). This is an unlearned response in which the animal does not have a choice whether to respond or not to the UCS. After several presentations of an initially neutral stimulus with the

Figure 5.1 Emperor penguins nest in pairs very close to other nesting pairs, but different pairs ignore each other.

food, such as the sound of a bell, the animal will eventually salivate to the sound of the bell, as Pavlov showed. The bell has become a conditioned stimulus (CS) that now elicits the conditioned response (CR) of salivation.

The adaptive significance of this kind of learning is that the new CS (formerly a neutral stimulus) becomes a signal or substitute for the UCS. For example, if an animal is threatened or attacked by a predator in a formerly neutral place, the animal will learn to avoid that place in the future. Thus, the place becomes associated with the threat, leading the animal to avoid it as it would the predator. In this instance, classical conditioning is *aversive;* that is, it leads to a response that is adaptive because the animal avoids unpleasant consequences.

Hollis (1984, 1990) hypothesized that one adaptive function of classical conditioning is to prepare animals for important events. Some of her studies focused on territorial defense in a fish, the blue gourami (*Trichogaster trichopterus*). The male gourami defends its territory vigorously because females usually mate only with territorial males. When confronted with an intruder, the territorial male swims toward the intruder with fins erect. If the intruder does not retreat, a battle ensues in which serious injury is possible.

Hollis reasoned that any behavior or trait that would promote successful territorial defense should be favored by natural selection. So, for example, a gourami that anticipates an upcoming battle would be able to prepare better for defense. In an experiment, a territorial gourami was trained with classical conditioning: 10-second light (CS) preceded a viewing of another male gourami for 15 seconds across a glass barrier, acting as a signal that the viewing was coming. After experiencing this situation for several trials, the conditioned males were tested with actual encounters with other males, but with the 10-second light preceding the removal of the barrier between the fish. The results showed that the conditioned males were superior in territorial defense. As soon as the light came on, the conditioned males approached the barrier with their fins already erect. While fighting, they bit their opponents more often than they received bites. Thus, the data supported the idea that classical conditioning can function to prepare the male gourami for an aggressive encounter, thereby giving it a better chance of defending its territory and gaining mating success.

Instrumental Conditioning

The systematic study of what is now called instrumental conditioning began with the work of an American psychologist, Edward L. Thorndike (1874–1949), in the late 1800s. Thorndike (1898) set food outside a wooden puzzle box that housed a hungry cat (see Figure 5.2). In order to get to the food, the cat had to press a lever that released a latch on the door to the box. Initially, when put in such a place, a cat becomes agitated and displays a variety of unsuccessful behaviors—reaching between the slats, pushing and pulling, and so on. This is the trial-and-error learning phase of what came to be called **instrumental conditioning.** Eventually, the cat accidentally releases the latch, escapes, and gets to the food. When this situation is repeated, it takes less time on the following trials for the cat to get out of the box. In other words, with more experience, the cat learns to get out very quickly after it is caged.

Both classical and instrumental conditioning involve learning "associations." However, whereas classical conditioning leads to an associ-

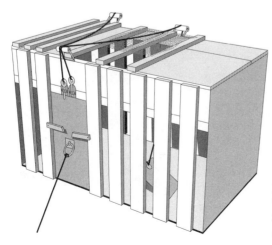

Figure 5.2   Thorndike's puzzle box from which a cat had to learn to escape to get a food reward.

ation between two stimuli (the UCS and the CS), instrumental conditioning leads to an association between a stimulus situation (the puzzle box) and a response (escape). In Thorndike's original analysis, the function of the reward is to strengthen or reinforce the escape response. In studies of learning and conditioning, **reinforcers** are now defined as any events that follow a response and serve to increase the probability of that response's occurrence.

In the 1930s and 1940s, B. F. Skinner (1904–1990) focused the attention of researchers on the phases of instrumental conditioning that come after the initial response is discovered and acquired. Specifically, Skinner and many others studied how associative responses are strengthened and maintained once they are learned. These procedures are referred to as **operant conditioning.** Skinner (1938, 1953) developed his operant chamber ("Skinner box") to control an animal in this situation. For example, in many of Skinner's studies, a rat learned to press a bar because a bar press was followed immediately by food presentation (see Figure 5.3).

Though early studies on conditioning used only a few species (primarily mammals, like rats and monkeys, and birds, such as pigeons), more recent research has broadened the range of species known to be capable of instrumental conditioning. Boycott (1965), for example, demonstrated that the common octopus (*Octopus vulgaris*) could be conditioned to prefer some food items (e.g., crabs) while avoiding others (fish). These outcomes have enabled researchers to investigate the visual and tactile abilities of the octopus. Other researchers have demonstrated operant conditioning in arthropods such as spiders and bees.

Operant conditioning is the basic process underlying how animals (including humans) often acquire and perfect their skills. The animal continues to respond, receive feedback, and respond again until a goal

Response
lever

Food cup

Figure 5.3 A rat in an operant chamber.

is reached. When we say "practice makes perfect," we are essentially talking about operant conditioning in its simple and more complex forms. Research psychologists have spent an enormous amount of time and effort studying the factors that speed up and slow down operant conditioning and that strengthen and weaken acquired responses. Most often, this has been done with relatively few species (e.g., rats and pigeons) under highly controlled laboratory conditions.

Instrumental and operant conditioning have many variations, two of which will be discussed further here.

Shaping.   All of us have probably observed domestic or circus animals performing behaviors that they would never perform or learn in the wild. How can we condition an animal to exhibit such behaviors if the behavior never occurs naturally? In several of his publications, Skinner (e.g., 1953, 1958) was the first to describe the process of **shaping** by means of the method of successive approximations. A hungry pigeon is placed in a small cage that has a target key placed at the level of the pigeon's eyes. When grain is delivered to the pigeon, a light illuminates the grain. The pigeon in the box learns that the light coming on signals the delivery of food.

Next comes the shaping process, the goal of which is to have the pigeon learn that pecking the key causes food to be delivered. This is accomplished through successive approximations of the desired result. First, any movement toward the key is rewarded with grain. Once this movement is consistently performed, then a reward is given only when the pigeon stands in front of the key. Finally, the bird is rewarded only when it pecks the key. After this response is learned and performed consistently, other responses can be shaped through successive approximations, including behaviors the animal would never perform in its natural environment (e.g., turning around in circles, doing figure eights, or preening). (See Figure 5.4.)

Thus, the essence of shaping is to begin by rewarding the behavior that is most like the desired behavior. After this behavior is repeated consistently, only those behaviors that are closer to the desired behavior are rewarded. Thousands of experiments have demonstrated how unusual responses can be shaped in a variety of species. Shaping by successive approximations is a very common event in the natural environment and in human learning—so much so that we generally take it for granted. Shaping is the process underlying the way in which human children gradually acquire many basic skills, such as swimming, riding a bicycle, pronouncing words, and writing the alphabet.

Aversive Conditioning.   Animal learning can also occur in response to unpleasant, or aversive, stimuli. When used to condition animal behavior, the general process is called aversive conditioning. In classical

Figure 5.4 A pig can be shaped to perform unusual behaviors using the method of successive approximations.

conditioning, the aversive factor might be a UCS such as a mild electric shock. In operant conditioning, the painful event follows a specific response. When an aversive stimulus follows a specific behavior for the purpose of getting rid of that behavior, the process is known as learning through **punishment.**

Under what circumstances can punishment work to eliminate behavior? After performing many studies of the effects of punishment and aversive control on animal behavior, Azrin and Holz (1966) described five factors that appear to be important for using punishment successfully:

1. *Intensity.* Strong aversive events suppress behavior better than weak ones. Estes (1944) had hungry rats learn to press a bar to obtain food. When the same rats were given an extremely intense electric shock after pressing the bar, they learned not to press the bar again—ever!

2. *Consistency.* Punishment works better when it is certain, that is, when the undesired response is punished every time it occurs, not just occasionally.

3. *Immediacy.* As in other forms of learning, punishment is more effective when it follows the response immediately after it occurs rather than later.

4. *Suddenness.* Punishment is more effective when it is most intense right from the start. Beginning with mild punishment enables the learner to get used to it.
5. *Brevity.* Surprisingly, punishing events are more effective when they are brief rather than long in duration. Longer durations may allow the organism to adapt to it.

Based on the preceding summary from Azrin and Holz (1966), it should be clear why using punishment effectively to remove undesirable behavior in everyday life is often difficult: the "rules" that make punishment effective are hard to administer. Punishment is particularly effective in quickly eliminating an ongoing occurrence of undesirable behavior, but, by itself, punishment does not help the learner replace the target response with behavior that is more appropriate. For this to occur, the desired behavior must occur and be reinforced in some way.

When parents and animal trainers use punishment too frequently to control behavior, other outcomes may occur instead of the results that are desired. Children and animals that are frequently punished can become fearful, anxious, and passive. Moreover, if one person always delivers the punishment, the child or animal may come to fear and avoid that individual. In addition, many animal species will strike out aggressively at stimuli or people that deliver painful experiences. Therefore, when punishment is used, it should be employed with a great deal of care and precision in order to be effective.

Insightful Learning

From 1920 to 1955, American psychology was dominated by Watsonian radical behaviorism. This was behaviorism's "golden age." Behaviorism was an attempt to view animal and human behavior in purely objective terms: only concepts referring to observable events outside the organism and behaviors readily observable by anyone were permitted in this system. All behaviors, including learned responses, were viewed as almost completely determined by experience and environmental events. In Watson's view, there was no room for concepts that referred to hypothetical events inside the organism, thinking, planning, or any kind of subjectivity. Learning was conceived as a process wherein one kind of stimulus came to substitute for another through the laws of classical and instrumental conditioning. However, there were sporadic challenges to this view, especially from European scientists who never completely accepted the conditioning and reinforcement analysis of behavior.

In 1913, the German scientist Wolfgang Kohler (pronounced *kurler*) became director of the Anthropoid Research Station on the island of Tenerife near Gibraltar. A colony of chimpanzees was maintained for study on the island. Planning to stay there only a few months, Kohler decided to do some research on the chimpanzees' abilities to solve problems. With the outbreak of World War I in 1914, Kohler was marooned on the island and remained there until 1920.

In one of his typical studies (Kohler 1925), an animal was placed in a cage with various objects scattered around—sticks, boxes, rocks, and so on (see Figure 5.5). Hanging from the ceiling and out of direct reach was a bunch of bananas that the chimps really loved. Initially, of course, an animal tried to jump in order to reach the fruit. Or the animal would throw something at it in an attempt to knock it down. Eventually, some chimps would solve the problem—put boxes on top of each other, climb to the top of them, and reach the bananas.

In one of his most famous studies, the two-stick problem, a banana was placed on the floor far enough from the cage so that one stick could not reach it but two sticks fitted together end-to-end could. When a male chimp, Sultan, was confronted with this situation, he tried each stick but soon gave up in frustration. Sultan sat on a box, then picked up the two sticks and played carelessly with them. Sultan's keeper then reported the following to Kohler:

> While doing this it happens that he [Sultan] finds himself holding one rod in either hand in such a way that they lie in a straight line; he pushes the thinner

Figure 5.5 In Kohler's classic studies, chimps sometimes solved problems suddenly with what appeared to be "insights."

one a little way into the opening of the thicker, jumps up and is already on the run towards the railings to which he had up to now half turned his back, and begins to draw a banana towards him with a double stick. (Kohler 1925, p. 127)

Kohler called this sudden solution to the problem **insight**. He concluded that typical learning concepts could not explain this process because it was abrupt, rather than gradual, and unprepared (involving no prior learning). Kohler thought that such insights represent sudden, holistic perceptual reorganizations in which the animal sees "all at once" meaningful relationships among stimuli that were not perceived before. An insight yields a unified, meaningful, and novel relationship among objects. He was convinced that the trial-and-error behavior typical of instrumental learning could not account for this kind of complex problem solving.

This theory of insight learning turned out to be problematic because, as others have pointed out, it is difficult to know whether an "insightful" response is truly new. Other researchers (e.g., Birch 1945; Schiller 1952; Chance 1960; Epstein, Kirshuit, Lanza, and Rubin 1984) determined that insights occur only when the animal has had some prior learning experiences or has had familiarity with the objects involved in solving the problem. Chance (1960) specifically showed that familiarity and experience with problem elements (sticks, boxes) enormously affected how a task was tackled by the animal.

Insight learning combines previously learned information from unrelated situations to solve a problem in a new situation. To demonstrate this, Schiller (1952), like Kohler, had chimps become familiar with putting sticks together end-to-end in order to reach distant bananas on the ground, outside their cages. At other times, the same chimps learned to stack boxes on top of each other to reach bananas hanging from the ceiling above their cages. When these chimps were then presented with bananas hanging from a very high ceiling, they were able to solve the problem by putting the poles together, stacking boxes on top of each other, climbing up the boxes, and then knocking down the bananas with the pole. Chimps that did not have prior experiences with stacking boxes or with poles could not solve the problem.

Thus, apparent insights might actually be the result of a cumulative process involving a combination of trial and error with previously learned behaviors. Indeed, intelligent animals such as chimpanzees have the ability to draw on behaviors that have already been learned and to put these behaviors together in a meaningful, adaptive fashion. Thus, Kohler was probably incorrect about insights being totally unprepared, but he did make the important observation that problem solving can sometimes be sudden rather than gradual.

For many years, the Gestalt psychologists (of which Kohler was one) were a thorn in the side of traditional behaviorists, for they offered demonstrations and experiments that were difficult to explain exclusively by simply referring to principles of conditioning and reinforcement. Insightful learning, for example, appears to generate a learned response that is not primarily a function of either rote practice or reinforcement.

Spatial Learning

Spatial learning involves learning the layout of the environment and remembering where activities took place or where objects were left. The direct relationship of learning and memory to survival can be illustrated dramatically by the results of studies of one species of bird, Clark's nutcracker (*Nucifraga colomiana*). Because learning experiences often accumulate slowly during development, we sometimes take such experiences for granted and miss the importance of specific experiences as they influence survival and adaptation. Clark's nutcracker was studied by Balda and his associates (Balda 1980). The nutcracker, pictured in Figure 5.6, buries seeds in the fall and retrieves them in the winter as they are needed. One bird may store as many as 9,000 seeds in sites that are spread over several square kilometers. Amazing as it might seem, evidence shows that the bird is able to retrieve the seeds later because it remembers where it put all of them! The exceptional memory for food caches in Clark's nutcracker is by no means unusual in birds, but this is one species that is highly dependent on its memory of specific locations for its very survival during the winter. Balda and Kamil (1989) were able to show that other bird species that were less dependent on storage of seeds for survival did not remember as well as Clark's nutcracker. Thus, this work demonstrates that natural selection evolves traits that enable

Figure 5.6   A Clark's nutcracker.

the species to survive. Other species that have similar spatial learning abilities were described by Shettleworth (1983). Spatial learning ability appears to have developed the most in those species for which the benefits for survival from those abilities are critical.

Food-hoarding birds can forget. Studies have shown that the longer the time since a nut was stored, the more likely forgetting is to occur. This forgetting is actually adaptive because, with more time, it is likely that any nut will be taken by another animal. Thus, food-hoarding birds are more likely to retrieve nuts that were buried more recently because these nuts are still likely to be available (Shettleworth 1984; Kamil and Clements 1990).

With rats, spatial learning, as in the learning of mazes, used to be classified as a form of instrumental conditioning since trial-and-error behavior is involved in the early stages of maze learning. However, more recent research has shown that the abilities of rats go beyond those revealed by the old T-shaped choice point (left or right?) maze. Olton and Samuelson (1976) presented rats with an eight-armed radial maze like that pictured in Figure 5.7. All eight arms had food at the end of each arm. With 20 trials in the maze, rats learn to visit each arm to get food, and they also learn not to reenter an arm they have already visited. From a human perspective, you might think this is a trivial problem: just go

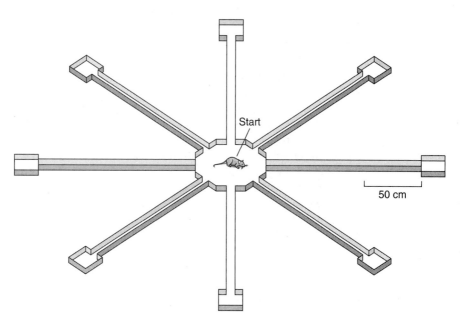

Figure 5.7 An eight-armed radial maze used to study learning in rats.

in a circle and visit each arm in turn, all the way around. But rats don't do this! Instead, the order in which they visit each arm is almost random. The researchers also eliminated the possibility that the rats were using odor cues (smelling their own odor in arms they already visited) by dousing the maze with aftershave lotion that obscured any other odors.

Traditional stimulus-response learning principles are hard-pressed to explain this kind of performance. Rather, it appears that species such as food-hoarding birds and rats form a kind of "cognitive map" of their environment (a term originally coined by Tolman [1948]). With experience, the animal develops a cognitive representation of spatial relationships in its environment. The animal then uses its cognitive map to retrieve the food.

Menzel (1971) demonstrated similar abilities in a colony of chimpanzees. Chimps were carried through an out-of-doors compound on a route filled with twists, turns, and backtracking. While en route, food was hidden before their eyes in 18 locations. Afterward, each chimp was released at the center of the compound to find the food. Each chimp found most of the food, but what is of chief interest here is how they searched. Chimps went to each hiding place in a pattern that minimized the distance they traveled from place to place, not in a pattern resembling the path they experienced when they observed the food being hidden.

In a second experiment, fruit was hidden in 9 of the 18 places while a vegetable was placed in the other 9. When released to search, almost all of the chimps' first 9 searches went to the fruit locations since chimps prefer to eat fruits over vegetables. Apparently, chimps can form cognitive maps much like food-hoarding birds and rats.

Finally, though insects and spiders are not renowned for their learning abilities, a great deal of evidence indicates that spatial learning is typical in many arthropod species. Weiss and Schneirla (1967), for example, showed that ants can use learned visual and kinesthetic cues to master a maze even when one of their most preferred cues (pheromones) is removed. Honeybees are very adept at learning the locations of nectar and pollen. Spiders learn and remember the locations of prey caught on their webs. When the prey is removed without disturbing the web, spiders still return to the exact locations where prey was originally found and keep searching for the missing food.

Observational Learning

When a learner learns by observing the behavior of another individual (the model), learning is inherently social: this is **observational learning.** Although learning with models can take several forms, psychologists have been particularly interested in situations where observational learning takes place with no obvious reinforcement to either the model or the learner, a form of observational learning traditionally called imitation. Scientists also find it intriguing that, after observing the model, the imitator may perform the observed behavior quite a while after the original observation took place (days or even weeks). Both of these characteristics of imitation—no obvious rewards and delay in responding—have caused theorists to regard this phenomenon as a distinct form of social learning that is found in relatively few species.

Imitation is easiest to observe in humans and other primates, especially the great apes (chimpanzees, gorillas, and orangutans), though it has been documented as occurring in other species such as rats, birds, and dolphins. Many reports exist of how chimpanzees have exhibited spontaneous imitation in settings where the chimps have been raised by humans. In one early study by Hayes (1951), a female chimpanzee, Viki, put cosmetics on her face in front of a mirror, screwed lids off cans, and put a pencil in a sharpener and turned the handle. Viki was not rewarded for these activities. Instead, these behaviors often occurred spontaneously, well after Viki had observed humans performing the same behaviors.

Although theoretical aspects of imitation remain controversial, many psychologists have concluded that imitation is an innate capacity of those animals that demonstrate it. The adaptive advantages of imitation and all forms of observational learning are obvious. Entire complex acts can be acquired quickly and efficiently, whereas operant conditioning of the same behaviors would be long, difficult, and filled with trial and error. Observational learning bypasses much of the trial-and-error phase of learning and allows the animal to avoid the potential dangers of making errors during the trials. More about observational learning and imitation appears in Part 4 of this book, where we will focus on primates and their evolution, abilities, and adaptive behaviors.

Explanations of insightful learning, spatial learning, and observational learning phenomena illustrate how cognitive factors have increasingly made their way into modern learning theories. Psychologists no longer feel that all learning phenomena can be accounted for by just a few conditioning processes. The studies we have reviewed also illustrate the general ecological principle that animals tend to evolve abilities and strategies that assist them the most in survival in their natural habitats.

Adaptive Differences in Learners

In the early part of the 20th century, behaviorists typically studied learning in animals while taking for granted two important assumptions. One assumption was that learning was a *general process* independent of the species that was learning. In other words, it was assumed that any form of conditioning obeyed the same laws, regardless of the traits of the learner. The second assumption, sometimes called the principle of *equipotentiality,* was that what an animal learned depended completely on experience and nothing else. In other words, any stimulus could potentially be connected to any response with the same ease. In summary, these two assumptions stipulate that learning is pretty much the same in all species.

If these assumptions were in fact true, learning could be studied and understood completely by studying only a few species under laboratory conditions. This enterprise is exactly what the early behaviorists largely did until the 1950s—study learning primarily in rats and mice in a strictly controlled laboratory environment. Starting in the 1950s and 1960s, however, biologists, ethologists, and some psychologists began to challenge these assumptions with new data from animal species other than rats and mice—data from animals in more natural settings. The new data appeared to show that learning in many species is a process heavily influenced by the characteristics of the learner, not just the characteristics of the learning situation. In the remainder of this chapter, we will examine some of these ways in which the learning process depends on the learner.

Instinctive Drift

Earlier in this chapter, we discussed the work of B. F. Skinner in demonstrating the power of shaping procedures for developing unusual behaviors in pigeons. Two of Skinner's students, the Brelands (1961, 1966), went further and showed how more unusual behaviors could be learned by pigeons, rats, chickens, pigs, raccoons, and humans just by using the procedures of shaping (and a great deal of patience).

However, the Brelands also found that instinctive responses would sometimes interfere with the conditioning process. When the Brelands tried to train a pig to put a token in a piggy bank, for example, the pig would repeatedly push the token on the floor with its nose (the "rooting" response). Similarly, chickens would scratch on the ground repeatedly in the middle of a learning task that had nothing to do with scratching.

One of the most dramatic examples of this kind of **instinctive drift** occurred when the Brelands (1961) tried to train a raccoon to pick up coins and put them in a small metal box. The raccoon easily learned to pick up one coin, put it in the box, and receive a food reward. But problems developed when the raccoon was required to pick up two coins and put both in the container to get the reward:

> Not only could he [the raccoon] not let go of the coins, but he spent seconds, even minutes, rubbing them together (in a most miserly fashion), and dipping them into the container. He carried on the behavior to such an extent that the practical demonstration we had in mind—a display featuring a raccoon

putting money in a piggy bank—simply was not feasible. The rubbing behavior became worse and worse as time went on, in spite of nonreinforcement. (Breland and Breland 1961, p. 682)

The point here is that the organism is not empty. Each species brings with it a host of tendencies and potential reactions that may emerge when the appropriate environmental conditions encourage their manifestation. Such tendencies may augment or interfere with the learning process as we see it, but these reactions have generally been designed by natural selection to assist the animal with its survival in its natural habitat. Pigs and their relatives are born diggers because roots and other underground plants make up a large part of their diet. Raccoons often find their food through foraging by touch for small crustaceans at the bottoms of streams.

Preparedness

Seligman (1970) challenged the generality and equipotentiality of the learning process with his concept of learning **preparedness.** According to him, each species has genetic predispositions to learn in certain ways and not in others. Thus, an animal may not perform on a task very well because its heredity has prepared it to learn in ways not conducive to the particular task. Or an animal may find other learning tasks rather easy because it is already well prepared by genes and evolution to learn that task. Preparedness has received support from many areas of research, two of which we will examine here.

Avoidance Behavior.   Through the procedures of classical and instrumental conditioning, an animal can learn to avoid situations that are painful or unpleasant. Thus, an animal will tend to avoid situations that have produced painful consequences in the past. However, a great deal of avoidance behavior in many species is built in, with the animal performing an avoidance response without much prior learning. For example, young birds will flee from hawklike silhouettes and many primates appear to fear and avoid snakes, in both cases without prior relevant learning experiences. These largely unlearned responses make sense in terms of natural selection because they would protect an animal from learning to avoid a dangerous predator through trial and error. Imagine if this were not so: a prey species like a deer would likely have to be attacked by a mountain lion in order to learn to avoid it. Unfortunately, instead of learning, the deer would be the lion's lunch.

Bolles (1970) concluded that how an avoidance response is learned in an experiment depends directly on how similar the desired response resembles those avoidance tendencies in the animal that are already built in. So, for example, rats require only about five trials to learn to run from one box to another in order to avoid a painful electric shock, but they need hundreds of trials to learn to press a bar to avoid the shock. This finding is consistent with the fact that, in their natural habitats, rodents typically run away from threats.

Learned Taste Aversions.   One area of the study of learning that has produced a great deal of research and controversy involves animals learning to avoid something they have eaten or drunk. What will happen if we feed a rat something that has a certain taste, and afterwards we make the rat ill? What will the rat learn? If you say that in the future it will avoid eating something with that taste, you are correct. This is a learned taste aversion, a variation of classical conditioning.

But some animals learn taste aversions much more readily and quickly than they learn other behaviors under typical laboratory conditioning situations. Generally, in the laboratory, an aversive event (such as an electric shock) must follow the eating by only a few seconds or the animal will fail to make the association. The animal will probably need several repeated unpleasant experiences to learn to avoid the food entirely.

In contrast to this well-established laboratory fact, studies on the learning of taste aversions in wild rats have shown them making the same association even when the sickness follows the eating by as long as seven hours! Furthermore, they can learn the aversion from one experience, without repetitions (Garcia, Hankins, and Rusiniak 1974). Wild rats that have survived even one poisoning attempt become bait-shy and are very difficult to poison. The mere taste of something is an important cue that enables rats to select and eat nourishing foods and avoid harmful ones. Apparently, their nervous systems are innately organized in ways that allow them to learn taste aversions very quickly because their very survival might depend on it. Thus, Seligman's concept of preparedness implies that rats are a species whose evolution and ecology have prepared them to learn taste aversions very quickly. Rats are omnivores, capable of eating any food source they encounter, but it also pays rats to be cautious with novel foods for which the consequences of eating are unknown. Thus, rats often avoid novel foods (if given a choice) or sample them in very small amounts.

That rats are prepared by evolution to acquire taste aversions efficiently should not be so surprising. On the other hand, rats are not prepared by evolution to press a bar to avoid an electric shock. While a rat can easily learn to avoid an electric shock by running away, it takes many trials for it to learn to press a bar to avoid it.

Similarly, pigeons can learn very quickly that a light coming on in an operant chamber signals that pecking a key gets the pigeon food. They can also readily learn that a tone signals a shock is coming, enabling them to avoid it. But the same pigeon has difficulty learning to associate a tone with getting food and a light with shock arrival. Thus, for the pigeon, the difficulty of learning depends on how genetically prepared it is to deal with relationships among the particular stimuli with which it is presented (Foree and LoLorde 1973).

Parent-Offspring Recognition.   Preparedness may be indicated in many biases that affect learning in a particular species, and usually the bias reflects an adaptive advantage for the animal. So, for example, bees can easily learn to associate sugar water with colors; this makes sense because flowers of different colors may yield different amounts of nectar in bees' foraging areas.

Another area of learning that reveals biases is the process by which parents and their offspring learn to recognize one another. Parent-offspring recognition develops early and quickly in two species of swallows, the bank swallow (*Riparia riparia*) and the cliff swallow (*Hirundo pyrrhonata*), but is less advanced in northern rough-winged swallows (*Stelgidopteryx serripennis*) and barn swallows (*Hirundo rustica*). Does this make sense? An examination of their lifestyles by Beecher (1990) showed that the first two species nest in large colonies whereas the latter two have solitary nests. In colonial species, it is important for parents and offspring to learn to recognize one another quickly after hatching because many other birds are nearby. On the other hand, in solitary species, the parent and offspring birds are unlikely to see other members of their species. Thus, the difference in parent-offspring recognition can be readily understood in terms of preparedness.

Modern biologists have concluded that a relationship between the ecology of a species and what an animal can readily learn makes sense. Many studies since the 1960s have supported this contention.

Summary

Learning is a process by which long-lasting changes in behavior are acquired as a result of experience. As an adaptive mechanism, learning ability benefits animals in adjusting to unpredictable circumstances that occur during their lifetimes.

There are many different types of learning, six of which were described in this chapter. In the simplest form of learning, habituation, an organism learns not to respond to a stimulus when that stimulus is repeatedly presented. In this way, the animal learns to ignore stimuli unimportant for survival.

In classical (Pavlovian) conditioning, an animal learns to attach a response it already makes to a new stimulus (CS) by pairing the new stimulus with a stimulus (UCS) that already elicits the response. The CS functions as a substitute for the UCS, allowing an animal to prepare itself for future action.

In instrumental conditioning, an animal discovers in trial-and-error fashion that performing a certain behavior is followed by reinforcement. Once a response is acquired in this way, it can be maintained and strengthened through the procedures of operant conditioning. Through careful and patient instrumental conditioning procedures, unusual behaviors that an animal would never normally perform can be shaped. When a specific behavior is followed by a painful event with the intention of getting rid of that behavior, this is learning through punishment. While psychologists have delineated the variables that can make learning through punishment effective, in the everyday world the use of punishment effectively to control behavior is often difficult.

Insightful learning combines previously learned information from unrelated situations to solve a problem in a new situation. Because such insights occur quickly and unpredictably, they have proved difficult to study. But, as Kohler's original studies of insight showed, insightful learning can be very important in the adaptive behaviors of intelligent animals such as chimpanzees.

In spatial learning, an animal learns and remembers where something is. Food-hoarding birds often have remarkable spatial memories, enabling them to find nuts or seeds buried days and weeks before. Observational learning, in which an animal learns entire sequences of behavior by observing another animal, is perhaps the most efficient learning form of all since it bypasses much of the trial and error and repetition of simpler types of learning.

The learning process is also influenced by the characteristics of the learner, which vary greatly among species. Even well-trained animals may exhibit instinctive drift when innately organized behavior patterns interfere with learned behavior. Different species are also prepared by genes and evolution to learn more easily in some ways rather than others. Rats, for example, easily learn to associate a taste with becoming ill, an ability that has obvious advantages for rodents in their natural habitats. Similarly, those bird species for which learning to recognize their parents is important early in development are usually adept at learning recognition.

Part 2

Making a Living in the Wild

Before an animal finds a mate and passes its genes on to a new generation, it must grow, mature, and survive in the environmental conditions with which it is confronted. In many species, survival may be difficult, with a high probability that only a few individuals will survive. In the next four chapters, we will survey the many lifestyles and adaptive behaviors that enable animals to make a living in the wild. For some species, the main problem is simply to locate a food supply, and their behavior is geared to pursuing their food to wherever it leads them. Some species migrate over long distances between habitats that offer them desirable resources at different times of the year. For other species—predators—the food supply is other animals that have evolved effective ways to avoid being eaten. While predators and prey compete against each other for survival, individuals of the same species also compete with each other for food, territory, and mates. Still other species have evolved communication abilities and group living that give competitive advantages to the individuals who live in such groups.

CHAPTER 6

Foraging and Migration

The most immediate problem for any animal is to find food and water. In the next two chapters, we will survey many of the different strategies that animals have evolved for locating, selecting, handling, and storing a food supply. In this chapter, the focus will be on foragers, those animals whose food supply ordinarily does not offer resistance to being eaten. In Chapter 7, we will deal with predators whose food displays considerably more reluctance about being consumed. Traveling from one place to another, sometimes over great distances, has evolved in some species as part of the solution for maximizing food resources as well as for finding mates. In the latter part of this chapter, we will examine migration as a survival strategy. Some species have evolved exceptional abilities for navigating by using subtle environmental cues. These abilities, such as the use of the earth's magnetic field by birds and sharks, have only recently begun to be understood.

The most fundamental problem any animal faces for its everyday survival is obtaining a supply of food. The term *foraging* encompasses all those behaviors that an animal uses to find and capture the food it needs to survive. In this chapter, we will discuss species for which the food supply offers little resistance to being eaten, for example,

plant, seed, worm, and insect eaters. Factors involved in migrating behaviors will also be discussed in this chapter, since the availability of a
food supply often appears to be implicated in the evolution of migration
as a survival strategy.

Cost-benefit analyses of foraging behaviors in many species have
given the behavioral ecologists some of their most notable successes in
applying optimality models to animal behavior. When such models are
applied, the scientist treats an animal much like a human economic
consumer. Typically, individuals who shop for food using money will
presumably minimize cost (money spent) while maximizing the intake
of desirable food products to the greatest possible extent. However, there
are constraints in this situation, depending on each individual's economic situation at the moment. For example, an individual with a dire
need for food but little money will behave differently than a person who
is well fed and wealthy. Thus, the needy individual cannot afford the
time and energy to be too choosy about diet, whereas the well-off individual can afford to be extravagant and fussy.

In the animal kingdom, "money" is the effort (energy) and time an
animal must spend in order to obtain food. Similar to the human situation, many constraints or limiting factors will impinge upon an animal's decisions in foraging for food. According to cost-benefit analysis,
if the time and energy cost of obtaining a particular food item outweighs
the benefits (energy and protein intake) to be gained, the animal will
seek food that is easier to obtain: energy intake must outweigh energy
output or the animal will not survive. Moreover, when faced with alternative food sources, the animal should prefer the food source that provides the greatest benefits relative to costs. As with our human example,
how the animal behaves at the moment may vary, depending on its circumstances. A starving animal will be less selective about food that is
easy to obtain, whereas a well-off animal may be interested in only a few
food sources while ignoring others.

Foraging and eating behaviors are particularly amenable to cost-
benefit analysis because, unlike reproductive outcomes, foraging events
are short term, and scientists can measure calories taken in minus calories spent during a given time period for an individual animal. Keeping
these principles in mind, let us turn to some examples of how scientists
have studied foraging behaviors and how they have tested the basic cost-
benefit model.

Locating Food

Some aquatic animals obtain their food simply by straining food from
the water they live in (e.g., clams). There are even some vertebrates that
use this method, such as the flamingo whose beak filters small crus-

taceans from the mud and water of shallow pools. The largest animals on earth, baleen whales, have large, specialized plates (called baleens) in their mouths, which also function to filter out small crustaceans.

However, for many species, a primary problem in obtaining food is simply to locate it. In general, most food sources are not scattered evenly over the environment. Instead, food (whether seeds, plants, or insects) tends to be concentrated in certain areas or patches. Because of this, many animals have evolved highly sophisticated sensory systems to locate either the food source itself or the patches where the food may be found. An example of this specialization is found in honeybees (*Apis mellifera*), which use vision to locate their primary food source—the nectar produced by flowers.

Flowers are designed by natural selection to be maximally reflective in the ultraviolet wavelength so that they can attract the bees (see Figure 6.1). This happens because, whereas the bees depend on flowers for food, the flowers in turn depend on the bees (and other nectar eaters like hummingbirds) to carry pollen from flower to flower for reproduction. Therefore, honeybees see the shorter, ultraviolet wavelengths of sunlight that are undetectable to human eyes. This process of **coevolution,** in which flowering plants and insects have evolved together in mutual dependence, explains why flowers exist in nature. Plants, like animals, have evolved their attributes for survival and reproductive advantages, not just to be beautiful for our appreciation.

Moving to another example, the food supply of chipmunks (*Tamias striatus*) is primarily seeds from trees. Chipmunks look for seeds at particular sites around their den, but the supply of seeds at each site fluc-

Figure 6.1   A flower pictured as humans see it (left half) and perhaps as honeybees see it (right half). Because honeybees see ultraviolet light, which we do not, they may see flowers differently than we do.

tuates greatly because of the effects of wind, rain, and other animals. Consequently, chipmunks check their supply of seeds at several sites to find where foraging for seeds will be best. In these circumstances, an optimality model predicts that chipmunks should check alternative foraging sites more often when the current foraging site decreases its food output (Stephens 1987). To verify this hypothesis, Kramer and Weary (1991) performed an experiment. Chipmunks were presented with artificial food sites, namely, trays of sunflower seeds. The experimenters manipulated the number of seeds that appeared on different trays and, as predicted, chipmunks spent more time investigating seeds at alternative trays as the number of seeds on any one tray decreased.

Chipmunks illustrate that an animal may leave its customary eating area when the food from that area falls below a certain stable level. But other factors may also impinge on the decision to move to another food patch. These factors include the difficulty of getting to a new location (it might be far away) and the risk of encountering predators. So, for example, Giraldeau and Kramer (1982) showed that, as the distance between a seed tray and the chipmunk's burrow increased, the longer the chipmunk would stay at trays nearer the burrow. In the chipmunk's natural habitat, this kind of behavior makes sense because travel time outside the chipmunk's nest greatly increases the risk of predation by snakes, weasels, or raccoons.

In fact, some species of animals value their need for safety above other needs. For example, the collared pika (*Ochotona collaris*) is a small, tailless, ratlike mammal closely related to the rabbit (see Figure 6.2). Pikas will feed exclusively on mediocre to poor sites near their nests, even though a meadow rich in roots and plants may be nearby. Holmes (1991) concluded that the pikas do this primarily to avoid predation; they stay near the safety of their burrows, which are typically dug among rocks and piles of boulders that provide protection. Holmes also showed that when the pika's habitat was modified by providing long rows of rocks away from their nests, individual pikas would travel farther away.

Some animals may find their way to food sources by following their companions. In large colonies of some birds, for example, adults can observe other birds returning with food for their offspring. Greene (1987) found support for this hypothesis by observing ospreys (*Pandion haliaetus*), or fish hawks. Ospreys nest in colonies along the North American coast and feed on schools of fish whose locations are unpredictable. Ospreys are more likely to fly out after seeing another osprey return with a fish. They then fly out in the direction from which the successful forager returned. Greene also showed that those ospreys that took their cue from a successful hunter were themselves successful more often than those that foraged on their own.

Some researchers have proposed that changes in an animal's diet are related to the development of a **search image** of the food item the animal is seeking. Basically, the idea is that with increasing experience at finding one kind of food, the seeker forms a clearer picture or image of what it is looking for, making it easier for the animal to spot its food.

Figure 6.2   The collared pika, a rodentlike member of the rabbit family.

When Dawkins (1971) studied chicks from domestic chickens (*Gallus domesticus*) feeding on colored grains of rice, he found that for some birds the rice was made easy to spot by placing grains on a contrasting background. Other chicks had to detect grains on a matching background. At the beginning of a test period, the easy-to-see grains were quickly seen and eaten by the chicks, whereas the camouflaged grains took the chicks a longer time to detect. However, by the end of the test period, the chicks were eating the camouflaged grains just as fast as the conspicuous ones. These results support the search image hypothesis. Similarly, many studies of predators and prey have shown that predators get better at finding their prey with greater exposure to it.

On the other hand, there is a body of evidence that supports a different idea: when looking for hidden food items, foragers may simply take more time to look carefully for the items rather than to form an actual search image. Gendron (1986) found that bobolink quails (*Colinus virginianus*) reduced their hunting speed as their laboratory "prey" (different-colored dough pellets) increasingly blended into the background. It is likely that both processes—forming a search image and changing the search rate—are used by foragers to the extent that such strategies give the animal success.

Food Selection

In general, most animals have a diet consisting of a wide range of food sources; however, they prefer some kinds of food over others. Researchers have found that animals will feed exclusively on their favorite food if that food is readily available. As the most preferred foods become less available, the animal will be less fussy and partake of secondary choices. Thus, the decision about what to eat depends only on the availability of the most preferred foods, not on the abundance of less preferred foods (Pyke, Pulliam, and Charnov 1977).

The fussiness of some animals is well illustrated by Glander's study (1981) of mantled howler monkeys (*Alouatta palliata*) that live in the forests along rivers in Costa Rica (see Figure 6.3). These large monkeys primarily eat leaves. However, they are very adept at avoiding those leaves that are both low in nutritional value and that contain toxic substances. The monkeys seek out rare, more nutritious leaves that take some time and effort to find. Furthermore, of those trees whose leaves

Figure 6.3 The mantled howler monkey of Central America, whose calls are among the loudest animal sounds in nature.

they do eat, the howlers are very selective about the particular leaves, preferring smaller, young leaf growth over larger, more mature leaves. Whereas a howler appears to be wasteful when it eats only part of some leaves and discards other parts, Glander was able to show that the howlers are actually discarding the parts of leaves that are most toxic.

Generalists versus Specialists

In their selection and pursuit of food sources, some animals have evolved as generalists (omnivores) that can eat many different types of food, while others have become specialists that eat only one or a few types of food. Each strategy has advantages and disadvantages. Neither strategy— generalist or specialist—is inherently superior to the other. Rather, what works best depends on the circumstances the animal is in. Generalists (like earthworms, rats, wolves, and bears) can switch from one type of food to another, depending on food availability, but they are not highly efficient at getting any one type. Thus, generalists find food in a relatively short period of time, because they eat many different things, but generalists take more time in capturing and consuming their food because they're not specialized to do so. On the other hand, specialists like the koala, giant panda, or anteater are very efficient at handling their food but do not have the ability to switch to other food sources in lean times.

With time, specialization of diet tends to evolve changes in the species' physical characteristics so that the body may accommodate dietary changes. For example, koalas of Australia eat and digest leaves from eucalyptus trees that are indigestible and even poisonous to other animals. The giant panda has evolved a thumblike sixth digit on its front paws, which assists it in stripping leaves from the bamboo shoots it eats (see Figure 6.4). Anteaters have evolved giant, powerful claws to break into concrete-hard termite mounds, and long sticky tongues to capture the termites within.

Optimality Models

Food selection has also been studied in the laboratory, primarily with small birds that are easy to keep and monitor. Starlings (*Sturnus vulgaris*) serve as one example. They are birds that feed on worms and leatherjackets, the larvae of worms, in the soil. During the summer, these larvae are plentiful and easy for the starlings to find. A busy parent starling may make as many as 400 trips a day to get such food for its young. Behavioral ecologists studying the starling have asked, How many such worms should the parent get and carry in its beak on one trip? What should the "load size" be?

We should expect starling parents to be efficient and economical in this feeding task. In other words, they should use a load size that maximizes the amount of food they can get for their young each day. One worm per

Figure 6.4 The giant panda has evolved a bony projection from its wrist that functions much like a second thumb to assist the animal in stripping leaves from bamboo shoots.

trip would be really inefficient, like going to the store once for each item on a grocery list. But should they always carry the biggest load possible? Probably not, because the more worms the starling has in its beak, the harder it will be to get new ones in its beak, and the bird will waste time dropping some. Thus, the way to behave efficiently is for the starling to carry more larvae the farther away it has to go to get them, up to a certain limit. It only pays to make a long trip for larvae when the starling brings back many of them.

Kacelnik (1984) actually tested these ideas with a clever experiment in which he first trained starling parents to get mealworms from a tray and then manipulated the rate at which the worms appeared. As predicted, load size increased with an increased distance of the tray from the nest, supporting the cost-benefit model. As distance (or time) for foraging increases, it pays to get a larger load of worms. The starling can't afford to travel far for a small load, but it also cannot afford to spend long times searching ineffectively. The optimal load is somewhere in between—the load that will maximize the net rate of food delivery to the chicks. Evolution will favor those birds for survival that can effectively feed and raise their young to adulthood. Thus, over the long term, evolution has produced modern starlings that are very good at maximizing the delivery of food to their offspring.

Handling and Consuming Food

Finding food is not always the last step before consumption. Squirrels get very good at finding nuts but they also must learn how to open them. Each young squirrel must learn specific techniques for cracking open different species of nuts; these techniques are acquired through trial-and-error practice. An adult squirrel will have mastered these techniques and spends minimal time cracking them open. Similarly, young oystercatchers (*Haematopus ostralegus*), a shorebird, must learn how to open shellfish like clams to get at the meat inside. Norton-Griffiths (1969) found evidence that these birds are taught these techniques by their parents during the first year after hatching.

Animal Cultivators

Most of us probably don't think of animals as food cultivators or "farmers," but there are instances of such behaviors in nature, especially in ant species. For example, leaf cutter ants (genus *Acromyrmex*) cut fresh leaves, which they transport back to an underground nest (see Figure 6.5). Instead of eating the leaves, the ants chew them up and provide them to a garden of special fungus that they cultivate for themselves as food (Weber 1972).

Ants of the genus *Crematogaster* form associations with particular species of acacia trees. These trees have large, sharp thorns that protect the plants from large plant eaters. The ants chew holes in the walls of the

Figure 6.5   Leaf cutter ants bringing leaves back to their underground nest.

thorns and live inside them, and the ants get their food from glands on the tree's leaves that secrete nectar. The result for the tree is that it gains protection from leaf-eating caterpillars and other insects because the ants will attack and sometimes eat any invading insects.

Other species of ants form symbiotic relationships with aphids, butterfly caterpillars, and other insects that provide the ants with food in the form of sugary liquids that they excrete. The ants in turn protect their "cattle" insects from predators and, in some species, even take them into their nests to live with them! Some species of symbiotic aphids have become so dependent on their ant caretakers that the aphids have lost their own ability to protect themselves (Holldobler and Wilson 1994).

Some species of mammals also cultivate plants to some extent. Prairie dogs encourage the growth of grasses they eat by pulling out the varieties of grass that they don't eat.

Storing and Caching

When food is eventually obtained, it can be used immediately as an energy source or it may be stored or cached for later use. One way for an animal to store food is to turn food immediately into fat stores in its body. For animals such as seals and penguins, additional fat reserves are not just desirable but are essential. Without them, they could not survive the cold environments in which they live. On the other hand, with birds that take flight (unlike penguins), fat stores in the body may be costly by impairing their ability to fly. Consequently, many birds store food in caches or special chambers.

Many animals take food back to a nest or burrow either to eat the food immediately or store it for later use. As previously discussed with pikas, this behavior often reflects the animal's attempt to minimize the risks of predation, especially in the case of smaller ground animals like rodents. However, chipmunks and squirrels need to store food in the summer in order to survive the winter when the seeds and nuts they eat are no longer available. Squirrels dig holes around their nest site and bury the seeds and nuts for later retrieval. While squirrels store large amounts in a few locations, chipmunks prefer storage in special chambers near their burrows. In any event, both squirrels and chipmunks are relatively inactive during winter months and awaken only occasionally to eat from their stores. Many rodent species have cheek pouches that allow them to store large numbers of seeds and nuts and bring them back to their nests.

Desert rodents store seeds inside their burrow passages. Kangaroo rats (*Dipodomys phillipsii*), for example, get all the water they need from the seeds they retrieve and store. Desert ants in North America bring hay and grain to storage areas large enough to enable them to survive severe droughts during which it may not rain for years.

Once a cache of food is hidden or buried, the animal must face the problem of finding the food at a later date. Species such as red squirrels and many rodents can locate their hidden food by smell alone. Many species of birds, on the other hand, can remember exactly where they hid food, even when they store as many as a hundred seeds or nuts per day. In fact, some birds like the tit will retrieve the most preferred items they have hidden first and will not revisit the locations they have already emptied out!

Optimality Models

On the west coast of Canada, northwestern crows (*Corvus caurinus*) feed on whelks, large mollusks covered by a tough shell. When it finds a whelk, the crow picks it up, flies, and then drops it on rocks below until the hard shell breaks to expose the meat inside (see Figure 6.6). Crows tend to select only the largest whelks (which have more meat and break more easily), and they average about two trips (drops) per whelk. Zach (1979) made careful measurements and observed that the crows drop the whelks from a height of about 5.2 meters (17 feet). The behavioral ecologist would ask, why this particular height?

An optimality model of foraging assumes that the crows are behaving in an efficient manner, which maximizes results while minimizing effort. If the crow flies higher, the whelk is more likely to break when dropped. But it is harder to aim when higher, and the breaking may scatter pieces all over the place, or else it may bounce the whelk to a hard

Figure 6.6 A whelk, which a crow can crack open by dropping it on the rocks.

place to reach. If the crow flies lower, it will need to drop the whelk more often to break it but will need less energy to fly each trip. Zach (1979) not only observed the crows but also calculated how much actual energy is consumed by the crow when carrying and dropping the whelks at different heights. (This can be done when you know the height of the drop and the approximate weights of the whelk and the crow.) The 5.2 meters turn out to be the optimal height. Thus, the crow chooses the dropping height that comes close to minimizing the total vertical flight (total amount of energy) needed to break each whelk.

Migration as a Survival Strategy

Migration in animals is a periodic journey to a specific location that alternates with a return journey to the place of origin. The ability of some species of animals to do exactly this has intrigued naturalists for many decades. Although all the details of both the evolution and mechanisms of animal migration are not understood, we should keep in mind that scientists presume that these behaviors are subject to the same Darwinian principles of evolution that govern other behaviors.

Many animals strike out from their birth site to seek a new location that provides food and mating opportunities. However, naturalists call this journey dispersal rather than migration because it is not oriented toward a specific location and is not cyclical.

Costs and Benefits

According to theory, we should assume that the advantages of migration for lifetime survival and reproduction will necessarily outweigh the combined risks. We assume this is so despite the fact that large numbers of animals die each year in the migration effort. Fisher (1979) estimated that half the migrating songbirds that left the coast of Massachusetts each year did not return and that less than half of all waterfowl species that went south in one year failed to return to their breeding grounds in the spring. Whereas each end of a migration route may offer an animal considerable benefits, the cost of making the trip itself is enormous. Some of the most obvious costs include the extra energy it requires to travel and the dangers in the terrain or water that is crossed (predators and obstacles). In addition, the time of year that animals typically migrate (fall and spring) often have unstable weather patterns, including wind and rainstorms, which can make travel hazardous. Finally, a migrating species must compete anew each year for a territory at the site it migrates to, while nonmigrators often keep the same territory year-round.

The main functional theme of migration is that each different place at which the migration ends must be better for lifetime fitness and reproductive success at different times, and these different times are often during seasonal changes. In other words, for reasons of survival or reproduction, migrating must gain the animal more than staying in one place does. The gains may represent one or several factors, such as more mating opportunities, a greater food supply for the animal and its offspring, and avoidance of predators. In the final analysis, migrations are almost always related to food or "energy profit" in some way.

There are many theories about how migration evolved in different species, but in most of these theories it is assumed that it evolved, at least in part, to enable an animal to breed in an area good for breeding but not good for survival the rest of the year. A typical migratory pattern is for an animal to move back and forth between a summer breeding area and a winter denning area. Even snakes, not usually thought of as migratory animals, may travel several miles to join a communal wintering den. A spectacular migration is that of the monarch butterfly (*Danaus plexippus*). It spends the summers all over North America and migrates up to 2,500 miles a year to winter in large colonies found in a few mountains of Mexico. During the winter months, these insects simply rest together on trees, neither flying nor eating (see Figure 6.7).

If an animal migrates south in North America in order to get a better food supply, why does it go back north in the spring and stay through the summer? Why not just stay in the warmer climate? The most common answer here appears to be reproductive benefits. For bird migrators, the

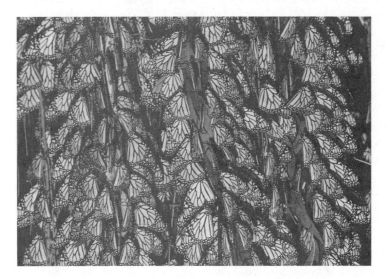

Figure 6.7   Thousands of monarch butterflies may rest on one tree during the winter before returning north in the spring.

north yields longer daylight hours from spring to fall. This, in turn, gives the birds more time to find mates and to obtain food for their young. Typically, the birds breed and feed their young at precisely those times when more food is available. Thus, short northern summers are rich in food such as new plant shoots, grasses, and insects, and many small mammals serve the birds well. In addition to these advantages, the northern migrators typically are confronted with less predation than in the south. Furthermore, the synchrony of breeding (all members of one species breeding at about the same time) lessens the chances that a predator will capture any given individual. Generally, the farther north a bird species breeds, the larger number of offspring it will have (Welty 1975).

Not all migratory journeys are annual. The eel and the hagfish, for example, typically take several years to make their journey to their species' breeding grounds. The migration of fish and reptile species, primarily for reproductive purposes, will be discussed further in Chapters 10 and 11.

Migration in Birds

Because they can fly over large bodies of water, birds are the champion long-distance travelers in the world today. The arctic tern (*Sterna paradisaea*), for example, travels each year from pole to pole and back again, even though it is only the size of a pigeon. These terns breed in the Arctic regions of North America and Asia in the summer and travel down the Atlantic along the coast of Africa to the Antarctic. One tern may travel up to 30,000 miles a year, a distance greater than the circumference of the earth. About half of all bird species that exist have some kind of migratory movement each year.

Many other species of birds migrate between North and South America, or between Eurasia and Africa, and the functional reasons why they do this seem clear: greater food availability and better weather. But scientists are also concerned with the question of mechanical or proximate causes: How do the birds know when to leave or return? How do they get to their destinations without getting lost? How do they return to their original location, sometimes even the same tree, each spring? Although navigation and orientation mechanisms in all migrating bird species are not completely understood, some species have been studied in considerable detail in the last 30 years.

Migratory patterns in birds are studied by first capturing a bird and recording its age and sex as well as the place and date of capture. Then the researcher attaches a plastic or metal band or tag to the bird's leg to identify it and lets it go. When a banded bird is later captured hundreds or thousands of miles away, it is hoped that the one who finds the animal will return the band to the address indicated on the band itself. Obviously, many bands are never returned, but enough are sent back so that information about the species accumulates. The location where the bird was found yields information about the direction of flight and places traveled to. Using these methods, it was discovered, for example, that the common American mallard duck (*Anas platyrhynchos*) summers in North American marshes and lakes and winters in the southern United States. When flocks of migrating birds are studied, radar can be used to estimate the number of birds in a flock, and the altitude, speed, and direction of their flight.

How do birds "know" when to migrate? Migrating birds have internal "biological clocks" that are set by an external, seasonal stimulus. In most birds, the clocks are set by the **photoperiod,** the length of time the sun shines during the day. A typical pattern is for birds to sense the days getting shorter in the fall. The decreasing amount of sunlight stimulates the pituitary gland in the bird's brain to excrete certain hormones, which underlie the bird's preparations to migrate. When this happens, the birds begin to overeat to increase their stores of fat (energy), which they will need to migrate successfully. Some species store all the energy they will need to make the entire flight to the other location (e.g., parulidae warblers and some hummingbirds) while other species stop along their migration route for food as they need it (e.g., white-throated sparrows, *Zonotrichia albicollis*). Preparation for the coming migration is also indicated by restlessness and greater activity of the birds. Thus, when day length gets short enough and the weather is favorable, migration begins. Similar biological events happen to the bird in the spring when the increasing length of daylight initiates a return flight.

Navigation in Birds

Those processes that enable an animal to find its way from one specific place to another are encompassed by the term **navigation.** Typically, navigation involves certain cues from the environment (e.g., landmarks) and either the innate or learned ability to use those cues. The knowledge an animal has about its current location relative to the goal of its migratory journey is the animal's **map sense.** Its knowledge about the direction to travel is its **compass sense.**

The most obvious method to find the way from one place to another is to use familiar landmarks or visual features in the environment (called **piloting**). Birds usually can use such landmarks close to their home, and visual features such as ridges and valleys probably enable birds such as hawks and eagles to get around in their environments. But landmarks alone cannot explain how many species of birds navigate over long distances or over large bodies of water where there are no discriminating features. In addition, landmarks cannot explain how birds successfully migrate for the first time, before they have ever seen any of the potential landmarks! And what do experienced birds do when they are blown off course by a storm into a territory that is unfamiliar? The truth turns out to be both complex and subtle. Many species of birds are capable of using those directional cues that are available, some cues we humans are not even aware of.

Sun Compass.   The most common direction indicator for birds is the sun and its path in the sky. Schmidt-Koenig and Schlichte (1972) fitted homing pigeons (*Columbia livia*) with frosted lenses over their eyes so that the birds could not see anything clearly beyond 3 feet in front of them, but they could see where the sun was. When released 8 to 12 miles from their loft, the birds returned to within a short distance from the loft. As time progresses during the day, the sun travels across the sky from east to west, and pigeons take these changes in the sun's location into account by using their internal biological clock. It tells them where the sun should be at each daylight hour. Thus, the birds used the sun to find their way home, even when they could not see landmarks.

Laboratory experiments reported by Keeton (1974) demonstrated how birds can maintain their sun compass even when the sun's position changes during the day. Birds can be housed in a chamber where the experimenter manipulates the lighting that the bird is exposed to. The bird reacts to the artificial light as if it's the sun. When the light exposure cycle is shifted by 6 hours away from the normal sun cycle, the birds changed their direction of initial flight to their home site by 90 degrees. This appears to be an ability used by homing pigeons and birds that migrate during the daytime.

Star Position.   Despite the apparent necessity of using the sun, some birds engage in migratory flights primarily at night when the sun obviously cannot help them (e.g., the European blackcap, *Sylvia atricapilla*). These birds typically use the position of stars that are relatively fixed in the night sky, such as the north star Polaris, to navigate. To demonstrate this, Sauer (1957) used an indoor planetarium to manipulate the night sky and star patterns that his captive birds (sylviidae warblers) could see. The birds exhibited migratory restlessness when the stars pointed toward the south. But when Sauer shifted the star pattern used by the birds 180 degrees, the birds' restlessness shifted along with it. Finally, under a cloudy sky or with no stars visible, the birds were still active but their orientation was random, indicating that they needed the stars to navigate.

Emlen (1975) replicated Sauer's results using indigo buntings (*Passerina cyanea*). In addition, he showed that the bird's early experience with a night sky star pattern determined which pattern it used the rest of its life. So these birds are not born with a star map in their heads but, rather, have a predisposition to learn whatever sky pattern they see when they are growing up. Then they use that learned pattern to orient themselves and navigate between destinations for the rest of their lives.

Geomagnetic Cues.   Human beings can see the sun and stars just as birds do, and they can use these celestial bodies to navigate as birds do. But birds can respond to one kind of information that is completely unavailable to us through our own senses—the earth's magnetic field. To illustrate, Southern (1972) experimented on young ring-billed gulls (*Larus delawarensis*) in darkness so that no stars or celestial vantage points were visible. These birds, which fly south, tended to do so even though they could not see the sun or stars.

With homing pigeons, Larkin and Keeton (1976) had magnets fitted to their backs. These served to disrupt the bird's detection of any hint of the earth's magnetic field, if in fact it could be sensed (see Figure 6.8). When released, these birds flew in a random pattern and in no particular direction. These results indicate that, when sun or stellar cues are absent, some migrating birds can still use geomagnetic information to guide them in the "right" direction. Moreover, Walcott, Gould, and Kirschvink (1979) found the existence of an organ along the midline of the pigeon's brain that contained magnetic granules, which may be the detectors of the magnetic field.

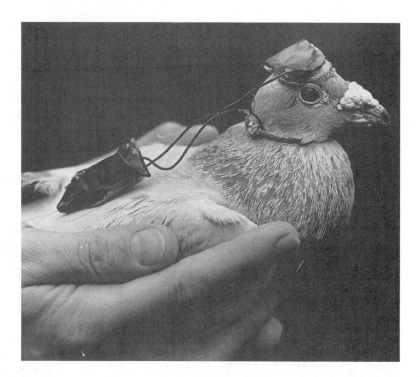

Figure 6.8   A ring-billed pigeon with a magnet attached to its back.

It isn't the direction of the magnetic field that the bird responds to since the magnetic lines of force run both north and south to the poles. Rather, the bird detects the dip or inclination of the magnetic lines toward the poles. The lines of force are actually vertical over the poles. At the magnetic equator, however, the lines of force are horizontal, making that field useless as a compass for birds.

Thus, birds like the homing pigeon and nocturnal migrators have evolved the ability to take advantage of whatever cues are available to them in order to successfully orient, migrate, and navigate to a new location. Homing pigeons will use a sun compass to find their way home on sunny days, star position on clear nights, and geomagnetic cues if the other cues are not available. These birds can normally navigate no matter what the prevailing weather conditions are.

Finally, recent evidence also indicates that scalloped hammerhead sharks (*Sphyrna lewini*) in the Gulf of California follow electromagnetic "roads" to travel from distant feeding grounds back to undersea mountains where they congregate and mate. In the next chapter, we will discuss how some shark species use their electrical sensitivity to detect prey (Klimley 1995).

Migration in Mammals

The mammals that are most like birds are bats. While some species stay in one location with a colony year-round and hibernate through the winter, others migrate southward in the winter just like birds. Typically, bats travel at night and do not need vision to travel well since most species of bats can use echolocation and prominent landmarks to navigate. Migration in bats probably developed primarily as a response to needs for food since most bats eat insects that are only plentiful in warmer climates.

The number of species of migrating mammals is much smaller than the number of bird migrators. Many species of mammals hibernate or den up for the winter, staying in the same area year-round. However, some do migrate, like the migration of the bighorn sheep (*Ovis canadensis*) in the American Rocky Mountains. Its journey is typical of many mammals, especially larger herd animals such as the American elk, caribou, and bison and the African wildebeest and elephant, and is primarily a response to food supplies. In the summer, the sheep travel to the highest part of the mountains where many green plants grow and where few predators can follow. In the winter, the sheep travel lower, to the foot of the mountains, where some vegetation is present to get them through the winter.

Wildebeests (*Connochaetes taurinus*) are typically scattered all over the eastern Serengeti Plain in Africa from December to February. This is the rainy season; when it ends, there is less water and gradually less edible vegetation. As a result, the animals start forming huge herds at the remaining water holes, herds also containing zebras and gazelles. They then move west in search of new grazing lands. At this time, the male wildebeests become territorial and try to secure small herds of females along the migration route for breeding, but these herds last only as long as there is vegetation to eat. Thus, the wildebeest migration appears to be primarily related to food and water availability.

In North America, the migrating mammals that make the longest journeys are also hoofed animals (or ungulates) like the wildebeest. The largest of these are caribou (*Rangifer tarandus*), which breed in the spring on the Arctic tundra. When winter comes, the food for caribou on the tundra (mainly mosses and lichens) dies, and the ground freezes. This forces the caribou to go south to the edge of the forests where they can feed on other vegetation. The average individual caribou makes an annual journey of about 700 miles, and along the way some are preyed upon by wolves.

Smaller mammals such as rodents typically do not migrate. They stay within a home range that does not extend very far from their nests or burrows. Consequently, rodents primarily use landmarks and familiar objects to keep track of where they are. Drickamer and Stuart (1984) showed that deer mice (*Peromyscus* species) apparently orient themselves toward tall objects like trees to find their way back to their nests in the winter.

Though rodent travel is exceptional, one of the most famous journeys is undertaken every four or five years by lemmings (*Lemmus lemmus*), a rodent native to Norway. Their trek is really dispersal rather than migration since lemmings typically strike out in all directions rather than focusing on reaching any particular destination. The lemming journey is not a mass rush to commit suicide by jumping over cliffs, as is recorded in legend and folklore. Rather, lemmings breed very fast, and their populations tend to build up in a particular area over a period of a few years. When the population of lemmings is so large that the surrounding vegetation cannot support their numbers, they strike out in all directions, eating much of the vegetation in their path, sometimes continuing until they reach the sea. This journey offers a real feast to local predators such as hawks, eagles, and foxes.

Mammals that travel over oceans and undersea offer difficult challenges to the researcher. One way in which valuable information has been gained is to attach radio transmitters to an animal so that it can be tracked with electronic receivers. In this way, the migratory routes and seasonal patterns of a number of large animals, like polar bears, sea turtles, and whales, have been documented.

California gray whales (*Eschrichtius robustus*) are around 40 feet long and weigh 16 tons. These baleen whales feed by filtering small creatures through gigantic strainers called baleen plates located in their mouths. Their yearly migration back and forth from the Alaskan Arctic to the Baja Peninsula off California makes them the whale with the longest migration route—up to 12,500 miles a year. Grays stay near the western North American coast probably to use the shallow water and visual cues to navigate their routes.

In the winter, gray whale calves are born in coastal lagoons off Baja. During these months at Baja, grays often do not eat at all, living on their body fat and losing as much as one third of their body weight. Then during the spring, adults and young travel to the Bering Straits to feed extensively from June to October. The gray whale illustrates dramatically how a migrating animal can use one site almost exclusively for feeding and the other for reproduction, with very little overlap in the two sites' functions.

Another marine mammal with a long migration route is the elephant seal (*Mirounga augustirostris*). Recent evidence (Stewart 1996) has shown that these large seals, like the gray whales, migrate back and forth from breeding areas near the Baja Peninsula to foraging areas in the Bering Sea—twice a year! While elephant seals do not travel as far north as gray whales, the seals' total annual distance traveled is over 13,000 miles for the males, a distance comparable to that of the gray whales. More details about the life cycle of the elephant seal will be presented in Chapter 10.

Summary

Foraging for food is a behavior to which cost-benefit analysis has been applied with notable success. Because food energy can be measured precisely and all behaviors constantly consume energy, costs and benefits for foraging can be assessed in individual animals.

The first problem for a hungry animal is to locate a food source. Many species have developed sophisticated sensory systems for locating their food, such as the honeybees' ability to detect the ultraviolet light reflected by the flowers they seek. Small mammals such as chipmunks forage at several consistent food sites near their dens so that they don't come to depend on only one source. Pikas may feed primarily on poorer food sites to minimize predation. With experience, foragers become more adept at locating their food.

In general, foragers prefer some food sources over others and will fall back on less preferred foods only if forced to by circumstances. Some species, such as mantled howler monkeys, spend time and effort to find a few highly preferred types of leaves that maximize nutrition and are free of toxins. Being a specialist or a generalist eater has advantages, depending on the situation. Specialists deal with their food very efficiently but eat only certain foods, whereas generalists profit by being able to switch food sources, depending on their availability.

Optimality modeling has frequently been applied to foraging behaviors, such as studies of starling parents obtaining worms for their young. As the parent bird travels farther away to obtain worms, the number of worms it returns with is larger. Using this strategy, starling parents maximize the rate of food delivery to their offspring.

In many species, food must be handled, processed, or stored before it is eaten. Leaf cutter ants feed chewed-up leaves to a fungus they cultivate for food. Other ant species form symbiotic relationships with trees or other insects that provide them with food. Chipmunks and squirrels store food in the summer that enables them to survive the winter. Other rodents may store food for droughts. Some bird species can remember exactly where they stored seeds or nuts even when the storage locations number in the hundreds. Optimality models have shown that birds such as crows can behave in ways that minimize energy loss during flight to obtain food.

Migration represents the cyclical journey of a species, usually every year between breeding and foraging grounds. These journeys have evolved because food or mating opportunities are abundant at different places during the year. Banding birds and tagging other animals have gradually revealed migration routes and patterns. For many migrating birds, the proximal stimulus for migration is the photoperiod, or length of daylight.

During migration, an animal must have some means for finding its destination. This process of navigation involves different environmental cues and sensory processes, depending on the species. Homing pigeons, for example, use the sun's position in the sky to find their way. Migrating warblers and indigo buntings learn to use the pattern of stars at night to fly in the right direction for their migration. Birds such as gulls and some pigeons can also use the dip in the earth's magnetic field to fly in the right direction when sun and star cues are not available. Migration by large land mammals such as caribou and wildebeests is engendered by food and water availability. The longest migrations among mammals are performed by marine animals, such as sea turtles, seals, and whales.

CHAPTER 7

Predators and Prey

Television programs about animals typically portray nature as an eternal war between predators and prey. Lost in the violence and sensationalism are the subtleties of this struggle: the long periods of learning that predators must undergo to hunt successfully, the many failures that hunters experience relative to their successes, the amazing sensory abilities used by prey animals to avoid predators.

Many predators, such as large cats and crocodiles, are at the top of the food chain. This means that they prey on other animals but are not preyed upon themselves—except by us. We tend to view these top predators as kings of the hill and rulers of their domain; but interdependence, not dominance, is a key to understanding predator-prey relations. Both predator and prey species have evolved many of their traits and behaviors because of interactions with one another. Over geologic time, the predator's weapons become sharper and more effective as the prey's defenses become quicker and more alert. Where will this evolutionary arms race end?

It's a fact of existence that animals must eat other living things, or things once living, in order to survive. **Predators** are organisms that survive by eating other living animals; their **prey** are those other animals. People think of predators primarily in terms of large, ferocious carnivorous mammals like lions, which prey on helpless herbivores like zebras. But this impression can be misleading. Many small and even microscopic organisms are predators, and, technically speaking, even some kinds of plants and fungi are predators! One of the last books that Charles Darwin wrote was *Insectivorous Plants,* which surveyed the many species of plants that attract, capture, and digest insects as their primary source of energy.

When a predator organism preys on one species in particular, both predator and prey may gradually evolve body structures and complex strategies to defeat each other's survival strategies. This process is known as **coevolution**, and it occurs when the changes that evolve in both species are a consequence of the interactions of predator and prey. In this chapter, we will first review adaptations that allow predators to locate, capture, kill, and consume their prey. Then we will examine the prey strategies that have evolved to make the predator's tasks more difficult. Finally, at the end of the chapter, we will return to questions about evolution and coevolution.

Predator Behaviors

Prey Selection

Predators often have a choice of which prey to attack from a host of possibilities, and the traditional assumption is that predators generally pursue animals that are old, young, or slow and diseased. Wolves, for example, only rarely capture a healthy, adult moose or even a healthy calf. On Isle Royale, an island in Lake Superior, studies showed that 50 percent of the animals killed by predators had lung disease even though only 2 percent of the entire population had the disease (Mech 1970). With some group predators, decisions about what to hunt may be made before the hunt begins. This may be typical of African wild dogs and spotted hyenas, though researchers are not in complete agreement about how much cooperation and planning is involved in group hunting species.

Decisions about what to hunt often reflect what predators have learned from experience. Ryan and Tuttle (1983), for example, showed that captive fringe-lipped bats (*Trachops cirrhosus*) consistently visited electronic speakers making the sounds of edible frog species, but the same bats avoided the speaker when it emitted the sounds of a poisonous toad. This preference likely came about from the bats' earlier experiences with frogs.

As discussed previously in Chapter 6, prey selection may also depend on whether an animal is a generalist or a specialist. Although generalists can often select from a variety of potential prey, the generalist predator will usually demonstrate definite preferences among readily available prey. African lion prides, for example, generally prefer zebras and wildebeests as prey, and they ignore smaller animals on their hunts. On the other hand, a lone, nomadic lion may have to be less fussy and prey upon whatever it runs across, including those smaller animals. If the generalist's most preferred prey becomes scarce, the generalist has the advantage of being able to switch to other prey. However, it appears that some hunters such as hyenas and wild dogs probably switch prey merely for the sake of variety rather than due to any dietary pressures.

Figure 7.1   The ears of an owl are asymmetrical, giving it the ability to detect prey more precisely.

Locating Prey

The most common methods that predators use to detect prey are vision, hearing, and smelling. Predatory birds that hunt during the day, like eagles and hawks, rely almost completely on vision and usually have a poor sense of smell. On the other hand, owls, which hunt at night, rely more on their acute hearing abilities. The ears of owls are arranged asymmetrically, allowing them to precisely pinpoint the location of a rodent on the forest floor on the basis of sound alone (see Figure 7.1). Moreover, owls capture and eat young skunks and thus appear to be totally indifferent (or insensitive) to the skunk's noxious odor.

Bats use a variety of sounds to communicate and locate objects, some of which are in the range of human hearing. Contrary to the old saying "blind as a bat," bats see perfectly well in ordinary daylight. In addition, many bat species (but not all) use high-frequency sounds to navigate and to catch insects on the wing—in total darkness. However, it wasn't until 1938 that Donald Griffin showed conclusively that bats emit high-frequency sounds that humans cannot hear.

In subsequent work, Griffin (1959) and other researchers investigated the amazing ability of bats to use the echoes of their own vocalizations to navigate their environment, a process now called **echolocation.** One of the most common bats studied is the little brown bat (*Myotis lucifugus*) native to New England. These tiny bats, weighing only 7 grams, sleep during the day, feed on insects at night, and hibernate at group roosts during the winter. The main source of food for bats are insects, especially large, nocturnally active moths. Echolocation is also used by dolphin species to communicate, navigate, and catch prey under water, much like bats do in the air.

Figure 7.2   The pit organs of a python detect heat and help the snake locate prey very precisely but may miss a cool-skinned frog.

Some species of animals that hunt at night on the ground, like the sand scorpion (*Paruoctonus mesaenis*), detect prey through ground vibrations. Inhabiting the Mojave Desert, this scorpion has poor vision and hearing, but to make up for these deficiencies, it has vibration sensors in its legs that are very sensitive to any movements in the sand. Brownell (1984) showed that these scorpions could accurately orient themselves toward the source of vibrations, using information from all eight of their legs to pinpoint the location of potential prey.

Many species of snakes (all of which are cold-blooded) use body heat to detect their prey. Rattlesnakes (species of the family *Crotalidae*), for example, have heat receptors in round pits located between the nose and each eye (see Figure 7.2). A rattlesnake can detect a mouse's body heat and accurately strike at it with its poisonous fangs in total darkness.

Sharks have evolved very acute abilities in several sense modalities to help them detect and locate prey. For instance, sounds from sources as far as a half mile away may attract their attention. As the shark swims nearer to the prey, it can use sense organs along the sides of its body to detect wave motions in the water caused by the prey's movements. As it gets closer still, the shark uses both scent and vision to zero in on the prey's location. In addition, many species of predatory sharks and rays have sensors that detect the weak electrical fields given off by the fish they hunt. Kalmijn (1971) showed that sharks can detect their prey even when the fish are motionless and buried under the sand at the sea's bottom. There are also varieties of fish (e.g., the electric fish, *Gymnarchus niloticus*) that generate their own electric fields around their bodies. This field enables the fish not only to get around objects in murky water but also to detect the presence of other fish nearby (Hopkins 1974).

Capturing Prey

Once the prey is detected, there are two common approaches for capturing it: stalk and ambush, or consistent pursuit. Stalk and ambush are typical of predators like wolves, tigers, leopards, and lions. These animals are capable of bursts of speed over short distances but generally they cannot outrun their prey. On the other hand, African wild dogs and spotted hyenas generally do not hide from their prey; they can run for miles and often do so until their prey tires out.

Cheetahs, the fastest land animals on earth, are both stalkers and pursuers. They cannot run at full speed very far but may run up to 70 miles per hour briefly to catch their prey, after inching as close as possible to it. If cheetahs fail during this period, they must rest for at least 15 minutes before they can try again.

Some predators adopt a more patient strategy; they offer a lure to make their prey come to them. The angler fish (of genus *Antennarius*) dangles an appendage that extends from its nose that resembles a small fish while it lies still on the bottom of the stream. Other fish are attracted to the lure, and when they come to close to it, they are suddenly gobbled up by the angler. Similarly, the alligator snapping turtle (*Macrolemys temmincki*) lies on the bottom of a stream with its mouth wide open and its tongue sticking out. The end of its tongue has a wormlike growth that the turtle wiggles to attract fish.

Many species of spiders can create an environment that will trap prey for them. Spinning webs is the common strategy. Resting on the web's periphery, the spider detects prey by the vibrations that insects make when they get caught in the web. However, the web merely holds the prey, and usually the spider needs to use additional silk to subdue its prey before it can escape or else use a poisonous sting.

Hunting in Groups

Social Carnivores.   Some predator species take advantage of the benefits of hunting in groups, and the most well known of these animals are lions, various canids, and hyenas—the social carnivores. Lions (*Panthera leo*) hunt in female groups and can thus hunt larger prey (e.g., zebras, wildebeests). These group hunters vary in their degree of cooperation during the hunt; they are far less cooperative and coordinated as a group than African wild dogs or hyenas. Schaller (1972) found that group lion hunts are twice as successful as solitary hunting ventures, but more than half of the lion pride's prey was scavenged from hyena kills. When a kill is made, the adult male lions in the pride eat first, despite the fact that they usually do not participate in the hunt. This occurs because female lions do not dispute the male's right to eat first since a male is much bigger and stronger than a female and could harm her if she made a move against him.

Making a kill is no guarantee that the predator will be allowed to eat it. It's true that hunting in groups increases the odds of a successful capture, but this advantage must be weighed against the potential cost of having to share the proceeds with others. Although lions are able to bring down larger prey such as giraffes and cape buffaloes when hunting in groups, each individual at a group kill actually consumes less meat than lions that have hunted alone (Schaller 1972).

After a hunt, the cubs are the last to feast, and when food is scarce, as many as 80% of the cubs may die of starvation. Why hunt together, then, if the whole pride isn't well fed? Perhaps because there are other advantages to group hunting. For example, groups are better able to drive off intruders. Therefore, each pride of lions can better defend a territory. The long-term benefits of holding a territory may outweigh the short-term losses of not enough meat (this is discussed further in Chapter 9).

The spotted hyena (*Crocuta crocuta*) was studied in detail by Kruuk (1972a). Hyenas live in clans of about 10 to 60 animals of both sexes and all ages. Each matriarchal clan has a territory with a central den. On a hunt, hyenas typically make a herd of zebras or wildebeests run in order to spot slower animals. Then they select an individual and chase it exclusively, ignoring all others. Wildebeests can run much faster than hyenas, but the group is relentless, chasing its prey at 25 to 35 miles per hour for miles. Their success rate on hunts is about two successes out of three attempts, a higher rate than that of lions.

Some predators may have to compete with other predators even after a kill has been made. Jackals and vultures are notorious thieves and can often sneak in for a bite of what others have killed. In the Serengeti Plain of Africa, spotted hyenas and lions regularly steal each other's meals. In the past, researchers often assumed that lions were predators and hyenas were scavengers; they made this assumption because they often arrived at the scene of a kill to find a noisy group of hyenas encircling a group of lions feeding off a dead zebra. However, evidence indicates that, frequently, the hyenas had made the original kill and the lions were the thieves (Kruuk 1972a). One hypothesis about the hyenas' well-known barrage of sound is that they make their calls specifically to attract other hyenas to the kill site before lions show up.

African wild dogs (*Lycaon pictus*) are much smaller than lions or hyenas but are the most successful organized group hunters on the African plains. Schaller (1972) estimated their success rate to be around 90%. Like hyenas, they pursue an animal such as a gazelle for miles until the prey tires. African wild dogs eat only their own kills and generally do not scavenge.

A cheetah (*Acinonyx jubata*) can outrun a lion, but because it often hunts alone, the cheetah can only attack relatively small prey (e.g., Thomson's gazelles). This is especially true of female cheetahs, which are usually solitary animals except when they are raising their young. However, groups of two to six male cheetahs may form and take advantage of group hunting opportunities to catch larger prey or to make catching faster prey more likely. Cheetahs lose some of their kills to hyenas and lions on the African plains, but because cheetahs hunt exclusively during the daytime whereas hyenas and lions are active primarily at night, cheetahs keep most of their own kills.

The largest social predator of North America is the gray or timber wolf (*Canis lupus*), which hunts deer, moose, bison, sheep, elk, and, occasionally, small game. A typical pack of five to eight members uses scent to detect potential prey. Once prey is detected, wolves follow the pack leader to the prey's location, attempting to surprise their victim with stealth and ambush. It used to be thought that wolves were great pursuers, following their prey over long distances, but evidence now shows that they usually give up pursuit after a half mile (Mech 1970).

Group Predation in Other Species. While we often identify group hunting with the large carnivores, cooperative hunting also occurs in many other species. Mated pairs of Harris hawks (*Parabuteo unicinctus*) usually hunt together in the American Southwest, and sometimes they also hunt with their subadult offspring, much like a wolf pack. Bednarz (1988) charted several kinds of group hunting tactics used by the hawks. For example, one bird will flush a jackrabbit out of the brush while the others wait to catch and kill it. Or the group may suddenly surprise a rabbit and attack it together. When the rabbit is running, the hawks may attack in relays. These tactics enable hawks to kill rabbits that may weigh two to three times as much as an individual bird. Even further, Bednarz (1988) was able to show that the larger the hunting group was, the more meat there was for each individual bird because group hunting was so much more successful than individual hunting. And regardless of a hawk's contribution to bringing down prey, all individual hawks shared in eating the kill, though often adults waited until the juveniles finished eating before they did.

Humpback whales (*Megaptera novae-angliae*) hunt in groups by first surrounding a school of fish and then emitting bubbles. These bubbles act as a sort of barrier to the fish, causing the prey to swim away from the bubbles into a more closely confined area. When all the fish are concentrated together, the whales will attack as a group, swallowing as many fish as they can (Earle 1979).

Some species of spiders live in communal webs, which they build together. These spiders attack prey together, drag it back to the center of the web, and feed on the prey as a group (Buskirk 1981). The advantage of such a situation is that more spiders can build larger, thicker webs, and communal webs provide reduced reaction time in getting to the prey.

One of the most devastating of group hunters are several species of army ants, as described by Franks (1989). A colony of one of these ant species consists of a queen, workers, larvae, pupae, and eggs. However, the colony has no permanent home. Instead, each night the entire colony stops and forms a "bivouac" in which as many as a half million worker ants hook their legs and bodies together to form a cover for the queen and her eggs. In the morning, the workers leave the bivouac and move outward along the paths of least resistance. Any animals encountered by the army are stung, divided up, and carried back to the rear. Few animals can stand in the way of this onslaught. There are no leader ants in these maneuvers; rather, those in the lead position constantly return to the swarm and are therefore replaced by others. The ants do follow a trail of chemicals (pheromones) laid down by the outermost ants.

Handling Prey

In Chapter 6 on foraging, we looked at the special techniques some animals have developed for handling food items once they have been located. Obviously, some predators have evolved special ways of handling their prey once it has been captured so that it is easier to consume. For example, snakes immobilize their prey by suffocation or toxins. Then they swallow their prey whole, but they must orient their prey's body for easy swallowing—usually head first. Some fish can immobilize their prey by using a built-in "stun gun"—delivering a paralyzing electric shock. Lions immobilize their prey by delivering a killing bite that severs the spinal cord or by clamping their own mouth over the mouth and nose of the prey animal, thereby suffocating it. When a dog holds something in its jaws and quickly snaps its head from side to side, it is displaying its killing ability (Norris and Mohl 1983).

Some predators store prey for later consumption. For example, leopards and cougars hide their prey and return to it later, sometimes leaving the prey high in a tree where other carnivores cannot reach it. Red foxes make multiple food caches, burying different prey in different locations. Shrikes are nicknamed "butcher birds" in recognition of their habit of skewering small rodents and insects on sharp sticks or barbed wire fences. There are even anecdotal reports of spotted hyenas dragging carcasses into water. Although alternative explanations for this behavior have not been ruled out, this too may be a form of food storage. Finally, storage may also require special handling, as in the case of spiders that wrap their prey in silk.

Defenses against Predation

Edmunds (1975) gives us a helpful scheme for discussing modes of defense against predators in the wild: the distinction between primary and secondary defenses. A **primary defense** is something built into the structure and behavior of the animal, like a turtle's shell; it is present regardless of whether a predator is in the vicinity or not. A **secondary defense** (e.g., running away) occurs only when the animal is actually faced with a predator.

Primary Defenses

Camouflage.   A fairly widespread primary defense across nature, especially in the young of many species, is for an animal to have a color or visual pattern that blends in with its environment, making it hard to detect or locate. For example, young deer, lion cubs, antelopes, and birds often blend in better with their habitats than do their adult counterparts. Using Darwin's principle of natural selection, it's easy to understand how nature has selected the young for this kind of camouflage (technically called **crypsis**). Some insects make use of an extreme form of camouflage by evolving a body that actually mimics the appearance of part of their environment, such as a stick, leaf, or flower.

Erichsen, Krebs, and Houston (1980) performed a clever laboratory experiment to test whether even a crude amount of camouflage could make a difference in deterring predation. In their study, they used the great tit (*Parus major*), a bird that eats small, brown mealworms. They manipulated the camouflage by putting the mealworms inside of straws that were either clear (the tit could see the worm) or opaque. Other straws contained inedible pieces of brown string that looked like the mealworm.

The straws passed by the birds on a conveyor belt. This gave them only a few seconds to decide which straw to take. Often, a bird could choose half of a worm in a clear straw or take a chance on finding a larger, opaque straw that might contain a larger, whole mealworm. However, deciding on the contents of opaque straws took time, and the extra cost in decision time of 2 or 3 seconds, plus the possible error by the bird, were enough to make the bird strongly prefer the smaller worms in the clear straws. The results of this experiment demonstrate that even simple, crude camouflage (the resemblance of the larger worms to the string) was sufficient to deter the tit from trying to eat the larger worms.

Kettlewell's studies (1965) of the peppered moth (*Biston betuaria*) of Europe provide dramatic support not only for the principle of camouflage but also for the capacity of some species to change quickly in response to environmental pressures. Several hundred years ago, most of these moths were white with black specks on the wings, though darker variations also occurred. These moths avoided predation from birds by resting during the day on light-colored trees that provided effective camouflage. In 19th-century England, however, white trees in the coal country became blackened with soot. Consequently, Kettlewell reasoned, the light-colored peppered moths that rested on these trees were eaten by birds, whereas moths that were darker tended to survive more often—their camouflage was better. Thus, over a few generations, the surviving peppered moths gradually became much darker in color as more of the darker moths reproduced successfully while more of the lighter ones were eaten (a process called **industrial melanism**). The darker habitat and predation by birds were the selective factors that created the darker moth population. Kettlewell's conclusions were supported not only by the natural history of the moth in England but by his own experiments replicating the same effects. For example, when he released an equal number of dark and light moths in the countryside, he discovered that out of 190 moths taken by birds, 164 were dark and 26 were light. When the same numbers of each kind of moth were released in the industrially polluted coal country, three times as many light moths were taken as dark moths. Cook, Mani, and Varley (1986) showed that in recent years the number of darker moths has declined as air pollution has been reduced.

Penguin species also use camouflage as a defense in the water. When penguins swim, their dark backs face up and their white bellies face down. Consequently, this pattern makes the penguin difficult for predators to spot from above and below. The darker backside blends in with the darker depths in the water while the white belly blends with the lighter sunlit background from above, a pattern called **countershading.** Many marine animals have carried camouflage in water to its ultimate solution—transparency! These include many species of jellyfish and the larval stages of many fish.

Some animals can actually change their color to match the appearance of their habitat. Although the chameleon is familiar to most people, the greatest color changer is the cuttlefish (*Sepia officinalis*), which is not a fish but a smaller relative of the octopus and squid. These mollusks (a distinct phylum of animals) can change from their normal zebralike stripes to dark brown, white, or a mottled brown-white pattern matching the sand they rest on, and they do it very quickly, making them nearly invisible to predators and prey (Holmes 1940).

Individual fox squirrels (*Sciurus niger*) of the eastern United States do not change their colors, but there is tremendous color variation within the species (called polymorphic coloration). Their colors include shades of gray, tan, and black, with combinations of these colors often found on the same individual. Kiltie (1989) related the variations in color to the history of wildfires in the region. Wildfires, which blacken the ground and tree trunks, give a selective advantage to darker-colored squirrels that are preyed upon by hawks. Thus, the southern states, in which Kiltie found more wildfires burning, also had a larger population of darker squirrels. However, he surmised that when wildfires don't occur for awhile and the forest regrows, the advantage for survival likely shifts to the lighter-colored squirrels. Thus, both darker and lighter forms exist genetically in the squirrel population because, depending on the environmental circumstances, each color variation may be advantageous at different times.

Warning Displays.   In some species, coloration is designed to have just the opposite effect of camouflage—to stand out as a warning display (called **aposematism**). That is, distinct coloration can function as a warning to potential predators that an attack will not be worth the consequences. A skunk with sharply contrasting black and white stripes falls into this category, as do the unmistakable sounds of a rattlesnake's rattles. The brightly colored patterns on some insects often inform birds that this insect is not edible, as in monarch butterflies. Brightly colored or contrasting stimuli can also serve to startle or surprise a predator, giving the prey time to escape.

Some moth species (genus *Catocala*) are unusual in that they have both camouflage and warning displays built into their coloration! These moths have forewings that match the pattern of the trees they rest on during the day, causing them to be unnoticed by birds (see Figure 7.3). But if a bird gets too close, the moth will expose its normally folded hindwings to reveal a distinctive eyelike pattern, which can startle a bird predator long enough for the moth to fly away.

What about zebras? Why do these animals have such bold stripes? What is the advantage? If anything, their boldly distinctive stripes appear to make them stand out. However, this may not actually be so for

Figure 7.3 Moths of genus *Catocala* use camouflage on their front wings and a warning display on their normally covered hindwings.

the zebra's natural predators. The theory is that the stripes make it difficult for a predator to detect the body's contour, a defense called **disruptive coloration.** Thus, it is the patterning in this case, not the color, that provides zebras with their camouflage.

Mimicry.   Sometimes the body of a harmless animal evolves an appearance that imitates a dangerous animal, gaining the aversive animal's alarm or defensive value. This can take many different forms, some of which are named after the scientists who first discovered them. **Mertensian mimicry,** for example, occurs when a prey species comes to resemble something dangerous to the predator (see Figure 7.4). This strategy can be particularly effective when the real animal that is imitated is potentially lethal to the predator. Some flies resemble dangerous bees, and some snake species behave like rattlesnakes—shaking their tails, hissing, and engaging in apparent striking movements—even though they are not poisonous. And, as we have already mentioned, moth or butterfly wings may resemble gigantic eyes to startle or send away predators.

When a palatable insect comes to resemble an unpalatable one, this is called **Batesian mimicry.** Figure 7.5 shows how much the viceroy butterfly (*Limenitis archippus*), an edible insect for birds, resembles the monarch butterfly, which is inedible for most birds.

Figure 7.4   An example of Mertensian mimicry: the body of a caterpillar resembles the head of a snake, putting off potential predators.

Figure 7.5 Mimicry in insects: the appearance of a viceroy butterfly (left) mimics that of a monarch butterfly (right).

A more rare kind of insect mimicry is called **Mullerian mimicry.** This occurs when two unpalatable insects come to resemble each other, each species taking advantage of the aversive effects of the other. The queen butterfly (*Danaus gilippus*) resembles the monarch, and both species contain toxins absorbed from the plants they feed on. Why would different but equally toxic species converge in this way? One theory is that each species is less likely to be eaten by mistake if the predator (mainly birds) has to learn to avoid only one visual pattern rather than several.

Lifestyle.   Primary defenses may also be evident in an animal's typical daily lifestyle. For example, many small animals avoid predators by simply hiding out of sight or by coming out only at night when diurnal predators will not pursue them. In addition, living in groups gives many animals survival advantages against predators. For example, herds of four-footed mammals and flocks of birds allow some individual members to eat while others are vigilant for potential predators. For animals like the Thomson's gazelle, vigilance appears to be the chief factor that determines whether a cheetah will catch it. Fitzgibbon (1989) showed that a cheetah will attack the less vigilant gazelle when pairs of gazelles are equidistant from the cheetah.

The advantage of vigilance in numbers is also clear in examining hawk predation on flocks of birds. Hawks are less likely to catch a bird from a larger flock than from a smaller one because the hawk is liable to be spotted earlier by some birds in a larger flock, allowing the birds to fly away before the predator gets too close (Kenward 1978).

Many of the larger four-footed animals of the African plains also protect themselves against predators by living in groups, often with other species. Wildebeests, zebras, giraffes, and many antelope species may graze together; while some eat, others watch. This makes it difficult for predators to approach a potential victim without being spotted and an alarm being given. The unaware, weak, old, injured zebra may fall easy prey to a pride of hunting lionesses, but a full-grown, healthy adult zebra in the herd is rarely in any danger.

Vigilance is not the only advantage of living in groups. A milling flock or herd may create confusion in a predator, allowing potential prey to escape before the predator selects a victim.

Secondary Defenses

An easy way to remember secondary defenses is to associate them with three *f*-words—*flight, fight,* and *freeze*. These words encompass a vast range of responses that different species use to cope with predators when they show up on the prey's doorstep.

Flight. The most widespread strategy in nature for coping with a predator is to run, fly, swim, or jump away—to flee. For many four-legged mammals (and one two-legged bird, the ostrich), running away is the principal if not the exclusive mode of secondary defense. Consequently, many of these animals have evolved highly proficient sense organs to detect approaching predators and lightning reflexes and high running speed to elude them. We have come to think of the cheetah—capable of speeds up to 70 miles per hour—as a supreme predator that can outrun any of its prey. But keep in mind that on many of its hunts the cheetah is unsuccessful. Many more of its prey animals escape the cheetah than it catches because the animals it typically pursues, such as Thomson's gazelle and other small antelopes of the African plains, can also run very fast, and the cheetah cannot maintain its maximum speed for very long.

Thomson's gazelles (*Gazella thomsoni* or "tommies") sometimes display an unusual way of running called **stotting.** The tommy jumps high into the air with all four legs at once (see Figure 7.6). They seem to do this primarily when they detect an approaching predator, but evidence appears to show that tommies stot to cheetahs but not to wild dogs. Researchers aren't sure exactly why or when tommies stot in relation to cheetahs, but one possibility is that the tommy is signaling the cheetah that it has been detected, making the cheetah more likely to give up and leave the area. Another possibility is that the tommy stots to signal the presence of the cheetah to other tommies (Caro 1986a, 1986b). Of course, it's possible that stotting might serve both informing and warning functions.

In most birds, flight reactions are innate to any fast-moving, approaching stimulus. In some species of birds (as well as reptiles and cats), the individual will display an apparent size increase by puffing up

Figure 7.6   Stotting in Thomson's gazelle.

its breast or extending its wings just before flying away. This "bluffing" behavior may serve to startle and stop an approaching predator, gaining the bird valuable time to slip away.

Parent birds will sometimes behave as if they are injured in order to draw a predator's attention away from a nest where fledgling birds reside. This **flagging behavior,** of course, puts the parent bird at greater risk from the predator. So, why do they do it? It's easier to understand if we view flagging in terms of reproductive costs and benefits. The parent birds may breed only once a year, and they make a heavy investment of time and resources in hatching, feeding, and protecting their young. If their young do not survive, the parents may not breed again for another year. Seen in this light, flagging appears to be a small risk for the parent if it results in the offspring's survival.

While some prey species can outrun or outlast their persistent predators, others must quickly find a protective structure to hide in. Otherwise, they will be caught and consumed. Many members of the rodent family (e.g., beavers, rats, and squirrels) typically have prepared hiding places or nests into which they can quickly withdraw. Some birds that don't fly well (like pheasants) and other rodents simply try to find whatever ground cover that might hide them, such as bushes, holes in logs, or high grass. However, turtles don't need to be fast, and they don't need to find a shelter because they carry their protective structures with them on their bodies. Similarly, some species of armadillos have their own protection; they can roll themselves into a tight ball that exposes only armored skin to predators.

Perhaps the strangest and most fascinating flight strategies occur in some worms, reptiles, and insects. For example, some lizards and worms will allow parts of their bodies to break off in a predator's grasp while the rest of the animal escapes. Later, the animal will regrow its missing part.

As noted earlier, bats are particularly good at catching flying insects, like moths, in total darkness by using echolocation. But some nocturnal moths (of family Noctuidae) have evolved unusual and effective ways of avoiding predatory bats. The hairs on the side of the moth's body can detect the high-frequency sound waves emitted by the bat at frequencies of 20 to 100 kHz (outside the range of human hearing). In addition, the ears of these moths are designed to detect the sounds of bats and little else— they're "bat detectors" (Roeder 1967). Given this sensory information, the moth can react in two different ways, depending on the distance of the approaching bat. When the bat is detected from up to 60 feet, the moth will turn away from its current path, which frequently takes the moth out of the bat's range of detection. If the bat is closer (less than 6 feet), then the moth will dive wildly and erratically, reducing the chance that the bat can zero in and catch it (Roeder 1967). Thus, the typical moth can detect the bat long before the bat is aware of the moth (Fenton and Fullard 1981).

More recent work by May (1991) and other researchers has shown that several flying insects, including green lacewings, katydids, praying mantises, and locusts, are also able to detect high-pitched ultrasonic sounds and take evasive action. When these species were experimentally presented with directed high-frequency sounds as they were flying, they consistently changed their flight paths in response to the sounds.

Fight.   While fleeing and escape are the most universal responses to a predator, many species have developed aggressive counterattacks to drive predators away. Even nonaggressive prey animals will use an aggressive defense if they are cornered and flight is no longer possible. The arctic musk ox (*Ovibos moschatus*), which is really a kind of sheep, uses a group defense when confronted by a pack of wolves. The oxen form a circle with their horns pointed outward while the young are protected in the center (see Figure 7.7). Many nesting birds also attempt to protect their young. Parents may be observed diving and chirping loudly at other animals that approach their nests, a behavior called **mobbing.** If a group of baboons or chimpanzees is approached by a large cat, the males will gang up on and harass the cat until it leaves their area.

Some of the most effective defenses in nature involve the use of chemicals or toxins. The most toxic mammal most of us are familiar

Figure 7.7   Arctic musk oxen form a circle as a defense against group predators such as wolves.

with is the striped skunk (*Mephitis mephitis*) of North America, which has little to fear from any predator on the ground. The foul-smelling liquid, which it can spray as far as 6 meters but only 2 meters accurately, deters any animal that comes too close. On the other hand, as previously mentioned, large owls do not have a very well developed sense of smell. Therefore, they are indifferent to the skunk's odor and will gladly eat baby skunks if they can catch them.

Similarly, some beetles, such as the bombardier beetles of genus *Brachinus,* can spray predators with noxious fluids or toxins. The bombardier's fluid is ejected when two chemicals, stored separately in the beetle's body, combine explosively and result in a liquid spray nearly as hot as boiling water. Such a spray keeps the beetle safe from ants, frogs, and birds but not from all other insects.

Like the monarch butterfly, some animals can borrow the toxins of plants and other animals and use them to protect themselves. For example, the hedgehog (*Erinaceus europaeus*) will eat a toad, remove the poisonous toxin in the toad's skin with its tongue, and concentrate the toxin in its own saliva (Brodie 1977). It will then lick itself all over, using the toad's poison to protect itself from its predators.

Freeze.   Fleeing or fighting seem to be rather natural and inevitable responses to predatory aggression. But other animals have evolved passivity and stillness to a high degree as ways to avoid getting caught or being eaten. For example, freezing while remaining silent and odorless are the only defenses a newborn deer has. This is why, when confronted by a nearby predator, a mother deer will typically leave her young alone. The predator may have great difficulty in finding a well-hidden, still, and odorless deer fawn; a wolf may walk right by it! The young of many mammal species have these instincts, including the young of predators like the hyena.

Perhaps the ultimate freezing strategy is that of the opossum (*Didelphis virginiana*), which not only can freeze when confronted by a large predator but actually loses consciousness! The opossum takes advantage of the fact that most of the predators it might meet (such as coyotes or wolves) will only attack and eat animals that move or resist, so it feigns death to avoid its demise. Its **tonic immobility** can last a few minutes while the predator sniffs and prods its unresponsive victim, then moves on. On the other hand, a mother opossum protecting its young is a formidable fighter, well equipped with teeth, claws, and snarls.

Evolutionary Arms Races

The evolutionary arms race refers to the fact that improvements in prey tactics to avoid predation tend to result in reciprocal improvements in the predator's methods of obtaining prey. Clearly, this is a mutually dependent relationship. Such arms races tend to improve the fitness of both kinds of species because, as Darwin's theory indicates, only the most fit individuals are likely to survive and reproduce.

As we have seen in this chapter, many predators have evolved effective strategies for obtaining prey, while prey species have evolved many effective defenses against predators. One consequence of this arms race is that, with time, predator and prey species may become dependent on one another and, to some extent, evolve together, a process called coevolution. The process goes on all the time in living species.

The fate of two species may become so intertwined that their population densities will vary predictably together. For example, in Canada and Alaska, the population of a wild cat, the Canada lynx (*Lynx lynx*), tends to closely parallel that of its major prey, the snowshoe hare (*Lepus americanus*). Lynx populations tend to be highest in the years just following the years when the snowshoe hare is at a maximum. The traditional explanation for this phenomenon is that lynx predation reduces the hare population so much that time is required for the hares (and thus the lynx) to regain stability.

However, more recent evidence suggests another possible explanation. On an island with no lynx at all, snowshoe hares were found to undergo the same cyclical rises and falls of population density as those hare populations preyed on by lynx. This finding suggests that the hare cycle may be the factor controlling the lynx population and not the reverse.

Why don't predators simply wipe out all the prey they eat, or, if the prey species improve enough, why don't the predators disappear? There is a host of potential reasons as to why predator and prey evolve and survive; this has been discussed in some detail by Dawkins and Krebs (1979) and Slatkin and Maynard Smith (1979). One possibility they put forth is that some predators consume their prey "smartly" in order to avoid depleting their resources. This is certainly the approach that human beings often take with their farm animals, but it is a more difficult argument to make with individual animals that are generally not aware of the statistics on prey depletion.

Another possibility is that the only predator-prey relationships that have survived are those that are, in fact, stable. The unstable ones in the past have led to group extinctions. In other words, some prey species may have been wiped out by predators that evolved hunting skills that were superior, whereas some predator species may have disappeared when their prey evolved superlative abilities to elude them.

So what explains why some predator-prey relationships in the world today are so stable, like the lynx and the snowshoe hare? One hypothesis is that the prey species' abilities always stay just enough ahead of the predator's abilities so that both survive. Dawkins and Krebs (1979) describe this idea as the "life-dinner" principle: rabbits run faster than lynx because, whereas the lynx is running after its dinner, the rabbit is running for its life. The cost is obviously greater for the rabbit if it fails to escape than it is for the lynx if it fails to catch the rabbit.

It also seems clear that many prey species stay ahead of their predators because prey species reproduce faster and, therefore, can evolve more rapidly. We see the extreme of this principle in rodents and insects; they typically have short gestation periods and/or produce very large numbers of offspring relative to their predators. For example, a moth lays hundreds or thousands of eggs per year, whereas a bat that preys on moths typically has one offspring per year.

Another factor involved in the stable relationship of predators with their prey is the role that learning plays in predator behaviors (as was discussed in Chapter 5). Predators such as the social carnivores have to spend years learning what, where, and how to hunt from their group members. Prey species, on the other hand, often have to learn much less (if at all) in order to escape or avoid predators. There is much more of a long learning and developmental period with large predators, and this survival strategy is costly in terms of time and invested energy. Thus, the predators never really multiply into vast herds because the adults must invest considerable time in training their young. At the same time, prey species produce large numbers of offspring and lose their less fit members to predators, but the more fit members survive and continue to reproduce, staying enough ahead of their predators to avoid extinction.

Summary

Many animals in nature survive by hunting and eating other animals. Predator animals usually show strong preferences for the kind of prey they pursue. Predator generalists eat a variety of prey, enabling them to switch from one prey animal to another. Predators typically have highly developed sensory systems that enable them to locate their prey. Bats, for example, use echolocation to locate insects while flying in total darkness.

Predators typically capture prey either by stalk and ambush or dogged pursuit. Large, slower predators such as lions and leopards must get close to their prey before suddenly rushing forward, whereas wolves and hyenas may run for miles until their prey tire. Other animals may use lures or traps to capture prey.

Social carnivores take advantage of the benefits of group hunting, which enables them to hunt more efficiently and to capture prey larger than an individual animal could catch. Lions, spotted hyenas, and wild dogs are group hunters that compete with each other on the African plains. Group hunting strategies are also apparent in Harris hawks, humpback whales, and army ants.

Once captured, prey animals often have to be processed or handled before they can be eaten. While some animals subdue their prey with electric shocks or toxins, more often predators use weapons such as claws and teeth to deliver a killing blow. Some predators like leopards also store their prey when they cannot eat all of it at once.

Defenses against predators can be classified into two general categories: primary defenses, which are built into the animal's morphology or behavior; and secondary defenses, those behaviors that occur in the presence of a predator. Camouflage is a primary defense in which an animal avoids detection by blending in with its habitat. Other species may employ warning displays or distinct coloration to warn predators to stay away. In mimicry, the animal's body comes to resemble a dangerous animal, gaining that animal's defensive advantage. The primary defense for many species is their lifestyle. Strategies such as hiding and living in groups lessen the likelihood that an animal will be caught by a predator.

Secondary defenses can generally be classified as either fleeing, fighting, or freezing. The most common defense, flight or running away, is the only secondary defense available to many four-legged mammals such as antelope species of the African plains. Some flying insect species avoid predation by bats by detecting the bat's echolocation signals and altering their flight paths accordingly.

Other species defend themselves by fighting back. Whereas some animals use physical aggression to defend themselves, skunks and bombardier beetles spray noxious chemicals to deter predators. Other animals neither flee nor fight but, instead, freeze into a still position, effectively discouraging predators that pursue only active or fleeing prey.

Many species of predators and prey have established relatively stable relationships that have existed for thousands of years. Those "evolutionary arms races" that are not stable tend to disappear when either the predator can no longer catch the prey animal or the predator gradually wipes out all the prey. Generally, prey species stay ahead of their predators because they breed faster and in larger numbers.

CHAPTER 8

Competition and Territoriality

According to Darwin, each individual animal tries to maximize its own survival and reproductive success. While some individuals are successful, others of the same species are not. Because the resources that animals need for survival are often scarce and unevenly distributed in the environment, individuals of the same species, and sometimes of different species, are forced to compete with one another for the same resources. As we shall see in this chapter, competition takes many forms— sometimes involving direct encounters between aggressive animals, but more often involving rituals and behaviors that minimize the risk of injury from other members of the species.

In many species, the most fit individuals are able to corner more resources for themselves by establishing and defending a territory, the boundaries of which other individuals typically respect. As we shall see, territoriality is not an instinct or inborn drive; rather, it's a strategy that animals often use when the benefits outweigh the costs. Thus, territoriality becomes an advantage only when the cost of defending the territory is exceeded by the benefits to the defender.

Aggressive relationships do not occur simply between prey and predator species. Often they occur *within* species; animals of the same species compete for the same resources needed to survive, all vying for food, mates, and territory. The term **agonistic behavior** refers to this animal competition—fighting and aggression that is not involved in prey-predator relationships. Though it is commonly identified with overt aggression and fighting, agonistic behavior also includes threats and submission, chases, defensive territorial displays, and marking. Most often these activities involve members of the same species, usually but not always males, competing for the same resources.

Competition for Food

Competition within a Species

Animals must adapt their behavior to the availability of resources in the area where they live. Although animals generally prefer areas rich in resources, competing with other individuals for those resources can be costly in terms of time and energy. Let's imagine for a moment a very rich habitat that might attract many members of one species. Squirrels, for example, are attracted to richly wooded areas with trees bearing nuts and fruits. If many or all squirrels go to the rich area, they will have to compete for the resources, and the competition itself expends time and energy. If things get too crowded and competitive, it may pay late arrivals to go to a poorer, less crowded habitat to avoid the competition. Thus, the "best" place to go at a given moment in time depends on where all the others have already gone. As the number of competitors increases, it becomes more difficult to obtain rewards in any habitat, although resources will be more available in the better, richer habitats.

Severe competition for resources may even take place between sibling animals as they are developing together in the same nest or den. In some species of birds, for example, the first bird hatched is often the largest chick because it is fed by the parent birds for some days prior to the other egg or eggs hatching. In some species (e.g., the black eagle, *Aquila verreauxi*), the oldest bird pecks and eventually kills its sibling. In other species (e.g., the great egret, *Casmerodius albus*), the younger sibling often dies of starvation because the oldest offspring monopolizes the food delivered by the parent birds. In either case, the parent birds do nothing to stop the aggression and continue to deliver food to the largest bird.

Mock, Drummond, and Stinson (1990) concluded that the most fundamental factor common to these "siblicidal" species is competition for resources (primarily, food). This conclusion is supported by the fact that, when additional food is provided, nestling mortality diminishes. In addition, in all of these species of birds, food is always presented to the nestlings in small morsels directly from either parent's mouth. However, research has shown that when the morsels of food are larger, less fighting occurs. In other words, fighting wastes time that is better devoted to eating.

Thus, siblicidal competition is encouraged by a shortage of food, by the slow delivery of food in single small morsels, and by the ability of the largest nestling to monopolize and defend each morsel (Mock et al. 1990). In terms of evolution, these siblicidal behaviors have evolved in part because the largest, most aggressive nestlings are the ones that survive and pass their genes on to their offspring, thereby perpetuating the cycle of aggression.

There is another form of competition that is perhaps even more extreme than killing one's siblings: cannibalism (for which the polite name is **intraspecific predation**). We human beings regard eating our own kind as an evil aberration of behavior, and, moreover, we probably prefer to believe that it occurs rarely in other species. However, in the animal kingdom, cannibalism is neither as rare nor as aberrant as scientists once thought. Research has revealed that in many cases cannibalism has evolved not just to gain food but also to eliminate competitors. For example, in some species of beetles, the parents will eat enough of their newly hatched young to ensure that the remaining hatchlings have enough food. Even guppies (*Lebistes reticulatus*), a favorite among fish pets, will consume their young if the fish are placed in a small aquarium.

Embryonic sharks will eat each other while still in the womb! According to the "icebox hypothesis," evolution has stocked the shark's womb with extra offspring specifically for the purpose of feeding the one that is the strongest and fastest growing. Cannibalism is common in social insects where, according to Wilson (1975), it serves to conserve nutrients and regulate colony size. Termites eat their dead and injured. Kruuk (1972a) also reported cannibalism in competing clans of spotted hyenas.

One way some animals help their offspring compete successfully in a tough world is to eliminate the offspring of competitors. In some species of birds such as herring gulls, the parents will not hesitate to eat or destroy the eggs and young of other members of the same species. However, in other species, cannibalism may be primarily a function of the ecological circumstances of the animal. Wolcott and Wolcott (1984), for example, found that red land crabs (*Gecareinus lateralis*) became cannibalistic on younger crabs only when the available food supply was poor. A more extensive survey of predation within species of mammals is provided by Polis, Myers, and Hess (1984).

Competition between Species

Whereas most species must compete primarily with their own kind for resources, competition also occurs from time to time between different species that use or prey on the same resources in the same habitat. This is true even though most organisms of different species do not interact with each other, even when they live in relatively close surroundings.

Lions, hyenas, and wild dogs of the African plains all compete to prey on the same large herd animals, mainly zebras and wildebeests. Hyenas may not get to eat their kill if lions show up and drive the hyenas off. Once the prey animal has been eaten by the predator, vultures and jackals compete for the remaining carcass. Similarly, in the United States, badgers and cougars may fight over carrion, and squirrels and birds may compete for the same seeds during the winter.

Competition between closely related species can affect the habitat and eating habits of each species, sometimes to the disadvantage of one or the other. This idea was first formulated by the Russian biologist G. F. Gause. According to his principle of **competitive exclusion,** when two species compete with each other for the same limited resource, one species will usually be more effective at obtaining and using the resource. In turn, this superior species will eventually exclude or eliminate the other species in situations where they occur together. Though Gause's own work involved demonstrating the principle with various species of one-celled organisms (genus *Paramecium*) that competed for food, the principle appears to hold true for many interspecies interactions.

The typical consequence of the exclusion principle is not that the less competitive species is destroyed or killed but, rather, that it is forced to occupy a less preferred habitat. Randall (1978) tested two related species of voles (rodents similar to mice), *Microtus montanus* and *M. longicaudus,* in outdoor enclosures that provided both grass and shrub habitats. When each species was tested separately under these two conditions, each preferred to spend most of its time in the grass. But since *M. montanus* normally lives in grass while *M. longicaudus* lives in shrubs in the natural environment of these mice, *M. montanus* is a more aggressive species, for it excludes or drives away *M. longicaudus* from the grass it prefers to live in.

Animals that are closely related, live in the same area, and eat the same food do not always drive each other away. This phenomenon was revealed in a classic study of the exclusion principle by MacArthur (1958). He studied five closely related species of small warbler songbirds (genus *Dendroica*), all of which occupy the same New England forests and eat insects, often in the same tree. The question was, how do these species manage to occupy the same habitat if the exclusion principle applies? MacArthur showed that each warbler species had a separate feeding area in a tree, with the Cape May warbler feeding on insects primarily at the top of the tree, the yellow-rumped warbler at the bottom, and the other three species at varying areas in between (see Figure 8.1). Thus, rather than trying to exclude each other, the warbler species live in harmony by preying on insects at different locations on the same tree. They therefore eliminate the necessity of spending energy on aggression and defense.

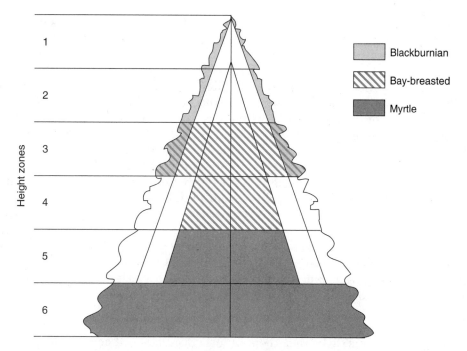

Figure 8.1 Different eating areas of three species of warblers inhabiting one tree.

Competition for Mates

Aggression and agonistic behavior can increase the individual's reproductive success. Generally speaking, aggression can help the individual to achieve reproductive success in four ways: (1) helping the individual obtain a mate, (2) guarding against a mate having sex with other individuals, (3) increasing the individual's chances for fertilization, and (4) reducing the offspring's competition. We will look at some examples of how these situations work in the following paragraphs. How competition for mating and reproductive success affects natural selection and evolution will be discussed in Chapter 10.

Assessment Processes

The term **assessment** refers to the process whereby animals size each other up or assess each other's strength and fighting ability. In many species, the process of assessment ensures that animals of unequal size or fighting ability do not engage in fighting. After all, a real fight risks possible injury to either party, and many animal species have evolved ways to avoid unnecessary and uneven conflicts.

Let's look at the male red deer or stag (*Cervus elaphus*) of Scotland, for whom the assessment process is complex. When competing for females, males engage in a three-stage process of assessing each other.

In the first stage, the males roar at each other vocally. A faster roar indicates an animal in better physical condition and with superior fighting ability. Upon hearing such a roar, a stag with a noticeably slower roar usually withdraws from confrontation (Clutton-Brock and Albon 1979). When an agonistic encounter is resolved in this way without actual fighting, it is said to be **ritualized.**

If males roar at about the same rate, they then engage in the second stage in which they walk some distance, one next to the other. Presumably, this allows each to assess the other rather closely. Many challenges end at this stage because one challenger likely perceives the other as being larger or as having more formidable antlers (see Figure 8.2). Thus, in these deer, as in many other species, the parallel walk is a ritualized test of strength that allows neither animal to be injured, just as long as one of the two contestants backs down.

Stage 3—an actual, serious fight (called **rutting**)—only occurs when the two protagonists are about equal in stature. When this is determined, the preliminary rituals escalate into actual fighting in which the deer charge each other, their antlers crashing together. Male deer can seriously hurt each other simply by pushing and shoving, by using skillful footwork, and by using their deadly antlers to poke an eye out or puncture the op-

Figure 8.2 Male red deer engaged in a parallel walk in order to assess each other's strength before possible fighting.

ponent's hide. Size and skill seem to be the determining factors, but in the case of an equal match, it is not easy to predict a winner; hence, the rut.

Rutting requires a great deal of energy, and it comes with many risks. Although we humans might not view rutting as worthwhile, a male deer likely would because it may be the only way to obtain the herd of females to mate with. That is, it may be the primary means of passing one's genes into the future. However, the stags fight only if they have to. If there are clear signals (roars) or assessment information (on the parallel walk) that one protagonist is the stronger, they will not fight and the weaker will generally withdraw.

Competition for females by displays of force often occurs in many species. For example, buffaloes, wild sheep, and goats butt their heads together. Beetles have pushing contests where the larger one usually wins. Frogs and toads may have wrestling matches to determine who mates. In many primate species (like baboons and macaque monkeys), size is often less important, and aggressiveness (where an animal won't give in and fights very fiercely) is more critical. (We will take a closer look at several primate species in later chapters.)

Costs and Benefits

The cost-benefit analysis of behavioral ecology is also very helpful for understanding aggressive behavior in this instance. Generally, for an animal to fight for a resource or payoff, it has to be worth it. In other words, the potential reproductive benefits must outweigh the potential costs (injury). Thus, when a resource is less valuable, we should expect fighting to be less likely to occur. In the situation where a challenger confronts the occupier of a territory, for example, we would normally expect the challenger to give way to the territory defender, if plenty of other resources are available. On the other hand, all animals in the wild are strongly driven by evolution and genes to reproduce, to pass their genes on to subsequent generations (remember—those not strongly driven to do this are no longer with us). So if the resource, such as obtaining a mate and reproducing, is highly valuable, we would expect to see animals willing to fight to obtain their share—that is, to fight for their genetic success.

To further illustrate these points, let's examine lions (*Panthera leo*) of the African plains. Each pride of hunting females, with their youngsters, is usually defended by one to seven males who are often (but not necessarily) genetically related (e.g., brothers). What determines which male gets to mate with a female in heat? Usually, only three factors matter (Schaller 1972):

1. *Age*. Older, weaker lions give way to younger.
2. *Size*. Smaller, weaker males give way to the larger and stronger.
3. *Whoever gets there first!* If two or more males are about equal in age and size, then it is a matter of which one encounters the female first.

Now let's use a cost-benefit analysis to try to understand this arrangement. What is the cost of fighting? It appears to be rather high because male lions are very powerful beasts that can hurt each other quite easily, and they risk severe injury in real battle. What are the reproductive benefits of fighting over one female in heat? Not very great. As it turns out, the probability of surviving offspring being produced from one mating is extremely low in lions: 1 in 3,000 matings actually leads to a cub that lives and survives to adulthood! In addition, there are other females in the pride, some of which may also be available for mating. Therefore, male lions within the pride are not going to risk injury by challenging another male for only one occasion of mating. All each male has to do is make sure that, occasionally, he's the first lion in line. The others will give way for exactly the same reason. However, this doesn't mean the males within a pride never fight.

What happens when two equally matched males encounter a female in heat at the same time? They will probably fight, though only briefly. The male lions that dominate the pride will vigorously defend the entire pride against any outside, wandering males. Often they will gang up on the outsider, and this defense lasts until the male intruder is driven away.

As we have seen, male lions within the pride generally do not fight much because the costs of potential injury outweigh the benefits of potential reproductive success for any particular mating opportunity. On the other hand, we should expect to see animals engage in fighting when the payoff is great (as when the potential for reproductive success is high), making the risk of injury worth it. In many species, most, if not all, of the adult males have battle scars, and many die each year in combat over females. These battles are most fierce when the males have real weapons—whether teeth, claws, antlers, or sheer physical strength—and one victorious male gets to mate with many females while his competitors do not mate at all. In these cases, fighting is worth it because the victorious male obtains a great deal of reproductive success. As we shall see in Chapter 10, the elephant seal can only mate with a harem of females if he succeeds in keeping other males away from his beach.

Territoriality

One widespread strategy for securing resources that occurs in the natural world is **territoriality.** Specifically, the ones who arrive on the scene first will find the best habitats and try to keep newcomers out, thereby securing the richest resources for themselves. A **territory** is any area that an animal will defend. Often a territory is a smaller area lying within the animal's **home range,** that larger area in which the animal carries out its normal activities of looking for food and mates. Within the home range and territory is a **core area,** the den or nest and its immediate surroundings where the animal often spends most of its time, sleeps, or keeps its young.

Territoriality is demonstrated when an individual animal, a mated pair, or a family of animals claims exclusive use of a space and uses agonistic behavior to defend the territory against **conspecifics** (members of the same species). Animals keep others out by patrolling the boundaries of the territory and by using certain displays or signals, scent marking, harassment, and sometimes overt aggression, as we shall see. A few individuals will capitalize on the best resources, making others use the poorer habitats.

What defines territorial behavior, or territoriality, has been described in detail by Huntingford and Turner (1987). They indicated four basic components:

1. Defensive behavior is confined to a particular place, the territory (i.e., the animal does not engage in defensive behaviors all the time).

2. The defended area is used exclusively by the resident defender unless it is deposed by a newcomer.

3. Defense involves agonistic behavior such as warnings, threats, displays, and sometimes aggression.

4. When an animal intrudes into another's territory, the intruder behaves submissively toward the resident, and not all intruders into an animal's territory are attacked. Animals typically recognize familiar neighbors that have their own territories and respond to them without threat when they accidentally stray into the resident's area. It is new strangers that could potentially take over the resident's territory that are most often attacked.

Territoriality is a common strategy in a large number of species, including many birds that are seasonally territorial. The first birds to arrive stake out the best resource areas and nest there. Subsequently, they drive out any new arrivals to the poorer habitats. If the old occupants die or leave, new birds rapidly move in. When all the acceptable (good and bad) habitats are full, no new "settlers" are permitted, and new arrivals become "floaters," never building a nest because they are not permitted to do so.

According to Huntingford and Turner (1987), there are two main factors that generally determine who wins territorial disputes. First, when the resident and intruder are equally matched, the resident will generally win a dispute and keep its territory. And second, when the resident and intruder are not equally matched, it is generally size that wins the dispute; smaller animals tend to give way to larger ones. Why does the intruder give way more easily than the resident? One possibility is that the resident fights harder because it knows how valuable the resources in its territory are, whereas the intruder does not.

Many studies have shown that, should a resident in a prime habitat leave or die, the territory is quickly taken over by a new resident. This is true of the great tit (*Parus major*), a bird of the English countryside that likes to breed in oak forests (Krebs 1971). When the oak forest habitat is satiated with breeding tits, each of which has its own territory, latecomers and floaters are forced to nest in hedgerows and bushes, and, consequently, their reproductive success is less than ideal. But when a resident tit in the woodland area leaves, it is replaced by a hedgerow resident very quickly.

With low population densities and ample resources, animals that are territorial typically encounter each other only accidentally and may not be hostile to each other. For example, the coati (*Nasua nasica*) is a kind of South American raccoon that lives a largely solitary life. Each coati (pronounced ko-OT-ee) has an individual feeding and denning area, but if they encounter each other by accident, they simply exchange friendly communications and go their separate ways. Thus, since they are not competing for the same resources, there is no reason to fight or be defensive (Kaufman 1962). Similar results were obtained by Ims (1987) in studies of territorial female gray-sided voles (*Chlethrionomys rufocanus*), a kind of field mouse. When extra oats, corn, and sunflower seeds were provided to these voles, the territoriality and aggression between females decreased.

In the long run, evolution tells us that, within the populated habitats, some individuals will have the best territories—they will tend to be the stronger, more aggressive, or larger individuals. We should expect that, on the basis of evolution, average reproductive success should increase with habitat quality (more food available, more young raised), and success should decrease as the number of competitors increases, since then the resident has to spend more of its time on defensive actions to keep others out.

Establishing Boundaries

Scent Marking.   You might think that territoriality would lead to a great deal of aggression and fighting among animals. However, in the competition for food resources (unlike competing for mates), this tends not to be the case. Often animals merely need to threaten aggression to achieve the result of keeping competitors out. In many instances, they accomplish this by using a system of marking their territories with scents (from chemicals called pheromones). In effect, these scent markings act as a clear signal to other members of their species to "keep out or else." Thus, territoriality—with or without aggression—tends to become a stable system (in most species) for the distribution of resources to the most fit individuals that can successfully occupy and defend their areas.

Three of the most common methods in mammals for marking territories are using urine, using feces, or marking with special built-in scent glands that have evolved specifically for this purpose. Let's briefly examine an animal that uses all three methods, namely, the spotted hyena of Africa (*Crocuta crocuta*) (see Figure 8.3). These animals live in female-dominant groups that roam around fairly large territories looking for prey on the hoof as well as carrion. To mark their territory conspicuously, both male and female hyenas defecate and urinate together in special areas at the boundaries of their territory called **latrines,** then smear it around with their paws. The feces turn white and are very conspicuous . But hyenas also employ what is called **pasting** to mark their well-traveled hunting routes. The hyena has two glands just inside its anus that secrete a white, smelly substance. When traveling across fields of grass, the stems of grass pass underneath their bodies. When stimulated in this way, the animal will open its anus and deposit the white secretion onto the stems. Other clans of hyenas only rarely trespass these territories and will be chased out if they're seen.

We can also see marking occur with wolves (*Canis lupus*). These animals use urine to scent-mark the boundaries of their territory. Wolves not a part of the pack risk injury and death if they enter this territory, and most of the time they won't take that risk. This minimizes

Figure 8.3   Spotted hyenas near the boundary of their territory.

within-species aggression. Many territorial wild cats do the same thing. Many species of wild deer mark their territory by rubbing their heads against trees and bushes, leaving scents from glands located near their eyes.

Generally, neighbors respect territorial boundaries. Occasionally, some may need reminders to keep out, but actual aggression by the resident animal is rarely used because most intruders will respect the markings or displays. With weasels and stoats, for example, scent marking will almost always cause an intruder to withdraw immediately from the resident's territory. Clearly, these animals use scent marking as a system of mutual avoidance. Indeed, in some cases, territoriality may lead to animals avoiding one another completely, creating few or no contacts between individuals.

Mammals that do not use scent marking are typically large and live in trees. This includes many monkey species. For these animals, urine or fecal marking is impractical because gravity brings all the urine and feces down to the jungle floor while the animal inhabits trees and branches. So monkeys often use loud vocal calls in conjunction with visual displays to delimit their feeding area. And, as is the case with hyenas, intruders are usually chased out.

Calls are not always used to threaten, however. The young of some species (e.g., rodents, wolves, dogs, and bats) will use calls to summon their parents. These stress calls often lie outside the range of human hearing and quickly mobilize the parents to come to the rescue. These calls may also be inaudible to other species. This can be a real advantage if a nearby predator species cannot hear the distress call, while the parent can.

Aggressive Displays.   Although scent marking of territory is common in mammals, not all mammals use it, and it never occurs with birds. Instead, many species signal "keep out" visually by exhibiting certain gestures, body postures, or actions. In some species, the simplest aggressive display is an apparent increase in size. Many species of fish and lizards puff up their size when they feel threatened. The same kind of response can be observed in the domestic cat; it arches its back and its fur stands on end when it encounters a threatening situation. Another common aggressive display is for the individual to expose its weapons. Crabs will spread their claws when encountering an intruder. Similarly, many mammals like dogs and baboons open their mouths and bare their teeth or fangs when threatened. The pitch of an animal's call can also be a display cue. For example, lower pitches often indicate that the intruder has a large body size. Davies and Halliday (1978) taped the croaks of toads (*Bufo bufo*) and played them to other male toads. The lower the pitch of the calls, the less likely was the listening toad to approach the caller.

Whereas many species often use aggressive displays to demark their territorial ownership, such displays may also be used by social animals to indicate their dominance over another member of their group. The role of displays in dominance relationships will be discussed in the next chapter.

Costs and Benefits

Territoriality is a very old topic in the study of animal behavior, but it is only more recently that behavioral ecology has begun to have a better understanding of resource defense (territoriality). This is due to the fact that scientists are examining it in terms of costs and benefits. This approach began with the work of Brown (1964), who made the general point that an animal would be territorial if the gains of territoriality outweighed its costs. More specifically, he concluded that territoriality would be adopted when the resources of the territory were economically dependable; that is, when the animal could count on the regular support from the resources of the territory as opposed to the lack of regular resources when not being territorial or when wandering.

Territoriality has frequently been studied in hummingbirds and related sunbirds. In these bird species, it is easy to measure or estimate quantitatively many of the cost-benefit parameters because the birds feed almost exclusively on nectar from flowers. Therefore, the amount of energy in a given quantity of nectar can be measured precisely, as can the exact amount of nectar consumed by a bird. Gill and Wolf (1975), for example, examined in detail the economics of feeding territoriality in the golden-winged sunbird (*Nectarinia reichenowi*), which lives in the mountains of Kenya and is similar to the hummingbird pictured in Figure 8.4. They found that different sunbirds defended territories that

Figure 8.4   A hummingbird sipping nectar from a flower.

varied in size, but each territory contained about 1,600 flowers. After taking careful measurements of the nectar content of the flowers and the costs of the bird's metabolic activities, Gill and Wolf concluded that the main benefit of defending a territory is that the defender gets all the nectar and does not share any of it with other sunbirds. Effective defense of the 1,600 flowers provides all the nectar that the individual bird needs and, in a sense, means that each visit to a flower produces more nectar for the bird. The more nectar from each flower, the less time the individual needs to forage for other flowers, and the more time and energy there is to devote to defense of the territory.

The main point here is that the more economically dependable (or valuable) the resource is (e.g., the more nectar there is in the flowers sought by hummingbirds), the more territorial and aggressive the bird will be. When plenty of the resource is available, the bird then has the energy to defend its territory, and, therefore, it is worthwhile to do so. However, when resources are scarce—when the bird is in a poorer habitat—the gain from excluding others (aggression and territoriality) may not be enough to pay for the cost of defensive behaviors. Thus, the bird will not be territorial because such behavior is too expensive.

Birds also tend not to be territorial when resources are plentiful for all individuals. In this situation, competition and territoriality are not necessary; they are just wasteful. So we should expect to see territoriality when there are normal variations in the supply of resources, not when there is too much or too little.

Behavioral ecologists like to push the envelope a little further and try to calculate the "optimal" territory size for a given species. If we know exactly what an animal is working to obtain to satisfy its needs, it should be possible to use that information to determine how large an area the animal needs to reach its goals. As we have already seen in the example of sunbirds, studies have shown that the size of the territory depends entirely on the number of flowers. Because sunbirds are territorial and stay where they are year-round, they try to minimize their daily energy cost by using the resources confined to their 1,600 flowers. Some smaller hummingbirds, on the other hand, try to maximize their energy gain every day because they will need extra energy to migrate over long distances. Thus, the two groups optimize their food input in different ways because the different needs of each species are affected by whether they stay in a territory or migrate.

Evolutionarily Stable Strategies

Of course, when two competing animals encounter one another, there may be no fighting and aggression at all—one may simply give way to the other. In such a **submissive display,** an animal is communicating to an aggressor or resident that it will not compete for resources. Often this communication is made either with sounds or body language that is largely built in or innate. Dog puppies, for example, will usually roll over on their back, display their belly, and lie still if approached by any strange, large dog. Adult dogs and wolves display submission by lying down, flattening their ears, and not challenging another dog that displays aggressively. Dogs will not usually attack another dog giving a submissive display (see Figure 8.5).

Submissive displays pose some theoretical problems for the theory of evolution. If the more aggressive individuals are, in fact, the more successful ones, how could submissive displays ever evolve? In other words, how could more submissive individuals succeed in passing their genes on to subsequent generations if, in fact, it is aggressive behavior that gives an individual a competitive advantage?

Scientists began to better understand the evolution of conflict and displays with the work of Maynard Smith and Price (1973) and Maynard Smith (1974, 1976). Maynard Smith introduced the concept of an **evolutionarily stable strategy** (ESS). An ESS is a way of behaving that gradually becomes the dominant strategy in a population of animals over time. The word *strategy* does not imply deliberate, conscious acts when applied to animal behavior as it does with human behavior. Rather, it's simply a typical pattern of behaving. Once the ESS is adopted by nearly all population members, it cannot be challenged by any alternate strategy; that is, it becomes stable.

Figure 8.5   An aggressive display (left) and a submissive display (right) in wolves.

Maynard Smith and his colleagues were able to show that neither pure aggression (i.e., all members of the population being aggressive) nor pure submission is an ESS. The explanation of why this is so goes as follows: If aggressive animals (called hawks) are successful and breed profusely, they will reach a point where all of their aggressive offspring will be constantly fighting with each other. As a consequence, many will die in the process. In fact, if all the hawks are equally matched, 50% will lose (though not necessarily die) in aggressive encounters. Therefore, when most of the individuals in a population are hawks, it will pay an individual to be a submissive dove when challenged by a hawk. Thus, with more hawks, the advantages for reproductive success will revert to the doves.

On the other hand, when there are mostly doves, it will pay more to be a hawk and to dominate the submissive doves that will not offer the hawk resistance. So, at any given moment in time, the optimal strategy for the individual depends on what the other individuals are doing. Under these circumstances, it will also pay individuals to be capable of a **mixed strategy,** that is, to be a hawk or a dove depending on the circumstances the individual is confronted with.

What do these strategies have to do with territoriality? It turns out that, in the long run, there is an optimal ESS, called the **bourgeois strategy,** that cannot be defeated by other strategies; this strategy, a variation on the mixed strategy, says, "Be a hawk if you're in your own territory, but be a dove if you're in someone else's territory." Many species of animals follow this ESS. Thus, agonistic aggression in many species is related to ownership of the territory. Davies (1978), for example, showed that the resident speckled butterfly (*Pararge aegeria*) always wins in encounters with an intruder. Moreover, when two males were both tricked into ownership of the same territory, they would fight over it.

Of course, residency doesn't always predict which animal will win a competition. In some species, the critical factor appears to be strength or size: weaker, smaller animals give way to stronger, larger ones. Riechert (1984) performed laboratory experiments with female funnel-web spiders (*Agelenopsis aperta*) of varying size. When a pair of spiders met, the larger spider would immediately attempt to fight, but the smaller spider would retreat. When they were about the same size, then the intruder would give way to the resident spider.

Summary

Animals of one species frequently compete with one another for food, mates, and territory. Competition for food can take extreme forms, such as siblicide and cannibalism, when resources are scarce. While human beings regard such behaviors as aberrant and unusual, these extreme forms of adaptation are perfectly understandable in the context of evolution and are less rare than previously thought.

Animals of different species, such as the large carnivores of the African plains, may also compete with one another over the same prey for food. The principle of competitive exclusion predicts that, when one species is more successful than another at competing for the same resource, the less successful species will be forced to pursue the resource at a new and probably less desirable location. On the other hand, some species of songbirds, rather than fight each other, will live together on different levels of the same tree as long as insect prey are available at every level.

Many species will also compete vigorously for mates. Although individuals may occasionally fight over potential mates, a number of species have evolved elaborate rituals to minimize aggression. Animals will assess each other's fitness, often leading to the withdrawal of the less fit animal. Fighting is most likely to occur when competitors are evenly matched. When a match is uneven, the potential risks of death and injury make a less fit animal reluctant to fight. So, for example, two or more resident males within a pride of lions will rarely fight over mating because the costs of injury vastly outweigh the reproductive benefits of one mating opportunity.

A frequent strategy in nature for controlling food and mating resources is territoriality—defending a desirable location against intruders. Aggressive encounters between residents and intruders are often prevented by some form of territorial marking. In scent marking, a territorial animal or its group marks the boundaries of its territory with urine, feces, or excreted substances, as in the hyena, which uses all three. Birds and tree-dwelling mammals use visual displays or vocal calls to mark their territories. For many animals, aggressive displays simply consist of puffing up in size or displaying teeth, claws, or other weapons.

Animals tend to be territorial when the resources of the territory are economically dependable and the benefits of excluding others outweigh the costs. The relationships between the costs and benefits of resource defense have been studied extensively with hummingbirds and sunbirds. These studies lend strong support to the idea that resident animals will vigorously defend their territories in proportion to the resources that the territory provides.

The study of aggressive and submissive displays has led to the development of the concept of an evolutionarily stable strategy (ESS), a strategy that cannot be defeated by other strategies as long as most population members adopt the ESS. In general, because an optimal strategy depends on what other individuals are doing, being a hawk or a dove all the time is not usually an ESS. Rather, in most populations, it will profit individuals to adopt some form of mixed strategy such as, "If you reside in the territory, be a hawk; otherwise, be a dove."

CHAPTER 9

Communication and Living in Groups

As humans we take communication, especially verbal communication, for granted. It's an integral part of social interaction, parenting, media, art, education, entertainment—virtually every aspect of our lives. Human language and culture originally evolved out of biological evolution but are no longer subject to the laws of biology alone. For nonhuman animals, communication must ultimately serve the functions of survival and reproduction. Over geologic time, different animal species have evolved many ways of communicating that take advantage of all their sensory capacities—hearing, seeing, touching, smelling, and tasting. The role of communication in facilitating reproductive success will be explored in subsequent chapters; how communication serves adaptation and survival is surveyed in this chapter.

For animals that enjoy the advantages of living in groups, communication is essential, and in group species communication abilities have often evolved to amazing and subtle levels. Elephants, for example, communicate with low-frequency sounds that biologists have only recently begun to understand. In the latter part of this chapter, we will see how communication abilities enhance the advantages of group living.

A nimal species across the world use a bewildering array of sounds, gestures, chemicals, and other means to communicate with each other as individuals and in groups. However, not every sound or gesture may be a communication. **Communication** refers to a process in which one individual, the "sender," sends a signal to other individuals, the "receivers," and, in turn, a receiver responds to the original signal in some way. The response may not be the one the sender would prefer, but, for communication to occur, the signal must be received—leading to some sort of response. Evolutionary biologists assume that communicative behaviors evolve because, on the average, the responses given by receivers confer some advantage to the sender.

In the animal kingdom, the purpose or intention of the communication must be inferred by observing the communication process. Sometimes the purpose appears to be clear and simple while at other times communications may serve multiple purposes that are not always clear. Also, the word *intention* is not meant to imply that the signaler "consciously" decides to send a signal. Whereas each communication contains a sender, a signal, and a receiver, the sender and receiver are usually but not always the same species.

As our definition of communication implies, the process of communication is generally adaptive or advantageous to the sender but not necessarily to the receiver. Even so, on a given occasion an evolved signal may be costly to the sender and advantageous to the receiver. For example, though a cricket's chirps generally are intended to attract a mate, the chirping may instead attract a predator (Cade 1981). Thus, while chirping obviously did not evolve in crickets to attract predators, the chirping is a communication to the predator—regardless of the cricket's intention—because the signal was received and responded to.

In the latter part of this chapter, the focus will be on how communication systems have evolved to support the ability of some species to enjoy the benefits of living in groups rather than to live solitary lives. How individual animals communicate with each other for many other purposes is discussed in other chapters in this book; for example, in foraging (Chapter 6), for defense against predators (Chapter 7), for marking territories (Chapter 8), in sexual attraction and courtship (Chapter 10), and in rearing the young (Chapter 12). Here we will discuss the basic channels of communication used by animals and their general adaptive functions.

Channels of Communication

The most familiar channels of communication are sound, visual displays, and touch. Though our primate ancestors probably depended a great deal on the use of scents and their powers of olfaction (smell) to communicate, modern humans rely primarily on hearing and vision. Nevertheless, the use of chemical trails for communication still remains the dominant mode for many species of insects like ants and for a large number of land mammals. Wolves and other canines are notable for their use of "multichannel" communication—scents, sounds, visual messages, and touch. Wolves (*Canis lupus*) mark their territory with scents in their urine that communicate "Keep out!" to other wolves. Their howling warns intruders, and it can bring the pack together. An erect tail by an alpha (leader) wolf in the pack shows dominance. Finally, a wolf pup will lick an adult's muzzle to beg for food.

Less common are two other channels of communication: electric fields and substrate vibrations. A few species of fish in South America and in Africa actually use self-generated electric fields to communicate with members of their own species, to attract mates, and to display aggression. Some species have learned to send vibrations through objects to communicate with their own kind. For example, some male spiders will vibrate the strands on the webs of female spiders to communicate their desire to mate.

In general, the modes of communication used by a particular species of animal are going to "make sense" in terms of the demands put on that animal by its environmental circumstances. For example, small nocturnal animals will use sounds and/or scents to communicate, rather than visual displays, since precise visual information is often not obtainable in the dark. And while many species of birds depend greatly on visual cues and visual communication, birds that live in dense bushes typically depend more on sounds.

Sound

Acoustic signals of animals are typically produced either by expelling air over a membrane, by forcing it through a resonance tube, or by rubbing body parts together. Crickets, for example, make their chirping sounds by drawing a filelike projection on one wing over a scraper on the other wing, much like stroking a comb with a fingernail (see Figure 9.1). Male frogs and toads use vocal cords to produce their croaking sounds, which attract females. The male can amplify these sounds by inflating a large sac beneath its chin with air.

Signaling by sound has two notable advantages for communicating: the signal can radiate in all directions at once, often around obstacles, and sound signals can be easily turned on and off. Loud sounds can penetrate quite a distance, day or night. Sounds are also flexible in that typically they can be modulated (in pitch or in loudness, for example) to indicate different messages. On the other hand, the downside of sound messages is that they usually require considerable energy to produce, and they can often be overheard by unintended receivers such as predators.

Mammals and some bird species are unique in their use of different vocal sounds to signal the presence of different kinds of predators. For example, California ground squirrels (*Spermophilus beecheyi*) use chattering sounds to warn of the presence of ground predators, but they use whistling sounds to signal the presence of large birds. Variations among the chattering calls indicate whether the ground predator is a snake, a badger, a cat, or a dog (the latter two being indicated by the same call). Similarly, Seyfarth, Cheney, and Marler (1980) showed that vervet monkeys (*Cercopithecus aethiops*) use several different calls in response to

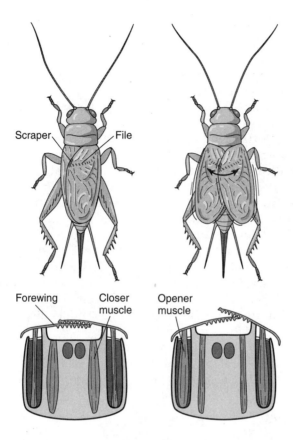

Scraper   File

Forewing   Closer muscle   Opener muscle

Figure 9.1   How a cricket produces sound.

different primary predators such as leopards, eagles, and pythons. A leopard call caused the vervets to run for trees, the eagle call made them look up and run for bushes, and a snake call made them look down. These monkeys responded the same way to a playback of tape-recorded alarm calls as they did to real calls in nature (Marler 1985).

Whereas most animals that communicate with sound use short and simple vocalizations termed **calls,** a few species use complex vocalizations. The most complex auditory signals in nature are generally used by vertebrate animals, mainly birds and mammals such as primates, bats, and cetaceans (dolphins and whales). How the males of many species of birds use complex calls or songs to attract the females of their species is discussed in some detail in Chapter 2.

The sounds made by cetaceans began to receive greater attention from scientists and the general public when the "songs" of the humpback whale (*Megaptera novaeangliae*) were recorded (Connor and Peterson 1994). Humpbacks grow to a length of about 50 feet and can reach a weight of 65 tons. The humpback song is an ordered pattern that usually lasts from 6 to 30 minutes. Yet, as with songbirds, it is only the male humpbacks that sing in their tropical, warm-water breeding grounds. Whereas beluga and bowhead whales produce the richest and most variable repertoire of sounds of any sea creatures, humpbacks can produce series of songs lasting as long as 22 hours! These songs contain a wide variety of sounds, sometimes characterized as snores, groans, yups, chirps, cries, eehs, and oohs, and can sometimes be heard as far as a hundred miles away.

All humpbacks sing approximately the same song in one of three ocean regions (North Pacific, North Atlantic, and Southern Hemisphere), and the songs slowly change from season to season. However, individual variations are identifiable within each song, suggesting the possibility that the songs help identify individual animals. But why sing? What are the songs really for? Because only the males sing, most researchers believe that the function is primarily sexual, perhaps to advertise sexual availability, attract females, and put off other males. But the songs are very long and complex, and the precise functions of humpback songs and their singing are not well understood.

Bowhead whales (*Balaena mysticetus*) live in social groups of up to 15 animals. Clark (1991) found that bowheads call to each other to maintain herd cohesion since individuals tend to be widely dispersed over an area reaching up to eight square miles.

The most complex form of sound communication known is human language. This method of communication and its relationships to the animal kingdom will be discussed in the last chapters of this book.

Visual Messages

Though displays can be auditory rather than visual, the word *display* is often associated with visual signals, and many species of animals communicate by using visual displays. A behavior becomes a display when its pattern is adapted in physical form or frequency to function as a social signal (Drickamer and Vessey 1992). Many displays have evolved into patterns of behavior that are very stereotyped and constant. The advantage of this outcome should be clear: the display can be identified easily and immediately by the receiver with little chance of error.

Visual messages have several advantages. They can be transmitted very quickly, they can convey a lot of information, and they are highly directional. In addition, when the message is largely conveyed by the sender's own body parts and coloration (as in sexual displays by birds), there is little cost in energy. On the other hand, visual messages typically cannot be conveyed over long distances and are easily blocked by objects between the sender and the receiver. Therefore, visual messages are not practical in the dark unless the sender can produce its own light.

A few species can actually signal by producing light with their own bodies rather than reflecting light. Male fireflies (genus *Photinus*) flash specific light patterns from their abdomens to attract females of their own species. Different species have different flash patterns. When a female resting on a leaf or branch recognizes a male's pattern, the female flashes back to the male, and soon the male lands to mate with the female. Carlson and Copeland (1978) showed that the females can flash their pattern perfectly the very first time, without any prior experience. Lloyd (1965) showed that this undertaking can gain a male reproductive success—or death. The females of one particular species (*Photuris versicolor*) can mimic the flash response of closely related species and lure males to them. These firefly femmes fatales then eat the deceived males!

Some fish can also signal by generating their own light. Flashlight fish (genus *Anomalops*) can turn on a light under each eye by dropping a flap of tissue that exposes a chamber underneath containing bacteria that make light (McCosker 1977).

Among the more unusual forms of visual communication are the signals used by cephalopod mollusks—squids and octopuses—as they change their appearance and color rapidly (Moynihan and Rodaniche 1977). Although some of these color changes can be used defensively to blend the animal in with its background (as also occurs in chameleons and one fish, the flounder, *Bothus ocellatus*), squids and octopuses also use these changes to communicate with other members of their species.

Touch

Tactile communication is very limited because the sender and receiver must be in close physical contact in order for it to occur. For this reason, touch is often used in conjunction with other channels. Touch has the distinct advantage of not usually requiring any specialized body structures in order for it to occur: the individual can use any body parts or the whole body to touch another individual.

Tactile communication appears to serve three important communication functions across many species. In humans, other primates, and some mammals such as cats, grooming communicates dominance and submission and serves to cement social relationships within social groups. (More will be said about grooming in primates in the later chapters of this book.)

A second important function of touch in many species is to initiate the giving of food from the message recipient to the sender. Chicks of many bird species peck at the beaks of their parents, causing the parent to give food to the offspring. In many other species of social insects and birds, similar behaviors will initiate the passing of food from one individual to another, sometimes from mouth to mouth.

Although ant communication is often identified with chemicals and scent trails, not all ant species depend on chemical communication. A third function of touch in some ant species is to initiate transport for one ant by another. One ant may pull or bite on the mandible of another in order to get a ride! When an ant of genus *Leptothorax* returns to the nest, it may lead another worker back to larger prey by having the follower rest its antennae on the leader's abdomen, a way of "leading it by the hand" to the prey site.

Chemical Pathways

Chemical messengers, usually called **pheromones**, are the most universal mode of communication. Using scents and chemical pathways is a less flexible method of communication than using sounds, but in general chemicals have many advantages: they are cheaper to produce than sounds, less risky in attracting attention, and they can last a long time. Chemicals are also indifferent to darkness and obstacles, and scents have the advantage in many cases of being detectable or meaningful only for the members of one's own species. Sounds, on the other hand, might be heard by friend and foe alike. Of all forms of communication, chemicals have the greatest potential range; sometimes they extend up to several kilometers in the air!

Pheromones have evolved to have characteristics that fit the situation for which they are used. The alarm pheromones of ants, for example, last only a few seconds but are dispersed widely and quickly through the air. On the other hand, the territorial scent markers left by beavers on the ground and on trees can last for many months. Thus, in most instances, natural pheromones are optimally designed to last as long as the organism needs them to last.

There are two general classifications of chemical messengers. We are accustomed to thinking of pheromones primarily as chemical **releasers** that affect the behavior of another individual, as in the chemicals used to mark territory or leave a trail. But in some species, chemicals also function as **primers** that directly affect other individuals' physiology. In a bee colony, for example, one pheromone given off by the queen (called "queen substance") gives the entire bee colony its identity. A more unusual example of priming occurs in the house mouse (*Mus musculus*). Chemicals in the urine of male mice cause females to abort fetuses that were impregnated by other males! This phenomenon was discovered by Bruce (1960) and hence is called the **Bruce effect**.

Communication by means of scents or odors is common among most species of insects and many land animals. A typical way in which ants communicate was illustrated by Holldobler (1977). **Recruitment** occurs in ants when one ant must recruit the help of another in order to complete a task. For example, fire ants (genus *Solenopsis*) often feed on other large insects, but several ants are needed to carry large prey back to the ant nest. An individual recruits a helper by first laying down an odor trail. After finding prey, the ant returns to the nest and lays a trail of scent along the way. The scent comes from a gland in the ant's ab-

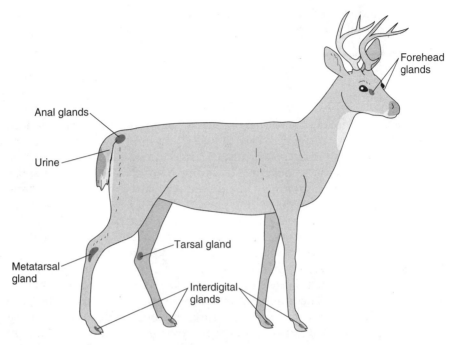

Figure 9.2   The odor-producing glands on the body of the black-tailed deer.

domen. This trail lures other worker ants to run along the trail to the prey and to eventually assist in bringing the prey back to the nest. The scent, however, does not persist long after the prey has been removed.

Scents are very important for land mammals that live in forests and dense vegetation. In many deer species, for example, communication with sound is impractical because it attracts predators. Visual communication is also less useful because the forest environment presents many obstacles to visual pathways. In these ecological circumstances, many forest species have developed highly specialized glands for producing chemicals used as markers. The black-tailed deer (*Odocoileus hemionus columbianus*), for example, has six different pheromone-producing glands: on the forehead, between the toes, on the inside and outside of its back legs, in the anus, and in the urinary tract (see Figure 9.2).

Functions of Communication

Currently, two main theories prevail for how and why communicative signals have evolved in animals. One theory states that the primary purpose of communication is to share information about what an animal is likely to do next (e.g., Smith 1984). Thus, for example, an animal would give a visual aggressive display so that the receiver of the message would know that the sender will behave aggressively if the receiver doesn't stand down. On the other hand, Dawkins and Krebs (1978) proposed a different theory that animals communicate primarily to manipulate the behavior of others to their own advantage, that is, to ultimately increase their own individual fitness. This idea is more consistent with the Darwinian view of evolution as the selfish pursuit of individual gene propagation.

Konrad Lorenz (1932) began the modern study of communication by classifying certain responses as *social releasers*. These are behaviors that have been designed by evolution to elicit instinctive social behavior patterns in members of the same species. How did these "releasing" behaviors evolve in the first place? The process by which behaviors become social releasers is called **ritualization**. The idea is that behavior that provides information to another animal will become habitual, stereotyped, or "ritualized" if it leads to that animal's responding in ways that are advantageous for the releasing animal. A classic example illustrating ritualization is how herring gull chicks (*Larus argentatus*) obtain food from a parent. The chick pecks at a red spot on the tip of the parent's beak. This causes the parent to regurgitate food for the chick. Both responses—pecking the red spot and regurgitation in response—are ritualized (invariable) and largely unlearned (Tinbergen 1951). (See Figure 9.3.)

Darwin (1873) described how communicative facial expressions in mammals may have originally evolved from responses used to protect

Figure 9.3   A herring gull chick pecks at the dot on its parent's beak, causing the parent to regurgitate food.

the sense organs. When a mammal narrows its eyes, flattens its ears, and raises its neck hairs (as in canids and primates), the sense organs are protected in times of danger. Other animals may have learned to interpret these responses as signs of aggression or fear and therefore reacted appropriately. These responses increased their effect on other animals as they became ritualized and somewhat exaggerated. Other behaviors such as vocalizations (e.g., barking in dogs) and facial markings (in many monkey species) may also assist in making the expressions more effective as means of communication. In fact, the absence of hair on parts of the human face may have evolved primarily as a part of successful communication.

Recognition Functions

One of the most basic functions of communication is to assist the individual in recognizing and identifying other individuals as members of the same species, the same population group, or the same family (called "kin recognition"). This recognition function reaches its most extreme form, perhaps, in the social insects (ants, termites, bees) where the entire colony is infused with one colony-specific chemical odor given to it by the queen. Individuals of the same species that do not have this chemical scent will be treated by all colony members as an enemy and as potential food.

By itself, recognition is not always communication since our definition of communication requires some intention on the part of the sender to affect a receiver in some way. Thus, when two animals that know each other as individuals just happen to pass by and recognize each other, this would not be classified as an act of communication. But whether or not recognition is always communication, there's no question that it is an important phenomenon. Cats, dogs, and their wild relatives typically mark their territories with scents, which are chemical messengers saying, "Strangers, keep out!" Territory holders can typically tell the difference between strangers and neighbors, and they usually are not aggressive toward neighbors.

It is also important for parents and offspring to recognize each other and for mated pairs to distinguish their mate from other individuals. Bird species typically do this by the unique songs or calls that they vocalize. When a female Emperor penguin (*Aptenodytes forsteri*) returns to the land after feeding in the sea, she is confronted with a colony of thousands of braying penguins, all of which look very similar. She and her mate find each other by means of unique characteristics in the sound they each make.

Primates can often identify individuals by means of distinctive facial characteristics. Gorillas, chimpanzees, and humans have so many variations in the size, shape, and configurations of facial features that visual identification of individuals is learned rapidly. Humans have the additional advantage of being able to produce speech and language patterns that are readily recognized as unique to an individual.

Group Coordination

The social calls made by members of the dolphin family are among the most complex and unique in nature. For example, killer whales (*Orcinus orca*) appear to be among a distinct minority of animal species that acquire communication signals largely through experience (the other animals being some birds, some seals, a few primates, other members of the dolphin family, and humans). The killer whale's ear canal is closed to the surface; it does not possess external ears. Instead, the animal "hears" with its lower jaw, which conducts sound to its extremely sensitive inner ear. Killer whales produce rapid clicking sounds in order to echolocate—to navigate their surroundings and to locate prey. They also produce whistles, squeaks, and screams, primarily to communicate with other members of their group (see Figure 9.4).

While some killer whales are nomadic hunters called "transients," other "residents" live in territorial social groups called **pods**, each consisting of about 10 to 20 whales led by a dominant female. Ford (1991) studied resident pods off the shores of British Columbia and was able to show that each pod has its own "dialect," or distinctive call repertoire,

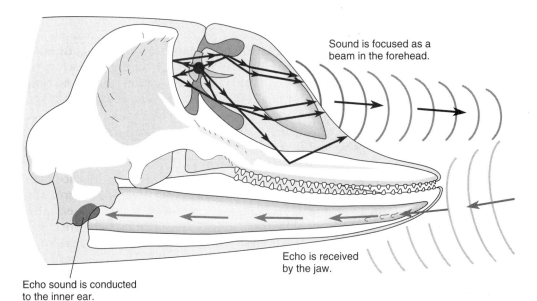

Sound is focused as a beam in the forehead.

Echo is received by the jaw.

Echo sound is conducted to the inner ear.

Figure 9.4   The killer whale's system for producing and receiving sound.

even though pods occasionally interact with each other. Each pod has a repertoire of about twelve calls that are nearly identical in sound when produced by any group member but that differ from the calls made by members of other pods. Since both male and female offspring tend to remain in the same pod for life (as long as eighty years!), it is believed that the pod's distinctive call repertoire is learned by youngsters imitating their mothers and other pod members.

The precise functions of all the killer whale calls in a pod are not well understood at this time. Some likely possibilities are the maintenance of contact among pod members, the coordination of behavior during group activities such as hunting (resident pods prey primarily on salmon), and the attraction of mates. (Though males remain in their birth pods, they mate with females in other pods.) Another function may be pod recognition since sometimes a hundred or more different killer whales from several pods congregate in the same area.

Alarm

Animals that live in groups can use signals to warn each other of danger. Even animals of different species that co-exist in herds or flocks often have alarm calls that are identical, though their other calls are clearly different. Thus, animals threatened by the same predators can benefit by having the same alarm calls. For example, Marler (1973) found that African red-tailed monkeys (*Cercopithecus ascanius*) and blue monkeys (*C. mitis*) used the same chirping alarm calls, although the male sexual calls differed markedly.

Some species, such as sea urchins (*Diadema antillarium*) and earthworms *(Lumbricus terrestris)*, produce chemical alarms that warn away members of their own species. Rottman and Snowden (1972) showed that mice and rats secrete an alarm pheromone in their urine when they are stressed.

Hunting and Foraging

In predator species that live in groups, effective communication can also increase the efficiency of hunting, making it easier for the group to capture larger prey. The African wild dog (*Lycaon pictor*) is a very efficient hunter on the African plains. Before each hunt for large game, the pack members have a "ceremony" where members engage in tail wagging, nibbling, lip licking, circling, and nose nudging. Such behavior may be important for coordinating group activities, getting all adults involved in the hunt, and possibly even communicating what kind of prey will be hunted (van Lawick and van Lawick-Goodall 1970).

Common chimpanzees (*Pan troglodytes*) of Africa live in large social groups in which individual members forage for leaves and fruit. Menzel

(1971) showed that individual chimpanzees can communicate the location of food to other chimpanzees and can also lead them to it. Though the leader uses no special signals or calls, its purposeful body posture and constant looking back at the others gradually leads the other chimps to the food.

Group Living

Many species of animals afford many advantages to their individuals when the individuals live together in groups. First, let's make a distinction here between **aggregations** and organized **societies**. Aggregations are groups of animals, like herds of four-footed animals, flocks of birds, and schools of fish. The animals stay and move together, usually for defensive advantages, but without definite structure, organization, or communication. In an organized society, on the other hand, there is often some division of labor, communication of members with each other, close proximity to each other, stability of composition of the group, and resistance by the group to intrusion by outsiders. Species that participate in this kind of society include human beings, chimpanzees, gorillas, baboons, wolves, lions, and wild dogs. Insects such as ants, termites, and some species of bees also live in organized societies but are often placed in a special category called **eusociality** because most species members are sterile and cannot reproduce.

Aggregations

Some species of animals live in loosely knit groups that afford individual animals many advantages involving vigilance, defense, and food gathering. An interesting study of an aggregate species, the raven (*Corvus corax*), was provided by Heinrich (1989). Ravens are large, black birds of the crow family. They are the largest of all songbirds (see Figure 9.5). They can make many sounds with their calls, including warbles, yodels, squawks, thunks, and yells, that can be heard a mile away.

Heinrich (1989) became puzzled by the fact that a group of 15 ravens, while eating a moose carcass, were yelling loudly together and creating quite a melee. Heinrich tested several possible hypotheses as to why the ravens were carrying on so loudly, despite two obvious costs: tremendous energy loss from yelling, and attracting other ravens to the same valuable food. In his investigations, Heinrich placed rich food baits in raven territories. He found that, whereas nonresident ravens always yelled at the food site, the resident raven territory owners (usually a mated pair) never yelled. He also found that the yelling brought other nonresident ravens to the same bait, too many for the resident ravens to drive off. Therefore, the baits were either eaten entirely by the quiet resident pair or by noisy crowds of nonresident ravens.

Figure 9.5 The raven, a large member of the crow family (Corvidae) of birds.

Clearly, the nonresident ravens yell to attract other nonresidents to the food site so that, together, they can override any interference by the resident pair of ravens. Here the benefits of obtaining a rich food source—even if it must be shared—outweigh the costs of yelling. Heinrich's interesting study (1989) also illustrates how animals will communicate information to conspecifics when it is in their selfish interest to do so.

Organized Societies

The organization of a socially structured species can be maintained in a number of different ways. With insects and many invertebrates, this usually happens entirely through chemical controls and some forms of communication. However, another common kind of organizational regulator in many animal societies is social **dominance**, that is, some individuals have priority over others in terms of access to food, space, and mates. The study of dominance hierarchies began in the 1920s with the identification of "pecking orders" in domestic chickens. Although dominance hierarchies are common in most species of social vertebrates, they also occasionally occur in some nonvertebrates such as crickets, wasps, ants, and shrimp.

Dominance relationships are often established through displaying or fighting. Once dominance is settled, the individuals generally do not duel again because the result of the match would likely be the same. The stability of the dominance hierarchy depends partly on the ability of individuals to recognize each other as individuals and to communicate the appropriate signals that indicate either dominance or submission.

Dominance in Birds.   Some species of birds are unusual in that their rank in a dominance hierarchy may be indicated by variations in their color or plumage rather than by behavior. Plumage differences that signal dominance in this way are sometimes called "badges of status." For example, Evans and Hatchwell (1992) studied male scarlet-tufted malachite sunbirds (*Nectarina johnstoni*), which inhabit Mount Kenya in Africa (see Figure 9.6). The males defend territories that contain flowers bearing the nectar on which they feed. In territorial defense, the males display red chest tufts, and those males with larger red tufts defend more flowers. Evans and Hatchwell (1992) manipulated tuft size experimentally by gluing feathers onto male birds. The birds with larger tufts gained more flowers, while others with reduced redness lost flowers to neighbors.

However, in other bird species, variations in plumage and color may not be related to status at all. For example, Whitfield (1986) showed that the ruddy turnstone (*Arenaria interpres*), a wading bird, varies greatly in

Figure 9.6 The male scarlet-tufted malachite sunbird of Africa.

its plumage and is territorial, but status is not affected by the bird's plumage color. Thus, plumage variations signal status in some bird species but simply aid recognition in others.

Some of the most interesting ecological studies of dominance and aggression have been done with birds. Here actual experiments in which critical variables are manipulated and controlled have been performed in addition to drawing conclusions simply from field observations. Rohwer and Rohwer (1978) conducted one such experiment with Harris sparrows (*Zonotrychia querula*). The color of the plumage of these birds varies considerably in the harsh winter months. Darker, blacker plumes are worn by the dominant and aggressive birds, which displace the more pale-colored birds from food supplies (see Figure 9.7). But "blackness" cannot be the sole factor determining which birds acquire more resources. If it were, less aggressive birds would evolve black plumes as a kind of bluff to get more food.

Rohwer and Rohwer (1978) attempted first to understand the differences in these birds by painting the feathers of lighter-colored birds black. Despite their new "bluff potential," these birds still failed to compete with the normal dominant black birds because they didn't behave aggressively enough to compete. Next, they tried injecting the submissive birds with the male hormone, testosterone, which is directly related to aggression in many species. With greater testosterone, the pale-colored, submissive birds behaved more aggressively, but it didn't help them because their opponents (the genetically darker-colored birds) didn't give in to pale-colored conspecifics. Only when the submissive birds were both painted black and injected with testosterone were they respected by the other birds and could therefore compete successfully. So, with these

Figure 9.7 Dominant (darker, left) and less dominant (lighter, right) forms of the Harris sparrow.

birds, darker plumage is a clear signal of greater aggression and dominance. And, in effect, the darker plumage acts to reduce aggression because the lighter-colored birds have learned to respect the sign.

In Chapter 7, we discussed mimicry (e.g., when one palatable insect imitates the appearance of another bad-tasting one to gain protection against predators). Considering this ploy, why don't the lighter-colored birds evolve darker plumage (without exhibiting more aggression) so that the other birds will "respect" them more? Why don't they bluff or cheat? In general, the coloration or display of an animal as found in examples of mimicry does not indicate an animal's intentions to members of its own species—only to those of other species. For animals within the same species, coloration and display must indicate the animal's real ability if it is to be an effective strategy. If this were not the case, all the Harris sparrows would gradually acquire dark plumage. True, there would still be differences in aggression, but the dark plumage would no longer have any meaning and therefore would signal nothing. Dark plumage *and* aggression go together in the Harris sparrow. Thus, the darker birds must back up their "badge" of aggression with real aggression when it is needed. We must remember that mimicry only works across different species, not within species, and that displays within species have evolved to communicate the animal's *real* strength, not its intentions, to members of the same species.

Dominance in Mammals.   In some mammalian species, dominance is related primarily to size, as, for example, in the American bison, *Bison bison* (Rutberg 1986). In many rodents, dominance appears to be primarily a product of the level of the hormone testosterone. Albert, Walsh, Gorzalka, Siemens, and Louie (1986) showed that castrated male rats that had been dominant lost their dominance after castration but regained dominance when they were later injected with testosterone.

Baboons (*Papio anubis*) have an ordered social structure based on dominance. Dominance is often enforced through aggression, threats, or aggressive signals. In baboons, the social relationships are more fluid and changeable than in other species. A new male can become dominant by defeating the most dominant male, called the **alpha** male, but pairs of subordinate baboons can also form temporary coalitions to gang up on or put off a more dominant male (Packer 1977). More will be said about baboon societies in Chapter 14.

Sometimes dominance relationships are established early in the animal's development and last for life. In some species, dominance status may actually be inherited from a parent. In baboons and macaque monkeys, for example, a young female's rank in the troop is determined by the rank of her mother. When the young female encounters a conflict, the mother will interfere, lending her status to the outcome of the conflict (Altmann 1980). If the mother has several female offspring, the offspring's ranks are ranked in reverse order, with the youngest ranking above the older daughters since the mother is most protective of her youngest. Most of the time, however, an animal's dominance status appears to be related to fighting ability, to the size of the animal, and to its weapons such as large claws and teeth. Of course, older animals tend to dominate the young for these reasons.

In small social groups, all the animals know each other, and in time a pair of group members establishes a stable dominance relationship. In wolves, for example, a pack has an alpha male and female who lead the pack on hunts, do the mating for the pack, eat prey first, and expect submissive gestures from other pack members.

Dominance can be viewed as solving a number of problems for, or giving several advantages to, the members of organized societies, including the less dominant animals:

1. It provides stability—every animal knows its place and what to expect from others.

2. Destructive aggression is minimized because animals are only rarely killed or seriously harmed in dominance contests, and once dominance relationships are settled, peace tends to reign. Moreover, submissive animals avoid aggression by exhibiting the appropriate submissive signals.

3. In the long haul, fitness of the species tends to be enhanced if only the strongest, most aggressive animals are allowed to breed (and the unfit are kept from breeding).

4. Dominance competition helps spread populations out (radiation) because dominant animals in many species will chase competitors completely out of their territory (e.g., deer and caribou, many wild cats, and territorial antelopes). Thus, dominance "losers" often do not gain reproductive success by staying in the group but may succeed if they leave and join another group.

Eusocial Insects

Ants, termites, and many species of wasps, bees, and aphids live in large colonies in which most of the individuals are sterile workers. Only a small number of individuals (e.g., the "queen" ants or bees) reproduce. This worker-queen division is only one type of organization. Many of these eusocial insects also have caste structures. A **caste** is a special group within the larger colony that performs only certain tasks (Wilson 1985). Typical castes may be responsible for reproduction (the queen), defense of the colony, foraging for food, and brood care. Different castes may actually differ from each other in physiology and appearance; for example, colony defenders are often larger, with more formidable weapons than members of other castes. These caste differences do not come from differences in genes but, rather, from differences in treatment early in development. Queens typically develop, for example, after being fed a special substance that no other colony members receive.

Ecological Factors in Group Living

Most species of animals in the world are not social—they do not live in groups. Cost-benefit analysis tells us that a social system can evolve when its advantages outweigh its costs. Thus, for most species of animals, living alone is the optimal way to maximize fitness. Keep in mind that this *individual* advantage is an essential part of the theory of evolution: individuals will survive whose ancestors have behaved in such ways that maximize individual reproductive fitness. In general, individuals do not sacrifice themselves for the good of the group (though there are qualifications on this that we will examine in Chapter 13).

Costs.   There is no doubt that living in groups incurs some costs not experienced by solitary creatures. Some of the typical costs are as follows:

1. *Increased competition* for resources occurs among group members because whatever resources are available—mates, nest sites, food, and water—must be shared and competed for. Thus, the large herd animals of the African plains are almost forced to wander because, in a group, they tend to eat up all the grass in one place very rapidly.

2. *Increased exposure to disease* and parasites occurs more quickly when animals live in groups. When one group member becomes ill, the likelihood that group mates contract the same illness sharply increases. This has been the chief factor in making the African wild dog (*Lycaon pictus*) an endangered species: together they suffer from susceptibility to diseases carried by domestic animals with which they come into contact.

3. *Interference with reproduction* and parental care also occurs because other animals often disturb mating and parenting, even if they do so unintentionally. For instance, bat and bird parents that live in large, crowded colonies often have difficulty finding their own young when they return to the crowded nesting site. As a result, some parents end up raising offspring that are not their own while their own offspring starve, though parents are able to find their own offspring successfully the vast majority of the time.

4. *Increased conspicuousness* to predators occurs among groups since groups of animals will take up more space, make more noise, and potentially draw more attention to themselves than solitary animals do.

5. *Overcrowding* may occur in group living if there are too many individuals in a small area. Many experimental studies have shown that the effects of overcrowding on animal populations are usually devastating, leading to hoarding by dominant individuals, a surge in aggression and violence, and the emergence of many unusual and maladaptive behaviors. In one classic study, Calhoun (1962) showed that laboratory rats living in overcrowded conditions displayed hypersexuality (trying to mate with any other rat), cannibalism, deviant nest construction, and extremely high infant mortality—even when plenty of food and water was available for all the rats.

Benefits.   From what we have discussed so far, you can imagine that the advantages the individual gains from group living are not always the same. Much depends on the species and the ecological factors to which it is exposed. But some advantages are more common in nature than others:

  1. *Increased vigilance*—the fact that groups may detect the presence of predators sooner than an individual—affords the individual greater protection. A larger flock of birds will spot potential predators earlier (on the average) than an individual will. Thus, hawks have fewer chances of catching a pigeon in a large flock than in a small one because the large flock takes off when the hawk is further away.

  2. *Dilution* refers to the advantage that, even if a predator attacks the group, each individual in a group decreases its chances of being the prey. For example, if a lion attacks a group of ten ostriches, the chance of each ostrich being a lion meal is only one in ten since the lion will kill only one ostrich. A more extreme example is the 17-year cicada (*Magicicada septendecim*), which lives for 17 years safely underground before all emerge to mate with other cicadas at the same time. Many of these will be eaten by birds, but, because they all emerge simultaneously, many individuals will survive.

  3. *Cover* refers to the fact that those animals near the center of the group (rather than at the edge) will probably do better. This creates the tendency for the group to bunch closely together and for late arrivals, who may be weaker or slower, to end up being the prey. Hamilton (1971) labeled this tendency for individuals to compete for the central position in a group and to use others as shields against predators as the **selfish herd**. Some studies have shown that, contrary to our intuitions, some individuals in fish species are actually in greater peril when at the center of a school. Some predators will split the school in two, then attack the tail—where some fish were at the center! So the relative safety of the location within the group depends on the method of attack of the predator.

  4. *Group defense* is another advantage. Many species will fend off predators much more successfully when they act as a group. In some species, part of this advantage comes from the **confusion effect**, whereby the predator may be momentarily put off by the commotion of group activity. This is probably the chief advantage of fish schools, where evidence has shown that, as the size of the school increases, hunting success by predators is reduced because the hunters hesitate or switch their target prey to a new individual and then miss both. As another example, songbird groups will engage in **mobbing** a nearby hawk, attempting to drive it off by diving and calling at it; one songbird acting alone could not do this. Mobbing tends to confuse and discourage the predator since it has been spotted. It also alerts others to the danger and provides learning opportunities for younger or inexperienced members to recognize and fear the animal that is mobbed. These advantages outweigh the obvious fact that individual mobbers place themselves in some danger from the predator.

5. *Group attack or group hunting* is an advantage enjoyed by predators that live in groups, like lions and hyenas. These groups can attack larger prey, such as buffaloes, which an individual animal would not even approach. Some dominance relationships still prevail here, however. In lions, for example, the female lions do the hunting and killing, but the larger male can eat first if it wants to; younger lion cubs eat last. In schools of fish, the fish in front of the school get the best meals.

6. *Exchange of information* about food is another advantage gained by many group species that forage together. Birds at the home roost may follow other birds to the feeding sites. Rats will follow other rats that smell like desirable foods. (This is similar to the way we know that someone has eaten pizza or garlic by smelling their breath.) As we have seen in ant colonies, the individual ant often discovers a food source such as a dead animal and then uses a chemical trail to lead other ants back to the site of the body. Many ants working together can often carry the entire dead animal back to the nest.

7. *Warmth* against the cold can be obtained by some species when they huddle together, slowing down heat dissipation. This occurs in many species of bats. They typically sleep together in large bunches in rather cold caves. However, since warmer air rises, the top of the cave may be surprisingly warmer than the rest of it, and this, coupled with group huddling, keeps the bats from freezing.

8. *Mating swarms* occur in some species, especially in insects and sometimes in sea creatures like squids. This activity takes place at a specific time of the year, making it easier for species members to find a mate.

9. *Division of labor* is another advantage that we see most clearly in organized societies like the eusocial insects (ants, bees, termites), where every member of the society has a specific task. Individuals within ant and termite societies have even evolved different body structures to fulfill their tasks (e.g., ants have warriors, queen caretakers, nursery workers, food gatherers, garbage collectors, etc.). These structures arise during development from food and temperature differences, not from different genes. (More will be said about eusociality in Chapter 13.)

10. *A richer learning environment* for the young is an advantage gained by many mammals, especially primates. The group provides more behavioral models, feedback, and stimulation for curious and growing youngsters. The same principle holds for rearing human beings.

Summary

The ways in which animals communicate have evolved because of the survival and reproductive advantages that communication affords the animals. The most common channels of communication used by animals include sound, visual messages, touch, and chemical scents. Whereas many species communicate with simple sounds or calls, a few species, such as bats, cetaceans, and primates, have evolved complex sound patterns that convey many meanings. Visual displays are typically used over short distances during the daytime, except for some animals, like fireflies, which can produce their own light. Tactile communication is especially important in social animals and in parenting. Chemical communication using pheromones is the most universal communication channel and has reached its most complex development in insects.

Communications become social releasers within a species when messages from a sender elicit largely built-in responses from the receiver. Such sender-receiver relationships are often involved in species mating patterns (courtship) and parenting. One of the most basic functions of communication is the recognition of members of an individual's own species. Group living animals such as dolphins and whales use complex sound messages to coordinate group activities over long distances. Other functions of communication include warning alarms and coordination in hunting and foraging.

Animals that live in groups can be categorized into three main varieties: aggregations, organized societies, and eusocial groups. Animals living in aggregations such as herds, flocks, and schools gain advantages like greater vigilance and defense but experience little group structure. Organized societies are often arranged around social dominance, with some individuals having greater access to resources than others. Dominance may be established by a variety of means, including displays, fighting, and inheritance from a parent.

The benefits of group living must outweigh the costs in order for it to have evolved. Some of the potential costs include increased competition, exposure to disease, interference with reproduction, and greater conspicuousness to predators. The many advantages of group living include increased vigilance, the dilution effect, greater cover, group defense or attack, exchange of information, and division of labor.

Part 3

Mating and Parenting

The theory of evolution tells us that individual animals should be strongly motivated to pass their genes on to future generations. Those individuals in the past who were not so motivated are not with us, nor are their potential offspring. Animals that are ready to reproduce, however, are often faced with formidable problems: finding a potential mate, persuading the individual to cooperate, keeping competitors away, finding a place to raise the young, and protecting and feeding the offspring as they develop. In response to these problems, different species have evolved an almost bewildering array of lifestyles and mating systems to maximize reproductive success in the circumstances in which they live. In the next four chapters, we will try to make sense out of this array by understanding the concepts and processes that explain what works best for individual animals.

Sometimes what works best can take an extreme form that, on the surface, contradicts our intuitions about how things should be. In these cases, scientists try to understand these apparent contradictions without discarding the fundamental concepts of genetics, evolution, and adaptation that already explain so much.

CHAPTER 10

Sexual Conflict, Selection, and Courtship

Some organisms, even some animals, reproduce without sex and without a sexual partner. These females lay eggs that reproduce the female's genetic pattern—they are clones of their mother. What, then, is the benefit of sex if a sexual creature bequeaths only 50% of its genes to its offspring while a clone carries 100% of its mother's genes? Why bother to have males at all? Yet the vast majority of animals and plants on this earth are sexual creatures that must contact a member of the opposite sex in order to reproduce. The answer to this question is very complex and is not settled in modern biology. It is likely that both historical and environmental factors, as well as genetic processes, played a role in making most current living species sexual by nature.

In this chapter, we will examine how sexual reproduction is viewed in the context of the theory of evolution, and how the theory accounts for sexual dimorphism—the differences in behavior and appearance between males and females that are typical of many species.

As humans, we might take for granted that, in order to reproduce, a male and a female must get together. But across nature, other methods for reproduction are used. Some single-cell organisms reproduce asexually, replicating themselves by splitting. Bacteria, on the other hand, reproduce sexually; two individuals are needed to produce offspring, but bacteria have no males and females. Therefore, any two individuals can share their genes.

What does it mean to be male or female? On the surface, we identify male and female humans by means of secondary sexual characteristics such as relative differences in size, shape, and muscle or body hair distribution. A more intimate look, of course, also reveals differences in the external sex organs. But for a more general definition that applies across many species of animals and plants, scientists need criteria that go beyond mere external appearance. For example, in some species, the females are larger than the males, so relative size is not a consistent indicator of sex across species. The largest animals that have ever lived on earth are blue whales that are female (over 100 tons in weight). In terms of genitalia, even the external appearance of the sex organs may not always help us. The spotted hyena female, for example, has sex organs that, superficially, look exactly like the male's.

A more reliable way to define the essence of male-female differences involves examining the kind of reproductive cells the individual produces on the genetic level (as described in Chapter 4). In biology, "femaleness" is defined by the fact that it is females that produce larger but fewer eggs (ova) to which more energy must be allocated, whereas "maleness" refers to the sex that produces smaller and mobile but many more reproductive cells (sperm). Generally (but not in every species), each sex makes the same genetic contribution to their offspring (50%), but females contribute more material to their reproductive cells and to the fertilized egg (zygote) as it develops.

Sexual Conflict

Picture a beach on an island shore in the Pacific Ocean near California. On the beach is a group of about 30 female northern elephant seals (*Mirounga angustirostris*). They are air-breathing, marine mammals, each weighing about 800 kilograms, or 1,700 pounds. During nine months of the year, the females swim to ocean depths of over 200 meters in search of squids, sharks, and small fish. Also on the beach is a lone adult male, weighing four tons (8,000 pounds)—almost four times more than the typical female. He is called a "beachmaster." When other males are not around, the large male mates with as many females in his harem as he can (see Figure 10.1). Any other adult male that attempts to come near the females is viciously attacked and chased away by the resident male.

Many questions might occur to you about this situation. For example, why is the male so much bigger than the female seal? Why does this resident male spend so much of its time chasing away other males? What does a female seal gain by staying on the beach with the other females?

Figure 10.1   A beachmaster elephant seal and one of the members of his harem of much smaller females.

Those who study animal behavior try to determine the answers to these essential questions by using Darwin's principles.

Each seal parent has a 50% investment in the survival of its offspring to adulthood. But before this survival occurs, many other things have to happen first, including choosing a mate, providing the developing embryo and zygote with nourishment, caring for eggs, and caring for the young. In these areas, a conflict of interest occurs between the sexes because only one parent, usually the female in most species, will carry the egg and eventually give birth. Consequently, each parent has a different "investment" in these activities (Trivers 1972). Females must allocate more of their resources to the offspring because they carry the young until birth. Thus, once one egg starts to develop, they (usually females) are invested in this one egg for the duration. Males, on the other hand, will behave differently to maximize their reproductive success: they have an investment in fertilizing as many eggs as possible, and they're prepared physically and behaviorally to do this.

Females can achieve reproductive success only by seeing that their limited number of offspring grow and achieve adulthood. Males can increase their reproductive success by finding and fertilizing as many females as possible. This is the main theme of sexual conflict. So, for example, while a human female is struggling for nine months to give birth to one child, the male (in theory) could be fertilizing hundreds of other females. A mere 5 milliliters of human sperm could fertilize all the fertile women in the United States! On the other hand, a human female produces only a few hundred eggs during her entire lifetime. Similarly, while the female elephant seal is pregnant for nearly a year and then has to care for her offspring, the male beachmaster can and does fertilize many other females in his harem. In short, male elephant seals contribute nothing more than their genes to their offspring.

For evolutionary biologists, the ultimate measure of an individual's success is the number of surviving offspring it produces. The theory of evolution tells us that individual animals will try to maximize their reproductive success, and natural selection will gradually produce surviving individuals who are good at doing just this. In order for the vast majority of species to reproduce, therefore, males and females of each species must get together and engage in sexual activity. But each individual is trying to maximize its own reproductive success, not anyone else's, including its mate's. **Sexual conflict** refers to the fact that, in order to maximize reproductive success, males and females develop and behave differently.

The consequence of all this is that reproductive strategies that maximize reproductive success often differ for males and females. Males in nature compete with each other for females because they're driven to impregnate as many as possible to maximize their reproductive success. Because of this competition, males are often larger and more aggressive than females, and they typically devote more effort to obtaining mates than to parental care.

Here is the typical pattern exemplified by the elephant seal: The females come on to the beach during the winter months to give birth and then afterward to come into heat again, provoking males to fight for them. During this time, a larger male beachmaster doesn't eat at all and tries to gather a harem of females to keep for himself. Males will challenge each other by inflating their large noses, roaring, displaying threatening postures, and eventually fighting. These fights can be truly vicious; large males damage each other by attacking each others' necks and chests with their large canine teeth. However, a successful male may have exclusive mating rights with as many as 40 females in his harem (LeBoeuf and Reuter 1988). The males fight for mating rights but do no parenting themselves.

Females are more limited by biology in maximizing their reproductive success—they can produce only so many offspring over time. Whereas a single insemination costs a male very little energy and soon afterward he can produce millions of tiny sperm all over again, female ova are much larger than sperm and more "expensive." The female elephant seal typically produces only one offspring per year. Therefore, giving birth on an island during the winter months provides some safety and isolation for the female. Females become part of a harem to obtain this security and to engage the most fit males, the beachmasters, in breeding with them.

Sexual Selection

Because females generally invest considerably more time and energy than males in reproduction, the males will compete to mate with the females. Whereas females put most of their reproductive effort (time, food, caretaking) into parenting, the males put most of their effort into finding potential mates, competing with other males for the mates, mating with females, and keeping other males away from the females. In those species such as the elephant seals in which males aggressively vie for females, **sexual dimorphism** will be noticeable—that is, males will look different and behave differently than females. As a result of countless generations of natural selection, only the largest, most aggressive male seals do most of the mating. Therefore, the large, aggressive adult male elephant seals gradually produced larger and more aggressive male offspring.

Sexual dimorphism is greatest in species where the males compete the hardest for females. With elephant seals, the most dominant and aggressive males will mate most often, passing more of their genes on to their offspring. LeBoeuf and Reuter (1988) found that fewer than one-third of the males mated successfully with females, and the top five males did half of the mating. This process—where males and females evolve different bodies and behaviors to maximize their individual reproductive potential—is called **sexual selection.**

Darwin was well aware of the role that sexual selection played in natural selection, and he first described its role in some detail in *The Descent of Man* (1871). Darwin realized that in many species some males are more successful than others in producing offspring because they have some reproductive advantage over the other males, not because they have any greater survival skills. In fact, the characteristics that promote reproductive success may actually be detrimental for survival. For example, males have a reproductive advantage when they can attract more females with their physical characteristics (e.g., adornments like the long tail feathers of the peacock) or with their behavior (e.g., the courtship flight of the male eagle). At the same time, these adornments and behaviors may make the animal more visible to predators and easier to catch.

Across nature, sexual selection takes one of two general forms. In **intrasexual selection,** members of one sex of a species compete vigorously with each other to acquire the right to mate with members of the other sex. This pattern is illustrated by the elephant seals. In this situation, the female awaits the outcome of the competition, but the males decide among themselves who shall mate. In the second form, **intersexual selection,** one sex of a species, usually females, chooses which male(s) with which to mate. Here the males still compete with one another but the competition is for female attention and acceptance.

Intrasexual Selection

We can see the first pattern in the form of the hoarding and guarding that is typical of the elephant seal and many species of deer, antelopes, sheep, and other herd animals. The male tries to capture a herd of females, and he aggressively tries to keep other males out. In some species like the elephant seal, the males actually engage in combat and can do serious damage to each other. In many other species, the males may engage in ritualized combat or trials of strength that do not involve fighting or serious risk of injury (e.g., butting heads in male bighorn sheep).

The dominant male then mates with the females as often as possible, but each individual female is willing to mate only at certain times. These times occur at regular cycles corresponding to the time when the female has an egg or eggs ready to be fertilized. A female that is ready to mate is said to be in **estrus,** or, more colloquially, "in heat." When the estrous periods of the female groups occur together at the same time of year (called **synchrony**), males have to corral the females only during the mating season and may be largely solitary for the rest of the year (e.g., the elephant seal and many deer species). When the females are not synchronized and can mate throughout the year, the male stays with the female group all year long, mating whenever the opportunity arises. This pattern of behavior is seen in lions, horses, many monkey species, and baboons.

Think how successful a male can be if he manages to father 30 to 40 offspring each spring for several years. He can really put his genes into the next generation! Males compete so hard for females because, from an evolutionary standpoint, the potential reproductive payoffs are so enormously large and are worth the loss of energy and risk of injury. So, in general, males have a greater reproductive potential than females for putting their genes into the next generation. Females are limited by how fast they can produce eggs, get them fertilized, and raise the young to adulthood. In theory, males do not have this limitation if they can mate with many different females.

As evolution proceeds, sexual conflict eventually results in sexual selection. Sexual selection means that males and females will eventually develop different physical and behavioral traits as they use different strategies to maximize their own reproductive success. In turn, sex differences in reproductive strategies within a species tend to lead to sexual dimorphism. Elephant seals are an example of extreme sexual dimorphism resulting in males and females that appear and behave very differently from one another.

In nature, male animals generally compete hard to mate with females, and we can expect that natural selection has produced traits in males that increase their mating success. We've already seen one way this is done: males of many species often fight each other for females, so better fighting ability tends to evolve in the males of some species as a result of sexual selection.

With respect to sexual dimorphism, males of a species are not always larger than the females. In fact, among most insect species and many birds, the females are larger. In general, when males are larger, the difference is due to sexual selection from males competing with one another for females. When females are larger, it's usually due to natural selection rather than sexual selection. For example, it may be advantageous for the female to be larger in order to lay more eggs or provide more resources to the young.

Intrasexual competition between males can take a number of forms, some of which are quite unusual as compared to the animals with which we are most familiar. Some of these forms include being "sneaky" instead of aggressive, variations on guarding and repelling, sperm competition, and dual male forms.

Being Sneaky.   What do you do if you're a sexually mature male elephant seal, but you're not large and aggressive enough to be a beachmaster? The main elephant seal strategy for obtaining mates, fighting other males for harems of females, will not be available to you. Is there no hope? In this case, an individual may be forced to use some alternative strategy to obtain reproductive success.

One of the alternate strategies used by many animals is **female mimicry.** A smaller, less fit male elephant seal may get the opportunity to mate with females by pretending to be a female. If small enough, the male might join a harem, avoid the resident male, and seek mating opportunities when he can. After all, the beachmaster cannot watch all the females all the time! Also, the smaller male might wait in the water off the beach until a female leaves the harem to return to the sea for food. As she draws near, he catches her. Thus, the beachmasters are not the only seals who mate. Other males may also get a chance to mate later in the breeding season. As the dominant beachmasters get worn out and return to the sea, other males rush in for the opportunity.

Less fit male bullfrogs use a related sneaky strategy when they become **satellites.** Fit male bullfrogs compete for females by lying in a pond and croaking loudly, calling receptive females to come. A smaller, less fit male will not be able to croak low enough or loud enough to attract a female but can still obtain some reproductive success by being a satellite male. The satellite stays near the larger, croaking male and tries to intercept approaching females before they reach the dominant male. According to Howard (1978), satellite frogs do not succeed often, and frequently the dominant males will chase them away.

In general, these kinds of sneaky alternate strategies do not work as well as the main strategy for a species, but they do obtain some reproductive success for the less fit animals, which keeps their genes active in the population gene pool. Alternate strategies for reproduction were once thought to be abnormalities in nature, but modern scientists now recognize such behaviors as simply alternative behavioral strategies that enable animals to obtain as much reproductive success as they are capable of.

Guarding and Repelling.   Whereas the competitive strategies discussed so far are typical of many mammals and birds, competition can become curious and fascinating with many species of insects and worms. Many males of these species use methods that not only maximize their own reproductive success but also lessen that of their competitors.

One method used by some insects is to guard the female until she is ready to mate, and, after having fertilized her, to prevent other males from mating with her. Some insects and worms have really taken this approach to extremes. For instance, after having fertilized the female, some species of butterflies (e.g., *Heliconius erato*) leave an odor on her that will repel other males. However, the ultimate guarding strategy is to remain in actual, physical contact with the female for as long as possible, ensuring that her eggs are fertilized by no one else's sperm; insects called walking-sticks may do this for days and weeks!

Sperm Competition.   Usually, the last male insect to mate with a female is the one that actually fertilizes the female's eggs. Therefore, some male insects, like the damselfly (*Calopteryx maculata*) studied by Waage (1979), have devices on their penis to remove the sperm already in the female's womb before they mate. This sort of struggle to be the male that actually fertilizes the female was first termed **sperm competition** by Parker (1970). Some males can seal up the female's genital opening with a copulatory plug so that other males cannot fertilize her. This will also make sure that their sperm is not lost (the insect version of the medieval chastity belt!). Versions of this also occur in some species of garter snakes and deer mice.

In other species, males will take action to actively interfere with the sexual success of other males. Some salamanders will mimic female sexual behavior, inducing other males to release their sperm on the ground. In some worms (such as *Moniliformes dubius,* a parasitic worm in the intestines of rats), the males, after mating with the female, not only seal her genital opening with a plug, but they proceed to mate with other males and seal up their genitals too!

In some species, a male can interfere with another male's reproductive success after the female has given birth to young offspring. Male lions that take over a new pride will often kill any young lion cubs that are the progeny of other males. It is believed that the new males do this in order to bring the females into heat so that they can mate with them sooner. Although the females in the lion pride certainly are not happy when their young are killed, they have little choice but to mate with the new rulers of the pride to ensure their own future reproductive success. This practice is also sometimes witnessed in horses and among some species of rodents, monkeys, and langurs (Hrdy, 1979).

Dual Male Forms. Some species have actually evolved two different alternative reproductive strategies in physically distinct animals (phenotypes) of the same sex. A good example of this is the coho salmon (*Oncorhynchus kisutch*), studied by Gross (1985). Each year these fish breed in North American streams and rivers on the Pacific coast. In order to reach these areas, males and females fight their way from the ocean, upstream, to breeding pools where they breed and then die. What is unusual is that males take one of two forms—either hooknoses or jacks. Those that mature at three years of age are called hooknoses and are large and aggressive. They will fight against other hooknoses for mating territories. Those males maturing at two years of age are the smaller jacks that are neither territorial nor aggressive. While the hooknoses fight for breeding territories that attract females, the jacks sneak matings (see Figure 10.2).

The concept of an evolutionarily stable strategy (ESS) was introduced in Chapter 8. Coho salmon illustrate that two different natural history strategies (hooknoses and jacks) may both be ESSs since, on the average, they are

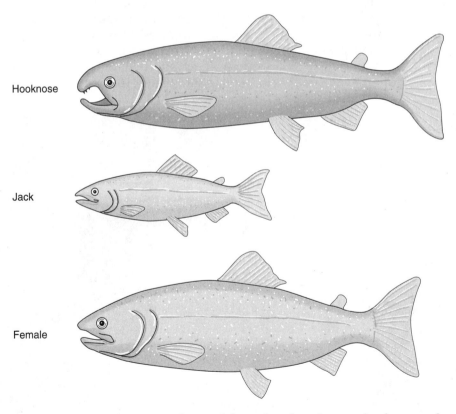

Figure 10.2 The two different forms of the male coho salmon, a hooknose and a jack, and the female, which has only one form.

equally successful. If one form were inferior to the other in terms of reproductive success, the inferior form would gradually disappear from the gene pool. But, in fact, the two forms balance each other. Think what would happen if most of the males were hooknoses: they would spend all their time fighting each other, allowing the sneaking jacks to mate more successfully. And if most were jacks, the larger, aggressive male hooknoses wouldn't fight because each would have a territory, and all would succeed in breeding because each would attract many females. So fighting and sneaking each work about equally well and are balanced in the coho salmon population, evolving two stable ESSs in the population (Gross 1985).

Intersexual Selection

Fighting, however, is not the only way for males to compete for females. A second way is to produce traits that the female finds attractive so as to make the females seek them out. Competition still exists among the males, but the competition doesn't involve fighting or aggression. Instead, it might relate to sounds (e.g., in songbirds, frogs, and crickets) or visual displays (e.g., in peafowl, lizards, crabs, and fireflies) that get the female's attention. Differences between male and female peafowl are examples of extreme intersexual selection and sexual dimorphism, resulting in males and females that appear and behave very differently from each other. Figure 10.3 pictures the peacock and

Figure 10.3 Peafowl: the spectacular peacock in display and the smaller peahen.

peahen.Researchers believe that the better appearance of one male as compared to another is probably related either to its superior ability as a provider or to its having "better" genes. We don't generally assume that the peahen selects a more dazzling peacock simply because it's more beautiful.

In intersexual selection, females are not passive receptors of sperm as they are in intrasexual selection. Think about their situation: Because females produce fewer eggs and must invest more parenting into them, they have more to lose than males if something goes wrong. Males can move on and inseminate many other females, but a female with only a few eggs that is unsuccessful in breeding may have to wait a whole year before she has another chance. Therefore, it generally pays for females (more so than males) to be fussy or choosy about whom they mate with. We should expect to see females trying to select males that can provide better material resources to their young as well as "good genes" for their future offspring, and that proves their fitness to her before she commits herself. In addition, we should see females having an investment in prolonging courtship displays, which would give her ample opportunity to observe the male's traits. This is true even for the female elephant seal, for she exercises some choice. Cox and LeBoeuf (1977) showed that the female will vocalize loudly when a less dominant male tries to mate with her, attracting another, more dominant male to drive the less dominant male off. She prefers to mate with only the best males.

In some species, the male defends a breeding territory that has resources advantageous for raising offspring, such as good shelter and food. In this case, the female doesn't so much choose a specific male as much as she chooses a good territory that has some particular male in it (and that was fit enough to keep it successfully). For example, the North American bullfrog female (*Rana catesbeiana*) seeks warm water with sparser, less dense vegetation in which to lay her eggs, and it is exactly these more precious territories that the males fight over. Therefore, the female will mate with whichever male occupies the best territory she can find. Female red-winged blackbirds and dragonflies are similarly fussy about locations.

In many species of birds and insects, the key selection factor for the female is the male being a good provider of food for the developing eggs or young. In some species, the male actually brings the female a piece of food during courtship. Among waterbirds, the male herring gull (*Larus argentatus*) brings a fish to the female. She will then mate only with males that bring her bigger pieces of food.

Trivers's theory of parental investment (1972) states that whichever sex invests more time, energy, and resources in parenting will be the "choosier" sex when selecting a mate. In general, this is the female in most organisms but not all the time. The theory predicts that, when it is the male that invests more as a parent, then the male should be the choosier sex. This is exactly what happens in some species of fish (sea horses and pipefish), birds (phalaropes and sandpipers), and insects (the waterbug). In these species, we see a sex role reversal with females trying to attract desirable males and males doing the parenting after the eggs are laid.

Intersexual evolutionary forces have produced some of the most complex and elaborate behaviors that we can observe in the animal kingdom. As succeeding generations of males of a species compete for female acceptance, sexual selection tends to maximize those traits in males that most attract females willing to mate.

In the 19th century, one of the most notable aspects of animal behavior with which naturalists became fascinated was the courtship behavior that many species engage in prior to mating. Courtship behavior may be divided into three general categories: courtship rituals, individual courtship displays, and leks.

Courtship Rituals.   **Courtship rituals** differ from **courtship displays** in that, ordinarily, a male and a female perform rituals together whereas in displays only one sex performs for the other. Each species has unique rituals and sequences of behaviors, some of which are quite complex. For example, a pair of birds may take turns engaging in a long series of behaviors that cost a lot of time and energy. Waterbirds are well known for such rituals, as, for example, in mallard ducks (Lorenz 1971).

Mallards (*Anas platyrhynchos*) mate from the late summer to the early spring so that the young can be hatched in late spring. Courtship and mating typically occur on water, often in social groups of ducks, relatively safe from predation. The female mallard begins the ritual by swimming and nodding around males or one particular male. This behavior elicits a set of responses from the male, including a grunt-whistle sound and the bending of his tail and head upward at the same time. The male, or drake, looks at the female and they get closer to each other. The male eventually leads the female away. They both engage in head pumping, which leads to the male following and then mounting the female by standing on her back. He maintains his balance by grabbing her neck with his bill (see Figure 10.4). Since male birds lack a penis, copulation occurs when the drake contacts the female's cloaca with his cloaca and releases sperm. Copulation may take only a few seconds (Lorenz 1971).

This description is brief and incomplete but shows how elaborate, coordinated, and synchronized the chain of ritualized responses can be, which lead eventually to copulation. (For another example, see the pattern for the stickleback fish described in Chapter 11.)

Most male mallard ducks engage in courtship rituals to get female mates, but some are not able to attract females. Instead, some will wait until a fit male is far enough away, seize a female (that has already

Figure 10.4   A drake (male mallard duck) mounts the female and grabs her by the neck to maintain balance before copulating.

paired with the fit male), and force his attentions upon her by grabbing the back of her head and forcing copulation. These "rapist" ducks deviate markedly from the norm of their fellow males, but they do succeed to some extent in passing their genes on to offspring. However, this is not the end of the story. What will the female's mate do in this circumstance, if she has already mated? If he arrives in time, he will try to chase the attacker off, as any honorable duck would. But what if he arrives too late? The female's normal mate will himself coercively mate with her immediately, without performing the normal rituals! This is the only chance the male has of lessening the probability of the stranger's success in fertilizing the female's eggs; it is the only way his sperm can compete with the rapist's.

Elaborate courtship rituals such as those in mallards are easier to explain than courtship displays, which will be examined later. Courtship rituals always serve some of the following distinct functions:

1. *Identification.*   If you're a bird, you want to mate with a member of your own species, not some other one! Many waterbirds such as ducks, geese, and swans live together, eat together, and have high resemblances to each other (especially the typically blander-colored females). Similarly, male and female sparrows of many distinct species often resemble each other highly. The female sparrow can identify the right male by the song it sings, but the male has to verify the identification of the right female by observing her behavior. Clearly, rituals and clear markings can serve to help the bird determine that it has found the proper mate. In addition toads and frogs, the male calls not only identify the species but also disclose the male's location to the female, indicating where she should go.

2. *Reduction of aggression*   In many species, potential aggression between the sexes must be reduced so that a mating pair can get together. For example, in many insect and spider species, the female is larger than the male and the male is about the size of her typical prey. To avoid being eaten, the male orb-web spider taps a signal on the female's web to calm her down before approaching her very carefully. In crab spiders (*Xysticus cristatus*), the male ties the female down with silken threads he ejects, and this actually serves to trigger her cooperation in mating. In other species, the female must enter the male's territory and perform the "correct" behaviors for him to recognize her as a potential mate.

In some insects, the male must present the female with a "gift" in order to attract her for mating and to reduce the chances that she will eat him. Kessel (1955) described the mating activities of species of balloon flies (family Empididae, order Diptera), which exhibit an amazing diversity of variations on the gift-giving theme. In some empid species, the male simply captures prey, presents it to the female, and then copulates with her as she is eating the prey. In other species, the male captures prey, "dances" in the air with other males, and females join the males to select one for mating. Here the prey item functions simply to attract females. In still other empids, the male captures prey, wraps it in silk to resemble a balloon, meets a female in midair, and transfers the balloon to the female. After landing on a plant, the female eats the prey while the male mates with her. Finally, in *Hilara sartor* species (illustrated in Figure 10.5), the

Figure 10.5   The male balloon fly (*Hilara sartor*) attracts a female with an empty balloon that he weaves from his silk.

male gives the female an empty balloon as the sole stimulus for mating! Presumably, the only advantage the female gains in this case are the "good genes" gained by choosing males that offer larger balloons.

3. *Fitness assessment.* Rituals give each animal the chance to size up the other as a potential mate. Females are typically more selective than males, and they therefore may reject a male suitor by breaking off the courtship rites prior to mating. In falcons and bald eagles, for example, the male performs aerial acrobatics while the female observes his skill, speed, and coordination. All of these factors may play a role in his later ability to provide food for the young. However, as the female assesses male fitness, the male assesses female readiness (or whether the female has already mated with someone else!). At the beginning of courtship, male birds are typically overaggressive and females are reluctant. The ability of each to overcome these orientations and synchronize their efforts indicates their readiness.

4. *Mating readiness assessment.* Neither animal is (physiologically) ready to mate unless it can go through all the rituals correctly. So courtship rituals can be viewed as a sort of "final exam" before mating actually occurs. Exchanging appropriate ritual behaviors brings the male and female into mating and reproductive readiness. There's no point in the female mating until she can produce eggs, and mating readiness and courtship rituals will appear in her behavior as she is ready to have her eggs fertilized. Of course, males are often ready to mate all the time and are just looking for ready females.

5. *Bonding.* Finally, in some species, it is important for the male and female to bond together as a pair because both will be involved in incubating the eggs and/or raising the young. Of course, this is not relevant in those species where the female raises the young without male assistance. On the other hand, in some bird species, the pair bond for life; this is the typical pattern in many species of waterbirds, including mallards.

In summary, elaborate courtship rituals are not so difficult to understand, particularly in waterbirds. Predators are not usually a problem on the water and the pair of birds usually have plenty of time for courtship. Furthermore, there are plenty of resources because they typically mate during the early spring when plenty of plant food is available.

Courtship Displays. More puzzling are the elaborate individual displays performed by some male birds, like peacocks, pheasants, and birds of paradise. Their displays are spectacular and colorful, potentially attention getting to predators as well as to potential mates. Why would such elaborate displays evolve if such feathers and motions serve to increase the chance that the male bird will be some predator's lunch? How could they be "adaptive" in some sense?

In more concrete terms, how could the elaborate visual displays like the peacock's feathers or the auditory displays of loud and complex birdsongs evolve? One theory was proposed by R. A. Fisher (1930) and is now called the "runaway evolution" theory. Fisher assumed that, in early evolution, the male peacock's ancestors possessed some characteristic related to their fitness that was attractive to females. In the case of the peacock (*Pavo cristatus*), the attractive feature was tail length. Perhaps the early males with longer tails could fly better or were simply larger birds. The idea here is that longer tails originally correlated with male fitness, and as the females selected for this trait, the tails got longer because of repeated selection. At the same time, the females were evolving a preference for longer tails! If they prefer longer tails and select on that basis, then it would be more likely that they would pass this trait on to their male offspring, which in turn would be preferred by other females and would therefore be more likely to reproduce. This creates a runaway process whereby peacocks' tails become longer; but there are limits to how far this can go. Tails will keep increasing in length up to a point where the length is balanced by survival disadvantages: if it gets too long, the tail will become an encumbrance to the male bird in terms of the food and metabolism needed by the bird to maintain itself and to avoid predation. Selection for greater tail length will then stop, and the tails will not get any longer.

The peacock is the extreme example of this. In the process of developing exceedingly long feathers, which it displays spectacularly to the peahen, it has practically lost the ability to fly. Peacocks can fly much like chickens, for short spans and over barriers, but neither very high nor far. Thus, the original function of the longer tail (indicating general fitness) may be lost when all members of the species evolve long tails. Nevertheless, the genetically determined female preference for long tails will still be there, and they will select on that basis.

Zahavi (1975) proposed an alternative "good genes" theory. He accepted the premise that longer tail feathers are a survival handicap but proposed the novel idea that peahens may prefer the longer tails because those peacocks that possess them have survived *despite* their handicap. In other words, peacocks must have better genetic qualities for health and survival; therefore, male characteristics such as long tail feathers signal to the female high male fitness in other respects. As such, males only express the so-called handicap (remarkably long feathers) when they are in good physical condition, which, in turn, is related to good genes, which the female should find desirable. Unlike the runaway theory, this theory requires that the longer feathers accurately indicate the greater fitness of males. This idea has received some support from Hamilton and Zuk (1982) and others.

Some evidence exists for both of these theories about peafowl, for they are not incompatible with each other. Still, these issues have by no means been settled (see Maynard Smith 1991). Even Darwin (1859) recognized that animals like the peacock presented a problem for those parts of the theory of evolution that emphasize survival skills. The peacock is a vivid example of how sexual selection may ultimately create animal characteristics that are good for reproduction (attracting mates) but may not be good for avoiding predators. Individual fitness always reflects all those traits that contribute to both survival and reproduction, and, in some cases like the peacock, the gains in reproductive potential may vastly outweigh the risks of predation.

Lek Displays.   In some species, males may congregate in groups on a display ground where they defend tiny territories adjacent to each other and try to attract females with colorful dances or displays. A congregation of males on such a space is called a **lek.** Lek males typically provide no resources, no nest, and no parenting to their offspring. All they do is mate and provide their genes. The female observes the males displaying together and selects the male she wishes to mate with. Usually, only a few males do all the mating.

Lek systems occur in several species of grouse, including the sage grouse (*Centrocerus urophasianus*), as studied by Wiley (1973) and others (see Figure 10.6). Early in the mating season, the males arrive at the

Figure 10.6   A male sage grouse dances in a lek to attract a female.

lek site, usually the same area every year. The best territories, near the center of the lek, are occupied by the most dominant males. When the females arrive and move through these areas, the males do a dance and display their feathers while the females mate with males of their choice. The females then leave, find a nest site, build the nest, lay their eggs, and raise their young by themselves.

It's still not really well understood why the males subscribe to the lek system and how such systems evolved because many males do not get to mate at all. However, from the female's standpoint, there appears to be some advantage: females seem to get the males with the "best genes." In addition, the lek may provide a relatively safe area in which to mate.

Lek systems, although certainly not common, also occur in some insects (e.g., Hawaiian fruit flies), some coral reef fish, and some mammals like the walrus, hammer-headed bats, and several species of antelopes. Different explanations may exist for how lek systems developed in these different species.

A strategy like a lek also occurs in many species of frogs and toads. Among these animals, the similar arrangement is called a **chorus;** it occurs when the males congregate to call for females. Typically, they produce loud croaking that attracts the females. There are definite advantages to this technique: it's easier for females who are farther away to hear; it makes it harder for predators such as owls and bats to locate a single frog; and, because of the dilution effect discussed earlier, a predator can take only one frog at a time, giving the majority of males a better chance to survive.

Alternative Reproductive Strategies

Hermaphroditism

Some organisms possess both male and female sex organs and are capable of exchanging both sperm and egg cells with a mate—a situation called **hermaphroditism.** This is a common pattern among sea slugs, snails, and earthworms. These animals have separate male and female copulatory organs, enabling them to exchange eggs and sperm simultaneously. Figure 10.7 shows how the sex organs are arranged on an earthworm. Self-fertilization can also occur but happens only rarely. In some hermaphroditic organisms (such as the sea squirt, genus *Ciona*), self-fertilization is actually prevented by the fact that the organism's sperm is physiologically incapable of fertilizing the eggs of the same individual.

What these animals have in common are slow movement and generally solitary lifestyles, which lead to difficulties in finding a potential mate. Consequently, hermaphroditism enables every individual to mate with any other individual of the same species in their rare encounters, and every individual can produce new offspring.

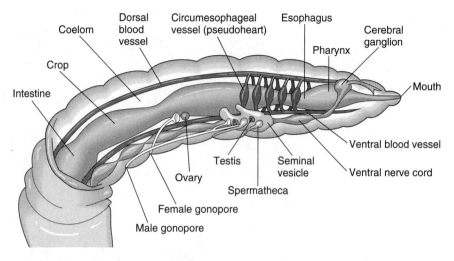

Figure 10.7   The arrangement of reproductive organs in the common earthworm, a hermaphroditic species.

Sex Change as a Reproductive Strategy

There are many species of fish for which it is quite normal for the individual to undergo a sex change during its lifetime. For example, among the blue-headed wrasses (*Thalassoma bifasciatum*) of the Western Atlantic are brightly colored males that vigorously defend their territories. Only the largest males are successful in breeding. However, all these male fish start off as smaller females! This change from male to female is called **protogynous hermaphroditism.**

Another similar example is the clownfish (*Amphiprion ocellaris*). It too experiences a sex change; however, unlike the wrasse, the clownfish's change is from male to female because the larger and older females can lay more eggs. These are usually monogamous fish that live in association with sea anemones (animals of phylum Coelenterta; a kind of animal permanently glued to a rock), which protect them from predators (see Figure 10.8). If for some reason the male loses its larger female mate and then a smaller male arrives on the scene, the older male will change its sex to female because it is the larger of the two fish! This is called **protandrous hermaphroditism.**

Why don't elephant seals do this too? They have the classic sexual dimorphic, male-dominated system: only the largest, most aggressive males breed. Why don't they start off as females and change sex later, like the wrasse? Actually, this is not too practical a procedure for mammals, in general, because the mammal female has a complex physiology that enables her to give birth to live young and to lactate, feed the young,

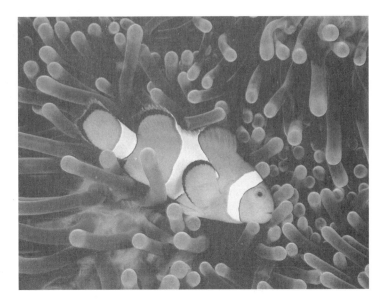

Figure 10.8   The clownfish lives in association with the sea anemone, which produces a poison that can stun other fish, but which the clownfish is immune to.

and take care of them. All sex-changing fish have simple sex organs that are easy to change, and all use external fertilization, which simply involves spraying eggs or sperm into the water. So, in these fish, a sex change simply means producing sperm instead of eggs or vice versa. Either way, external fertilization means just squirting the eggs (or sperm) in the right place. Thus, serial hermaphroditism works in these species because individuals can maximize their reproductive success by being one sex earlier in life and the other sex later. Mammals, on the other hand, use internal fertilization, which requires complex reproductive organs that would not be easily amenable to change in midlife.

Finding a mate, of course, is only the beginning of the reproductive process. In many species, the mother or both parents must cope with a variety of environmental problems for their young to survive. How animal parents collaborate in their efforts and provide critical experiences for their developing young will be examined in the next two chapters.

Summary

In general, female animals produce larger but fewer reproductive cells (ova) in contrast to males, which produce smaller but many more reproductive cells (sperm). Males have a greater reproductive potential than females because, whereas each male can mate with many females, the female must carry her offspring until birth and must often do most of the parenting. Consequently, a sexual conflict exists between the sexes in that each sex will maximize its reproductive success by behaving differently. This is illustrated by a male elephant seal beachmaster, which may mate with all 30 females in its harem during the mating season while each female mates only with the beachmaster.

During evolutionary time, sexual conflict leads to sexual selection: each sex gradually evolves distinct traits and behaviors that maximize its reproductive success. Thus, in many species like the elephant seal, the sexes are dimorphic in appearance and behaviors. Sexual selection takes two general forms—intrasexual and intersexual selection. In intrasexual selection, one sex (usually males) competes with others of its sex to gain mating access to members of the opposite sex that play a largely passive role. Mating patterns typical of intrasexual competition include male dominance through size and strength (as in elephant seals), being sneaky, guarding the female and repelling other males, and sperm competition. Less common but in the same category is the evolution of dual male forms (as in the coho salmon) when the existence of both forms becomes evolutionarily stable.

In intersexual selection, a member of one sex (often female) chooses to mate with a member of the opposite sex (usually male). Males compete with each other for female attention and choice rather than for access to females. As in intrasexual selection, such a process through evolutionary time can produce extreme sexual dimorphism, as in the extremely long and spectacularly colored tail feathers of the peacock in comparison to the far drabber peahen. Intersexual selection is typical of species that employ elaborate courtship rituals, individual male courtship displays, and lek displays. Attention-getting courtship displays have been a problem for evolutionary theory since Darwin's time because, as in the case of the peacock, sexual selection appears to contradict the forces of natural selection. Modern theorists have struggled to understand this "runaway" process within the context of Darwin's principles.

Some species have evolved various forms of hermaphroditism in response to sexual selective forces. Whereas some species of worms, for example, have both male and female sex organs, other species have developed serial hermaphroditism (sex change during their lifetime) to take advantage of the greater reproductive potential that is strongly associated with size.

CHAPTER 11

Mating Patterns

*Although some earlier thinkers regarded species'
mating patterns as innate and genetically determined, modern biologists have established that
the pattern that emerges in each individual case is
heavily influenced by the particular circumstances
the animal is in. This conclusion is supported by the
fact that a variety of mating patterns may exist in
one species, and an individual animal may display several different patterns in its lifetime.
Whereas the number of ways in nature for males
and females to get together is large and diverse, scientists have tried to bring this apparent clutter into understanding by identifying a smaller number of key principles
that bring order to the amazing diversity. That's what this chapter is about, and many
of the causal factors are related to principles already discussed in previous chapters,
such as territoriality and cost-benefit analysis.*

*Of course, an animal's behavior is also constrained by its physical and biological
limitations. As we shall see, sometimes these constraints limit an individual animal to
employ some mating strategies but not others.*

Through the principles of sexual conflict and selection discussed in
Chapter 10, animals have evolved many different reproductive
strategies. The mating system employed by a species can be viewed
as the way male and female urges to reproduce are played out in the particular conditions under which they live. In this chapter, we examine the
four major mating systems, some of their variations, and the ecological
circumstances that have influenced their development.

Some traditional terms used to describe mating patterns include
monogamy, polygyny, polyandry, polygynandry, and polygamy. In

monogamy, one male and one female form a pair: the two mate with no one else but each other. When each sex mates with only one mate per breeding season, but the mate changes from season to season, the system is sometimes called serial monogamy. However, some species do pair for life (or at least until one of the pair dies).

In **polygyny** (from Greek, meaning literally "many females"), the male mates with several females whereas each female mates with only one male. Here the female usually (but not always) provides the parental care. Polygyny is the most common and universal system in nature, used by the majority of species in all animal groups except birds. In **polyandry** ("many males"), the female mates with several males, and it is often the male that does most of the parental care. Polyandry is a very rare mating system, occurring in a few bird species, some insects, sea horses, and occasionally human beings. In **promiscuity/polygynandry,** both males and females mate several times with different individuals during the breeding season. Finally, **polygamy,** the most confusing and least informative term, is not itself a unique mating pattern; it describes a situation in which an individual of either sex has more than one mate. So polygyny, polyandry, and polygynandry are all polygamous.

Determining which mating system is typical of a species is not always easy or obvious. Rodents, for example, may mate only in underground dens where they are not easily observed, and nocturnal species may be nearly impossible to observe in their natural habitats. Consequently, scientists sometimes have to attempt to infer the animal's mating system from their other, nonsexual, social behaviors. So, for example, if a male and female pair are always seen together, and the male is neither seen with other females nor does he permit other males to approach the female, monogamy might be inferred.

However, direct observations of apparent mating habits may not always tell the actual story of reproduction. Not all eggs in a clutch laid by one female necessarily have the same father. Moreover, there is no guarantee that any one act of mating will result in fertilization. Yet, for identifying the particular mating system used by a species, it is often essential to determine who the father of the offspring is. Modern biochemical methods, such as DNA fingerprinting (whether with humans or another species), enable scientists to precisely identify the father. For example, DNA fingerprinting has revealed that some apparently monogamous species actually are not monogamous at all. The razorbill (*Alca torda*) is a bird that lives in seemingly monogamous pairs on North Atlantic coastlines. The mated pair defend their nest site in large colonies on the sides of cliffs. However, DNA fingerprinting of eggs from a specific pair revealed multiple fathers. Further investigation showed that away from the breeding colony are areas in which males gather, and females will visit these areas during their fertile period.

Even though they yield outstanding results, these advanced techniques for identification are generally impractical because of their great expense (conducting such a test on a single animal costs upward of $200!). Consequently, biologists still depend for the most part on data gathered from direct observations in order to draw conclusions about the mating system of a species.

Monogamy

Monogamy is defined by mating exclusivity but also tends to be associated with the male and female living together in the same territory and raising offspring together (Dewsbury 1988). Despite our familiarity with this concept in the human scheme of things, monogamy is a relatively rare mating pattern across nature. Kleiman (1977) estimated that fewer than 3% of all mammalian species are monogamous.

Several ecological factors increase the likelihood that monogamy will prevail over some other mating system (Wittenberger 1981). It is especially probable when both parents are needed to raise the offspring and when a missing parent seriously endangers the survival of the young. In this case, both parents have a high reproductive investment in staying with, and caring for, the offspring (as is described in more detail in Chapter 12).

In some species, female aggression against other females prevents males from mating with other females in the area, even if they wanted to. In species such as wolves, wild dogs, and marmosets, for example, the breeding female permits other females to be a part of the pack but does not permit them to reproduce. Similarly, in some situations, the male defends the one available female against all other males. This occurs especially in those species where males are in high density relative to females. Finally, monogamy also occurs when females are so spread out or scarce that males are unlikely to find more than one female during the breeding season.

When there is plenty of food for the young and predation is at a minimum, then one parent can raise the young successfully, and, consequently, monogamy is not necessary. In these circumstances, it is usually the male that "deserts" his mate and offspring. There are several reasons why it is usually the female that is left to do the parenting. One reason, as discussed in the previous chapter, is that the male can usually gain more than the female by deserting: he can maximize his reproductive success by mating with more females. A second reason is that most mammals have a relatively long gestation period before birth, and after birth the female parent must lactate in order to feed the young for some period of time (whereas males cannot feed the nursing young). Thus, female mammals are more adapted for parenthood than male mammals typically are. In addition, many mammals have quite long developmental periods during which they must grow and learn from experience.

Figure 11.1   The laboratory white rat, *Rattus norvegicus.*

Consequently, most mammal species are polygynous, with females doing most of the long-term parenting.

An Example of Mammalian Mating: The Lab Rat

To illustrate the complexity of mammalian mating patterns, let's look at the reproductive pattern in one mammalian species very familiar to most psychologists—*Rattus norvegicus,* the laboratory white rat (see Figure 11.1). Sexual behaviors in rats are largely controlled by hormones (internally) and environmental stimuli (externally). When the female rat is receptive to sex, her genitals emit an odor that attracts males. Then a definite sequence of behaviors ensues (adapted from Dewsbury 1978):

1. *Courtship behavior*—the male sniffs and chases the female, which may encourage the male by approaching him when she is receptive to mating.

2. *Pursuit*—the male pursues the running female.

3. *Mounting*—the male "mounts" the female from behind.

4. *Lordosis*—the female adopts a stereotyped posture in which the head and hindquarters are elevated, the back is arched, and the tail is deflected to the side.

5. *Intromissions*—the male inserts his penis into the female's vagina two to ten times but only for about one-fourth of a second each time, followed by rapid dismount.

6. *Ejaculation*—finally, the male rat grasps the female, engages in rapid thrusting, and ejaculates. Ejaculations do not occur without prior intromissions.

7. *Rest*—the male rat needs about five minutes of rest before starting over again, with increasingly longer rest periods with repetitions. The pair usually commit about seven complete intromission-ejaculation series before stopping for a long rest of at least a half hour.

If a satiated male is exposed to a new female, however, he can start all over again immediately! The ability of males to resume copulation with a new female is common in rodents and is called the **Coolidge effect,** named after—of all people—President Calvin Coolidge. Bermant (1976) reports the story as follows. When President and Mrs. Coolidge were visiting a farm, she was shown a group of chickens, one rooster with many hens. She was told that only one rooster was sufficient to copulate with all the hens every day. Hearing this, Mrs. Coolidge is said to have replied, "Please tell that to the President." When the President was informed of this situation, he asked, "Same hen every time?" When he was told no, President Coolidge nodded and said, "Tell *that* to Mrs. Coolidge."

Some male rodents normally seek out other females to mate with. However, most species of rodents are monogamous; because resources are scarce, both parents are needed to feed the young. Rat parental care is done mostly by the female, which must start suckling her blind and helpless young right after birth. Yet, in the laboratory, male rodents typically display virtually all the characteristic behavioral patterns of the mothers except, of course, lactation. It is not known if male rodents behave as such good fathers in the wild.

In other species, the male penis and female vagina will "lock" for as long as 20 minutes. In dogs, for example, there is a copulatory lock in which, after penetration, the male will turn around and male and female normally stand back to back. The female's lock will not permit the pair to separate until the male is finished ejaculating. The adaptive function of such an arrangement is related to the fact that female domestic dogs come into heat only twice a year and wild canids only once a year for less than two weeks of time. Under these circumstances, it is important for the female to insure insemination because she will not get a second chance.

Monogamy in Birds

Monogamy is the common pattern only in birds, where Lack (1968) estimated that it occurs in over 90% of species, though more recent evidence has tended to lower this figure, as we shall see. Both parents are often needed to protect the nest and feed the young until the young are independent, and most young birds are completely helpless until they can fly. Male and female birds (unlike mammals) are equally equipped to assist their offspring once they are hatched. In many bird species, both parents care for only one offspring per year because that's all they can handle (e.g., the Emperor penguin mentioned in Chapter 5). Nevertheless, some species of birds have developed alternate strategies, depending on their circumstances, as we shall see.

Some species of birds are renowned for the lifelong monogamous relationships that involve remaining together even when they are not breeding. Perhaps the most well-known examples are geese and swans;

they are legendary for their seemingly steadfast bond that dissolves only in death. However elegant or romantic this conception may be, the truth is that not all monogamies in the animal kingdom end because of forced separation or death. It has been estimated that about 21% of monogamous relationships in birds break up spontaneously, a sort of "divorce" in birds. In addition, recent evidence using DNA fingerprinting has shown that some female birds, such as the zebra finch (*Taeniopygia guttata*), even when paired with a monogamous male, still mate and have offspring by other males. These females may welcome or even seek out high-quality males to father their offspring, especially when already paired with a less fit male (Birkhead 1996). More DNA fingerprinting studies may reveal that true monogamy in birds is not as prevalent as was once thought.

As an example of a truly monogamous bird, let us examine reproduction in the sandhill crane (*Grus canadensis*), as described by Johnsgard (1981) and Tacha (1988). This bird grows up to four feet in height, has a six-and-a-half-foot wingspan, and weighs up to 14 pounds. Sandhills migrate between eastern Siberia across North America to the middle of the United States. Each year in February and March, many stop near Nebraska's Platte River where they flock and feed in the thousands. They eat a broad diet, including grains, berries, mice, frogs, lizards, snakes, and insects, spearing their prey with their long, sharp beaks (see Figure 11.2). Their migratory routes take them to old feeding grounds by long-established paths that the young learn from the older birds.

Figure 11.2 Sandhill cranes performing their courtship dance.

When young cranes leave the nest, they travel with other juvenile cranes for two or three years. It is in these groups that the young cranes usually meet and pair with their lifelong mates. During the breeding season, a mated pair separates from the flock to establish its breeding territory and nest. Sandhills are famous for their elaborate and spectacular courtship displays. Courtship usually begins with the pair exchanging unison calls during which they stand side by side and sing alternate notes. This leads to a complex series of springs, whirling dances and head pumps, stretching the wings forward, flinging sticks into the air, and bowing to each other. They also engage in vertical leaps in which each bird coils and then jumps into the air as high as 15 feet, with wings spread wide and flapping as many as five times before coming down. This courtship leads to mating, after which the pair will raise their young for several months, each parent bringing food to the developing youngster. Young sandhills can walk and follow their parents through the wetlands only a few days after hatching.

Polygyny

Polygyny, a situation in which a male mates with several females during the breeding season, is the most common mating system in the animal kingdom. According to Emlen and Oring (1977), polygyny with no male parental care often develops through a causal chain that begins with food resources existing in clumps or patches. As a consequence, females tend to exist only at these patches because their ability to raise offspring and have reproductive success depends directly on the resources. In this situation, males may compete for females in either of two ways: by competing directly for access to females or by seizing the rich clumps and keeping other males out. Thus, the most general condition that promotes the development of polygyny is the distribution of resources: when resources are concentrated or "clumped" in specific areas, a higher potential exists for polygyny. Emlen and Oring (1977) described the general forms that polygyny can take and the circumstances that lead to the evolution of each form.

Resource Defense Polygyny

When resources that females need to survive and reproduce are clumped in certain areas, it's to the male's advantage to defend the territory that the resources are in and keep other males out, retaining exclusive mating rights with all the females in that territory. The question that arises in this situation is, why do the females remain in this group rather than seeking out a more exclusive relationship with one male? Why do the females "share" one male, so to speak?

The fact is, the fitness of a female (i.e., her reproductive success) depends on the quality of the territory that she resides in—the availability of food, water, and safety for her and her offspring. It may pay for a female to choose to share a superior territory with other females rather than seek out a monogamous relationship with a male in poorer territory, even though other females also will be raising their young in the same area (Orians 1969).

The most typical pattern of polygyny for mammals, predominant in perhaps 60% of all mammalian species, is for females to live solitary lives in smaller territories within a larger territory defended by a solitary male. This is the typical pattern, for example, for tigers (*Panthera tigris*) of Asia and for most species of bears.

Variations on this strategy occur when females live in social groups but wander over a range of territory that is not defendable by a male. If the females' routes to waterholes and food sources are constant and predictable, it may pay for the male to occupy a territory along these routes and capture mating opportunities as females travel back and forth (Owen-Smith 1977). This is the typical pattern for an African antelope called the topi (*Damalisius levatus korrigum)* and for Grevy's zebra (*Equus grevyi*).

In general, ungulates such as gazelles, horses, sheep, antelopes, and wildebeests have to assess the female's readiness to mate by sniffing the female's urine and genitals. The male typically sniffs by curling the upper lip upward to expose odor-detecting membranes to the female odor, a behavior called the flehmen response or test (see Figure 11.3). The female's odors reveal her hormonal state and whether or not she is receptive to mating.

Figure 11.3   The flehmen response in ungulates is the male's test for a female's sexual receptivity.

Female Harem Defense Polygyny

This form of polygyny occurs when females aggregate in defendable areas, typically for reasons other than the territorial resources. Often they aggregate for the advantages of increased vigilance, mutual defense, and alarms, as already discussed in Chapter 9. In these circumstances, a male can defend a group of females against other intruding males and keep all the mating opportunities for himself.

When the group of females is relatively small, a single male can defend the group of females as a permanent harem within his territory. This is the typical pattern for some primate species, such as the black-and-white colobus monkey (*Colobus gueveza*) and langur monkeys (*Presbytris entellus*). Hrdy (1977) discovered that when a male langur takes over a harem from another male, he often kills the young offspring fathered by the previous male. This event brings the females into estrus sooner and allows him to begin to father his own offspring as soon as possible. This pattern is also typical of lion prides. (More will be said about infanticide and its possible explanations in the next chapter.)

When females are in larger groups, several males may team up to defend the territory and its females together, keeping exclusive mating rights for themselves. This is the pattern among mammals such as lions, chimpanzees, and red colobus monkeys (*Colobius badius*).

Seasonal harems occur when groups of females come into estrus at the same time (a phenomenon called synchrony). In this instance, males typically spend most of the year eating and building up physical stores of energy. At the breeding time, the male then captures a group of females, defends it against other males, and enjoys exclusive breeding rights with the females. This is the typical pattern for many deer species, such as the red deer (*Cervus elaphus*) discussed in Chapter 8. Female red deer are receptive to breeding for only about a month per year. A similar pattern was described for the northern elephant seal in Chapter 10.

Male Dominance Polygyny

In some species, territory and space are not really the causal factors in the development of polygyny: there is no clump of resources or harem of females to defend. Instead, the females are free to choose any males they want to mate with, but they all tend to choose the same ones! Specifically, they choose those males that are most fit. Other males are ignored by the females. In this situation, the males compete vigorously with each other for access to females, but only a few males do most of the mating.

This is the system used by lek species described in Chapter 10. While lek systems are most often identified with birds, they can also occur with some species of mammals. An example is the West African hammerheaded bat (*Hypsignathus monstrosus;* Bradbury 1977). During the breeding season, male hammerheads assemble in traditional display areas in the evening. Each male hangs upside down from a tree branch and defends a territory about 40 feet in diameter. Males cry to attract receptive females that fly to the lek area to "examine" the males. Bradbury (1977) reported that in 1974, of all the bats present at one lek, 6% of the males performed 80% of the matings. In this bat species, the male does no parenting, and females visit the lek only to select a male to mate with.

Scramble Competition Polygyny

In this form of polygyny, the males actively search for mates but do not engage in much overt contact or competition with each other (Emlen and Oring 1977). For example, consider mating in wood frogs (*Rana sylvatica*) as studied by Berven (1981). He found that in this species the females congregate in small ponds, sometimes on only one night of the year. The male frogs rush around trying to mate with any females they can catch. A similar pattern occurs for horseshoe crabs (*Limulus polyphemus*). The females come out of the sea to lay eggs on the beach on only a few nights each year. At these times, the males gather in the water off the beaches in large numbers and await the incoming females. A male will grasp a female with a claw, follow her to her nesting site on the beach, and fertilize her eggs once they are laid. There are so many males and females gathering simultaneously that it does not pay the male to be territorial or combative (Brockmann 1990).

The same kind of pattern may develop when females are widely separated by space. Schwegmeyer (1988) studied ground squirrels of the species *Spermophilus tridecemlineatus*. The male squirrels actively search for females in estrus but without dominance interactions and territoriality. Those males that are more successful in their search for females will be more successful reproductively, but individual male squirrels do not confront other males. This is also the typical pattern for American moose (*Alces alces*) and orangutans (*Pongo pygmaeus*). Orangutan females move over a large range, following the fruiting seasons of different species of plants. Males will pursue the females when they are in estrus, but, otherwise, male and female orangutans are not interested in one another (MacKinnon 1974).

Polygyny is the norm in mammals, making up about 97% of the mating patterns for mammalian species. Males are typically not involved in parental care but will try to mate with as many females as possible when females are available. If the female's territory is actually larger than the male's, the male can defend only one female and will be monogamous (e.g., most rodents and nocturnal prosimians). Even in these species, however, only 3% of the males actually help defend the young against predators, carry them, or help feed them (e.g., jackals and wild dogs do all three). Thus, if forced by environmental circumstances to be monogamous, the male will maximize reproductive success by investing some effort in parental care (common only in canids). But if not forced to be monogamous by circumstances, the male will maximize reproductive success the traditional way, namely, by mating with as many females as possible and leaving all parental care to the females (most mammals).

An Unusual Polygyny: The Stickleback Fish

To illustrate the considerable variety in polygynous relationships, let's examine the reproductive pattern of one species, the three-spined stickleback fish (*Gasterosteus aculeatus*), which reproduces in freshwater streams of Europe. These fish get their name from the sharp spines along their backs, which makes them inedible to most predator fish despite the fact that they're only 5 centimeters (2 inches) long. (See Chapter 1, Figure 1.4) This fish was virtually unknown to the scientific community until Niko Tinbergen (1952) published some of the most famous studies in the ethological literature on this species. In fact, ever since these studies began in the late 1940s, the stickleback has been the best-studied fish in the world because it's small and does well under laboratory conditions.

All the reproductive behaviors in the stickleback are to a great degree innately organized, but they must be done in a sequence controlled by **releasers**—particular stimuli that the male and female exchange during courtship. In the breeding season, male sticklebacks develop a red coloration on their undersides and begin to protect their nesting territory aggressively. The red signals to other male sticklebacks to keep away—or else. If another male appears near the territory, the stickleback will typically stand on its head to give the intruder a "blast" of its red underside; then it will aggressively attack the intruder if it stays around. Tinbergen figured this out by making models of fish and manipulating the models' characteristics, including size, shape, and coloration. He showed that it is specifically the redness in the stimulus, not its size or shape, that evokes defensive behaviors in the other males. The red coloration releaser doesn't even have to look like a fish.

Because predators usually avoid them, the male sticklebacks build their nests in relatively open habitats. They do this by digging out a small pit on the bottom of the stream, filling it with plant material, gluing it together with a fluid they secrete, and then swimming through it to turn it into a tube. Next, the male changes color again, turning off the red and changing its upper half to a blue-white color to attract fertile females. When a female comes near, a very involved series of actions occurs: the male does a zigzag dance; the female comes near the male; the male leads her toward his nest; the female follows; the male shows her the nest entrance by swimming through it; the female enters the nest; the male trembles, nudging the female's behind; the female spawns and leaves; the male swims into the nest and fertilizes the eggs (Dewsbury 1978).

The male may do this with several females, using the same nest. Therefore, this is a polygynous species. Each action by the male and female is the releaser for the next action in the pattern. None of these behaviors require learning or experience. The whole reproductive system is a complex interaction between sign stimuli or releasers from male parent, females, and other males.

Finally, the male resumes its red underside coloring and does all the parenting! He protects the nest and fans water over the eggs, aerating them. When they hatch, the male guards them and chases away intruders. If a young hatchling strays away from the nest, the male takes it into his mouth and then spits it back into the nest.

Though we're accustomed to thinking of the female always doing the parenting, across the animal kingdom this is not always the case. We can observe here that fish often do not have the same problem as many mammalian species: with fish, females often produce almost as many eggs as males produce sperm, so these females do not have a greater parental investment in their offspring than the males. Thus, sticklebacks have evolved a male parenting system, partly as a function of the fact that males are territorial and build the nest; that is, they "own" the place where the eggs hatch. This sex role reversal occurs occasionally in fish but is much less common (but not totally unknown) in birds and mammals.

Polyandry

Polyandry, where one female mates with many males, is a rare strategy across nature, occurring only in a few bird species, a few insect species, sea horses, and in a few human cultures. Whereas the incubation of eggs is common in many bird species, for the male to do all the incubating is highly exceptional but characteristic of polyandry.

How polyandry may have evolved is illustrated by some species of arctic wading birds that use "double clutching," such as the sanderling (*Calidris alba*) and Temminck's stint (*Calidris temmenckii*). With these birds, the male defends a territory and the female lays one clutch of eggs that the male fertilizes and incubates. Then the female lays another clutch that she sits on herself. So the pair raise twice as many offspring at one time. This can only work when resources (the insects they eat) are abundant during the breeding season, and it's only advantageous if the parents are in a hurry to get their young to adulthood, and they are, because the parenting season in the cold Arctic is very brief indeed. In addition, and consistent with the principle of parental investment, raising two broods is better insurance against predation (Oring 1981).

It is easy to see how double clutching might give rise to polyandry: as long as food is abundant, the female can really maximize her reproductive success by laying several clutches for several males. This outcome can be seen in another wading bird, the spotted sandpiper (*Actitis macularia*), a bird that inhabits northern seashores (pictured in Figure 11.4). Females compete for breeding territories, preferring to return to the breeding grounds where they were born (a phenomenon called **philopatry**). Spotted sandpipers have evolved a polyandrous system where the female lays as many eggs as possible during the breeding season. A female typically lays five clutches of four eggs—a total of 20—in just 40 days! Here reproductive success depends directly on how many males she can mate with and get to incubate the eggs since each clutch of four is laid in a different nest. Thus, the female lays her eggs, then leaves them to the male to fertilize and incubate (Oring and Lank 1982). The male typically mates with only one female in the breeding season because, after mating, he must take care of the offspring.

The American jacana (*Jacana spinosa*) is a large wading bird of Central and South America. The males occupy small territories; each female has a larger territory encompassing several males. Breeding females mate with a male, lay eggs in the male's nest for the male to incubate, provide no parental care, and simply leave afterward to lay more eggs for another male. The females are 50% larger than the males and just lay eggs (Jenni 1974).

As these bird species demonstrate, the female may increase her reproductive success more in a short breeding season by producing many

Figure 11.4 The spotted sandpiper, a polyandrous species.

offspring rather than by taking care of only a few high-risk offspring. In this situation, the ability of the female to lay new eggs to replace the lost ones will be favored by evolution. So polyandrous females do little nest building and spend more of their time feeding. When eggs are lost to predators or a tough environment, a well-fed female can produce a new clutch of eggs quickly.

Promiscuity/Polygynandry

Traditionally, the word *promiscuity* has been used to describe any mating system involving both sexes having multiple mating partners during the breeding season. However, promiscuity is a misleading term that implies, at best, random pairings of males and females and, at worst, moral disapproval of such a system. We will reserve the term here to refer exclusively to multiple matings by both sexes where there are no pair bonds.

Good examples of promiscuous species are found in members of the weasel family, such as the American mink (*Mustela lutreola*) pictured in Figure 11.5. In February or March, the male mink leaves his territory and travels in search of females. On his journey, one male may mate with multiple females and each female may mate with several males, but pairs stay together only to mate and males do no parenting. Fitness of the species is increased by the fact that the strongest males travel farther and mate more often than weaker ones.

Figure 11.5 The American mink, a ferocious little predator.

In some species with multiple matings, there is some nonrandom choice of male mates by females and some parental care by potential male parents. In this case, as suggested by Grier and Burk (1992), the system might better be called **polygynandry**—a combination of polygynous males with polyandrous females—rather than promiscuity.

The most well-known example of polygynandry is a small bird of the English countryside, the dunnock or hedge sparrow (*Prunella modularis*), pictured in Figure 11.6. This amazing bird species is worth discussing in some detail because it uses all the mating systems described in this chapter, depending on the circumstances the birds are in! How each mating pattern develops as a function of the bird's ecological circumstances was studied by Davies and his colleagues at Cambridge University (Davies 1983, 1985; Davies and Lundberg 1984).

Dunnocks eat small insects and seeds on the ground in dense bush and grass areas. In the spring, both males and females establish territories that they defend against the same sex but which overlap with the territories of the opposite sex. Typically, males try to obtain as large a territory as possible. A female, on the other hand, has a territory that contains enough resources for her and her offspring but no more. Thus, for females, the more concentrated the food resources in the territory, the smaller the territory is.

Territorial males associate with those females with whom their territory overlaps, but the actual mating system varies as a function of the size of the female territories and exactly how female territories overlap with the male territories. So, for example, when the male territory is ap-

Figure 11.6 The dunnock or hedge sparrow of England, a small songbird with each wing only about 3 inches long.

proximately congruent with one female's territory, the male and female will form a monogamous pair. Some male dunnocks actually achieve polygyny when a large male territory overlaps two female territories completely, and the male successfully keeps other males out. As in other species, polygynous and monogamous male dunnocks generally have exclusive mating rights with their females.

When the female's territory overlaps the territories of two males, the female and two males will form a polyandrous trio. Eventually, the two male territories will become one larger territory, but one (alpha) male will be dominant over the other (beta) male.

How does polygynandry arise? Sometimes several males will combine their territories that overlap the territories of several females. (Note that female territories never combine or fuse.) In other words, polygynandrous groups may form consisting of three males and two females or two males and up to four females. The precise composition of each group depends on the distribution and availability of food within the combining male territories.

Thus, when food resources are highly available, female territories tend to be small, and this situation encourages monogamy or polygyny to develop. When food resources are less available and more spread out, female territories are larger, and this situation encourages polyandry and polygynandry. Davies and Lundberg (1984) were able to show that, when more food was provided to some sparser areas, the birds actually shifted their mating system toward polygyny and monogamy.

During the breeding season, female dunnocks do all the nest building and the incubating of the eggs after they are laid. Before the females lay their eggs, they are persistently followed by males in search of mating opportunities. In polyandry and polygynandry, the alpha males attempt to mate with females but also try to drive away competing betas. As a result, the alphas succeed in getting about 60% of the mating opportunities whereas the betas get about 40%. Betas tend to be more successful in polygynandrous groups than in the polyandrous groups because, in the polygynandrous group, the alpha cannot be with more than one female at a time; thus, more females are available for mating. Similarly, betas tend to be more successful when female breeding is synchronous (all females breeding at the same time) than when they are asynchronous.

As we have learned earlier in this book, most females, like the elephant seal, prefer to breed with the most dominant males and often reject less dominant ones. Female dunnocks are unusual in that females actively seek out matings with the less dominant betas! What would the females gain by doing this? Cost-benefit analysis is helpful in understanding why this is so. For one thing, a male will help feed the female's chicks but only when the male has previously mated with the chicks' mother. Thus, by mating with beta males, the female can obtain their help (as well as the alpha's help) and raise more young successfully.

Davies (1983) showed that male dunnocks also exhibit sperm competition. Before copulating with a female, the male may peck at the female's cloaca for two minutes, causing it to become extended and eventually to disgorge sperm from any prior matings. Furthermore, beta males tend to peck at and destroy the eggs of females they do not mate with. So the female can help prevent the destruction of her eggs by mating with available betas. Finally, mating with betas also reduces the amount of harassment the female receives from betas that either persist in trying to mate with her or attempt to destroy her eggs.

Dunnocks illustrate vividly how the mating system employed by animals is primarily a function of the ecological circumstances that the animals find themselves in. While we observe that most species employ one mating system most of the time, and this may lead us to conclude mistakenly that a mating system is innate in the species, dunnocks show us dramatically that animals are capable of adopting whatever mating system maximizes their reproductive success and changing the system if it's to the individual's advantage. Dunnocks also illustrate how sexual selection and conflict can cause male and female dunnocks either to behave very similarly (as in monogamy) or very differently (as in the other mating systems) when it is to their individual reproductive advantage to do so.

Summary

The four varieties of mating systems reflect the extent to which either sex can have access to mating with more than one mate. In monogamy, neither sex can monopolize more than one mate. Monogamy tends to develop when both parents are needed for offspring care and survival. In many rodents, for example, the parents have large litters that both parents must feed after the young are weaned. Monogamy is the typical pattern only in birds. Most young birds are totally dependent on their parents until they can fly.

In polygyny, the male is capable of monopolizing matings with more than one female, whereas females are limited to one male during the mating season. Polygyny is the most common mating system in nature, with males typically but not always leaving parental care to the female.

Resource defense polygyny develops when food resources are clumped in certain areas that individual males can defend as their territories. In female harem defense, polygyny develops when females congregate in groups for reasons such as mutual defense, and a male can claim the group for mating by excluding other males. In the male dominance form of polygyny, females choose which male to mate with, but most choose only a few males. In lek species, for example, males display together at a site where all females watch and choose to mate with only a few males. Finally, in scramble competition, polygyny occurs as males—neither territorial nor combative—scramble to find and mate with as many females as possible.

Stickleback fish are unusual in that, while the species is polygynous, there is a reversal of parenting roles, with males doing the guarding and parenting of offspring. Sticklebacks also illustrate how courtship, mating, and parenting in many species are largely innate patterns of responses controlled by environmental releasers.

In polyandry, the female is capable of mating with more than one male, whereas the male is typically limited to one mate during the breeding season. The rarest of breeding systems, polyandry occurs in some arctic wading birds and especially in species for which egg and offspring loss are high. Here it is to the female's advantage to lay as many eggs as possible in a short time.

In promiscuity/polygynandry, both sexes have multiple mating partners during the breeding season, a pattern typical of weasels. The dunnock of England is a bird that exhibits all four of the mating systems described in this chapter, depending on the circumstances. One set of circumstances is how smaller female territories and larger male territories intersect. Although congruence of male and female territories leads to dunnock monogamy, polygyny or polyandry may develop when male and female territories overlap. Polygynandry may be achieved when two male territories that overlap are combined into one, and each contains at least one female (whose territories never overlap). Thus, larger female territories tend to encourage polyandry and polygynandry.

CHAPTER 12

Parenting

No creature on earth has a longer youthful development than human beings. Consequently, we spend more time with our parents than other species. Why is this so? If we are such an intelligent species, why does it take us so long to break away from our parents and become independent? This question about humans will be addressed more explicitly in Chapters 16 and 17 of this book. In general, the degree of parenting typical for a species varies greatly in nature, from no parenting in some animals to many years of parental supervision in others. In order for their offspring to survive and reproduce, parents in some species must commit considerable time, resources, and protection to their developing offspring. On the other hand, in other species, little parenting appears to be useful or necessary. In this chapter, we will survey the factors and theories that apparently explain variations in parental investment. As we shall see, specific parenting behaviors occasionally take on unusual forms— some of them, at least superficially, in apparent contradiction to offspring survival. Unusual or not, parental behaviors are assumed to have evolved over the long term because such behaviors maximize the survivability of the greatest number of offspring.

Reproductive success does not end with the birth of new offspring. Success is defined by the number of young that survive to adulthood and reproduce themselves. Survival to adulthood is often directly dependent on the quality of parental care delivered by devoted parents. In this chapter, we will examine theories of how parenting behaviors evolved as well as the range of parenting behaviors that occur after the young are born.

The Evolution of Parental Investment

In his classic book, *Sociobiology,* E. O. Wilson outlined four factors favoring the evolution of parental care:

1. *Saturated habitats.* Under crowded conditions where one species competes vigorously among its own members, intense parenting will be favored (e.g., the Florida scrub jay, described in Chapter 13).
2. *Harsh or stressful environment.* Parenting will be favored when the young cannot survive without parental care (e.g., as in the Emperor penguin discussed in Chapter 5).
3. *Specialized diet.* Parental help will be favored when the young need to learn what food to eat and how to catch it (e.g., in the case of lions and other large cats).
4. *Predation pressure.* Parenting will be favored, if not essential, when the parents are needed to protect the immature young while they develop, increasing greatly their chances for survival. This is perhaps the most common reason for the evolution of parenting, evident in the development of most bird and mammalian species.

As we shall see, the extent of parental care varies greatly in animals and is generally related to the complexity of the organism: more complex animals take longer to develop and consequently need more parenting. However, as the four factors outlined by Wilson imply, the extent of parenting in the individual case is also affected by other factors, such as the availability of resources and other pressures impacting on the parents. A better understanding of parental investment began with the work of Trivers (1972, 1974), who helped clarify the conflicting factors that affect parenting. Trivers defined parental investment as those behaviors that increase the chances of offspring survival at the cost of the parent's ability to produce and raise other offspring. Viewed in this light, parenting can be regarded as involving a conflict between the parents and between the parents and their offspring.

Conflict between Parents

As discussed previously in Chapter 10, males often are less invested in parenting than females because males can frequently maximize their reproductive success by mating with many females rather than by staying with one female. There are additional reasons for the prevalent occurrence of female care of offspring, as discussed in some detail by Gross and Shine (1981). One possible theory why natural selection works against male parenting is related to the paternal certainty hypothesis: females can always be certain their offspring are

Figure 12.1 The male cotton-top tamarin carries around its young offspring on its back.

theirs, whereas males cannot (Trivers 1972). Thus, according to this theory, when male confidence in paternity is low, the male should generally display little parental investment in the offspring. When confidence in paternity is higher, males will provide greater parental care (Ridley 1978).

For example, the male cotton-top tamarin (*Saguinus oedipus*), a species of small South American monkey, carries around and protects its offspring, usually sets of twins (see Figure 12.1). This parenting behavior on the part of the male partly reflects the great confidence that the male has in his own paternity since his relationship with his mate is monogamous (Snowdon 1990).

A second desert-first hypothesis is that one sex generally provides parental care because the other sex can depart first after mating, leaving parental care to the individual that is left with the eggs—usually but not always the female (Dawkins and Carlisle 1976). This idea is consistent with what happens in many fish species. Most fish species (79%) simply lay eggs that are fertilized by the male, with no care at all by either parent. In the other 21% of fish species, the young are more dependent and require care and protection until they reach a large enough size, and often it is the male who does the care after the eggs hatch. One critical factor here seems to be whether the fertilization is internal or external (Gross and Sargent 1985). When fertilization is internal (when the eggs are fertilized inside the female's body), the female usually does the parenting (in 86% of such cases), perhaps because the male can leave first. With external fertilization, the caretaking parent is most often male (70% of cases) since the female can leave after depositing her eggs.

Another critical factor here appears to be territoriality: male territoriality is most prevalent in externally fertilized species, as exemplified by the three-spined stickleback discussed in Chapter 11. Thus, in those species that use internal fertilization, parental care is typically provided only by the female after the male leaves. However, in cases of external fertilization, the male fish typically fertilizes the eggs after the female lays them and leaves (Gross and Shine 1981).

A third association hypothesis emphasizes that the mother more often is immediately able to help the offspring after they're born because she's more likely to be near at hand when they're hatched (Williams 1975). The father may not even be nearby when birth happens. This appears to be the most generally applicable explanation for the prevalence of female parenting, though there's no reason why more than one of the three hypotheses stated couldn't be operating.

Of course, many animals feature care by both parents, not just one. Such care is very rare in insects, relatively rare in mammals, occurs in about 22% of fish species having any parental care, and is common in birds. Gross and Sargent (1985) concluded that biparental care evolves from father-only care in fish but from mother-only care in mammals. Fish probably evolve biparental care when the female adds a significant amount of protection to the male's protection of the young, increasing their reproductive success.

In mammals, the evolution of joint male-female care may represent the necessity of having both parents attend to the young in warm-blooded species whose young develop with high metabolic rates. The male mammal may add a significant amount of care for the young, beyond protection from predators, since one parent could probably protect the offspring adequately. Care may include feeding the young (as wolves and wild dogs regurgitate food for offspring) or carrying them (as in marmosets, small monkeys of South America).

In many bird species, frequent biparental care probably is a function of the offspring's high demand for food. Certainly, male bird parents are just as efficient in bringing food to the young as are the females; with mammals, however, the male cannot lactate, so his ability to provide food to his developing youngsters is limited.

Conflict between Parents and Offspring

The interests of parents and their offspring do not always coincide. In general, parent animals are trying to maximize their own lifetime reproductive success. When parental survival and long-term reproductive potential are threatened by caring for current offspring, the parents may cease parenting and abandon them. After all, the adults can live to reproduce on another day. In addition, pressures and threats that may result in abandonment can also lead to other behaviors in some species: investment in a few offspring but not others, or, in extreme cases, infanticide and even cannibalism.

Trivers (1972, 1974) brought greater understanding to parent-offspring conflict by subjecting such conflicts to cost-benefit analysis. Typically, the mother's genetic investment in her offspring right after birth is always worth it: the cost to her of raising her young is small relative to the survival benefits gained by the young. But as offspring grow, they become more costly to her because they demand more of her resources, such as milk from lactation or catching more prey. These costs reach the point where the cost to the mother exceeds the benefits to the offspring, and the mother's genetic investment in future offspring is delayed or impaired.

The classic example of such a conflict occurs when young mammals are weaned off milk onto another diet. Lactation is more of a drain on the female's resources than the entire pregnancy period, and during lactation she cannot set aside energy reserves for her next pregnancy until the current offspring are weaned (Clutton-Brock, Albon, and Guinness 1989). Thus, it is to the mother cat's advantage to wean her kittens off milk and onto solid foods as soon as possible. On the other hand, the kittens are motivated to get all the support they can from their mother and prolong the nutritional advantages that come from her as long as possible. The actual time at which the mother can succeed in completing the weaning process is a compromise between her needs and the needs of her offspring.

The attachment of the infant rhesus monkey (*Macaca mulatta*) to its mother is very strong, but by the end of the first year, conflict is evident in their relationship. Typically, the infant can feed itself by six months of age, but it still attempts to nurse from its mother after one year. Once a new infant is born, the mother will no longer permit the older infant near her nipples. She may push the older infant away or even hit it if it bothers her too much. The infant may respond to this situation by throwing a temper tantrum (Berman 1980).

A Survey of Parenting Variations

Parenting can be classified along a spectrum of care ranging from minimum to maximum. Species whose young require little parenting care are called **precocial,** whereas those that require a great deal of parenting are called **altricial.** Parenting is most important and complex in altricial species, especially among those whose young require a longer developmental period in which to grow to adulthood and acquire critical learned experiences. Therefore, the more complex mammals and primates (like us) are altricial.

Little Parenting

The simplest kind of reproduction involves no parenting at all: many marine invertebrates just release eggs or sperm into the water, and the offspring survive on their own as soon as they hatch. Adult female butterflies do no parenting as such, but they typically deposit their fertilized eggs on just those plants that the young caterpillars need for survival.

A similar phenomenon is observed in large green sea turtles (*Chelonia mydas*). Many years after their birth, the adult female turtles will return to the same island and the same beach they hatched on to lay their own eggs (Carr 1967). It is thought that the smell and taste of the beach may stay with the females through the process of imprinting, but exactly how they do this is not well understood. The mother turtle lays her eggs in a ditch she digs on a beach, covers them up, and leaves, without meeting her young. After hatching on the same night, the young turtles must dig themselves out and run the gauntlet of predators between them and the water. In most species of sea turtles, sound is the hatchlings' primary guide to the water. Sometimes, however, sound cues may also be aided by olfactory (scent) cues.

The large green sea turtle is a highly precocial species, with the young having to fend for themselves from the moment they hatch. Young sea turtles experience a great deal of predation until they reach a size large enough to deter most predators.

It was formerly believed that alligators and crocodiles were much like turtles in their parenting (immediately abandoning the eggs after laying them), but more recent research has verified that mother alligators (*Alligator mississippiensis*) guard their eggs until they hatch, protect their young, and transport them to the water after hatching, usually by carrying them in their mouths. Once in the water, the young are on their own, having to avoid the larger adults that will eat them until they reach a certain size. This is a precocial species but with some initial parental care.

Precocial birds tend to lay larger eggs than altricial species so that the precocial chick will be more fully developed and independent when it hatches. Most vertebrate animals and insects display some minimal parental care, even if only placing the eggs in places favorable for development (as do butterflies) and staying with the eggs until they hatch. Birds' eggs contain a rich food supply in the yolk, enough so that the chick developing inside needs no additional food until it hatches. Insect eggs, on the other hand, have little yolk and are more dependent on their mother laying the eggs near an available food supply on which the larvae can feed after emerging. It used to be thought that maggots (the larval form of newly hatched flies) were produced by decaying flesh, but maggots on dead flesh simply represent the female fly's strategy of laying her eggs in a place where the maggots will have a food supply.

A few remarkable species of birds do not personally incubate the eggs. For example, mallee fowls (*Leipoa ocellata*) are large ground-dwelling birds of southern Australia similar to American turkeys. During the breeding season, mated pairs of birds build up huge mounds of vegetation covered by loose earth, standing 4 feet high and up to 14 feet wide. The vegetable matter that is sealed in begins to rot and generate heat. At intervals of about six days, the hen lays about 20 eggs in a hole at the top of the mound, and the heat from the mound incubates the eggs. During this time, the male tests the temperature of the mound periodically with its tongue! He piles on more earth to raise the temperature of the mound or removes earth to cool it to a constant temperature of around 92° F. The total incubation period lasts a long eight months, during which the male constantly guards the nest and controls the temperature. When the eggs finally hatch, the chicks must dig themselves out on their own and are largely precocial, receiving no help from their parents. Not all of the young make it; about 50% of mallee fowl eggs never hatch (see Figure 12.2).

Ample Parenting

Extensive parental care is characteristic of birds, mammals, and insects that live in colonies. Most birds are altricial, born naked and featherless, blind, helpless, and totally dependent on the parents for food,

Figure 12.2   The male mallee fowl guarding its large nest, which incubates the eggs.

warmth, and protection. Thus, parenting includes behaviors that occur before the young are hatched as well as after. One important decision made by parent birds is the choice of a nest site that offers protection for the eggs and young. For example, the kittiwake (*Rissa tridactyla*) is a gull that nests on tiny cliff ledges along Arctic shorelines. Large predator birds cannot get at the nests because of the unstable air currents blowing along the cliffs, and ground predators like foxes cannot climb the cliffs to reach the ledges.

Nesting Behavior.   A nest is a structure that parents create for incubating eggs and rearing the young. Nests are typically built by many fish and small terrestrial animals as well as by birds. Some insects merely dig a hole and leave enough food for the young after they are hatched. Dung beetles (e.g., *Kheper aegyptiorum*) dig a hole into which they put a ball of dung, on which they lay one egg. After hatching, a young beetle feeds on the dung. Similarly, some species of sand wasps (e.g., *Sphex ichneumoneus*) bury live animals, usually spiders, to provide food for their larvae. The wasp constructs an underground burrow, paralyzes its prey with a sting, and buries the prey with a wasp egg that lives off the spider once it hatches.

The greatest variety and complexity of nest building are exhibited by birds. The nest offers protection for the young against bad weather and predators. Protection can be gained primarily through four different strategies: location, camouflage, inaccessibility, and nesting in a colony (Welty 1962). For example, ground-dwelling birds like pheasants build highly camouflaged nests, but these nests are easily accessible. On the other hand, airborne birds generally have exposed nests that are relatively inaccessible by predators, such as the aeries of eagles and kittiwakes. Finally, the nests of colonial species of birds are often exposed and accessible, but these birds can nest in this way because protection is found in their numbers.

Many of the 90 species of weaverbirds of Africa and Asia build some of the most elaborate and intricate nests of all birds. These birds are small members of the finch family that live in a variety of habitats—some solitary in forests and dense undergrowth, others nesting in colonies and feeding in flocks on open plains. Their main weaving technique is based on their ability to hold down one end of a strand of grass with their foot while weaving and knotting the other end with their beaks (see Figure 12.3). The bird gradually weaves many strands together into a hollow ball that hangs from a branch or thick leaf. The entrance to the nest is typically at the bottom, making it difficult for predators to enter. An inner wall-like partition within the nest keeps the eggs from falling out. Some species even build their nests close to the nests of stinging insects like hornets to gain further protection from invasions by monkeys or other predators.

Figure 12.3 The nest of a weaverbird is constructed with abilities that are largely innate in these birds.

When a female bird lays its eggs, the parents may then have to incubate the eggs for days or weeks before they hatch. For many species of birds, incubation involves one or both parents sitting on the eggs to keep them warm enough for the embryo inside the egg to continue developing. As we've seen with the mallee fowl, some species have a complex incubation procedure. However, most species simply use their own bodies to keep the eggs warm. Some species possess brooding patches of bare skin that are designed specifically to transmit heat from the bird's body to the eggs. Those species that do not have brooding patches must provide heat in other ways. For example, the blue-footed booby (*Sula nebouxii*), a large seabird, incubates the eggs by standing on them with its large webbed feet, which maintain a constant temperature of 103°F. Once the chicks are hatched, the booby chicks keep warm by sitting on top of their parents' feet. Similarly, the Emperor penguin parent (discussed in Chapter 5) carries its one large egg on top of its feet to avoid placing the egg on the frozen ground of Antarctica.

Bird hatchlings are faced with the formidable problem of escaping from their prison—the egg—which is designed to withstand considerable stress. To escape the eggshell, the about-to-be-born chick has an "egg tooth" to help it break out. Essentially, this is a small, hornlike projection on the tip of its upper beak that it can use to crack the shell. This egg tooth disappears soon after hatching. Such a device demonstrates the relationship that birds have with many reptiles and snakes, which also have it.

When the young bird is finally free of the shell, the parent may eat or remove the shell if the young are to remain in the nest, since a bright

Figure 12.4 Goslings follow Konrad Lorenz after imprinting on him during the hours following hatching.

white shell might attract predators. However, they may simply abandon the shell if the chick can walk away following its hatching.

After Hatching.   Once hatched, most young birds are dependent on their parents for some time; in some species, attachment of the young to the parents is facilitated by a strong genetically organized process called **imprinting.** The studies of imprinting in birds are among the most famous in all of ethology. Konrad Lorenz discovered imprinting in geese and showed that, during a critical period of time after hatching, most waterfowl will "imprint" on whatever large object or organism is moving around them (Lorenz 1981). Usually, this is the mother bird, as in ducks and geese. But in the field, Lorenz substituted himself (see Figure 12.4). In the laboratory, we can use anything to imprint, even a featureless block of wood, as long as it is moving around in the young bird's view during the critical period after hatching (Hess 1973). This period varies but often is at its height around 8 to 15 hours after hatching.

In later studies, Johnston and Gottlieb (1981) were able to show that imprinting is also affected by the vocal calls made by the mother, particularly the assembly call that typically gathers the chicks to her side. Developing chicks can imprint to some extent on these calls before hatching while the chick is still growing in the egg (Gottlieb 1991)! While ducks imprint on a moving object, they may later abandon that object if it does not emit the maternal assembly call and some other moving object (e.g., a duck of another species) does make the call.

Imprinting can be regarded as a highly special form of learning that is biologically organized to occur only at a certain time during development and that produces an attachment that is relatively permanent. Its functional advantage to the species should be obvious: the young animal learns immediately whom to follow, watch, and obey. Only one day after hatching, the mother can lead all of her little ducklings (as many as 12) to the water and start showing them what to eat—usually plant material in the water and at the bottom of streams. Imprinting illustrates Lorenz's initial emphasis on built-in behaviors, or **fixed action patterns** (FAPs), which older scientists called "instincts." Accordingly, at a critical time, the imprinting FAP is released when the proper sign stimulus (i.e., the mother) is present.

The "fixedness" of FAPs has sometimes been questioned because of the wide range of individual differences in some species. Barlow (1968) proposed replacing "fixed action pattern" with "modal action pattern," which implies an average or typical response that is less fixed. However, since the term FAP is still widely used and is of such historical importance, I will continue to use it here, while recognizing that a FAP may be more or less fixed, depending on the species.

Birds typically incubate the eggs and raise their young at the nest site until the young are ready to fly and get food on their own. Most species are monogamous or polygynous, and within these possibilities are many variations. Sometimes both parents gather food and raise the young so that more young can be raised. Sometimes just the mother bird does the parenting, as is the case with many waterbirds. These animals typically are more altricial than reptiles since birds cannot fly immediately after hatching. On the other hand, young domestic chickens (which don't fly) are mostly precocial, being able to peck for seeds on the ground soon after hatching and to run away if threatened.

Many birds feed their offspring by putting insects or pieces of animal flesh in the young bird's mouth. Small bird parents may have to make more than 200 trips a day just to retrieve insects, worms, and larvae for their constantly hungry chicks. But there is a tremendous variety in all the techniques used to deliver food. Large seabirds often swallow their food (usually fish) when they catch it. Herring gull chicks peck at a red dot on their parents' bills, causing the parents to regurgitate the fish they caught. The brown pelican (*Pelecanus occidentalis*) opens its mouth wide, enabling the chick to retrieve food directly from its gullet. Parent albatrosses and spoonbills use a more drastic technique: grabbing hold of the chick's beak crosswise in their bills and pushing the food down the youngster's throat with their tongues!

Birds must perform many other parenting tasks during the development of their chicks. The body wastes of many young birds are expelled in a membrane-covered pellet called a fecal sac. The parents remove the sacs from the nest and transport them to another location. This procedure is important for the survival of many ground-dwelling or low-nesting birds whose droppings, if left in the nest, might attract predators to the nest site.

Many techniques are used to protect and defend offspring from predators. Terns, for example, will screech and swoop at a predator, trying to drive it away. Grebes can swim away with their young clinging to their backs. Grouse signal their chicks to freeze and remain motionless until the danger passes. If a predator comes too near a nest, many parent birds will display "flagging behavior." The most common form of this distractive maneuver is landing on the ground and hopping around as if injured, a behavior called a "broken wing display." Although the parent bird takes some risk of being captured itself, this risky behavior can be viewed as part of the parent's investment in the safety and survival of its offspring.

Parent birds may also play a role when the young finally leave the nest. Wood ducks (*Aix sponsa*), the only species of duck to nest in trees, call to their ducklings from the ground. The young, which cannot fly but which can swim, reach the ground by jumping out of the nest and half falling, half floating to the ground. The chicks are so light at this stage of development that they're not harmed by falling 15 feet or more. Pygmy nuthatches (*Sitta pygmaea*) of the American West, on the other hand, literally pull the chick out of the nest hole. The chachalaca (*Ortalis vetula*) carries its young from the nest to the ground by having the young cling to the parent's legs.

Some birds must instruct their young in how to catch prey and allow them to practice before they can function independently. For example, the parent belted kingfisher (*Megaceryle alcyon*) of the eastern United States catches a fish, beats it against a branch to render the fish unconscious, and then drops it in the water in front of its nest. The young kingfisher at first will dive awkwardly for this easy prey but gradually sharpens its diving skills to the point where it can catch fast and fully alert fish by itself (Bent 1940). Similarly, the mother spotted-necked otter of Africa (*Lutra maculicollis*) drops live, flapping fish beside her young pup before it can dive properly or catch fish (Mortimer 1963).

Insects that live in colonies, such as ants and termites, also have evolved highly complex care of their young. Ants build elaborate nests in which constant temperature and humidity are maintained. Specialized ant workers in the colony are responsible for brood care after the one breeding ant, the queen, lays her eggs. The eggs evolve through two stages, larva and pupa, before becoming adults ants. The wormlike larva is basically an eating machine designed to grow as rapidly as possible. In many ant species, the larva is largely helpless, having to be fed by the worker "nurses." The pupa is an interim stage during which the ant's anatomy is reorganized to form the adult that has a distinct head, legs, and sometimes wings. Other workers forage outside the colony for the food supply that nourishes the queen, the larvae, and the other workers. More will be said about ants and other eusocial insects in the next chapter.

The Most Parenting: Mammals

Mammals give birth to live young that must be weaned or get milk for a period of time from a lactating female. Only in mammals are the young supported exclusively by the mother's milk early in development. The mother's milk provides not only protein and calories but also vitamins, minerals, and immunity against some diseases. As we shall see in more detail in upcoming chapters, large monkeys and the great apes have the longest periods of development and parenting of any animals other than humans. Infancy in these species may last from a year and a half to over three years, sometimes encompassing a third of the animal's entire life span. These animals have long periods of parenting and socialization because survival and reproductive success as adults depends so much on learning. The dependence on learning in turn gives these species great flexibility in dealing with the habits, environmental conditions, and complex social systems within which they must function.

Marsupials, the mammals native to Australia, are unique in that gestation periods are very brief and the young are born very tiny and underdeveloped. A newborn red kangaroo (*Macropus rufus*), for example, is hardly more than an embryo with arms and a mouth. This newborn must travel on its own through its mother's fur from the urogenital opening to the mother's pouch. Once inside, it fastens itself to a teat (see Figure 12.5). The newborn remains and develops in the pouch until it achieves independence at about 230 days. Strangely enough, the mother red kangaroo mates again right after she gives birth, not after her current offspring leaves the pouch! While her ovum becomes fertilized immediately, the new embryo does not develop until the pouch is empty. Thus, a female that loses her developing offspring to predation or disease can begin the development of new offspring immediately because she has a fertilized egg "on hold" at all times. The unique characteristics of marsupial physiology may have evolved to enable marsupials to breed quickly when environmental conditions such as food and water are optimal.

Tutoring.   In large carnivores, primates, and human beings, the developmental period may be quite long and may involve extensive tutoring and instruction by the parents. Carnivores such as the large cats must be taught by their mother where and how to hunt. In the cheetah (*Acinonyx jubatus*), for example, practice begins early when the two-month-old cubs may be led by their mother to freshly killed prey. Like most kittens, young cheetahs are very playful at this age and practice pouncing, chasing, wrestling, and pulling with each other. Clearly, play is important for learning hunting skills. The most frequent form of play begins at about three months and consists of chasing and batting each other's hindquarters—precisely those behaviors involved in subduing prey (Schaller 1972). When accompanying the mother on hunts, the cubs may initially spoil the mother's attack by playing or bounding ahead of her while she

Figure 12.5   The tiny newborn red kangaroo—blind, naked, and underdeveloped—must make its way to its mother's pouch and attach itself to one of the teats.

is stalking prey. A cheetah mother displays amazing patience in these situations by sitting and waiting until the cubs come back to her. However, only three months after birth, the cubs are weaned and typically have learned to stay behind their mother, waiting for her to kill prey. When the cubs reach six months of age, the mother begins to bring back young living gazelles for the developing cubs to chase. From nine to twelve months, the cubs begin to hunt successfully and catch small game like hares while the mother watches. Still, the mother makes the final kill until the cubs are as old as fifteen months (Schaller 1972).

In other species, especially primates such as monkeys and apes, play and tutoring may also be very important for the development of social skills and sexual behaviors. Some of these species will be discussed in detail in Chapter 14 and after.

Group Parenting.   Group predators such as lions, wild dogs, hyenas, and wolves have additional advantages for teaching their young: more models to imitate and constant supervision by adults.

Some nonpredatory mammals also take advantage of the benefits of parenting in groups. Notable among these is the African elephant (*Loxodonta africana*). Female elephants live in groups of up to 25 individuals, including adult females and juveniles of both sexes. A group is typically led by an older female called a matriarch. A newborn elephant in the group is

Figure 12.6   A mother African elephant with its young calf.

typically surrounded by its mother's sisters and other relatives. Bonds within the group are very strong, and the bond between a mother and her offspring may last 50 years. The mother is very protective of her newborn calf, pushing it under her to protect it from danger and lifting it over fallen trees and out of holes (see Figure 12.6). The mother will wash the calf by squirting water over it and scrubbing it with her trunk (Poppleton 1957). While the baby elephant generally suckles only from its mother, the baby's other needs are often shared by other juveniles in the group. These helpers are extremely tolerant, indulgent, and protective of the developing youngster. One or another helper will guard the baby as it sleeps, or retrieve it if it strays, or help it if it falls down. The mother will continue to suckle the youngster for several years, even after the baby begins to eat vegetation. In summary, elephants are extremely social, group-oriented mammals that develop in the context of family support and cooperation.

Unusual Parenting Strategies

Unusual Brooders

Many species of animals have evolved rather unusual brooding and nesting strategies. For example, the frog *Rheobatrachus silus* actually broods its young in its stomach (Tyler and Carter 1981). After swallowing the

Figure 12.7 A male sea horse giving birth to many tiny offspring.

fertilized eggs, the young are hatched out of the adult's mouth! The female waterbug (*Abedus herberti*) lays its eggs directly on the back of the male, which carries the eggs until they hatch.

Sea horses (family Hippocampus) are small fish that swim in a vertical position and attach themselves to vegetation with their long tails (see Figure 12.7). A few days before mating, the male develops a pouch on its belly. He begins courtship by bringing his belly close to the female's belly, and the two intertwine. Shortly thereafter, the female will squirt thousands of eggs into the male's pouch; then they separate. The eggs are quickly fertilized because the male's sperm empties directly into the pouch. The lining of the pouch becomes larger and spongy, providing the baby sea horses inside with a nourishing fluid. In two weeks, the male experiences "labor" contractions and tiny baby sea horses emerge from the pouch. He may give birth to a thousand or more babies. Many babies are produced because so many are lost to predators or fail to find adequate food.

In summary, nature has evolved an extensive and mind-boggling variety of brooding and parenting techniques, and those that survive in living animals today exist because, for those species, these techniques work whether they are unusual or not.

Brood Parasites

Some species of birds have solved their parenting problems by laying their eggs in the nests of other birds, which then incubate the eggs and feed and care for the young. This process is termed "intraspecific" when the mother lays eggs in nests of the same species, and this practice is actually common in some waterfowl such as ducks, geese, and swans. Weigmann and Lamprecht (1991) were able to show that in bar-headed geese (*Anser indicus*) the genetic mother does gain some reproductive success by doing this while the host mother, on average, loses some reproductive success.

In other species, this form of **brood parasitism** is "inter-specific," and the mother lays eggs in the nests of a different species (Payne 1977). This process can be regarded as a form of predation, whereby the donor species gains while the host species loses. Although some species do this only occasionally, others like European cuckoos (e.g., *Cuculus canorus*) and American brown-headed cowbirds (*Molothrus ater*) are parasitic as a way of life. These species have evolved other behaviors that support their lifestyle, such as sneaking into the host bird's nest while the host is away and laying an egg in less than ten seconds (Wylie 1981). The cuckoo female usually removes one egg and lays one egg of its own in the nest of a host species like the reed warbler (*Acrocephalus scirpaceus*). The cuckoo egg is a little larger than the host egg but matches it in color and shading, an example of mimicry (Davies and Brooke 1988).

The parasite's eggs typically develop faster and hatch before the host's eggs. After hatching, the parasite chick does one of several things, depending on the species. The larger chick of the Euopean cuckoo maneuvers the host's eggs or chicks to the edge of the nest and dumps them out, thereby getting all of the host parents' food deliveries (see Figure 12.8). The young of the honeyguide (*Indicator indicator*) goes one step further, actually killing the host's offspring with its sharp, hooked beak.

Thus, in these species, brood parasitism is actually a form of predation. In other species, the parasite offspring are raised with the host's offspring. In those cases where the mouth of the offspring is a sign stimulus for parental feeding, the mouth of the parasite bird often resembles the mouth of the host chicks, acting as an effective stimulus for host delivery of food. For example, the mouth of the weaverbird chick (*Vidua macroura*) mimics that of a young finch (*Estrilda astrild*) (Lack 1968).

However, the host species does not always cooperate in these endeavors. Some potential hosts avoid parasitism by building nests that are highly concealed and by defending the nest if discovered. Some hosts recognize the parasite egg as strange and abandon or destroy it. European cuckoos are successful at parasitism partly because of the close resemblance of their eggs to the eggs of the host species.

How did this kind of parasitic strategy actually evolve? It probably began with some birds using the current or abandoned nests of other

Figure 12.8 The reed warbler host parent is much smaller than the parasite cuckoo that the host is feeding.

birds but still rearing their own eggs and offspring. If these eggs were then abandoned, some eggs may actually have been brooded by still other birds that took over the nest. This pattern may have gradually evolved into complete parasitism when the forces of natural selection favored those eggs and young raised by doting host species.

Infanticide and Cannibalism

Whereas we as humans see our own infanticide and cannibalism as inexplicable evils, such events in the animal kingdom can be viewed as adaptations for increasing lifetime reproductive success. A species that breeds many times during its lifetime should be willing to sacrifice short-term reproductive success to ensure long-term viability.

In some bird species, the parents usually lay more eggs than the number of offspring that survive. This is a common pattern in raptors—eagles, hawks, and owls. The first bird hatched in the nest is usually the largest because it is incubated earlier and fed first. The eldest chick is given most of the incoming food by the parents, and a second chick often starves to death. When the smaller chick is attacked and harassed by the older, larger one, the parents usually stand by and do nothing to interfere.

Why would such behaviors evolve? Why have two chicks if one is to die anyway? Two major explanations account for these events. One insurance hypothesis proposes that the second chick is produced as a form of "insurance" if the first chick doesn't survive. This explanation seems particularly applicable in those cases where the younger chick dies soon after hatching (Stinson 1979) when the eldest chick is strong and doing well, as in lesser spotted eagles (*Aquila pomarina*) and black eagles (*Aquila verreauxii*).

A second opportunism hypothesis appears to be more applicable in other species like the tawny owl (*Strix aluco*), where the survival of the second chick depends on the available food supply. The idea here is that when more resources are available, the parents can raise two chicks; however, when resources are scarce, the second chick is sacrificed. In lean years, the parent birds may also feed the carcass of the younger offspring to the eldest chick so that nothing goes to waste (Stinson 1979). Thus, having two chicks to start with may be an opportunistic strategy by which the parents can maximize their reproductive success in good years.

Whereas parents of some species may have to sacrifice some offspring when times are tough, in some arthropod species, the offspring actually eat the parent! Seibt and Wickler (1987) were able to show that the young of some African spiders (e.g., *Stegodyphus mimosarum*) are hatched on their mother's abdomen and eat their mother when they begin to mature. This form of sacrifice is more likely to be characteristic of species where the female breeds only once. Nevertheless, it may be the spider mother's final act of sacrifice for her young—making sure they start off in life with a good meal.

Natal Dispersal

The movement of a young animal from its place of birth to the place at which it first attempts to breed is referred to as **natal dispersal.** The average natal dispersal (for one species) is the average distance the young will travel before first breeding. Some animals remain close to where they were born; others move far away. At the very least, dispersal is important for preventing species inbreeding, which never helps the gene pool. Most animals will avoid mating with their relatives, though it can happen sometimes.

There are several principles here to keep in mind. First, the dispersal distance in most species always differs for males and females. In birds, for example, females generally disperse more than males because males tend to keep territories and sometimes one male offspring will "inherit" the territory from its male parent. In mammals, on the other hand, males disperse more because the male leaves the female after mating and is motivated to seek out more females that are further away. Male mammals often have territories, but these territories are usually large enough to encompass several smaller female territories, if females have territories at all.

So what is the consequence of all this? Simply this: members of the less dispersing sex tend to be more closely related to their geographic neighbors; and in the wild, it's one's genetic relatives that are willing to "help out" as a parent—rarely anyone else. So male birds help each other out in raising and feeding the offspring—if they are related as brothers, father and son, and so forth. On the other hand, female mammals are more likely to be each other's helpers since female relatives are most often the ones that live together or near each other, as in the case of lion females in the same pride that will suckle and take care of each other's cubs. (The reasons why relatives tend to help each other in the wild while nonrelatives do not are discussed in more detail in the next chapter.)

Summary

In many species, a major factor in reproductive success is the ability of parents to nurture and protect their young. Intense parenting is more likely to develop when environmental pressures are severe as, for example, in saturated habitats or when predation is frequent.

Across nature, females tend to be parents more often than males for several reasons. If females can nurture their offspring on their own, males may seek out other females in order to maximize reproductive success. However, males may engage in more parenting when they are more certain that the offspring are their own. When external fertilization is used (as in many fish), males may do the parenting because the female can leave first, but their roles are reversed with internal fertilization.

Parent and offspring needs may conflict. Whereas infant animals are typically concerned only with their own survival, adults typically try to maximize their lifetime reproductive success. Thus, current offspring may logically be neglected or sacrificed if adult survival is sufficiently threatened.

Parenting variations range from little or no parenting (precocial species) to ample parenting (altricial species). Precocial species include many insects, fish, and reptile species such as large turtles. Ample parenting is typical of most birds because young birds need protection and feeding until they can fly. Birds build nests to house the growing offspring and to protect them against predators and weather changes. Weaverbirds of Africa, for example, build elaborate, sacklike nests, and, like most birds, incubate the eggs with the warmth of their bodies.

Newly hatched waterfowl typically attach themselves to their parents by imprinting on them during a critical period after hatching. Many developmental responses like imprinting in birds are fixed action patterns (FAPs) largely programmed by innate abilities and released by specific environmental stimuli. Many birds must devote numerous hours to obtaining food for their young, protecting them from predators, and instructing them in choosing and hunting appropriate prey.

The young of mammals require the most parenting of any animal. Mammal infants are dependent on their mothers' milk until they grow large enough, and many mammals feature long developmental periods requiring parental care, protection, and tutoring. Some large mammals like elephants employ group parenting, which offers the young the advantages of multiple protection and care.

Some species have evolved unusual parenting strategies. For example, some frogs brood their eggs in their stomachs, and in sea horses it is the male that gives birth. Some birds are brood parasites, laying eggs in the nests of other birds that do the parenting. In some birds, more eggs and offspring are produced than can survive, perhaps to ensure that some will survive or to maximize the number of offspring if resources are plentiful.

When animals mature and leave their parents, male mammals tend to disperse further than females, whereas female birds disperse further than males. This difference appears to be related to territoriality, since male birds often inherit their father's territory, whereas male mammals often have large territories that encompass the smaller territories of several females.

CHAPTER 13

Cooperation and Helping

As we have seen in previous chapters, animal behavior is influenced by selfish genes, the adaptability of behavior, and the environmental opportunities that present themselves to the organism. These processes are generally understood within the context of Darwin's theory, which predicts that individuals will act in their own selfish interest with the result that the survivability of their own genes is promoted in subsequent generations. In this scheme of things, is there any room for unselfish cooperation, helping, and self-sacrifice? Apparently not, yet it is not difficult to find many instances of helping behavior among animals in nature. This apparent inconsistency between facts and theory demands resolution, and modern biologists have spent considerable time and effort trying to resolve the contradiction.

One approach, of course, would be to discard Darwin's theory and start over again, but to do this would be to ignore the countless phenomena that the theory of evolution explains so well. Consequently, modern theorists have generally taken a different approach—trying to find new principles that will help us understand apparent "unselfish" behavior within the context of the known principles of genetics and evolution. In this chapter, we will look at these efforts to understand cooperation and helping without discarding, but perhaps with modifications of, the modern synthetic theory of genetics and evolution.

Altruism can be defined as behavior that increases another individual's (the recipient's) lifetime number of offspring (reproductive success) at a cost to one's (the donor's) own survival and reproduction. In other words, altruism is apparent selflessness rather than selfishness. Attempts to explain such behaviors have taken a number of avenues, all of them attempting to preserve the theory of natural selection and at the same time explaining apparent altruism ultimately

255

as selfish behavior. Three of the main explanations we will label and discuss are mutualism, reciprocity, and kin selection.

Mutualism

Mutualism denotes a strategy in which two or more individuals cooperate with each other in order to gain more *for each individual* than they would gain if each were to act individually. There is nothing new in this idea, and nothing conflicts with any of the ideas central to the theory of evolution. However, this is not true altruism since the individuals involved do not sacrifice their own reproductive success. Moreover, mutualism occurs fairly often in nature. Thus, although mutualism is not altruism, it is cooperation.

Let's look at a typical pride of lions (*Panthera leo*) of the African plains, the most social of all cat species, as an example. Female lions can catch much bigger prey when they hunt together than when alone and are more likely to have a successful hunt when hunting together. In addition, lactating females will permit cubs other than their own to nurse, and, during a hunt, a female may stay at the nest site to protect all of the young. Many of these advantages can be accounted for with mutualism since all the females in the pride gain from such an arrangement.

Similarly, a pair of male lions can take over a pride from the resident male much more easily than one can (this occurs even when the invaders are not genetic brothers), and they can keep the pride for themselves much more easily against a lone male intruder. In such cases, though one male lion will still be dominant, this male will accept the other male as a partner and permit it to mate with receptive females, if the other male gets to a receptive female first. Although we are accustomed to assume that prides of lions are ruled by one large, dominant male, there are documented cases of prides having as many as seven resident adult males. As with female lions, the cooperative strategy of male lions can be accounted for to some extent by the gain all individuals receive from collaborating. But again, this is not really altruism since all cooperative males gain reproductive success by using this strategy.

To cite another example, we move to the open plains of the southern United States. It is there that we find the prairie dog (actually, a kind of ground squirrel, *Cynomys ludovicianus*). Prairie dogs live in social groups in underground passages that they dig out and maintain over periods of years. The tunnels they dig have entrances, multiple passages, and alternate exits. If, for example, a predatory snake invades the tunnels, the prairie dogs can escape by running out the exits. Both coyotes and badgers prey on prairie dogs when they can, but both also have difficulties. Badgers (*Taxidea taxus*) can dig through the prairie dog nests but are too slow to catch them. Coyotes (*Canis latrans*) can catch the dogs

Figure 13.1 Badger-coyote cooperation in pursuing prairie dogs that live in underground dens.

on open ground but cannot dig them out. Occasionally, a badger and a coyote will team up to their mutual advantage. While the coyote guards one exit, the badger will start digging the nest out at the entrance (see Figure 13.1). In this way, both animals gain a better chance of obtaining a meal, though they do not share their kills. This is an example of interspecific mutualism, a highly exceptional event in nature to be sure (as long as we discount our pets as instances of mutualism). Of course, one instance of badger-coyote cooperation may also be one animal simply taking advantage of the other, but many instances of badger-coyote pairings have been observed.

Badgers and coyotes demonstrate how mutual cooperation can even be a strategy that occurs between species, not just within. Recently, this same idea has been used by some theorists to explain how human beings and dogs began to associate with each other. The modern domestic dog in all of its forms or breeds is descended from a species of wolf that began to associate with humans over 12,000 years ago. It is thought that initially these dogs probably served as guards and alarms for human encampments while the dogs gained a steady food supply. The breeding of dogs for specific behavioral and physical traits may have begun when humans began to take advantage of the dog's capacity for both speed and detecting scents for hunting purposes.

In summary, examples of mutualism are frequently found in nature, and such phenomena do not present a serious challenge to evolutionary theory. They represent instances of cooperation that benefit all individuals involved, rather than true altruism.

Reciprocity

Reciprocity is similar to mutualism, but cooperating animals in this arrangement cannot help each other at the same time. So, in **reciprocity,** animal B helps animal A now, while A helps B later—a sort of tit-for-tat arrangement. This occurs all the time in human relations but is more difficult to understand in animals because it is not immediately clear why A wouldn't just "cheat" and not bother to help B later.

Prisoner's Dilemma

The specific conditions under which reciprocity (sometimes called reciprocal altruism) could evolve as a stable strategy in a species were not clear initially. Trivers (1971) began to clarify the concept, and Axelrod and Hamilton (1981) made great progress by using a game called the **prisoner's dilemma,** which works as follows: two players, A and B, can choose either to cooperate or to "defect" (not cooperate), but A must choose first. This situation leads to four possible outcomes, summarized in Table 13.1.

The table shows that, in one game (each player making one choice), the greatest reward for A (5) occurs when A defects and B cooperates. However, mutual cooperation provides the greatest reward for both players together (a total of 6, or 3 for each player) but not for the individual. The game illustrates that how well one player does depends on what the other player does. This game serves as a sort of minimodel for how reciprocity might have evolved in nature. When two animals of the same species encounter one another, each can either cooperate (e.g., share resources) or be selfish. The question is, what happens as the game "evolves" and the same players continue to be given the same options?

Axelrod and Hamilton (1981) showed that the strategy that tends to win over time in repeated trials is tit for tat: cooperate on the first move, then do whatever the other player did on subsequent moves. Axelrod and

TABLE 13.1   **Prisoner's Dilemma Game Results**

Player A	Player B Cooperation	Defection
Cooperation	reward for A = 3	reward for A = 0
Defection	reward for A = 5	reward for A = 1

Hamilton (1981) argued that this outcome illustrates how cooperation based on reciprocity could get started in less social animals. Moreover, they argued, reciprocity can become an ESS (evolutionarily stable strategy) when rewards are maximized for the individuals that use it.

One of the main points is that reciprocity as a survival strategy will never evolve in asocial animals that meet only once by chance. The reason for this should be clear: once animal A receives aid from animal B, and they never meet again, it always pays A to cheat or defect. Asocial animals will never reciprocate and have no reason to evolve reciprocity as a strategy. Therefore, the question that arises mainly deals with the situation where A and B are social animals and will likely meet again in the future an indefinite number of times.

Costs and Benefits

Once established, reciprocity will tend to persist when individuals continue to receive opportunities to cooperate, when benefits to the receiver exceed the costs to the donor, and when donors recognize defectors and stop rewarding them. In the event that an individual defects and refuses to reciprocate, the animal should not be able to get away with it if reciprocity is to work—there must be some kind of effective retaliation against the defector (e.g., refusing to interact with the individual any further). For this to happen, the individuals must be able to recognize and remember cheaters, or they must be animals who frequently encounter each other in the same place. Thus, for reciprocity to be a stable strategy, the probability of the same individuals meeting again must be high, or defection may gain the individual a payoff that cannot be resisted. Let's look at some examples of species where reciprocity is typical.

The black hamlet fish (*Hypoplectus nigricans*) is an animal that has both male and female sex organs (a hermaphrodite). Near sunset, pairs of fish will get together to spawn or exchange eggs and sperm, but they do this in a certain way: they take turns alternately releasing eggs or sperm, back and forth, trading little amounts of egg and sperm for two hours. As predicted by the reciprocity model, the fish giving eggs (who has to go first) will stop giving eggs if it sees that its mate doesn't subsequently give eggs itself. If it gave all its eggs up at once, then the second fish could fertilize them with sperm but cheat and not give up its eggs later (Fischer 1980). Taking turns guarantees that each fish will succeed with both its eggs and sperm.

Several species of vampire bats exist in South America, and Wilkinson (1984) has studied one that lives in Costa Rica (*Desmodus rotundus*). At night, these small bats (weighing only 1 ounce) seek out large domestic mammals such as llamas or cattle. Generally, they open a small vein in the animal's shoulder, rump, or leg and lap up the blood as it oozes out. They feed exclusively on blood, and chemicals in the bat's

Figure 13.2   Vampire bats roosting together.

mouth prevent the blood from clotting (see Figure 13.2). Despite their horrifying name, these bats are harmless to humans, and the cattle they feed on do not even feel the wounds they receive or suffer any long-term ill effects. However, bats can infect cattle with rabies.

In the morning, these bats return to their group roosting places in hollow trees. Because each bat needs about five teaspoons of blood each night to survive, those who haven't managed to obtain a meal will beg for some regurgitated blood from the others. Often they obtain some blood from roost mates who are well fed.

Wilkinson marked 200 bats that roosted in 14 different trees; he spent 400 hours keeping track of their interactions. He noted 110 cases of blood sharing, most often a mother bat sharing blood with her offspring. But some bats gave blood to unrelated adults with whom they shared their roost. In every case, the blood-sharing interactions conformed to the predictions of reciprocity theory: individual bats only helped those that roosted near them (and whom they were likely to meet again), and those who were helped tended to reciprocate later.

A cost-benefit analysis helps us to understand what happens here. Whereas a starving bat may benefit greatly from a small amount of blood from a cohort, the well-fed cohort probably will not miss a little blood when it has fed well. Thus, when it helps, the donor may be making a good investment in helping its cohort that will then survive and maybe help the donor at some later date when the donor has the same problem getting a meal during the night. Those bats that did not reciprocate were not fed again later by their neighbors; as we have noted, cheating or failing to reciprocate must be punished or the system of reciprocity cannot work. This situation illustrates all three of the main requirements for reciprocity to occur: (1) the animals must be social and meet often, (2) cheaters must be remembered and not be rewarded in the future, and (3) the cost-benefit principle must apply (i.e., the gain to the recipient must be greater than the loss to the donor).

Evidence of reciprocity in nature is most obvious in the primates, including ourselves. Grooming in monkeys and mating collaborations in baboons, for example, illustrate reciprocity in action: one male baboon will solicit help from another in fighting a larger male for a female in heat, and while the helper fights the male, the original solicitor will run off with the female and mate with her! But this only occurs because the solicitor, on a subsequent occasion, will reverse roles with the helper (Packer 1977). This is true reciprocity, for in monkeys, baboons, and apes, memory is highly developed. Therefore, reciprocity can occur days and weeks later because these animals will remember who helped or who cheated. Furthermore, primates often live in structured social groups where frequent future meetings are inevitable, so cheating is not likely to pay off.

As we have seen, mutualism and reciprocity are cooperative strategies that are designed to provide a long-term gain for each individual involved. Neither really conforms to our original definition of altruism. When examined closely, though, neither contradicts the "selfish" principles of Darwin's theory. Can we really find instances of true altruism in nature?

Kin Selection

The silver-backed jackal (*Canis mesomelas*) lives in monogamous pairs on the plains and brushlands of Africa. The pair defend their territory, hunt together, and share food and parental duties (see Figure 13.3). It is common for the previous year's offspring to stay and help their parents with a new litter, including regurgitating food for the lactating mother jackal and her pups. They do this rather than going off and finding a mate, establishing their own territory, and having their own young. Why do these offspring stay around and help their parents? This situation appears to conform more to the idea of true altruism since the individual offspring apparently sacrifice their own individual reproductive success to increase that of their parents.

Figure 13.3   A silver-backed jackal.

Why animals might help in this way was not well understood until the 1960s when the most complex theory of cooperation and altruism was initially developed by W. D. Hamilton (1964). This theory, called **kin selection,** is organized around the simple observation that most of the cooperation, helping, and true altruism we see in nature are done by relatives of the recipient. Donors are much more likely to be seen helping recipients who are the donor's relatives rather than strangers within a species. Thus, the theory of kin selection seeks to explain some kinds of altruism ultimately on the basis of genes.

This is a difficult theory to explain briefly and to understand in its entirety, so let's try a less formal account first. With this theory, we must assume that in the population there are genes for "helping" that some individuals have more of, others less so. So, for example, if offspring jackals help their parents raise new youngsters, as they do (rather than having their own new offspring), this behavior must in part have some degree of heritability.

Second, Darwin's theory tells us that if genes for helping increase the reproductive success of the parents over those that are not helped, then the gene will spread into the population and there will be more helping genes. We have already discussed this consequence of natural selection in several different contexts: *whatever increases reproductive success will tend to become more frequent in the gene pool of the population.* That is, whatever works tends to proliferate, whatever doesn't tends to disappear—the principle of natural selection, in a nutshell. If those jackals that carry genes for helping are more successful at reproducing offspring than jackals without such genes, genes for helping will become a part of the population.

So far there is no contradiction with Darwin's theory, but neither of these principles answers the most difficult question here: what's in this system for the individual helper? Helping one's parents reproduce more means that the helper will reproduce less or not at all (conforming to our definition of altruism), a fact that, on the surface, appears to contradict Darwin's theory of natural selection. But does it? If we define "success" as having offspring come from an individual's own sperm or egg cells, then, by definition, the individual cannot succeed with altruism or helping—it can only lose. But kin selection theory does not define reproductive success this way. Rather, it redefines reproductive success as passing the *information* that genes supply on to offspring. To some extent, an individual's genetic relatives carry the same genes—the same information—as the individual does. According to this new definition of genetic success, the individual can experience some reproductive success by ensuring that its genetic relatives reproduce as well. Therefore, the term *kin selection* implies that an individual has a genetic investment in having its kin (genetic relatives) reproduce in addition to having its own reproductive success.

Inclusive Fitness

Now, there are a few technicalities involved in understanding this theory correctly. First, the degree of relatedness between individuals can be expressed as a number called the coefficient of relatedness or r, a short way of summarizing the proportion of genes that two individuals (on the average) will have in common. Note that the average genetic relationship between one individual and its offspring and that same individual and its siblings is the same, namely, 50%:

Relationship	Average r coefficient
parent-child	.50
siblings	.50
grandparent-grandchild	.25
half-siblings	.25
aunt/uncle-niece/nephew	.25
cousins	.125

The theory of natural selection says that individuals try to reproduce their own genes in the genes of the population. The individual can do this by mating and producing offspring. But when genes are regarded as information, an individual's relatives share many of those same genes. Therefore, another way to get genes into the gene pool is to have relatives reproduce. Kin selection refers to this process by which a behavioral act is favored by natural selection due to its beneficial effects on the relatives that share the individual's genes.

If the gene causes the donor to help the recipients, but the donor genes are not reproduced, the gene will die out, finally resulting in no helping in the population. But if the gene causes the donor to help the recipients, and helping *increases* this gene in the gene pool (through others reproducing), then helping will become part of the species' genes. Let's take an even more extreme example. Let's say a gene causes an animal to make the ultimate sacrifice, to die to save its relatives. When this individual dies, its individual genes will be lost, but there will be a net genetic gain in the population if the act saves more than two siblings ($2+ \times .50 = 1+$), more than four nieces and nephews ($4+ \times .25 = 1+$), or more than eight cousins ($8+ \times .125 = 1+$)! Another way to express this idea is with Hamilton's rule, $B/C > r$: the ratio of reproductive benefits to costs must be greater than r (heritability) for altruism to evolve over a long time.

Clearly, kin selection broadens Darwin's concept of fitness to include the individual's fitness plus the reproductive fitness of its close relatives since all of these individuals will produce similar genes in their offspring. Thus, the theory says that reproductive fitness should be redefined as **inclusive fitness,** which is the summed effect of all fitness sources including kin selection.

Let's return to our silver-backed jackal family. Moehlman (1979, 1987) studied these animals in the wild and found that the number of pups that survived to adulthood correlated highly with the number of helpers in the family. Actually, each helper increased the number of survivors on the average by a factor of 1.5 (i.e., for each pup that survived from a pair without helpers, 1.5 pups survived from a pair with helpers). So there was a definite gain in reproductive success for the parent jackals when they had helpers living with them.

On the surface, it appears that helpers gain no reproductive success, but helpers are 50% genetically related to their siblings. Thus, by helping their parents and promoting the survival of their siblings, the helpers do gain some reproductive success genetically. In fact, on the average, they gain about as much genetic reproductive success from surviving siblings as they would from their own offspring since their genetic relationship to their own offspring and to their siblings is the same (50%).

Influence of the Environment

The reproductive gains that come about through altruism and kin selection do not occur independently of the environmental conditions in which the animal is found. In general, we should expect helping to occur more in tough, demanding environments where it is difficult for a new, young adult to survive or find a mate on its own. This is exactly the kind of situation where helping behavior by relatives has been found most often in nature. The jackals, for example, live in a hot, dry environment where competition for scarce food resources is intense, where predators are numerous, and where group hunting is more successful than individuals going it alone. Resources are barely adequate for the two monogamous jackal parents to raise their normal litter of young. Therefore, it is very helpful if offspring from previous years are around to bring the young as much as 30% of their food, as well as to guard, protect, and teach the young their skills.

In addition, in this kind of environment, the helpers may also benefit from helping in ways other than immediate reproductive success. For example, the young helpers may gain valuable learning experiences in rearing the young, and they may become familiar with the home territory, part of which they might gain at a later time. These learning experiences may contribute to the helper's own breeding success at a later date and eventually increase its lifetime reproductive potential.

If the environment is plentiful with resources and helping is not needed by the parents, helping will not occur. Instead, individuals will find their own territories and try to reproduce on their own. We should expect to see altruism or helping occur when helping produces more offspring than not breeding at all. But we should expect to see no helping when resources are plentiful and the helpers are not really needed for the young to survive, that is, when not helping produces more offspring for the donor than helping does.

This theory, which has received wide acceptance in biology, is an extension of and not a contradiction to Darwin's theory, provided that we accept the new definition of fitness as inclusive fitness and regard genes as information rather than actual reproductive cells. This theory predicts that an individual will value another's reproduction to the extent the individuals are related, that is, to the extent to which they have genes in common. Relatedness matters in this kind of inclusive selection because natural selection is a matter of the survival and proliferation of some genes at the expense of others, and relatives share more genes than nonrelatives.

We can point to many other examples of this in nature. Ground squirrels and prairie dogs use alarm calls to warn the other animals in the nest of an approaching predator, thereby putting themselves in more danger from the predator (Sherman 1977). But this occurs primarily among related females (mothers, daughters, sisters) that occupy the same burrows; it doesn't occur much among strangers or unrelated males.

Tasmanian native hens (*Tribonyx mortierii*) have wife sharing as a common practice, even when one male is dominant and another submissive. This occurs most often when the males are brothers; both mate with the female, share nesting duties, and raise the young. Remember: brothers share half their genes (Maynard Smith and Ridpath 1972).

Kin Recognition

Finally, for this theory to work, of course, the animals have to be able to *recognize* their kin—to distinguish their relatives from other species members. There are at least three possible mechanisms for how kin recognition might occur, as described by Holmes and Sherman (1983):

1. *Recognition by place.* Animals recognize other animals as relatives by virtue of their being in a certain place. An animal might use a rule of thumb like, "Treat anyone in my home as kin." This rule probably would suffice for many bird species for which only relatives would normally be in the same nest. Of course, brood parasitic birds like the cowbird described in Chapter 12 can take advantage of the limitations of this mechanism by laying their eggs in the nests of other birds that fail to distinguish their own eggs from those of the invader.

2. *Recognition by association.* Some animals might learn who their kin is while growing up, by imprinting or by making learned associations to their kin early in life (as in the imprinting in many waterbirds, discussed in Chapter 12). Porter, Wynick, and Pankey (1978) found that young spiny mice (*Acomys cahirinus*) preferred to huddle together with their siblings rather than with unrelated mice pups. To assess the effect of early experience, Porter and colleagues (1978) separated litters of sibling pups after birth and established new litters of unrelated pups. These pups preferred to huddle in groups with their unrelated littermates rather than their actual siblings. Thus, in this species, sibling recognition appears to be created by the spiny mouse's early contact with other mice.

3. *Phenotype matching.* Animals may regard as kin those individuals most similar to themselves in some characteristic that is easy to see or detect, such as a visual feature or an odor—a process called **phenotype matching.** After all, if two animals are very similar in odor or appearance, they probably have some similar genes. Social insects like ants, termites, and bees identify their own group almost completely by chemical scents called pheromones, which are unique to each dominant queen ant, termite, or bee.

There is no reason why more than one mechanism might be operational in some species. For example, Holmes and Sherman (1982) did experiments on kin recognition in two species of ground squirrels. Their experiments showed that females tended to be more cooperative with other females they were raised with in the burrow (implying that recognition is learned to some degree), but they were most cooperative with their full siblings who they may have recognized phenotypically (supporting the importance of kin selection).

The occasional failure of recognition mechanisms gives us an account of why totally unrelated animals sometimes help each other: the

Figure 13.4   A Florida scrub jay.

donor may mistake the recipient as one of its relatives! The Florida scrub jay (*Apelocoma coerulescens*), for example, is one of the most studied birds in terms of helping behaviors (see Figure 13.4.) This is a medium-sized blue bird that lives in the patchy brush areas of Florida, where, in general, the habitat is scarce for resources, except in isolated grassy patches. Here the birds live year-round in monogamous breeding pairs in the same territory. About half the pairs go it alone. The other half have, on the average, about 1.8 helpers that assist in feeding the young, sounding warning calls, and defending the nest against predators. The helpers are generally one- to two-year-old birds related to the breeding pair:

- 64% are older children helping their parents
- 24% are children helping one parent (whose mate is gone)
- 12% are other relatives
- 4% of the helpers are unrelated birds

Woolfenden and Fitzpatrick (1984) discovered all this by tracking the birds carefully and by keeping detailed records over many years. The helpers are both male and female, but males tend to stay around as helpers longer.

So, what reproductive advantages are gained in this situation? Obviously, the breeders gain quite a lot: they can rear more young while the helpers assist in defending the nest and bring the young as much as 30% of their food. The helpers also gain some potential genetic profit: they help rear their younger siblings, which are as genetically related to them ($r = .50$) as would be their own offspring. Additionally, the helper may receive some training that it benefits from when it goes it alone. But is it really worth it to stay home and help rather than getting your own nest and offspring?

There is no question that the helper could do better if it had its own breeding and nesting territory, but that's exactly the problem with scrub jays: the habitat is saturated with its own species and there are typically no other nesting sites available. The optimal strategy for the species is influenced by the ecology or habitat constraints. In addition, male helpers in this situation can gain another benefit: often the territorial males can inherit part of the breeding space from their father, especially if they assist in making the territory larger. Thus, males tend to stay around longer than females, and females gain fewer benefits from helping, encouraging them to leave and seek out their own nests sooner.

If there were a lot more patches and resources available, the motive to help would disappear as every mature bird would try to establish its own nest. Thus, the helpers must gain some benefit or investment (future benefit) from helping in order for helping to evolve. Ultimately, this is consistent with Darwin's theory—there has to be something in it for them or helping would make no sense.

Returning to our initial question about the failure of recognition mechanisms, the study showed that 4% of the helpers were unrelated to the recipients. Most likely, if we accept our general kin selection theory, these are birds who mistook the recipients for their relatives. We should not expect the recognition mechanisms in these animals to be perfect and error free. Of course, as Krebs and Davies (1993) suggest, there are reasons other than recognition failure for unrelated helpers to help. Helping may be a form of payment for permission to remain in the territory, with the possibility of taking over later. The helper may also gain help later in time from the nest owner's offspring. Thus, there may be several long-term investments in being a helper.

Let us summarize some central points with regard to kin selection theory:

1. Helpers tend to be relatives of the breeders and therefore have some genetic investment in seeing the offspring survive.
2. Helping occurs only when resources are relatively scarce, and helping relatives becomes a reproductive strategy that competes successfully with going it alone.
3. Helping (at least in vertebrates) is usually not a permanent life condition but a temporary state of affairs that can change when the environment changes. Helpers often become breeders later.

Eusociality

The most extreme form of altruism in nature is primarily represented in insects, namely, ants, termites, and some species of bees, wasps, and aphids. These organisms have social systems that are so unique that they

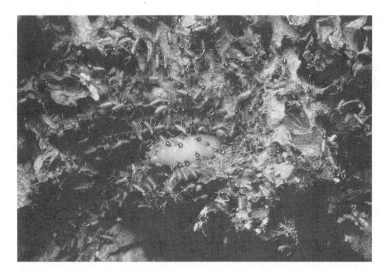

Figure 13.5   Eusocial insects: red termite workers supply food to the queen termite, the only reproducing female in the nest.

are described by a unique term, **eusociality.** By definition, eusociality always involves cooperative care of the young, division of labor into sterile **castes** or groups that perform functions not performed by others, generational overlap, and the production of many offspring. Thus, in a eusocial society, many members give up their biological capacity to reproduce (in other words, they're sterile) to a few individuals—their sisters, the other "queen" termites, ants, or bees. (See Figure 13.5.)

The main problem with the eusocial insects is accounting for how such a system could have evolved in the first place. These questions are by no means settled yet. There are several theories on how such eusocial insect systems could have evolved, and we do not have the space to address the technicalities of these theories here. While such theories are complex, a central assumption underlying all of them is that eusociality evolved partly as a function of kin selection. To clarify its relevance here, we will examine in some detail the life pattern of one eusocial insect species, the red ant, and one vertebrate species, the naked mole-rat, whose reproductive pattern resembles that of the eusocial insects.

Red Ants

The red ant (*Myrmica rubra*) is common in Europe and typifies most ant societies. In August or September, winged male and female ants mate in midair, the only stage at which the males exist at all! The males die soon after mating, and the fertilized female or queen ant lands, loses her wings, and digs a nest either under a flat stone, in an old stump, or in soil. The queen spends the winter alone in her nest without needing food yet, and lays some of her thousands of eggs in the spring.

In the summer, the eggs develop into larvae (a wormlike stage) that mature into sterile adult female workers, which live at most for three years. (In other ant societies, some larvae—fed a different diet—develop into soldier ants that protect the hive.) The matured workers bring food to both the younger larvae and the queen, who gradually lays more eggs. It is the sterile female workers in the ant colony that do all the work: they gather food, dig out further passages in the nest, take care of the young, feed the queen, and defend the colony from intruders (usually other insects).

After about nine years, the nest contains roughly 1,000 workers and the same queen, who has laid almost all her original eggs by now. At this point in time, the queen lays special fertilized eggs that develop into new winged females. She also lays unfertilized eggs that become winged males produced for a new nuptial flight and that will carry the hive's genes to a new location. When the old queen dies a few years later, the entire colony dies with her.

What is remarkable is that the three castes typical in ant societies (queens, workers, and soldiers) do not differ from each other genetically! Which caste the ant becomes is a function of the environmental conditions that prevail during the larval stage, typically, nutrition (what they're fed) and temperature.

Bee societies have a similar genetic arrangement. However, in bee societies, the workers often live only for three to ten weeks, making it necessary for the queen to constantly produce new workers. Whereas ants ordinarily have caste systems (individuals physically adapted to perform only certain tasks), bees typically do all the jobs of the hive but at different stages of their lives. So each bee helps clean the hive, look for flowers, feed the larvae, or attend the queen, but it does these tasks at different stages of its life. Thus, there is division of labor but not castes. (Note that not all ant and bee species are organized societies; some are solitary foragers, some are individual nest builders, some are predators.)

All of the members of one hive or ant colony are sisters, sharing many genes with each other and their queen mother. The eusocial insects (ants, bees, termites) have evolved with genetic relationships consistent with the theory of kin selection: sisters can sacrifice themselves for the nest kin because only the new queens (also their sisters) need to reproduce for all. Therefore, the entire nest can gear its activity to find food, protect the queen, or produce more eggs under the control of chemicals given out by the queen. Sometimes the behavior of insect societies can appear to us to be very intelligently planned and coordinated, but to an extent this is an illusion. All of the control is through genes and pheromones, not intellect. But, as a group and by some criteria, the ants can be regarded as the most successful organism on earth! It has been estimated that ants altogether make up perhaps one-tenth of all the animal biomass (physical mass) on the earth, including every mammal, insect, reptile, bird, worm, whale, elephant, human being, rodent, and cockroach you can find! There may be as many as 4 quadrillion ants on earth—a *very* large number!

Unusual Genetics

Ant genetics operate in a very strange way, and this method is the secret to its reproductive system and perhaps to why ants are a eusocial society. Like us, the female ants, including the queen, have DNA molecules that split into two parts (hence, they are called **diploid**), with each reproductive cell getting 50% of the queen ant's genes. So the sterile ant workers have half of their genes in common with their mother. But the male ant is different: a male is produced when the queen allows an egg to mature without fertilization. Therefore, the male has only half the genes of the female (called **haploid,** meaning "half")! Males are produced only when the queen matures and only for the purpose of spreading the hive's genes to a new location. In other words, males are used for nothing more than reproduction.

When the flying queen mates with a male (or sometimes several males) early in her life, the fertilized eggs receive 50% of her genes but 100% of the male's genes. Each genetic contribution forms a new female whose genes from the queen will differ across individuals but whose genes from their father will be identical. Although males cannot have sons (since males must mate with a queen to reproduce), they can have grandsons (when their daughters, new queens, lay unfertilized eggs).

When the queen produces new queens that will fly away and establish new hives, these new queens are the sisters of the sterile hive workers they have left, and the new queens have three-fourths of their genes in common with their sisters (since all got one-half of their genes from their mother but all of their father's genes). The inclusive fitness and kin selection principles already discussed try to explain why ants have evolved a society where most of the workers (and soldiers) are sterile and do not reproduce. Kin selection predicts that this kind of society can evolve when the offspring have many genes in common with the sterile workers. In other words, it's not necessary for every individual to be active sexually and reproduce individually if the system guarantees that the individual's genes will be passed on to the next generation through the reproductive mechanisms of others. An extremely high coefficient of relatedness can lead to the most extreme form of altruism—eusociality.

This kind of **haplodiploidal** arrangement in nature occurs only in the eusocial insects—ants, termites, aphids, and some bees and wasps.

These animals are so self-sacrificial for the hive or colony because, whereas one individual can be destroyed easily, its genes are secure in the other members of the hive and in the new queens that will eventually fly away and propagate the species. In those species of wasps and bees that are not social, we typically do not see the strange genetic arrangement of haplodiploidy.

Naked Mole-Rats

Are there any vertebrate animals for which the pattern of life is anything like that of the social insects? There is one—the naked mole-rat (*Heterocephalus glaber*) of East Africa. Neither a mole nor a rat, these are small, relatively hairless, pink, and almost blind rodents (pictured in Figure 13.6). They live their entire lives underground in burrows and tunnels that they dig with their large front incisor teeth, which can chew through rock-hard soil. They feed on roots and tubers that they encounter as they dig their tunnels. One colony of mole-rats may occupy tunnels that extend over 3 kilometers, take up an area the equivalent of 20 football fields, and consist of hundreds of football-size chambers. The mole-rats tend to live in and move to those chambers nearest their current food supply.

Figure 13.6   Naked mole-rats in their underground nest.

The social organization of naked mole-rats has been described in a book by Sherman, Jarvis, and Alexander (1991) and in an article by Sherman, Jarvis, and Braude (1992). According to these authors, although one colony may contain as many as 80 individual mole-rats, one female "queen," the largest animal in the colony, breeds with only one to three males in the entire colony. The other adult females function as workers but have undeveloped ovaries and so do not reproduce, much like ant and termite workers. The other males are capable of breeding but do not. There is also some specialization of function dependent on the size of the individual. Younger, smaller mole-rats search for food and transport nest materials through the tunnels. Older, slightly larger members clear the tunnels of debris (Honeycutt 1992). The oldest and largest individuals dig tunnels and defend the colony against snakes or other invaders by attacking them or trying to bury them in soil. (Many naked mole-rats are preyed upon by snakes.)

Chemical cues appear to be involved in how the colony functions but how these cues work is not well understood. Mole-rats also demonstrate a considerable repertoire of vocalizations in order to communicate with each other. When not caring for her large litters of young, the queen roams the tunnels at will and enforces submissive gestures from her willing subjects. If the queen dies, the largest remaining females may fight each other until a new queen is determined.

How could such a system as this evolve in a mammal that has a reproductive biology similar to that of other mammals? Part of the answer lies with kin selection theory. When genetic fingerprinting studies of a colony of naked mole-rats were performed, it was discovered that individuals in the colony had, on the average, 81% of their genes in common! Moreover, the breeding males that the queen mates with may include her brothers and male offspring (Faulkes, Abbott, and Mellnor 1990; Reeve, Westneat, Noon, Sherman, and Aquadro 1990). This inbreeding in mole-rats and their consequent high genetic relatedness may partly explain how they have evolved a eusocial system. The fact that all the colony members are closely related to each other produces exactly the conditions under which theorists would predict that group members could give up their individual reproductive potential to one individual, the queen.

But other environmental pressures such as their subterranean habitat and the dangers of leaving the nest may also have played a role in mole-rat evolution. In most species of mammals, one sex (usually females) will live near the area they were born in while the other sex (usually males) will disperse to a new area. In naked mole-rats, neither males nor females apparently leave their original nest colony, contributing to inbreeding and higher genetic homogeneity. It's understandable why they don't leave the nest. Above ground and in daylight they would be helpless against predators. The mole-rats' breeding system has evolved probably in part because dispersal and independent breeding are so difficult.

Summary

Altruism, or unselfish cooperative behavior between animals in nature, appears to fly in the face of Darwin's theory that individuals will self-ishly promote their own reproductive success. Consequently, biologists have developed several theories to explain how apparent altruism can actually be understood as a product of largely selfish motivations.

In mutualism, animals help each other and each individual benefits. In the case of lions, for example, two male lions can defend their pride of females more effectively than one can, thereby ensuring that each obtains greater reproductive success than in a situation where there is only one resident male.

In reciprocity, one animal aids the other first and the other returns the favor later. The problem here is to understand how reciprocity could evolve when the initial recipient of aid can "cheat" and not return the favor. Game theory and empirical evidence have helped clarify the conditions under which reciprocity evolves. For one thing, the benefits to the recipient must outweigh the costs to the donor. Reciprocity also evolves only in social animals that meet frequently and in situations where cheaters can be punished if they do not reciprocate. Reciprocity occurs in vampire bats, which donate ingested blood to their neighbors when only some bats are successful in a given night's foraging.

In some species, older offspring remain with their parents and help raise the current year's offspring. This situation is typical, for example, of silver-backed jackals and Florida scrub jays. Helpers here appear to conform more closely to the definition of altruism: individuals sacrifice their own reproductive success while increasing that of others. Such situations inspired the development of the kin selection theory of W. D. Hamilton, a theory basing apparent altruism on "self-ish genes." In kin selection theory, individual fitness is redefined as inclusive fitness—the summed effect of all individuals with the same genes. Thus, Hamilton's theory postulates that individuals can gain reproductive success by helping their genetic relatives (kin) reproduce. An individual helping its kin is more likely to occur under environmental conditions that make it difficult for the individual to raise its own offspring. The silver-backed jackal, for instance, lives in a tough environment in which monogamy and helpers are needed for the young to survive. In addition, for kin selection theory to work, animals must be able to distinguish their kin from other individuals; several mechanisms can account for kin recognition, including place learning, imprinting, and phenotype matching.

The most altruistic animals are the eusocial ants, bees, and wasps. In these species, individuals have given up their ability to reproduce to one individual in the colony—the queen. Workers are all sterile females, and males are only used for reproduction. Eusocial red ants benefit from division of labor, cooperative care of the young, and the production of many workers as needed. Biologists explain the evolution of eusociality with kin selection since ant workers in one colony share 75% of their genes in common rather than the usual 50%. The only mammals whose lifestyle resembles that of the eusocial insects are some species of naked mole-rats of Africa. They live in large underground colonies where one queen breeds while others tend the young, search for food, or defend the colony. Naked mole-rats in one colony share a large proportion of common genes because of inbreeding within the colony.

Part 4

Our Closest Relatives: The Primates

Primates are the order of mammals that includes not only our nearest relatives in the animal world but also ourselves.

Because of their similarities to humans, other primates have been of particular interest to biologists, anthropologists, and psychologists for many reasons. For instance, some living primates such as baboons and chimpanzees have served as models for how earlier humans evolved and behaved. Comparisons of humans with their closest genetic relatives reveal the unique physical and behavioral traits of humans. Primates also provide scientists with living subjects that sometimes can be studied in ways not possible with human beings (as discussed in Chapters 2 and 16), but which yield conclusions that may apply to humans. For these and other reasons, the last four chapters of this book focus on the lifestyles of a variety of primate species (including humans), the ecological circumstances under which their survival strategies evolved and thrive, and the relationships between primate and human behavior. Although few new principles are introduced in these chapters, the material presented here affords the opportunity for the student to apply most of the principles described in the preceding chapters to those animals that yield the most direct implications for understanding ourselves.

CHAPTER 14

Primate Patterns

In this and the next chapter, we will survey the lives of selected nonhuman primate species. As a group of mammals, primates display a great range of sizes, lifestyles, and adaptive behaviors. While some living species dwell on the ground and others in trees, primates in general have an evolutionary history of tree living. Primate adaptations to ground and tree living, and to a variety of food supplies, have led to the great variety in their behaviors and social structures.

In the current chapter, we will examine in some detail the lives of six living primate species, including two prosimians and four monkeys. In Chapter 15, we will move on to the lesser apes and the four living species of great apes (though there are a number of subspecies). Discussing primates in the order of prosimians, monkeys, apes, and humans reflects the order in which these groups of animals are presumed to have evolved, with living humans likely the most recent of primates to emerge.

What Is a Primate?

Primate Characteristics

Primates live primarily in tropical climates of South America, Africa, and Asia. Living primates display an amazing range of adaptive behaviors, habitats, reproductive strategies, and social organizations, as we shall see. The modern ecological understanding of how all the different primate lifestyles evolved began with the work of Crook and Gartlan (1966), followed by that of Clutton-Brock and Harvey (1977). An excellent summary of different primate lifestyles is presented by Smuts, Cheney, Seyfarth, Wrangham, and Struhsaker (1986).

Prior to 65 million years ago, the earth was dominated by dinosaurs, and the only mammals were a small group of animals about the size of a mouse, something like today's insectivorous shrews (see Chapter 3, Figure 3.4). Most mammals were probably nocturnal, as indicated by fossils with large eye sockets. After the dinosaurs perished around 65 million B.C., the mammals began to radiate into many different habitats. They also began to evolve into many new forms, which we now identify as being the ancestors of all modern mammals.

Primate evolution probably began when the small, shrewlike ancestors of all mammals became arboreal, that is, they started living in trees. In fact, many primate characteristics can be regarded as initial adaptations to living in trees. Other than being arboreal, the main distinguishing traits of primates are the following:

1. *Five-digit hands with a thumb.*   When a thumb can be opposed to the forefinger, gripping power, precision, and dexterity are greatly increased. These abilities reach their culmination in human beings, which have the most sensitive and agile hands in nature.

2. *Nonspecialization.*   While primates largely kept all of the separate five digits of their early ancestors, many other lines of mammals evolved more specialized uses for their limbs. For example, in seals and dolphins, hands became flippers adapted for swimming; in ungulates and cattle species, hands became hooves for running; in carnivores like wolves and cats, hands became claws and paws.

3. *Limb flexibility.*   Living in trees caused primates to evolve unique abilities to rotate their arms in their sockets and rotate the hand 180 degrees without moving the arm or elbow. Only humans, apes, monkeys, and some prosimians have these abilities.

4. *Nails rather than claws.*   Nails leave the hand and digits free to feel and explore the environment, whereas claws are generally better for running, predation, and defense.

5. *Visual acuity.*   Great visual acuity is needed in arboreal species because any mistake in reaching or moving could mean a quick death. Thus, moving away from the ground decreased the importance of sensing scents left on the ground and increased dependence on vision. (The same process took place in birds; some species of birds have very little sense of smell at all.) Gradually, primates achieved frontally directed eyes and stereoscopic (3-D) vision, with acuity enhanced by color perception. In general, color vision is typical for animals that fly (e.g., birds and flying insects) or live in trees, but not for animals that stay on the ground (though some ground-dwelling animals such as dogs possess slight, if not good, color vision).

6. *Upright posture.*   When primates began to stand up and look around, they were able to scan their environment; this probably was the first step in the evolution of bipedal walking. In addition, this process freed the hands to deal with what the eyes could see.

Primate Classifications

On this earth are about 185 species of living primates, the exact number changing from year to year as new species are discovered and, occasionally, earlier species become extinct. The majority of these species are monkeys, divided into two groups—the "Old World" monkeys of Africa and Asia and the "New World" monkeys of Central and South America.

Prosimians are the group of primates that evolved first and are most like the ancestors of all modern primates. These are mainly the lemurs of Madagascar and the tarsiers, lorises, and bush babies of Africa. These animals tend to be small, nocturnal, and arboreal and eat mainly vegetation or insects.

Apes are thought to have evolved from the ancestors of Old World monkey stock approximately 30 million years ago. More recently, the ancestors of apes diverged into several different groups. About 12 million years ago, the gibbons split off first, followed by orangutans about 10 million years ago. It is now believed that human ancestors diverged from gorillas and chimpanzees roughly 6 million years ago, but these dates are often revised in light of new anthropological findings.

The most obvious characteristic that distinguishes apes from monkeys is that apes lack a tail (even though some prosimians also lack tails). They also all have arms that are longer than their legs, which allow them to brachiate or swing from branch to branch in the trees, though gorillas and chimps live on the ground most of the time. What we usually call the "great apes" belong to the family Pongidae, which includes only four living species: the gorilla (*Gorilla gorilla*), the largest of all primates, with three subspecies; the orangutan (*Pongo pygmaeus*), with several subspecies; and two species of chimpanzees—*Pan troglodytes,* the common chimp, and *Pan paniscus,* the bonobo or pygmy chimp.

In contrast to the prosimians, the apes are also sometimes called anthropoid apes from the Greek *anthropo,* meaning "human being." It's the same *anthropo-* used in the terms *anthropology* and *anthropomorphism.* Sometimes zoologists have also lumped us and all the greater and lesser apes and most monkeys (but not the tarsiers and lemurs) into a suborder (under Primates) called Anthropoidea. Similarly, human beings, their ancestors, and the great apes are sometimes placed in a "super-family" called Hominoidea, the Latin word for "manlike." In any case, these words emphasize how closely related we are to the apes and the similarities between us.

The gibbons and siamangs (nine species) or "lesser apes" belong to the family Hylobatidae. These smaller apes generally use very loud calls to mark their territory, are primarily tree dwellers, and are among the most acrobatic of all the primates, swinging by their arms from branch to branch in the trees (an activity called **brachiation**). Finally, the family Hominidae contains only one living species, *Homo sapiens,* humans.

Prosimians

Modern prosimians comprise approximately 35 species of lemurs, bush babies, pottos, lorises, and tarsiers. Their ancestors developed around 38 to 65 million years ago, before all other primate groups. These early prosimians spread much further north and south than today's tropical species due to the fact that those parts of the world were considerably warmer. Whereas most prosimian species that exist today are in Africa and tropical southern Asia, the lemurs are confined to one island off Africa: Madagascar.

Relative to other primates, modern prosimians are typically smaller, furry, arboreal, and nocturnal. Their diet consists of insects or plants. However, they are less humanlike than monkeys and apes because of their longer noses, more developed sense of smell, and smaller brains.

Creepers: Lorises

There are a number of prosimian species that are specialized for nocturnal hunting of insects. The lorises of Southeast Asia are two of these species and consist of the slender loris (*Loris tardigradus*) and the slow loris (*Nycticebus coucang*), pictured in Figure 14.1. These species are arboreal, nocturnal, slow-moving, and solitary.

The slow loris has large eyes set close together, no tail, a dark line down the middle of its back, and dark patches around its eyes. Its fingers and toes all have nails except for the second toe on each foot. Instead, it has a claw that it uses to groom its head and neck fur and its ears. Lorises have a naked, moist snout and a keen sense of smell. They also have the most vertebrae of any primates, enabling them to bend their bodies around the branches they climb on. Because of their low metabolic rate, lorises have thick fur, which they must have to keep warm even in tropical weather.

Both species of lorises live in dense forest areas and move slowly and deliberately along tree branches at night, stealthily catching insects, lizards, and birds' eggs and occasionally eating fruit and berries. To their advantage, lorises are adapted to eating many foul-smelling and bad-tasting insects rejected by other species, such as caterpillars, ants, fleas, beetles, and millipedes. Thus, a large food supply is readily available to them. Though they live in the same environment inhabited by many monkeys, they do not compete with them because monkeys are only active during the daytime and eat mainly fruit. With their strong gripping hands, lorises can travel on top of or underneath tree limbs. During the

Figure 14.1   A slow loris.

day, the loris sleeps in the crotch of a tree branch, head tucked under, with its hands and feet always tightly gripping the branches. If danger is present, the main defense that lorises use is to freeze. In fact, they can maintain a frozen position for several hours. However, if a predator like a snake approaches too closely, they may simply let go of a branch and drop to the earth below.

Loris females bear only one offspring per year, and the mother initially carries it around on her stomach fur. Later the mother loris will leave her youngster on a tree branch early in the night and retrieve it after she has fed. After a few weeks, the newborn loris will follow its mother or cling to her back as they travel over long distances. It is from the mother that the young loris learns what foods to eat.

In summary, lorises are small, solitary primates adapted for living at night in a dense tropical forest. They have evolved large eyes and slow movements because walking around on tree branches in darkness is precarious. They have also evolved the capacity to eat almost any insect they encounter, even those unpalatable to other insectivores.

Leapers: Lemurs

Lemurs are diurnal prosimians that evolved only on the island of Madagascar, probably because there were no monkey or ape species to compete with them. Lemurs have basically adapted to all habitats of the

Figure 14.2   A ring-tailed lemur.

Madagascar forests, resulting in a considerable range of forms—from the 5-inch mouse lemur, which is solitary, territorial, and aggressive, to the 4-foot-tall indri, which lives in small, peaceful family groups and makes spectacular leaps from tree to tree.

A typical lemuroid is the ring-tailed lemur (*Lemur catta*), pictured in Figure 14.2. This lemur is about the size of a domestic cat, has a foxlike nose, yellow eyes, and a very distinctive long, furry tail. It makes a sound similar to a cat's loud meow, but can also scream, grunt, and bark. This is the most common living prosimian and the one most frequently found in zoos. It can live as long as 25 years.

Ring-tails live in troops of up to 25 individuals, eat primarily leaves and fruit, and can leap from tree to tree in the forests of Madagascar. They are also agile on the ground and can cover short distances in a few galloplike bounds, though they do not stay on the forest floor for very long. Safety for the ring-tail is in the forest canopy.

Ring-tailed lemurs communicate with each other by means of calls, and they also use extensive scent marking. Ring-tails have three sets of scent glands: on the inside of the wrists, high up on the chest close to the armpits, and around the genitals. Lemurs navigating through vegetation or tree branches will rub these glands against whatever they touch; scents from troop members establish a territory as their own. Males also scent themselves extensively before skirmishes with other males by drawing their long tails through their glands.

Female dominance hierarchies are typical of lemur societies and provide the stable structure that governs ring-tail troops. At the top of the hierarchy is one alpha female and her accompanying coalition of beta females. The alpha female and her betas have first choice over feeding and resting sites, and they generally control all troop activities. Such power coalitions are unique to primates and are also typical of chimpanzees, as we shall see in Chapter 15. Every ring-tail female knows her place; few disputes occur because lower-ranking females consistently give way to more dominant ones. The alpha female displays her rank by standing up on her back legs, staring, and strutting around. If offended or challenged by a lower-ranking female, the alphas and betas may grab the subordinate animal's fur, bite her, or swipe at her with fingernails. Ring-tails usually fight by trying to scratch each other with their sharp nails exposed on quick, open hands.

Female ring-tails generally stay in their natal troop for life, whereas males often migrate to other troops—a pattern typical for many primates. Males are submissive to females for most of the year and belong to their own all-male group within the troop called the "bachelor group." The male group has its own dominance order, but this hierarchy is not as stable and permanent as the females' because each year some males leave the troop while new members join from other places. Males settle their dominance relationships with postural displays, chasing, and much more scent marking than that used by females. The bachelor group follows where the females lead.

A ring-tail troop occupies a large territory, which it will defend with warning barks and shouts flung across the trees. Actual encounters between troops, however, tend to be short lived and bloodless since territories are scent marked and well defined, and interlopers tend to leave immediately when warned. There is little real aggression and violence in ring-tails.

In March of every year, the adult females go into estrus: the area around their genitals swells up and they release reproductive pheromones. These chemical stimulants provoke changes in the males, which cause them to produce more sperm. In turn, males become more active and violent toward one another. At the beginning of this period of estrus, early in April, individual females may go off with single dominant male "consorts" to become a pair, staying together, grooming each other, and cuddling for awhile. But eventually the male "mating frenzy" takes over. Chaos begins to reign: normally low-ranking males challenge their superiors; former male coalitions are abandoned; males from other troops challenge the alpha males; male consorts have trouble keeping their female mates—all in response to the overpowering female hormones (Budnitz and Dainis 1975). Thus, males fight a great deal, and younger, less dominant males may mate when the dominant males are occupied elsewhere.

The mating frenzy is further complicated by the fact that the estrous females actually prefer to mate with the less dominant males! Thus, ring-tails are unusual (unlike baboons and chimps, for example) in that social dominance is not strongly related to reproductive success. This phenomenon may partly reflect the idea that an optimal level of dominance and aggression leads to mating success; too much aggression in the male ring-tail is repellent to the dominant females, which can and do exercise some choice over mates. Furthermore, some older ring-tail males accompany the females throughout the year and do not associate with the bachelor group. These sensitive, mild-mannered males participate in the female grooming activities, are submissive to the females, and may be the females' preferred consorts during the mating season (Russell 1993).

After a four-month gestation period, the female usually bears only one offspring at a time (sometimes twins), and this occurs during the dry season. The infant must grow into a medium-sized juvenile before the rainy season comes or its survival will be imperiled. Infant ring-tails are born relatively helpless, except for their strong grip that enables them to attach themselves to their mother's waist. However, as the infant grows, it shifts to riding on its mother's back.

Young ring-tails have many lessons to learn. For example, infants learn what to eat and how to behave appropriately by observing their mother and other ring-tails as they forage for food and interact. One of the most important lessons is learning their place in ring-tail society. Male and female infants of alpha females are privileged from birth, inheriting their mother's status to some extent. On the other hand, infants of low-ranking females lead miserable lives, enduring a great deal of abuse, dominance attacks, and occasionally physical harm from more dominant animals. Thus, these infants must learn how to be submissive in order to survive.

Mother ring-tails often sit on the ground together, resting and grooming each other, and alpha and beta females are attended to by all troop members. Young female attendants, called "aunts," babysit for the mother and probably learn many effective mothering techniques from interacting with the mothers and their infants. Male infant ring-tails are more curious and inquisitive than their female counterparts, and they venture away from their mothers sooner. Eventually, they join the bachelor group; their status in this group tends to mirror their mother's status in the female group.

In conclusion, lemurs like the ring-tail represent a considerable advance in behavioral complexity from the earlier, ratlike solitary prosimians. Lemurs are highly social animals that live in structured groups in which individuals must learn how to fit. The sense of smell is no longer used primarily to find prey but for social communication and territorial marking instead. Sexual behavior, on the other hand, is still under the control of seasonal pheromones, which tend to disrupt the normal living patterns that exist throughout the rest of the year.

New World Monkeys

Monkeys were the second group of primates to evolve, probably from prosimian ancestors, about 38 to 53 million years ago. Monkeys feature larger and more prominent skulls, greater intelligence, and full-color, 3-D vision. Their world is less dominated by smells and more by visual information. The New World monkeys probably developed earlier, mainly throughout the Americas, though modern New World monkeys only survive in Central and South America. These monkeys are also sometimes called *platyrrhines* (meaning "flat-nosed"), as opposed to the Old World monkeys, which are referred to as *catarrhines* (meaning "downward-pointing-nosed").

Callers: Howler Monkeys

Howlers are six species of the largest and most widespread monkeys of Central and South America. All are arboreal and diurnal, live in the rain forest, and eat mainly leaves. The red howler (*Alouatta seniculus*) is pictured in Figure 14.3. Howler males weigh about 15 to 20 pounds, with

Figure 14.3   A red howler monkey.

females somewhat smaller. Both have prehensile tails that they can use to grasp branches or support themselves.

Howlers feed primarily on low-sugar, low-nutrition leaves that make up 50% of their diet. In fact, many of their adaptations are adjustments to how little nutrition the leaves provide. For instance, they have a specialized colon containing bacteria specifically for digesting leaves. They also help themselves by being fussy about the kind of leaves they eat, gravitating toward sugary fruits, young leaves, and unusually nutritious plants. Their slow-moving lifestyle and sleeping or resting for half the day also help them to conserve energy. Howlers do not travel very far each day because so much of their food supply is abundant and easy to find.

The calls made by the male howlers are among the loudest sounds made by any creature and can be heard by as much as a kilometer away. They have a prominent larynx that can be seen as a bulge beneath their chins that helps amplify their sounds. A group of howlers that occupies a territory will howl loudly at dawn, informing other groups of their location. The howling permits different groups to avoid each other as they forage for food, thus avoiding conflict and territorial disputes. If different groups do encounter each other, the males may fight over fruit trees, but actual fighting among howlers is comparatively rare because smaller, less dominant groups tend to give way to larger ones.

Where populations of howlers are relatively low, howlers tend to live in small groups of one to three females, their young, and one male. Where population density is higher, howlers may form larger groups of up to 20 individuals, including several adult males. Density and group size tend to be a function of the abundance of food. There is some division of labor within howler groups; all of the parental care is done by females, whereas males provide leadership and settle any disputes.

In summary, howlers represent a very successful adaptation of monkeys to a readily available food source—leaves. Their peaceful lifestyle is due partly to the development of loud howling, which minimizes the waste of energy on aggressive encounters.

Squabblers: Squirrel Monkeys

The small squirrel monkeys of northern South America are perhaps the most highly populated primate species on the continent. These monkeys have white faces with dark eyes, a dark mouth area, and long tails that are not prehensile but that help them keep their balance. (See the common squirrel monkey, *Saimiri sciureus,* pictured in Figure 14.4.) These monkeys are bold, curious, quarrelsome squabblers that are constantly active during the daytime.

Squirrel monkeys live in large, multimale troops in tropical rain forests, especially along the rivers where fruits and flowers they like to eat grow on vines. They also eat insects, which they can sometimes

Figure 14.4   The common squirrel monkey.

catch in midair with their quick reflexes. They tend to live high in the treetops since they are vulnerable to predators on the ground. Despite their noisome behavior, squirrel monkeys are not territorial, and different species may live together in the same trees without any overt aggression.

Each year a female gives birth to a single offspring, which looks just like its parents right from the beginning. The mother provides all parental care but sometimes gets help from other female friends that may either carry the young or watch over it when the mother is foraging for food. Adult females and their young travel from tree to tree without territorial constraints.

In summary, squirrel monkeys are typical small monkeys of South America. They are successful and widespread because of an abundant food supply, few predators, and little aggression within the species.

Old World Monkeys

The Old World monkeys, comprising the largest group of living primates, evolved originally in Africa and spread to southern Asia and as far north as Japan. These monkeys have provided researchers with the species of primates used most often in laboratory studies and medical research.

Lookers: Guenons

Guenons (pronounced "ga-NONZ") comprise about 20 to 25 species of primates (the exact number debated) and perhaps 60 subspecies of related monkeys, all of genus *Cercopithecus*. All are native to Africa, and most of these species are highly arboreal, living in the dense African jungle.

Blue Monkeys.   As one example of a guenon, let's examine the lifestyle of one species, the blue monkey (*C. mitis*), pictured in Figure 14.5. Blue monkeys are relatively small; males weigh about 12 to 20 pounds and females weigh 9 to 12 pounds. They live in the deep forests of central Africa and typically avoid strong sunlight by occupying the middle zone of tall trees. Blues are omnivores, eating many different plants, fruits, leaves, flowers, insects, and seeds. Adult females typically live in troops of 15 to 20 individuals dominated by one larger male, a pattern common to many forest guenons. The troop may have as many as ten adult, breeding females and has a territory that it defends (Butynski 1982).

The intense competition among males to obtain female harems accounts for the extreme sexual dimorphism in blues: males are nearly twice as large as females. Many males live solitary lives outside of troops, occasionally obtaining mating opportunities when they can find a female in estrus foraging away from the main body of the troop. Resident males may stay dominant in their troops for two years or more but are eventually displaced by more dominant males.

Tsingalia and Rowell (1984) found that troops can have more than one breeding male under certain conditions, such as larger troop size, greater dispersal of the troop in the jungle foliage, and having several females in estrus at the same time. Under these conditions, there is still

Figure 14.5   The blue monkey, one species of guenon.

only one dominant male, but he cannot prevent other males from associating with the females some of the time. Even so, intruding males must stay with the troop for some period of time because troop females generally will not mate with total strangers. When the troop is smaller and fewer females are in estrus simultaneously, one male dominates and maintains exclusive mating rights by keeping all other males away.

In dense jungle growth, it is important for troop members to be able to communicate with one another. Dominant male blues use a low-pitched, loud "boom" sound to communicate their location in the forest, and Brown and Waser (1984) showed that blues are especially sensitive to lower pitches. Males also make a loud "pyow" call in a regular rhythm of about five calls at once. These calls, sometimes called cohesion calls, are unique to each male and function to gather troop members and warn neighboring and solitary males to keep away (Rudran 1978). Males also use other calls to warn of approaching predators, and they use growls and snarls when engaged in aggressive encounters with other males. Females use their own calls to maintain group cohesion, alert troop members to danger, and initiate flight into the dense jungle. Blues also use visual communication through facial expressions, postures, and tail positions.

Most aggressive encounters within the troop involve the dominant male harassing and eventually driving off subadult males. Often these encounters of chasing, slapping, and biting occur over access to food (Rudran 1978). Even so, aggression between blue troops is relatively rare, occurring primarily when territories overlap and the overlap contains valued fruit trees. All troop members will defend the boundaries of their territory against neighboring troops. But, while troops are aggressive against rival blue troops, blues may associate and live near other monkey species, especially another guenon species like the redtail (*C. ascanius*) (Rudran 1978).

Among blue monkey females there is no obvious indication of the female's reproductive state. Breeding tends to be seasonal but exactly in which season varies across African habitats. Generally, a female that is receptive to mating takes the initiative and seeks out a male with her tail raised, grunting repeatedly as she approaches him. When she presents her hindquarters to him, he knows she is ready (Tsingalia and Rowell 1984). The males, which can mate at any time, usually mount the female immediately. The gestation period is 140 days, and the newborn blue stays with its mother exclusively for the first month. At two months, the infant's coat begins to acquire the adultlike grayness, and it may leave the mother for short periods of time. Later the mother will leave the infant in the care of other females as she forages alone. Since tree travel is vital, blue mothers encourage their infants by jumping to a new branch and waiting for the youngster to follow. Eventually, the infant learns the troop's territory and its aerial pathways.

New males that take over a troop may try to kill the resident troop infants that are not their own offspring. One possible reason males do this is to make more adult females available for mating at a sooner time, though other explanations are possible. Butynski (1982) estimated that such infanticides by males can shorten their waiting time by seven to thirteen months. However, sometimes females and their offspring can gang up on such a new male and chase him away before infanticides occur.

Guenon Evolution.   Guenon evolution presents researchers with some interesting problems for analysis. Most guenon species are highly similar in their basic body structures and habitats as well as in their food consumption and vocal calls. Given these similarities, why have so many different guenon species evolved? Part of the answer appears to lie in guenon differences in appearance: their facial colors and body markings are vivid and distinctive, as illustrated in Figure 14.6 for 12 of the guenon species.

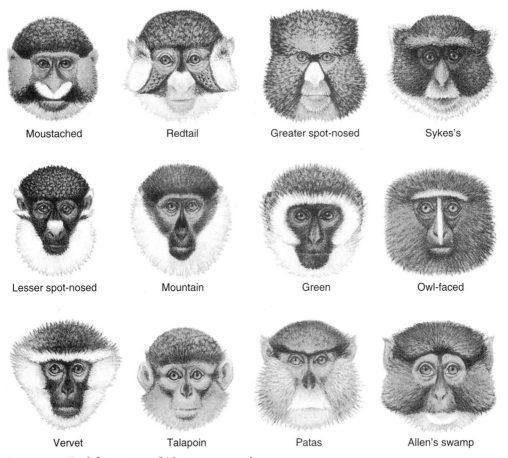

| Moustached | Redtail | Greater spot-nosed | Sykes's |

| Lesser spot-nosed | Mountain | Green | Owl-faced |

| Vervet | Talapoin | Patas | Allen's swamp |

Figure 14.6 Facial patterns of 12 guenon species.

Different species of guenons actually can interbreed, as they will do in captivity, but in the wild a guenon will generally breed only with another guenon that has the same facial pattern as itself (Kingdon 1980). Thus, it is these facial differences that inhibit interbreeding in guenons. But how did these facial differences arise in the first place? One possibility is that, long ago, habitats in Africa were once isolated long enough for different mutations to occur, producing different species, but these species became united later as Africa became one large, interconnected jungle continent (Kingdon 1980). Geological evidence shows that Africa has experienced extreme changes in climate and dramatic swings in yearly rainfall. Shrinking forests would tend to isolate guenon ancestor populations along rivers, whereas subsequent forest expansion would reunite long-separated guenon populations. If by this time facial patterns were distinct and different, these differences may have been sufficient to discourage interbreeding.

Kingdon (1980) suggests other factors that may have contributed to the evolution of distinctive facial patterns. Jumping around near the tops of trees in thick jungle growth is a dangerous activity. This may have encouraged guenons to switch from genital marking and pheromones (typical of many other monkey species) to facial markers. That is, monkeys displaying facially rather than with their hindquarters do not have to look back to see the impact of their signaling. In addition, a vividly colored facial pattern can convey a message to another individual without a static stare. Thus, in guenons, it is the facial pattern that matters more, not facial expressions (as in baboons or chimpanzees). Moreover, the vivid white marks on the faces of guenons (see Figure 14.6) can signal effectively even in the dim light of the jungle.

In conclusion, guenons have evolved physical characteristics and a lifestyle that permit them to live successfully in high and dense jungle growth, relatively free from predation and benefiting from an ample food supply. As a group of species, guenons occupy more habitats than any other African primate, making them the most successful primates of all if habitat variability and number of species are considered as the criteria for success.

Walkers: Savanna Baboons

Baboons are a number of species of monkeys that are adapted specifically for living and walking on the ground on all fours. The savanna baboon (*Papio cynocephalus;* see Figure 14.7) consists of four subspecies: Guinea, olive, yellow, and chacma (sometimes classified as separate species in older classifications). Baboons are the largest monkey species, the drill (*Papio leucophaeus*) being the largest of all, with males weighing up to 150 pounds. Adult savanna baboons are about two feet long, not including tail, and weigh up to 100 pounds, though adult males

Figure 14.7   A troop of savanna baboons.

are typically 70 to 80 pounds. They exhibit classic pronounced sexual dimorphism, with females typically one-half to two-thirds the male size. The arms and legs of baboons are about the same length, the shoulders are heavily muscled, and the tail is held upright, bending back toward the ground at about half its length. The males possess long molars and broad incisor teeth, large jaws, and 5-centimeter-long, daggerlike canines, which can truly do damage. Adult savanna baboons may live as long as 25 years.

Life of the Troop.   Savanna baboons live in socially complex bands of 30 to 50 individuals (called troops) in open areas, grasslands, and scrubby forests. Savanna baboons make a living by traveling constantly and foraging for whatever they can find or catch—either on the ground, walking on all fours or digging, or sometimes climbing trees, chasing small prey. However, they tend to climb rocks, trees, or high ground at night to sleep. They are eclectic omnivores, adapting readily to what is available but preferring ripe fruits, roots, tubers, seeds, and some leaves. They are also "opportunistic faunivores," eating small reptiles, other monkeys, young gazelles, rabbits, eggs, and insects.

Both sexes have padded and hairless ischial callosities—bare tissues on their rear ends that are hard (*callosity* is the same word from which we get "callous") and permit the baboons to sit comfortably on the branches of trees. When sleeping in trees, they typically sleep on their rumps on a branch away from the trunk of the tree, so that if any predator approaches (e.g., a snake or a leopard), the branch would sway.

Baboon troop society and organization are among the most complex and subtle in the animal kingdom. There is typically a pronounced dominance hierarchy for male access to estrous females, but the pattern of dominance behaviors among the males is highly variable and involves learned social maneuvers and teamwork, not just strength and aggression (Strum 1987). For example, males may temporarily form coalitions or partnerships against other dominant males, but these relationships tend to be short lived. In other words, males sometimes cooperate with other males, but never very frequently.

Females also have a dominance hierarchy within the troop among themselves, but normally females in estrus are perfectly willing to mate with more than one male during one estrus cycle. Which males get the most access to the female is primarily determined by the male dominance hierarchies.

A young female's rank in the dominance hierarchy is determined by the rank of her mother, in reverse order of age. Thus, the youngest offspring of each female are ranked higher than older offspring. By the age of two and a half, a juvenile female's rank with other females is permanently fixed (Altmann 1980).

Social bonds within the troop are aided by the considerable social grooming that always takes place. The typical baboon day begins and ends with extensive grooming, pictured in Figure 14.8. Mothers groom infants, mothers themselves are groomed by other females, and dominant males receive much more grooming than they give. Grooming itself consists mainly of separating fur and removing fleas and other insects.

There is usually a central hierarchy of several males, of which one is the alpha. This may be the largest male, or the one with the largest teeth, or the one that is most aggressive. Most dominance interactions occur through highly ritualized gestures, threat postures, and mock combat. Baboon facial expressions convey a lot of information and help to minimize aggression within the troop. Changes in some of these facial expressions as well as subtle vocal signals may indicate an entire change in the individual's emotional state. The adult male yawn, exposing its large canine teeth, is a sign of threat and dominance, as is staring and tooth grinding. These expressions are usually sufficient to stop another subordinate male in its tracks, preventing harm to either male. Sometimes, but not often, actual fighting and injury may occur. A subordinate shows submission by turning its back and presenting the rump to the dominant individual or by lying on the ground. When dominance relationships within the troop are stable over a long period of time, a troop experiences little aggression. But the stability may be interrupted by newly immigrated aggressive males or recently matured males.

Since baboons are not predators on larger animals, the large canines are primarily used for displays within the species and for defense. Therefore, the male hierarchy is very capable of protecting the troop against predators like lions, cheetahs, hyenas, and leopards. Along with some species of macaques, baboons are among the few primates adapted to

Figure 14.8   Grooming in savanna baboons.

stand and fight predators, not to just run away. In addition, the dominant male also directs troop movements. Different troops of baboons usually avoid each other, but intertroop aggression may occur when two troops are competing for the same resources, such as water or fruit trees.

Within the troop, daughters tend to stay with their mothers as long as they live, whereas males tend to leave the natal group around adolescence. They then go to another troop (preventing incest) where they will find their place in the dominance hierarchy.

Reproduction.   All primate females have a menstrual cycle during which the lining of the uterus is sloughed off. Thus, the menstrual cycles of human females and other primate females are homologous, probably arising from the same evolutionary origins. But unlike humans, females of baboons and other primates indicate their readiness for sex and reproduction at regular intervals in the estrous cycle. During this particular interval, baboons are said to be in estrus or "in heat." Female baboons have pronounced sexual swelling and redness of their genital tissues during estrus. Although the female may get the male's interest only when these tissues swell, it is actually scent pheromones (released at the same time) that are the real stimulus for sexual activity. Female baboons typically come into estrus about every 28 days throughout the year. They are receptive to sexual activity only at this time in their cycle, which may last five or six days.

During the time a female is in heat, she will present her hindquarters to a favorite male to elicit his attention, and she will exhibit a characteristic posture indicating her readiness to mate. Presenting the rear parts also occurs between other members of the troop as a sign of submissiveness, so its function is not exclusively sexual. In the wild, there is not much courtship behavior between these male and female baboons, though courtship behaviors such as play-chasing and grooming have been observed more frequently in captive primate populations.

The males are sexually ready at all times. The dominant male always has immediate access to estrous females, but other males may engage the female before and after the alpha male shows up. Whereas other males mate occasionally, the dominant male mates often (whenever he wants), assuring that his genes keep flowing through the troop. Females play some role in selecting their sexual partners but never select just one.

Other females show great interest in baboon babies and sometimes will harass the mother to be close to an infant. The gestation period is six months, and six to twelve weeks after birth, young baboons learn to ride on their mother's back in the "jockey" position when she is foraging on all fours for food (Altmann 1980). Males that are associated with a particular female may also play a godfather role to her offspring, which may continue well into the infant's second year. The male may hold, groom, carry, and share food with such youngsters (Smuts 1983a). Dominant males often settle disputes between females and do not permit older juveniles to harass infants. Adult males that befriend more females may actually have more reproductive success than those that do not (Smuts 1983b).

Male offspring typically remain with their mother until about the age of four, when they experience a growth spurt and develop larger canines. At this point, they acquire dominance over all females and soon leave the troop and try to join the males in another troop. Males may transfer between several troops after adolescence (Strum 1981).

Savanna baboons are the most widespread monkey species in Africa and are arguably the most successful monkey species surviving today. Their success is due to their great flexibility: they adjust to the diet, habitat, and social conditions they are presented with. They take advantage of many of the principal benefits of living in groups—effective defense against predators, some division of labor, social communication and bonding, and relatively stable group structures that minimize aggression within the troop. Living in the open and on the ground brings baboons into contact with more potential predators than many other monkey species. But group living has proved to be an effective counter to predation. Most predators, even lions, avoid baboon troops, and most baboons lost to predators are taken when they wander away from the troop or they're caught by surprise. It's no wonder that baboon society has been used so often as a model for the evolution of human beings. Undoubtedly, the success of baboons carries with it important implications for how our ancestors managed to survive when they, too, descended from the trees. More will be said about these implications in Chapter 17.

Summary

Primates are the order of mammals that includes prosimians, monkeys, apes, and humans. As a group, primates are characterized by five-fingered hands with thumbs, nonspecialized diets, great visual acuity, and often arboreal lifestyles.

The earliest evolving primates are prosimians, small primates such as lemurs, bush babies, pottos, lorises and tarsiers. Many prosimian species are nocturnal insect eaters. Lorises, for example, dwell in trees in dense forest areas of Southeast Asia. Their large eyes, slow movements, and ability to eat almost any insect have adapted them well to nocturnal life in the treetops.

The largest prosimians are the lemurs of Madagascar. Ring-tailed lemurs live in troops organized by female dominance hierarchies living in territories delineated by scent marking. The mating season in ring-tails is complex because females often prefer to mate with less dominant males. Young ring-tails learn social skills and what to eat by observing their mothers and other troop members.

New World monkeys evolved in the Americas. The largest New World monkeys are several species of howlers, which are primarily diurnal leaf eaters. Howlers mark their territories with loud calls. Their slow-moving lifestyle and lack of aggression probably reflect their low-energy diets that necessitate energy conservation. In South America, the commonest monkeys are the small squirrel monkeys constantly active at the tops of the rain forest. Their abundant food supply of fruits, flowers, and insects has ensured their widespread success across the continent.

Old World monkeys evolved in Africa and Asia. Among these are many species of guenons in Africa, one of which is the blue monkey. Blues exhibit extreme sexual dimorphism, with males about twice as large as females. Males compete vigorously to capture female harems, much like deer species. As a group, guenons are unusual in displaying many different species-specific facial patterns that apparently prevent interbreeding. While it is not completely understood how so many distinctive facial patterns would evolve, there's no question that such markings serve guenons well in communication and identification.

Baboons are the largest monkeys and the most adapted to living on the ground. The savanna baboon lives in large nomadic troops controlled by male dominance hierarchies. Whereas the dominant males have greater access to mating with females, they also provide the troop with defense against predators and with leadership. The success of baboons in Africa is likely related to their great flexibility, adaptability, and intelligence.

CHAPTER 15

Apes Great and Small

As of this writing, new information about apes is probably being discovered and published. Our pursuit of knowledge about the habitats, life patterns, reproduction, and social structures of the apes is a very recent enterprise, beginning in earnest only in the 1950s and 1960s. Consequently, many traditional ideas about the apes, especially the great apes, still exist, such as the assumptions that gorillas are violent and aggressive or that chimpanzees are exclusively vegetarians. Though bonobos were determined to be a species distinct from common chimpanzees early in this century, almost all of the meaningful facts we know about bonobo lifestyle in the wild have been gathered in the last 20 years.

Though resembling monkeys superficially, apes have evolved more recently and display more complex behaviors than most monkey species, perhaps due in part to their larger brain size. In this chapter, we will examine the general lifestyles of the lesser apes, or gibbons, and the four living great ape species—orangutans, gorillas, chimpanzees, and bonobos.

The small number of ape species surviving today have contrasting lifestyles, as we shall see. As we have learned throughout this book, the evolution of these different lifestyles, as well as the different physical characteristics of apes, have arisen in response to the environmental and ecological pressures that have impacted on their ancestors.

Swingers: Gibbons

Gibbons, or lesser apes, are about three feet tall and inhabit the tropical rain forests of Southeast Asia, Sumatra, Borneo, and Java. There are nine living species separated by seas and rivers. They are all arboreal, and they eat mainly fruits such as figs, grapes, and plums, young leaves, and, occasionally, birds' eggs. Since different gibbon species do not occupy the same habitats, gibbons have to compete for resources with birds and squirrels more than with other primates.

Each species has distinctive coat colors, facial patterns, and vocal patterns. Gibbons can stand and walk upright, but they usually move through the trees by brachiation—grabbing a branch with one long arm and swinging under it to the next branch. Gibbons are the great acrobats and trapeze artists of primates, capable of moving from one tree to another with great speed and skill; they can cross gaps between trees more than 20 feet wide (see Figure 15.1). Moreover, they can travel through thick vegetation as fast as a man can run on the ground. They are also capable of running on the ground from tree to tree on two legs.

Gibbons have evolved many adaptations in response to their arboreal lifestyle. Their need for quickness and agility have kept them relatively small; most gibbons weigh 12 to 20 pounds and are less than three feet tall. Their fingers are long, and their thumbs are reduced in size because their hands are used like hooks on the branches, and they must be able to release their grip quickly. As a result, on the ground they cannot pick up things with their fingers and thumb; instead, they must cup their hands and scoop up objects. Like baboons, gibbons have ischial callosities on their hindquarters, enabling them to sleep curled up on their sides on high tree branches. Unlike other apes, they do not build sleeping nests.

Figure 15.1 The white-handed or lar gibbon (*Hylobates lar*).

Gibbons are among the few nonhuman primates that form monogamous pairs, each couple living by itself with their offspring. Gibbons make loud warning calls unique to their species in order to indicate their territories and probably to maintain their pair bonds. In the morning, each family group vocalizes a loud chorus of calls, with the adult female's hooting call being the loudest. The largest of the gibbon species, the siamang (*Hylobates syndactylus*), has huge vocal sacs, which it inflates to amplify its calls. Evidence from breeding different species of gibbons with each other showed that the basic call of each species appears to have a large genetic component (Brockelman and Schilling 1984). Different gibbon groups may confront each other and shout at each other at the boundaries of their territories every few days or so, but fighting between groups is rare. There is no group defense; each individual simply flees a real threat. Leopards do not find it easy to catch a gibbon.

A gibbon couple normally gives birth to one offspring every two to three years after a gestation period of seven to eight months. A youngster clings to its mother's waist as she swings through the trees and forages for food. Often there are two youngsters in the family group, and there can be as many as four. The infant is weaned early in the second year and then participates in the social life of the group, which consists mostly of grooming and playing with infants. The siamang is unusual among gibbons in that the male typically displays high paternal care of the young (Rutberg 1983). Moreover, the adult male in a family group may take over care of an infant after the first year. Gibbons mature at about six years, and usually the same-sex parent drives the youngster away from the family group by the eighth year (Chivers 1980).

Though gibbons live in monogamous groups, recent evidence showed that lar gibbon females (*Hylobates lar*) occasionally seek matings with males other than their monogamous mate. Reichard (1995) found that, in three lar families in Thailand, 88% of the females' copulations were with their monogamous partner but 12% were with other males. Like the bird species discussed in Chapter 11, female gibbons appear to do this in order to breed with males of superior quality to their current mate, even though they stay with their mate.

In conclusion, because they live high in the trees, are quick and agile, and have an unlimited food supply, the gibbons enjoy almost total freedom from predators. Because of their many species and higher numbers than other apes, they can be regarded as the most successful of modern living apes. The gibbons have fully exploited their ability to swing through the trees very quickly by remaining small. Relative to the other apes, gibbons have little sexual dimorphism, reflecting the fact that males do not compete aggressively with each other for females. Rather, males pair up with females that accept them.

Orangutans

Orangutans (*Pongo pygmaeus*), sometimes called orangs for short, were probably the first of the great ape species to evolve some ten million years ago. Modern orangs are now found only in the tropical rain forests of Sumatra and Borneo, and, because of their solitary lifestyle, shy character, wide dispersal, and the challenges of their habitat, orangs are very difficult to study in the wild.

Adult male orangs weigh about 165 pounds on the average, stand nearly five feet tall, and have an eight-foot arm span. Female orangs are about half the size of the males, and they maintain a solitary life (as do males) when they are not carrying around their infants (MacKinnon 1974). Though orangs are the heaviest tree-dwelling animals in the world, they can walk on all fours on the ground, albeit awkwardly. In trees, they move around very slowly and deliberately, using their gripping hands and feet with equal adeptness. Being careless could result in a bone-breaking fall. Orangutans can live longer than 60 years but probably average 40 to 50 years in the wild (see Figure 15.2).

Orangs eat mostly fruits, and they supplement their diet with leaves, shoots, and young plant buds, occasional birds' eggs, and insects. They feed throughout the middle of the day, seeking out fruiting trees such as the arillus with its large and juicy fruit. Unfortunately, these trees and others like it are uncommon and widely scattered over a large territory. Moreover, some of the fruits bloom at only certain times of the year, and others bloom only at multiyear intervals. Con-

Figure 15.2   The orangutan.

sequently, orangs have to continually search for these fruits. Individual orangs have to spread out over large spaces for each to find enough food and have a chance at survival; this may explain why orangs remain solitary animals for the greater part of their lives. They appear to have very good memories for food locations.

Older male orangs develop large pouches hanging from their throat that can be puffed up with air, giving their heads a very large appearance. These pouches have no apparent function beyond amplifying the males' loud territorial calls. Males can emit a long series of calls consisting largely of sighs and grunts lasting as long as three minutes. These loud calls probably inform other orangs of the male's location, keeping other males away and attracting receptive females. Adult males inhabit a territorial range that includes as many smaller female territories as possible. Adult males are aggressive toward other males that come into their range. When adult males do meet, they may exhibit violent displays, staring at each other, inflating their cheek pouches, calling, and charging each other. Usually one male will flee, but occasional biting and grabbing fights can occur.

The only time male and female adult orangs socialize is for mating. Female orangs mature sexually at about ten years. Like all primates, female orangs have a menstrual cycle that makes certain days optimal for fertilization. However, orangs do not show the genital swellings that accompany ovulation as do baboons and chimpanzees. And, unlike other nonhuman primates (and more like humans), female orangs apparently do not have an estrous cycle associated with their menstrual cycle. In other words, females will mate throughout the menstrual cycle, though they tend to mate more at times of maximum fertility. When the female is receptive to mating, she may associate herself with a male for several weeks, traveling with him and mating only with him during this time. While seven years may pass between a female's offspring, the female tends to associate herself exclusively with one male. In some ways, human behavior resembles that of orangs more than it resembles that of gorillas and chimpanzees (Schwartz 1987).

A newborn orang is cared for exclusively by its mother. A baby orang is vulnerable and helpless and may cling to the mother's fur for as long as the first two years of its life. The mother may suckle the infant for as long as six years, and the youngster may stay with its mother for as long as eight years. Gradually becoming more self-sufficient, each juvenile achieves independence and establishes its own territory during the adolescent years of seven to ten. Juvenile and adolescent orangs are more social than adults and will sometimes play together.

In conclusion, orangutans are the most solitary of all the apes. This lifestyle probably evolved in response to the orang's dependence on hard-to-find fruits that are spread widely and sparsely over its territory. Orangs conserve energy by living in the trees that grow their food supply, by moving and traveling as little as possible, and by minimizing active social contact.

Gorillas

Ever since their discovery by European scientists in the 19th century, gorillas have been largely maligned as aggressive, dangerous, and destructive. Nothing could be further from the truth. Despite their formidable appearance and large size, gorillas are among the shyest and gentlest of all primate species. They live in small family groups in which there is little aggression and where the principal activities are eating and sleeping. Much of our information about how gorillas live comes from classic studies made by George Schaller (1963) and Dian Fossey (1983) in the 1960s and 1970s.

There are minor differences in size, body shape, and coloration between the three subspecies of gorillas (the mountain, eastern lowland, and western lowland) but nothing of great importance. In general, gorillas live in lowland or mountainous tropical rain forests where vegetation is thick and plentiful. They feed primarily on ground plants like bamboo shoots, leaves, stems, and fruits and must forage for food about one half of each day to sustain their large bodies: one large gorilla can eat up to 70 pounds of vegetation per day! Male gorillas can weigh from 300 to 600 pounds and stand up to 6.2 feet tall, whereas females are about half this size. The large males have extremely powerful arms but short legs relative to human males. And unlike orangutans, gorillas cannot grasp objects or tree limbs with their feet. They're more dependent on their massively powerful arms to reach and pull down most of their food without having to climb trees. This holds true for both males and females. Gorillas can stand erect but usually walk on all fours, using their knuckles for support. Gorillas can live as long as 50 years (see Figure 15.3).

Gorillas live in groups of 8 to 24 individuals, with typically twice as many females as males. Each troop has one large, silver-backed male who is dominant and who leads the troop and decides where the troop rests and sleeps. The group may also contain several younger males without silver backs. When traveling, the troop tends to move single file through the jungle with the silverback in the lead.

Gorillas possess an extensive and elaborate array of threat gestures. When the dominant silverback tightens his lips and stares at another gorilla, he usually gets a submissive reaction. He can also indicate his displeasure by growling, emitting a series of panting sounds, baring his teeth, and strutting stiffly around on all fours. These displays usu-

Figure 15.3 Dian Fossey with her group of mountain gorillas.

ally get immediate attention from troop members who stay out of his way. Large males can also make a loud "pock-pock" sound by beating their cupped palms against their chests. This action may indicate threat but also can accompany sexual arousal, play, or frustration. The pounding can advertise the male's size and strength without actual aggressive contact between males.

The male threat display to a male challenger or an intruder is truly impressive. A large male gorilla can roar ferociously, pound its chest, and charge an opponent. One blow from the fist of a male gorilla could shatter human bones, but gorillas primarily use their tremendous upper-body strength to pull down the vegetation that they eat. From a four-legged stance, a male gorilla can perform one of three kinds of charges: In the bluff charge, the male will run at an angle past his adversary. In the rush charge, he runs directly toward his adversary but stops short. In the slam charge, he runs directly into his adversary with his powerful shoulders. These charges may be accompanied by screams, roars, and tooth displays. Although challengers to the silverback's dominance may exchange slams with the silverback, all-out fights between males are extremely rare, and dominance displays are usually sufficient to settle the issue.

To display submission, gorillas usually cower on the ground with their backs exposed and belly covered. They may tuck in their lips (similar to human lip biting) and avoid the dominant animal's gaze. Yawning is also a submissive gesture (Hooff 1962). Younger animals in the troop groom the dominant silverback to get in his good graces and secure him as an ally. Female adults generally do not groom the silverback because they already have his protection.

Most gorillas nap during the hottest part of the day in temporary nests they build. At night, the adults build more elaborate nests by bending down long stalks of leafed plants, intertwining them at the center, and forming a circular bed as wide as five feet. Once completed, adults sleep alone while youngsters sleep with their moms. Some gorillas sleep directly on the ground, and others roll out of their nests during the night. Thus, nest building may actually represent a vestigial or holdover behavior from an earlier arboreal stage in gorilla evolution since gorillas do not seem to really need their nests (Dixson 1981). Unlike baboons and chimpanzees, gorillas do not have the hard rump pads that would enable them to sit on tree limbs and other hard surfaces. Sleeping on beds of soft leaves has eliminated the necessity for any such pads in gorillas.

Adult females that are ready to mate usually do so only with the highest-ranking male in the troop that is not a relative. Since males are not sexually aggressive, often it is the female that solicits attention from the male when she is receptive to mating. The female is normally in estrus about three days a month during which time her genital odors change in ways that attract males. The female may elicit male attention by presenting her rump to him or staring at the male with stiffened limbs. He may get her attention by beating his chest or strutting around. Gorillas can copulate front to rear or face to face. They typically copulate right in the middle of the troop, during the day, and their activity may provide other members of the troop with important observational learning experiences.

Females give birth only once in every three to five years since several years are needed for the female to wean and rear her new youngster. During this time, the youngster learns the social structure and experiences of its group. The mother is not able to get pregnant again until she stops lactating and her youngster matures. Infant gorillas nurse from their mothers from two to four years after birth.

Gorilla mothers are among the most caring and devoted in all of nature. Mothers groom their infants and handle them extensively from birth. The mother will scratch, rub, nibble at, and lick her infant, which clings to her underside fur for a few weeks after birth and rides on her back later. Infants typically engage in a great deal of solitary play that includes spinning on vines, doing somersaults, climbing, jumping, running, sliding down slopes, wading in water, and playing with objects.

Youngsters may also play together by lunging at each other, chasing, tackling, wrestling, and mock biting. The dominant male will put up with a great deal of attention from infants, including tugging at and clinging to his fur. Infant gorillas in the wild climb up trees and vines and sometimes sleep on the branches when they are young, but adults generally stay on the ground.

Young male gorillas begin to acquire their silver backs around the age of 11 to 13. When males become silverbacks, several possible outcomes may follow. The male may leave the group and remain solitary for awhile. Or the male may stay with its natal family and team up with the dominant male to keep any intruding males out. This situation gives the younger male the advantage of occasionally getting to mate with younger females and perhaps eventually taking over the troop from the dominant male. When female gorillas mature, they usually move out of the troop to join lone males or other established groups. This prevents inbreeding from occurring.

Since females in gorilla families are usually not related to each other because they come from other families, female relationships do not form the core of the group. Instead, what bonds the group together is each female forming a bond with the dominant male silverback. Females try to attach themselves to the larger males for its important advantages: predator defense, greater foraging opportunities, and protection of the female's infants. In a troop, the larger male can also keep competitors out, break up fights, and baby-sit while the mother forages. The dominance of the silverback male is the great stabilizing force in gorilla troops, keeping peace between unrelated females, protecting the infants, and deterring predators. Because of their huge size, gorillas have few predators in the wild.

Common Chimpanzees

The complete taxonomic classifications for human beings and common chimpanzees, with whom we share nearly 99% of our genes, are summarized in Table 15.1. Note that the classifications are exactly the same up to the family level. The common chimpanzee has yielded some very interesting and provocative information for biologists and anthropologists and has provided substantial evidence that chimps are probably the second-brightest species now living on this earth.

Genetically, the primate that is most similar to us is the chimpanzee, for which we are also its closest living relative (King and Wilson 1975). There are two different chimp species— the one most people are familiar with from the media, and the bonobo, which has been studied only recently. Stating that chimpanzees are our closest living relatives does not mean we humans are descended from chimpanzees

TABLE 15.1:   **Taxonomic Categories for Humans and the Common Chimp**

Classification	Human	Common Chimpanzee
Kingdom	Animalia	Animalia
Phylum	Chordata	Chordata
Class	Mammalia	Mammalia
Order	Primates	Primates
Suborder	Anthropoidea	Anthropoidea
Superfamily	Hominoidea	Hominoidea
Family	Hominidae	Pongidae
Genus	*Homo*	*Pan*
Species	*sapiens*	*troglodytes*

or any other ape in evolutionary time. It does mean that chimps and the other apes and human beings are all descended from common ancestors that are no longer on this earth. This was a common misunderstanding of Darwin's theory in the 19th century. When these ancient animals began to diverge into different genera and species, there were no human beings and there were no chimps or gorillas on the earth. Human beings and the great apes are all distinctly modern animals who have evolved relatively recently, but we do share common ancestors not that far back in evolutionary time—perhaps as recently as three or four million years.

Much of what we now know about chimpanzee behavior in the wild started with the classic studies by Jane Goodall. She lived with a chimpanzee colony in a savanna setting in Gombe, Tanzania, and for several years during the 1960s she observed behavior patterns never recorded before. Much of her work is summarized in books she wrote such as *In the Shadow of Man* and *The Chimpanzees of Gombe*. Two of her most important initial discoveries were that chimpanzees use tools and eat meat. Several other researchers have since studied chimps in other habitats, including the Boesch studies in the Ivory Coast. Here forest chimps live in a denser, thicker, more humid habitat where resources are somewhat more available than in Gombe, Tanzania. We would expect to see differences in behavior as a function of habitat differences even though the animals are all of one species.

Vital Statistics

The only wild places left where there are chimps are in West and central Africa, north of the Zaire River, from Senegal on the west coast to

Figure 15.4   Common chimpanzee.

Tanzania on the east. They tend to live in humid forests, woodlands, and sometimes mixed savanna, eating mostly ripe fruit and some leaves. Females are about 28–33 inches tall, averaging around 70 pounds; males are a little larger, 30–36 inches tall, up to 90 pounds, in the wild (see Figure 15.4). They can grow much larger and be obese in a zoo setting, with the males growing up to 190 pounds. Like baboons, males have larger canine teeth than females and sometimes use them in fights or defense. Chimps have arms that are longer than their legs; their coats are basically black in color, with graying starting at 20 years. They live up to 45 years in the wild. There may be as many as 200,000 chimps left in Africa.

Chimps prefer a fruit diet and they love bananas, but in the wild they adapt to whatever is available to some extent. Normally, they spend at least four hours a day eating, often eating leaves for two of those hours. They do not store food; they eat all they can get when they get it. They will also eat social insects (ants, termites), seeds, and small birds and mammals if they can catch them, but they usually can't. Like gorillas, chimps sleep in nests made up of leafy beds, which they normally remake every night. Adults sleep alone but mothers sleep with their offspring. Like gorillas, chimps walk on their front knuckles, fingers folded inward, and spend most of their time on the ground.

Chimpanzees are capable of an amazing variety of facial expressions, body gestures, and calls to indicate dominance and submission and, we presume, their emotional state. When calling at a distance they use hooting sounds, and the dominant males may also drum by hitting the bases of trees with their feet and hands.

In terms of sexuality, chimpanzee females are much like baboon females. They're in heat or estrus for about two weeks, every five to six weeks. During this time, they will present their hindquarters to the male to elicit his attention. Preferences here are complex. Early in the estrous period, the female will mate promiscuously with any available males. However, later in the same period, she will mate only with dominant males, and if she is approached by a subordinate male, she will call for the dominant male that is nearby. There is no breeding season. The gestation period is about eight months. The young tend to stay with their mother until the age of six or seven, though the female may breed again after the youngest reaches two years of age. Females are not sexually mature until about eight or nine years old (much later than baboons) and first become mothers at about ten or eleven years old, often later in the wild.

The average male chimp may not be as strong as Arnold Schwarzenegger but is much stronger than an average male human. Male chimps do not usually fight with male siblings, but they are always initially aggressive to other males until dominance is settled. The male chimps that live in a group form a loose dominance hierarchy, but, for reasons we shall see, males also tend to form larger group associations with each other. Subordinates indicate their submission by bobbing and crouching in front of a dominant male, making a sort of panting-grunting sound and sometimes baring their teeth in a "fear grin." The dominant males approach other males with a charging display, hair erect, sometimes dragging and banging a branch or club. The males test each other this way, sometimes actually fighting, but the dominance relations change and things are not always constant. Usually, some kind of understanding is eventually reached. After this precarious reunion occurs among males and dominance is settled, males may engage in mutual grooming and then travel around together as pals for awhile. When traveling, dominant males lead the way and drum or pound on large trees to let the group know the direction of travel.

Communities and Parties

Chimps live in two kinds of groupings, parties and communities (or colonies). A party consists of three to six individuals, often related, such as mothers and offspring, or sisters and offspring, or closely related males. These animals tend to stay together most of the time. These parties are typically a part of a larger community of 15 to 120 individuals whose territory may encompass up to 150 square miles (or about a 12 × 12 square).

One difference of chimps from baboons and most other primate species is that males stay in the community they are born in, for life, whereas females migrate to a new community. A female has a successful migration when she establishes her own core area (small territory) within the range of a new community whose females tolerate her and eventually accept her. It is important for the migrating female to assess the probability of success in joining the new community as well as the probability of the new community's success, since her life may depend on it. On the other hand, it is not that important for her to assess the fitness of individual males in the new community! Why not? Because the female will generally mate with any available male.

A migration to a new community will not always be successful but does succeed more often when the new female does certain wise things, like enlisting the protection of some resident males for awhile or teaming up with a member female, especially a dominant or core female that may protect her. In fact, older females in the group will even adopt abandoned infants and youngsters, take care of them, and raise them as if they were their own, as well as take a new migrating female under their wing.

How the chimp parties and communities behave depends a great deal on the available food supply. In times of food scarcity, chimps tend to travel around alone or in small groups or parties to forage for whatever each can catch. The parties tend to act independently in this situation, but they stay within the community's territory. When food resources are plentiful, things start to get really interesting and unique in chimpanzee communities. In this situation, the community males may form larger parties of 8 to 40 individuals. If this traveling group comes to the territorial (community) border and spots another party of chimps from an alien community, both communities will scream and holler, and the smaller party will beat a retreat or risk an aggressive attack.

The Ivory Coast male chimps are also very adept at group hunting, tracking down monkeys for food (Boesch and Boesch 1989). Hunting for meat takes place at least once a week, and during the rainy season it may happen every day. The chimps have learned to prefer larger, 25-pound colobus monkeys that have more meat, are slower and easier to catch, and are abundant. The monkeys can jump quickly from tree to tree— something the chimps cannot do—so the chimps can only catch monkeys by working in groups, and they're only successful less than 50% of the time. In general, forest chimps share their food more, cooperate more on hunts, and use tools more than savanna chimps, probably because of the greater availability of food.

Hunting parties assemble and leave in silence, without the usual array of chimp vocalizations and hooting. After locating a potential monkey that is unaware of their presence, four to six experienced males silently surround the tree the monkey is in; each performs a different role to catch the monkey. One, the driver, will climb the tree the monkey is in, trying to surprise it and keeping it moving. Blockers take up positions in the surrounding trees to cut off the monkey's escape. Chasers spring up the trees, trying to catch and kill the monkey. Finally, an older male ambusher anticipates where the fleeing monkey will go and waits for it. When caught, the monkey is torn limb from limb, and parts of it are shared in order of seniority.

Chimps Go to War

In some chimp communities, "border patrol" parties will visit the community boundary and sit for two hours. If nothing happens, they will travel on to some other area. But if they spot a lone alien chimp, or a small group, they may stalk, chase, and attack the loner together as a group, eventually resulting in some chimps holding the victim down while the others beat him to death. These chimp "lynchings" are relatively rare, but they illustrate well why male chimps tend to stay with other males in the community and why the dominant males tolerate and form relationships with subordinates. Thus, in the larger community, the males will eventually seek each other out and hang out together in groups. Once dominance relationships are agreed on, the familiar males will form alliances and support each other in conflicts, some of which they initiate themselves.

These "raiding parties" illustrate that sometimes the chimps behave like female lions: they seek out and destroy other individuals; unlike the lion, however, they are seeking members of their own species that are not in their community! You can call this "murder" or "war" among chimps, but the unique aspect here is that groups of chimps hunt for and kill members of their own species from other communities, not for food.

Some naturalists have tried to analyze this situation in terms of kin selection and inclusive fitness principles. Because they remain with the group, male chimps within the community tend to be related to each other genetically. Thus, to whatever extent they share genes, they will also share genetically in each others' reproductive success. This may help explain why male chimps are so cooperative and social with other males. Chimps are the *only* nonhuman primate males who stay with the group, who cooperatively share females, who are communally territorial, and who will "go to war" to protect their turf, sometimes using sticks and branches as weapons.

Thus, male chimpanzee society is more like human society in some ways, compared to other primate societies, in that it is less organized and more free-flowing, less constant and predictable and more complex. Relationships are less permanently defined and can change over time. Chimps also engage in a humanlike behavior exhibited by no other apes: committing murder. It has also been documented that the male chimp "gangs" may occasionally attack lone alien females and their offspring but not usually. Typically, for example, if the male gang encounters a lone male and female, they will attack only the male. We don't really know if these behaviors have evolved out of competition for feeding space or for mating rights, but there is on record an instance of one community "gang" gradually picking off all the males in an alien community and then taking over its territory.

Thus, chimps exhibit some behaviors that were previously thought to be uniquely human and are very much like the behavior of warlike human tribes: they fight for territorial expansion, ultimately resulting in greater food resources and more female mates.

The Other Chimpanzee: Bonobos

Because of their similarities to chimpanzees, bonobos were not classified as a separate species until 1929. Until the 1980s, they were generally known as "pygmy chimpanzees," a misnomer since bonobos are not much smaller than chimps. Female chimps and bonobos weigh about the same, averaging around 70 pounds, whereas the average male bonobo is slightly smaller than the average male chimp, weighing around 80 pounds. Relative to chimpanzees, bonobos have a slimmer build, narrower shoulders, longer legs, and a smaller head (see Figure 15.5). Wild populations of chimps and bonobos do not mix since chimps are found only north of the Zaire River in Africa and bonobos are found only south of the river and only in Zaire.

Figure 15.5   The bonobo.

Until very recently, bonobos were the most mysterious and least studied of the great apes. They have been studied in the wild only since 1974, starting with research by the Badrians at Lomako Forest in Zaire (e.g., Badrian and Badrian 1984) and taken up by a team of Japanese researchers led by Takayoshi Kano at a different location in Wamba, Zaire (e.g., Kano and Mulavwa 1984). Studies of interactions among bonobos living in a captive colony were also performed by de Waal (1989).

Bonobos display several interesting physical and behavioral differences from common chimpanzees. Bonobos find it easier to walk upright than do chimps, especially when carrying large pieces of fruit. Whereas chimps generally avoid water and find rain oppressive, bonobos do not fear water and like the rain. This difference may be related to the fact that there is generally much more water in the bonobos' environment than in the chimpanzees' because bonobos tend to live closer to the river and swampland (de Waal 1989). Bonobos also have some weblike tissue between two toes, indicating that watery environments may have been more common in the bonobo's evolutionary past than in the chimpanzee's.

Like chimpanzees, bonobos live in large communities that have smaller parties that stay together most of the time. But, unlike chimps, bonobo society is dominated by females, and males do not generally travel together or bond with each other. Instead, social bonds are between adult females and between females and males. So, for example, whereas males do not generally share food with each other, bonobo females will forage together and share their findings (de Waal 1989).

Bonobos are unique among nonhuman primates in their use of sexual activity to hold their society together. Unlike all the other nonhuman primates, female bonobos are generally receptive to sexual activity all the time, not just when they are in heat. Females can be in a sexually receptive state 75% of the time. Thus, as in human females, bonobo sexual receptivity is relatively independent from the menstrual cycle (de Waal 1989).

While the chimpanzee mating act is very stereotyped and always performed in the same manner, bonobo sexual activity is extremely variable. Moreover, females not only have sex with males but they also have sexual contact with other females, including rubbing their genital areas against one another. Females habitually use sex to avoid or deflect potential conflicts, especially those that might occur over food. The vaginal opening in bonobo females is more frontally oriented than in other primates, and male and female bonobos often mate front-to-front, more often than any other nonhuman primates. Kuroda (1984) found that female bonobos often receive food from males immediately after sexual intercourse (de Waal 1989).

Male bonobos are every bit as sexually oriented as the females. Males who greet each other after not seeing one another for awhile may mount each other, embrace each other face to face, and engage in mutual penis rubbing.

Thus, sexual activity in bonobo society is so frequent because it is used for more purposes than simply reproduction. Sex is used to avoid aggression or to reconcile bonobos after aggression has occurred (de Waal 1989). When tension or conflict builds between two animals, one animal will often invite sexual contact and the other rarely refuses. There is no rape in bonobo society, that is, no large animal will engage sexually with a smaller one without consent. Thus, sexual responses in bonobos do not indicate dominance by one animal but, instead, help to maintain harmony in the group.

Can Apes Use Language?

Modern psychologists and biologists have been very interested in determining how unique human language abilities are by testing the language capacities of the great apes. This work started back in the 1950s when Hayes (1951) raised a chimp in his own home and taught it to actually say a few words like "cup" and "mama." But chimps and the other apes really do not have the vocal apparatus to produce the variety of sounds that humans can. So researchers sought other approaches. Of course, apes in the wild do not communicate with each other using any kind of language, though they do have elaborate vocal calls to signal to each other.

In the late 1960s, the Gardners began work on teaching American sign language for the deaf (ASL) to a young female chimpanzee, Washoe, who learned over a hundred words with signs (Gardner and Gardner 1969, 1975). Premack (1971) taught another chimp, Sarah, to use colored pieces of plastic with symbols on them to communicate. Rumbaugh, Gill, and Glasersfeld (1973) taught their chimp, Lana, to press buttons with symbols on them to gain access to food and drink from vending machines or to get human companionship. Lana succeeded in acquiring a vocabulary of several hundred words, using verbs and pronouns. But her conversations were entirely pragmatic: once she obtained her immediate goal, conversation ended. She showed no curiosity in extending her knowledge of the world or how things work. This contrasts severely with human infants, who use language to gain information about all aspects of the environment.

In subsequent research, similar kinds of studies were performed on the other ape species. Using ASL, Patterson (1978) studied language abilities in a gorilla named Koko (see Figure 15.6), and Miles (1983) studied a young male orangutan, Chantek. The most substantial ape language abilities of all have been displayed by a bonobo, Kanzi, who was able to learn symbols faster than other apes, without many repetitive drills (Savage-Rumbaugh, Revcik, Rumbaugh, and Rubert 1985).(See Figure 15.7 on page 517.)

Figure 15.6   Koko and her caretaker, Dr. Francine Patterson.

There's no question that apes can learn the meanings of individual arbitrary symbols, whether they are presented in ASL or as plastic chips. The question that obsessed early researchers was the extent to which apes could acquire the grammatical rules of language, an achievement that human children accomplish in early childhood with little active instruction. Once children learn the grammatical rules, they can spontaneously generate new, meaningful sentences they have never heard before.

The early researchers were perhaps naively optimistic on what language abilities the apes really possessed. A more realistic assessment of the issue began with the work of Terrace (1979, 1982), who studied another chimp, Nim, and who also looked carefully at the old tapes of ape-human interactions from other researchers. Through his observations, he concluded that chimps could not really create new sentences and largely just imitated their captors word for word. This started a heated controversy in the literature between Terrace, the Gardners, and others, some of which still has not been resolved. Because of this, more recent research has focused on the limitations of ape language in addition to the abilities. The Rumbaughs, for example, have questioned whether chimps really use symbols in the same way humans do, though some studies appear to imply that they do (e.g., Savage-Rumbaugh, Rumbaugh, and Boysen 1980).

The questions and controversies in this area are by no means over, but several tentative conclusions can be drawn:

Figure 15.7   Kanzi, a bonobo possessing the most remarkable ape language abilities discovered so far.

1. Apes can learn to remember and use symbol systems to communicate their needs to humans and other apes, systems that we devise and that apes in the wild would never use.

2. To some extent, the apes can string together the symbols in novel ways that communicate effectively (i.e., they can be creative with the symbols, producing strings they never heard before).

3. These learning abilities far exceed the abilities of all other nonhuman primates.

4. On the other hand, the "sentences" apes create are short and very simple, consisting of a few words; they cannot produce the long, complex strings uttered by any two-year-old human child.

5. The only symbols apes understand refer to simple, concrete objects or actions and a few "connector" words; they do not acquire symbols for abstract concepts that the average human child learns all the time.

6. Finally, this whole topic is viewed now as much less important than it was 25 years ago, when some researchers were perhaps naively optimistic and were almost convinced that chimps could learn almost anything human beings could, provided they were taught appropriately.

The ape language studies have solidified the conclusion that the human brain has genetically programmed, innate structures that promote and accelerate normal language acquisition in every child.

Thus, there are aspects to language structure, syntax, and production that only human beings can deal with, as far as we know. To study these aspects, we have to study humans because no other model exists. Dolphins are relatively intelligent and can also readily learn sign and signal systems, but there is no reliable evidence that they can and do use anything like human language.

Summary

Modern apes include relatively few species, found only in Africa and Southeast Asia. The "lesser" or smaller apes are gibbon species adapted to living and traveling in trees. The lifestyle of gibbons typically features monogamy, some male parental care, and vocal calls to mark territories, as in, for example, the largest gibbon, the siamang. Their monogamous lifestyle may reflect the need for parenting during a long developmental period reaching maturity at six to eight years.

Orangutans are the heaviest animals in the world to live in trees. These slow-moving great apes live a solitary lifestyle that is probably created by the fact that their preferred food (certain fruits) is dispersed widely in their environment. Males are territorial and compete for mating with females, but otherwise adults are solitary and only females parent.

Although large in size and formidable in appearance, gorillas live in peaceful family groups led by a dominant male, called a silverback. Their massively strong arms and shoulders are used to pull vegetation down for food and nest material. The dominant male uses vocalizations, gestures, and threat displays to control group behavior, but actual fighting between gorillas is rare. The dominant male creates group stability by providing females and their young protection and structure within which the young can develop successfully with many models to learn from.

Common chimps are the closest genetic relatives to humans living today. Though chimps have long been familiar to us in circus acts and movies, the serious study of chimps in the wild began with Jane Goodall in the 1960s. Chimps eat mainly fruits and leaves but are also opportunistic foragers for insects and small mammals. Wild chimps live in large communities composed of smaller family groups called parties. Chimp society is unusual in that males stay in their natal community for life while adult females migrate to a new community. Males within a community form friendships and loose dominance hierarchies. Sometimes well-fed chimps may form hunting patrols that forage for meat and patrol the borders of their territory. Some patrols may capture and murder males that are not community members.

The other chimpanzee species, the bonobo, is physically similar to the common chimp but lives in a different kind of society dominated by females. Bonobos use sexual behaviors to promote social bonding and minimize aggression. Like human females, bonobo females are receptive to sexual activity most of the time, not only when they are in estrus.

Starting in the 1960s, scientists showed great interest and optimism in studying the language capacity of apes. Chimps, gorillas, and bonobos have demonstrated some ability to use signs or symbols to communicate their needs. But studies of the last 20 years have lessened the earlier optimism about ape language abilities and have focused more on their limitations. Human language abilities appear to exceed that of the apes after the age of two years.

CHAPTER 16

Learning and Early Experience in Primates

What can monkeys and apes tell us about ourselves? Although this provocative question has inspired a great deal of research on primate behavior, other scientists have studied these animals because primates themselves are intrinsically interesting. On other occasions, researchers pursue their intrinsic interests only to find out later that their work has profound implications for understanding human behavior. It is the area of human childhood and development where nonhuman primate studies have, perhaps, been most valuable to psychologists. Many experimental studies that cannot be performed with human children (either for ethical or practical reasons) can be conducted with monkeys or apes, yielding information about primate development that may be useful for understanding aspects of human development.

In this chapter, we will examine some of the key aspects of development shared by most primates—learning processes, forming social attachments, and play. As we shall see, though nonhuman primates are not capable of all the achievements of the human species, primates in general have many experiences in common starting from birth. We share with other primate species the necessity of having certain early experiences in order for maturation and development to proceed normally. Many of the factual details and theories about these fundamentals derive from our knowledge gained from studying nonhuman primates.

Though human beings have the longest developmental period of any animal, the other nonhuman primates are not far behind in the length of time and the intensity of parenting they need in order to mature. In this chapter, we will try to understand both the advantages and the costs of being an animal that takes a long time to reach adulthood.

The Primate Advantage: Observational Learning

As we have seen in the previous two chapters, most species of primates are intensely social animals. They often live in groups, have family relationships, and have long developmental periods during which the young acquire social skills. Like other mammals, primates are capable of learning by the principles of operant and classical conditioning described in Chapter 5. However, primates can also learn by first observing other individuals perform behaviors, then by remembering what they see, and finally by trying the same behaviors themselves.

A famous instance of this was brought to the attention of the public by Itani (1958) and Kawai (1965). Japanese macaque monkeys (*Macaca fuscata*) live on the shores of Koshima Island off Japan. One female, called Imo, learned to take sweet potatoes to the water to remove sand from the potatoes before eating them. She also learned to take handfuls of wheat and put them in the water; in this case, the sand sank to the bottom while the wheat floated, allowing her to pick up clean individual grains to eat. Over time, other monkeys apparently learned to do the same thing by observing Imo. Though Green (1975) later pointed out that the monkeys may also have learned through simple operant conditioning principles administered by the monkey's human caretakers, there is no question that these new behaviors spread rapidly through the monkey population until almost all the adult monkeys had adopted Imo's washing behaviors (see Figure 16.1).

Figure 16.1 A Japanese macaque, Imo, washing a sweet potato, is observed by a younger monkey.

This is **observational learning,** and it has some characteristics that make it a distinct and very efficient form of learning, as described briefly in Chapter 5. In simpler forms of learning, the individual learns largely through responding in a trial-and-error fashion until learning occurs. This process often takes time and numerous repetitions, and it can be dangerous in the wild if mistakes are made. Observational learning can bypass the dangers of hazardous errors; an entire cluster or series of responses can be acquired all at once, saving time and energy. There may even be a delay between the actual observation and the later performance, requiring the observer to have a good memory. In addition, not every response has to be reinforced or rewarded separately. Observational learning appears to be a hallmark of learning in primate species, giving them a degree of adaptability and flexibility rarely rivaled across nature.

In observational learning, each animal in a social group can take advantage of what other individuals already know, for example, what to eat, where food is to be found, and how to get it. When individuals in a group build up a large repertoire of such learned and socially transmitted behaviors (which they learn from each other and across generations), it is called **tradition.** We are accustomed to thinking that only human beings have traditions, but, to the extent that groups of other animals pass acquired knowledge and skills to other group members, they also have traditions, like the Japanese macaque.

Tool Use and Tutoring

In the history of animal behavior, one factor that initially received a great deal of attention was the ability of some species to use tools. Jane Goodall's chimpanzees, for example, strip the leaves of a stick and poke the stick into a crack in a log or a termite nest. When a few insects have crawled onto the stick, the chimp will pull it out and have a nice little snack. But chimps do much more than this; they invent other tools as needed. Of course, humans create and use tools all the time. Thus, tool use was formerly considered to be a sign of exceptional intelligence attributable to only a few species—human beings and their closest relatives.

The problem is that tool use keeps showing up in other species that are not supposed to be that smart! For example, the sea otter rests on its back in the sea and cracks shellfish open by smashing them against a rock lying on its chest. The Egyptian vulture picks up rocks and drops them on ostrich eggs to break open their tough shells. The woodpecker finch of the Galapagos Islands uses sticks much like the chimp to extract larvae from dead wood and may modify the stick before using it by shortening or bending it to fit better.

Recent evidence about one species of crow (*Corvus moneduloides*) indicates that they also may have to be admitted to this group. Hunt (1996)

Figure 16.2   A New Caledonia crow can make a barbed probe that it uses to snag insects it cannot reach.

studied crows that are native to New Caledonia, an island group east of Australia. Apparently, the crows make hooks and probes out of twigs and leaves to search for insects hidden under bark and in holes. For a hook, the crow nips a twig at its base and removes the leaves and bark. Probes are hard, slim leaves with a toothlike projection on the end (see Figure 16.2). The crows catch insects by dragging the barbed end under bark.

The importance of observational learning and imitation for tool use is illustrated by the work of a husband-and-wife team of researchers, the Boesches, who have done field studies with wild chimpanzees in the forests of the Ivory Coast (Boesch, 1991; Boesch-Achermann and Boesch 1993). These chimps typically seek out highly nutritious large nuts for their diet, but the nuts have thick shells and are hard to crack open. The chimps have learned to use a hammer-and-anvil method by hitting the nut with a tree branch against a rock or hard surface. Not only do young chimps apparently learn this method by observing adult chimps (usually their mothers) but the Boesches also observed chimp mothers actively instructing their young in nut-cracking techniques by correcting their errors and demonstrating the proper method (see Figure 16.3). This kind of active instruction is rare in the wild and was once thought to be unique to humans. Other recent

Figure 16.3   An adult female chimp teaches youngsters how to crack open a large nut.

studies of chimps indicate additional ways in which the abilities of chimps and other primates have challenged our concepts of human uniqueness.

Modern scientists can no longer regard tool use as a simple indicator of intelligence because it seems to have little relationship to central nervous system development or complexity. Rather, tool use appears to serve as an adaptive mechanism in those species that have not developed the biological, morphological, or specialized physical means to get their prey. For example, anteaters and pangolins have long snouts, sticky tongues, and sharp claws that allow them to dig up termite mounds. Through evolutionary time, they have adapted their bodies to their specialized food supply, but, unfortunately, now they can eat only insects.

On the other hand, chimps, woodpecker finches, Egyptian vultures, otters, some monkey species, some crows, and humans have not changed their bodies but instead have evolved behaviors to cope with varying foods through tool-using behavior that doesn't restrict them to one kind of food, keeping their diet general and flexible. Thus, in the long run, tool use has been a great advantage for humans, enabling them early in their evolution to compete with aggressors by inventing weapons, to protect themselves from aggressors and elements by inventing new housing materials, to hunt food animals by inventing traps, and to gather food crops by inventing agricultural tools.

Thus, the modern view is that the use of tools is not a simple sign of intelligence but is a sign of generalization rather than specialization. Humans are the most generalized species in the animal kingdom, partly due to unique intellectual and language abilities, but also due in part (in terms of the evolutionary past) to our ability to manipulate objects in our environment to suit our purposes and to invent tools to solve our problems. But we are not the only tool users in nature. Other species have also developed generalized abilities rather than changing their physical morphology to suit a specific food.

Innate or Learned?

Is the tendency to imitate or learn by observation learned or innate? Scientists still argue over this question, but evidence shows that the tendency to imitate is probably innate to some extent, even in species more primitive than primates. For example, Turner (1964) studied pecking for grains of food in newborn chickens. Chicks will begin to peck as soon as they can stand up and walk around, and they normally display no color preferences in pecking. When the chicks in the study were just 30 hours old, they were allowed to observe a mechanical hen peck at either green or orange grains. Afterward, when the chicks were allowed to feed on grains of many different colors, they chose the green or orange grains that had been pecked by the mechanical hen. Moreover, they did this more than two-thirds of the time. Having had no opportunities for learning imitation prior to this experience, the chick's tendency to imitate was clearly innate.

In a sense, the efficiency, speed, and safety of observational learning serve as substitutes for the innate or instinctive responses that many other species have. Observational learning does occur in species other than primates (e.g., dolphins, otters, and seals), but it is comparatively rare across nature and is confined mainly to mammals and birds. The vast majority of other animal species depend more on instinctive, built-in responses to protect themselves from predators and danger.

The Critical Role of Early Experiences

Some of the most important contributions of psychology to the study of animal behavior are experimental studies of the effects of early experiences on development. These studies with animals have great value for us because we cannot (and would not want to) study experimentally the effects of early experience on human development. In this area, the study of early experience in primates is particularly valuable because these animals share so much of our biology, evolution, and genetics. Therefore, we can presumably learn a great deal about ourselves by studying closely related species.

Harlow's Work

In the 1950s, the psychologist Harry Harlow and his colleagues performed perhaps the most thorough and elaborate series of studies ever conducted regarding the effects of early experience on the social development of monkeys. Most of these studies involved using the classic **method of deprivation** (or isolation), which involves depriving an animal of experiences it would normally have. (This research was conducted at a time when there was less concern about animal rights and welfare. It remains a difficult judgment for some people whether the treatment of the infant monkeys in these studies was justified by what was learned from the research.) In his studies, Harlow used rhesus monkeys (*Macaca mulatta*). The results of his research were reported in a variety of publications (e.g., Harlow and Zimmerman 1959; Harlow, Harlow, and Suomi 1971) but are conveniently summarized in a short book Harlow wrote called *Learning to Love* (1971).

Rhesus monkey mothers normally carry their infants around clinging to their bellies, allowing the infant monkey to nurse at will. With growth and maturity, the infant begins at first to explore its environment visually and then actively, but always staying near its mother. If startled or frightened, the infant quickly returns to its mother. At about two to four years of age, the rhesus youngster becomes independent of its mother and begins to behave like a normal adult.

Contact Comfort.   Initially, Harlow's early studies were inspired by the idea that primate infants (including humans) become attached or emotionally bonded to their mothers because their mothers breast-feed them. If true, the implication of this assumption is that breast feeding should be much better for the child's emotional development than bottle feeding, where the bottle is detached from the mother. This led Harlow into studies in which infant monkeys were separated from their natural mothers soon after birth and were then raised under controlled conditions where critical environmental variables could be manipulated independently of each other.

One classic study involved infant monkeys and two types of surrogate mothers that were simply wire vertical dolls that did not move in their cages. In Figure 16.4, we see an infant monkey with two such artificial "mothers" in its cage, one covered with wire and having a bottle attached to feed the monkey, the other being a wire model covered with soft terry cloth wrapping.

What Harlow found was that the infant monkey would, of course, return to the wire mother's bottle to be fed, but it would spend most of its time clinging to the cloth surrogate mother. Moreover, it would run to the cloth mother when frightened or upset. The implication was that the infant monkey needed the comfort of a warm, soft mother figure, and

Figure 16.4   An infant rhesus monkey with surrogate monkey mothers.

this need for **contact comfort** was responsible for the process of infant attachment to its mother, not the feeding. Those monkeys reared with a cloth surrogate mother also developed further toward normality than the wire-raised monkeys.

Mason and Berkson (1975) added to Harlow's work by manipulating the movement of a cloth-covered "mother." As compared to stationary surrogate mothers, the movement led to even more normal development of the infant monkeys, causing them to interact more with other infant monkeys.

If we generalize these findings to human development, as many psychologists have, we can conclude that what is essential for human development is the touch, warmth, and protective security that the mother's body offers the young infant, regardless of whether or not the infant is breast-fed. The need for contact comfort, or touch and warmth, in early infancy is now recognized as an important physical-psychological experience for all normally developing primates, including human babies. This was just the beginning of Harlow's extensive research program on social and emotional development in monkeys.

Peer Relations.   According to Harlow's research, there are actually five different love systems in monkey development: infant love, peer love, heterosexual love, maternal love, and paternal love. In his laboratory at the University of Wisconsin, Harlow set out to find the critical experiences involved in the development of these love systems. In one series of laboratory studies, he raised young monkeys in infancy with their mothers but held them in complete isolation for varying lengths of time later before introducing the monkey to a normal peer population of

Figure 16.5 A socially deprived monkey receiving "therapy" from a young female monkey.

monkeys the same age. As monkeys develop, they interact more with peers, especially in play activities. Social isolation from peers and normal play experiences had drastic effects on the infant's social development. The effects were largely permanent (unchangeable) when the monkey was isolated for nine months or longer. In these cases, the monkey would end up being overaggressive, sexually inadequate, and largely rejected, ignored or punished by other monkeys. In addition, the animal would typically exhibit some abnormal behaviors such as rocking and swaying, self-clasping and self-mutilation, and banging its head against the cage walls. It simply never learned to get along with the others.

The potential effects of social isolation could be corrected if they were caught before approximately six or seven months of age. In this case, it was found that social development could be "normalized" if the young monkey was placed among other normal three-month-old monkeys who functioned as sort of monkey therapists (see Figure 16.5). With attention from the therapists (young, nonaggressive females were the best therapists!), these monkeys made a complete recovery. Attention usually consisted of the females holding and comforting the infant when it was upset, encouraging it to explore its environment, and giving it realistic feedback when its behavior was unacceptable (e.g., ignoring or avoiding the infant when it was behaving badly). In fact, "therapy" was effective if it took place for only two hours a day, three days a week, for one month (Suomi, Harlow, and Novak 1974).

How much normal social experience is necessary to produce a normally functioning adult? Harlow and Harlow (1962) concluded that even a few minutes each day with peers was enough to elicit normal social behavior. The ability of organisms to stay on the appropriate developmental track with only a minimum of appropriate experiences is sometimes referred to as the principle of resilience. The process of normal development is receptive to a fairly wide range of experiences for healthy development to proceed normally.

Mother Deprivation.   Another part of Harlow's research concerned finding out what kinds of mothers the female monkeys would make if they themselves were deprived of normal mothering during infancy. In his lab, he raised a population of "motherless mother monkeys" who, at adulthood, had their own infants. With their first infant, these "mmm's" were terrible mothers. In general, they would ignore or arbitrarily sit on their infants, throw them against the wall of their cages, and sometimes try to kill them despite the infant's pathetic attempts to cling to its mother and stay near (see Figure 16.6). Without a doubt, the social isolation during the development of the mother monkey had seriously impaired her ability to be an adequate mother.

Harlow followed through on this population and discovered something even more surprising. When these same terrible mothers were permitted to have a second offspring at a later time, the normal mothering pattern emerged in the mothers' behavior in full force! In fact, they proved to be good to adequate mothers, feeding and protecting their young, as well as giving them warmth. How can this be explained? Harlow suggested that the first birth and experiential interactions the mother monkey had with her first offspring gave her enough experience to enable the innate mothering pattern in the mother monkey to emerge with the second birth.

Harlow's students also did studies on infant monkeys that were initially raised by their normal mothers for a period of time and were then separated from them. The effects of these separations, which occurred after the infant attached itself to the mother, were truly drastic and horrible (Mineka and Suomi 1978). Infant monkeys typically developed a disability roughly identical to the human psychiatric syndrome sometimes called **anaclitic depression,** where they became very passive, sad, upset, tearful, and depressed, as do human infants in the same situation (Bowlby 1973). These depressions continued for months and seriously slowed down normal development on all levels. A reunion with the

Figure 16.6   A mother monkey who was herself deprived of
normal mothering does not treat her first offspring well.

mother brought the infant back to normal when it took place soon after
the separation. Kaufman and Rosenblum (1967) obtained similar findings with infant macaque monkeys. When separated from their mothers
at five to six months of age, the monkeys became agitated for a day or so,
searched and cried for their mothers, and then became severely depressed. After a week there was some recovery, but some behaviors remained abnormal.

Implications

One implication of Harlow's research is that normal monkey peer relationships, including the heterosexual mating pattern, do not develop without social interactions during infancy, including ample opportunities for observational learning to occur. If the period of time
without these interactions goes on long enough, it permanently warps
the individual monkey's personality, preventing him or her from ever
becoming a functioning heterosexual adult. Harlow and Harlow
(1961) even contended that peer development is more important than
rearing the animal with the mother, at least for rhesus monkeys. In-

fant monkeys raised alone with a cloth surrogate mother needed only 20 minutes of daily contact with other infants in order to exhibit normal social behavior later.

On the basis of all this evidence, it seemed clear to Harlow that monkey development—and probably human development—is critically dependent on the social learning experiences the infant has with its mother and peers during childhood. Isolation has severe, destructive effects on the typical adaptive social patterns in these animals. Thus, the love systems in the monkeys are organized hierarchically, in an order, with infant love leading to peer love (friendships), peer love leading to adult heterosexual relations, and adult heterosexuality stimulating the adult parenting patterns. Harlow's work also demonstrates vividly the interaction of experience with genetic potential. Although the mothering pattern is innate in monkeys, really harsh experiences of deprivation can prevent this pattern from being expressed. Therefore, genes do not guarantee that a behavior will occur. Genetic factors must interact with the normal environmental conditions for the normal adult patterns to develop and become visible.

Deprivation in Human Children. How much can we generalize these findings to human development? Are there any nonexperimental data drawn from human experience that we might use as a basis of comparison to Harlow's studies? As it turns out, there are. Back in the 1930s and 1940s, American orphanages had developed a notorious reputation for their care of children (or lack thereof). A number of researchers looked at the development of children who had been raised in orphanages where a lot of isolation occurred, where children often received little attention and stimulation, and where mothering and bonding in early infancy were often missing. Goldfarb (1943, 1945) traced the history of children who had lived in such institutions from birth to three years of age. How did these children turn out later in life? Often they turned out like the deprived infant monkeys: socially inept, cognitively retarded to some degree, passive, lacking self-control and tolerance for frustration, and constantly in need of care. Moreover, they could not form close personal relationships with other people.

Provence and Lipton (1962) studied human infants who had been raised in institutions from birth to two years of age. They found that motor skills (that depend primarily on maturation of the nervous system) had developed normally, but cognitive skills (dependent primarily on learning and practice) were markedly behind developmental norms.

Another set of data consistent with these findings comes from information about the backgrounds of people who have antisocial personalities, people who behave impulsively or hurt other people without twinges of conscience. What do we find in these people's early childhood experiences? Typically, there is the lack of a mother figure, social isolation, child abuse, and a significant lack of constructive social learning experiences. Roff (1974), for example, found that adults diagnosed with antisocial personality disorders had experienced more neglect, rejection, and abuse as children than a comparison group of adults diagnosed as normal or neurotic.

Steele and Pollock (1968) studied the backgrounds of parents who had abused their infants or small children. Over a period of five and a half years, the researchers determined the backgrounds of parents from 60 families in which child abuse was well documented. Information was obtained through interviews and home visits through social workers, relatives, and parents. Consistent behavior patterns were revealed for the abusing parents: overly high expectations for young children and disregard for infants' needs, limitations, and helplessness. The parents themselves had typically been reared with the same patterns of extreme parental demands, constant criticism, and physical punishments. The parents as children had been deprived of basic "mothering" experiences such as tenderness, appropriate emotional interactions, and awareness of their needs. These parents lacked the social skills that would have enabled them to seek help from friends or relatives and lived adult lives that were relatively asocial and isolated.

Preventing Deprivation Effects.   Can children in peril from social deprivation be helped if discovered? To answer this, Skeels (1966) did a study where he compared children who stayed in an orphanage with others who left the orphanage to live in an institution where they received "mothering" from mentally retarded adults and older children. In a period of just one and a half years, the IQs of the orphanage children went down an average of 26 points while the IQs of the children who had been transferred rose 27 points. Although we may not think of an institution for retarded children as an ideal setting in which a child should develop, it apparently provided a more varied and stimulating environment for the children, with many more opportunities for healthy emotional and social development and individual attention. When Skeels studied the same two groups of people over 20 years later as adults 25 to 35 years old, he found that all of the original transferred children were self-supporting, half had completed high school, and most were functioning as normal adults. Of the adults who had stayed in the orphanage, on the other hand, half had not completed the third grade and some were still institutionalized. While Skeels's findings have not always been replicated in other settings, there's no question that social deprivation in early childhood is destructive to human development.

Harlow's experimental studies with monkeys and Skeels' nonexperimental research with humans dovetail beautifully: each set of data agrees with and reinforces the other. From Harlow's data, we have a better understanding as to how and why human infants do not develop fully or normally when they are isolated and ignored in impersonal institutions where they receive only custodial care. From Skeels's longitudinal study, we have learned how long term and destructive such effects are and that, like Harlow's deprived monkeys, such effects may not be reversible if they go on long enough.

The Role of Play in Development

Play is easier to define with examples than with concepts. In any case, in animals it consists of bodily movements involving leaps, running, climbing, throwing, wrestling, and other movements, either alone, with objects, or with other animals. Depending on the species involved, play may be primarily social interaction (e.g., wrestling, chasing, mock fighting), exercise (e.g., throwing, climbing, running), or exploration (sensory inspection and manipulation). One of the problems in providing a clear definition of play is that it involves the same behaviors that take place in other circumstances—dominance, predation, competition, and real fighting. Thus, whether play occurs or not depends on the intention of the animal, and intentions are not always clear from behavior alone.

Play appears to be a developmental characteristic of animals with fairly sophisticated nervous systems, mainly birds and mammals. Play has been studied most extensively in canids (e.g., Bekoff 1973a, b) and primates, including human children. A good survey of play across the animal kingdom is the book by Fagen (1981). Exactly why animals play is still a matter debated in the research literature, and the reasons may not be the same for every species that plays. Determining the functions of play is difficult because the functions may be long term, with beneficial effects not showing up until the animal's adulthood.

It may be helpful here to try to understand play in terms of the cost-benefit analysis of the ecological approach.

Costs and Benefits

Play is not without considerable costs to the individual animal. Play is usually very active, involving movement in space and at times noise-making. Therefore, it results in the loss of fuel or energy that might better be used for growth or building up fat stores in a young animal. Another potential cost of this activity is greater exposure to predators since play is attention-getting behavior. Greater activity also increases the risk of injury in slipping or falling.

The benefits of play would have to outweigh the costs or play would not have evolved, according to Darwin's theory. Some of the potential benefits relate directly to the healthy development of the brain and nervous system. Rosenzweig (1966) raised two groups of young rats under different conditions. One group developed in an "enriched" environment involving the rats in living with and playing with other rats, toys, and maze training. The other group lived in an "impoverished" environment in individual cages, in a dimly lit room, with little stimulation. At the end of the experiments, the results showed that the actual weight of the brains of the impoverished rats was less than that of those raised in the enriched environment (though they were fed the same diets). Other studies (e.g., Greenenough and Green 1981) have shown that greater stimulation not only affects the size of the brain but increases the number of connections between nerve cells. Thus, active play may provide necessary stimulation to the growth of synaptic connections in the brain, especially the cerebellum, which is responsible for motor functioning and movements.

Play also stimulates the development of the muscle tissues themselves and may provide the opportunity to practice those movements needed for survival. Prey species like young deer or goats, for example, typically play by performing sudden flight movements and turns, whereas predator species such as cats practice stalking, pouncing, and biting.

Play allows a young animal to explore its environment and practice skills in comparative safety since the surrounding adults generally do not expect the young to deal with threats or predators. Play also can provide practice in social behaviors needed for adult courtship and mating; this is typical of many monkey species where play consists of, for example, mock mounting behaviors even prior to puberty. Learning of appropriate social behaviors is especially important in species that live in groups, like young monkeys that, as we have seen in Harlow's studies, need to learn to control selfishness and aggression and to understand the give-and-take involved in social groups. They need to learn how to be dominant and submissive because each monkey might have to play either role in the future. Most of these things are learned in the long developmental periods that primates have, during which they engage in countless play experiences with their peers. (See Figure 16.7.)

There is a danger, of course, that play may be misinterpreted or not recognized as play by others, potentially leading to aggression. This is especially true when play consists of practicing normal aggressive or predatory behaviors. Thus, many species have evolved clear signals to delineate playfulness. Dogs, for example, will wag their tails, get down on their front legs, and stick their behinds in the air to indicate "what follows is just for play." With this **metacommunication** (a message about a behavior to follow), even dogs that are strangers to each other can be playing in just a few minutes.

Burghardt (1982, 1984) has pointed out that play appears to be associated primarily with altricial species in which the young have a long period of parenting and development, as compared to more precocial

Figure 16.7   An illustration of monkeys playing.

species that function on their own soon after birth. A long developmental period gives the young a time frame in which adultlike behavior is neither expected nor needed—there is "time to play." These altricial species with the longest developmental periods turn out to be the ones with the most sophisticated nervous systems and more advanced learning abilities. No species plays in adulthood more than human beings do, and humans are the species with the longest developmental period and the most complex nervous systems. These facts suggest that play has long-term developmental functions, though exactly which functions are not yet agreed upon by scientists.

Play in Primates

Fontaine (1994) found data to support the hypothesis that play has the function of promoting the development of physical flexibility in arboreal monkeys. He performed a field study of five species (from five different genera) of South American monkeys. This physical training that play provides serves to adapt monkeys to function better in the trees they inhabit. Whereas many theorists have been primarily concerned with the long-term benefits of play (such as developing adult skills for fighting and avoiding predators), Fontaine suggests that play in monkeys may also have short-term benefits to the individual monkey, enabling it to master its physical environment. Monkey play illustrates well how a behavior may serve several adaptive functions simultaneously. If there are immediate gains as well as long-term gains from infant play activity, it is easier to see how the adaptive benefits of play can outweigh the costs.

In human children, play appears to serve many functions, as it also might in other primates. Play stimulates the development of the nervous system and thinking abilities. This takes place early in infancy through exploration and learning about objects and progresses to problem solving and learning more complex concepts in later childhood. As in monkeys, play also is important for normal human social development. Children learn to understand other people and the give-and-take of social interactions. Through role playing and fantasy, children achieve some practice in adult roles before they actually have to perform in these roles. Play also permits children to work out their emotional problems, such as coping with anxiety, in situations that are nonthreatening.

Scientists have not ruled out the possibility that the young (and occasionally adults) of some species may play just for the fun of it, as we know humans do. Animals may play because they find the activity pleasurable. But this idea would only account for the proximate or immediate cause for play, not its evolutionary or survival function. The "play for the fun of it" hypothesis is very difficult to test experimentally since it postulates that animals would engage in play for its own sake and not for some developmental outcome to be measured later.

Do Animals Think?

The original edition of Donald R. Griffin's book *The Question of Animal Awareness* was published in 1976 and stimulated great interest in the mental lives of nonhuman species. After decades of dominance by behaviorists in psychology, Griffin (1981) urged researchers to take a more liberal, open-minded attitude about mental experiences in animals. Of course, the prospect of studying conscious experiences that themselves are not observable by others is fraught with difficulties. We can only observe the consequences of consciousness and thinking and try to make inferences about the underlying mental structures. Yet psychologists have actually been doing this for years with human beings. Thus, Griffin argued, we should not be so reluctant to apply the same methods and inferences to nonhuman animals.

Self-Recognition

If animals think in ways that are analogous or similar to the ways in which humans think, then we should find that thinking in the great apes. In other words, if they don't have it, we have little reason to think that other animals have it too. The rise of modern cognitive psychology has focused the attention of researchers on mental processes in animals as well as human beings. Although the study of thinking or consciousness experience in animals as well as in humans is extremely difficult, some of the most interesting and important studies of animal thinking have been performed with the great apes.

As an example, research in this area was stimulated considerably by the work of Gallup (1970, 1977) on self-recognition in chimpanzees. In these studies, chimpanzees were presented with full-length mirrors for the first time. Initially, chimps react to their images in these mirrors as if the image is another chimp (e.g., with threats and vocalizing), but these responses decrease until, after three days, the chimps begin to use the mirror to investigate themselves! They explore parts of their bodies they normally cannot see, such as their backs, the tops of their heads, and the insides of their mouths.

Gallup interpreted these behaviors as indicating that the chimps had correctly identified the images in the mirror as themselves. But to further support this interpretation, Gallup put the chimps asleep and, while they were sleeping, put red dye marks on their faces. When these chimps awakened in front of a mirror and saw their own images, they would touch and rub the marks on their own faces as they watched in the mirror. The presence of the marks greatly increased the time the chimps would spend observing their own reflections. Other control group chimps were also marked with the dye but had no previous experiences with mirrors. These chimps reacted differently, largely ignoring the dye marks. Gallup interpreted these behaviors as indicating that mirror self-recognition was learned by the chimps during the ten-day exposure to the mirror.

What is remarkable about this task is that, so far, only three other species have reacted to the mirror as the chimps do: bonobos, orangutans, and human children older than 18 months. Hundreds of other primate species have been tested, including gorillas, baboons, monkeys, and gibbons. These species display no self-directed behaviors in front of the mirror, even after 21 days of mirror stimulation, and they largely ignore any dye marks.

What does all this mean? Traditionally, naturalists and biologists since Darwin and Romanes have discussed the continuity of consciousness from simpler organisms to more complex. Human beings have been placed in a class by themselves and have been assumed to have a unique experience of consciousness. Gallup's research and the many studies that followed up on them imply that there may be a discontinuity of conscious experience or awareness in animals, but such a difference is not simply between humans and all other species. Instead, we may have to admit that a few other primate species—chimps, bonobos, and orangutans—have some aspects of self-awareness and consciousness in common with us.

Figure 16.8   Alex, a gray parrot, and his friend, researcher Irene Pepperberg.

Concept Learning

Griffin (1981) also urged that scientists not have preconceptions about animal abilities but see what the mental potential of each species is. One of the most dramatic demonstrations of having an open mind has been the work of Irene Pepperberg (1990) with an African gray parrot (*Psittacus erithacus*) named Alex (see Figure 16.8). Most of us are aware that parrots can learn to imitate human speech sounds very accurately, but it has been generally assumed that parrots and related birds have no comprehension of the meaning of English words. Alex has proven this assumption to be wrong, at least for one bird species. Alex understands concepts such as "blue" and "triangle," and he can pick out one object that is both blue and a triangle when the object is mixed with other objects. Over the years, Alex has acquired more than 70 labels for objects, colors, shapes, and actions, and he can apply the labels correctly to what he sees.

The research with Alex demonstrates vividly how preconceived assumptions about explanations for behaviors actually prevent the advancement of knowledge in these areas. As long as scientists assume that birds cannot learn labels and concepts, they do not bother to investigate what the animal can actually do. Thus, part of the value of Griffin's books on animal awareness and consciousness is to encourage researchers to put aside preconceptions and see what animals can really do. In many ways, work in this area has just begun, and the mental and intellectual potential of most species has yet to be investigated.

Summary

Primates and some other social species enjoy the advantage of being able to learn by observing others. When learning is transmitted to group members across generations, animals are said to have acquired traditions. Chimpanzees, for example, learn to use tools to crack open hard nuts by observing adults manipulating the tools in their presence. Tool acquisition and use also occurs in many animals as a general adaptive mechanism, reaching its most extreme development in human beings, the greatest tool manipulators and generalists in nature.

Primates have provided scientists with the opportunity to study the effects of early experience on development in ways not possible with humans. Harry Harlow, for example, performed classic experiments on the socialization of monkeys in the 1950s. Using the method of deprivation, Harlow found that depriving infant monkeys of typical social experiences had drastic effects on later behavior. Socially isolated infant monkeys could be rehabilitated by their peers if they returned to the group before six months of age, but longer isolation tended to have permanent effects. The monkeys became overaggressive, sexually inadequate, and rejected by other monkeys. Harlow showed that nonmothered female monkeys that became mothers themselves treated their infants with neglect and abuse. In addition, infant monkeys that had formed a strong attachment to their mothers and were then separated from them suffered severe depressions and other behavioral abnormalities when the separation continued.

Harlow's work is important not only for understanding primate socialization but also for its implications for human development. Social isolation has severely destructive effects on primate development. This conclusion has been reinforced by (nonexperimental) studies of children raised in isolative orphanages in the 1930s and 1940s. The long-term effects of early social deprivation in these children were similar to the effects observed by Harlow in his studies of monkeys.

Because many animals engage in play behaviors when they are young, play is thought to have important developmental functions in many species, though which functions is not always clear. One difficulty is that, while the potential costs of play activities are immediate (e.g., loss of energy and greater risks of predation and injury), the benefits of play may not appear until years later. Some of the benefits of play are thought to be brain growth, coordination, practice of predatory or escape responses, and acquisition of appropriate social behaviors. In primates, including humans, play appears to serve multiple functions.

The study of thinking and consciousness in animals is a relatively recent development in the behavioral sciences. Speculations about animal consciousness were stimulated by studies of self-recognition in primates begun by Gallup in the 1970s. Gallup and others showed that chimps would use mirrors to examine their own bodies. Only human infants, bonobos, and orangutans exhibit similar behaviors. Other research, such as that performed by Irene Pepperberg with a gray parrot, appears to show that some bird species may have mental abilities greater than once assumed. These studies have encouraged researchers to be more open-minded about the cognitive abilities of animals.

CHAPTER 17

Evolutionary Psychology

A discussion of primate behavior would be incomplete without Homo sapiens. Yet there is no way to encompass the great diversity and complexity of human behaviors in the space of one chapter. Thus, the purpose of this last chapter is something more limited: to examine human behavior in the context of ecology and evolution. How did the human species emerge from the rest of the animal kingdom? What unique features of human behavior distinguish us from other primates? What behaviors in modern humans can be understood as having evolutionary origins or influences? The answers to these questions are by no means settled, but the application of evolutionary theory to human behavior has experienced a great increase of interest from scientists during the last 20 years. Psychologists and biologists are devising new ways to understand the origins of modern humans from their primate roots. Comparisons between humans and the great apes, at the genetic as well as the behavioral level, are yielding new insights about what makes us uniquely human. And the new evolutionary psychology is stimulating developmental and social psychology with new controversial explanations for some aspects of human behavior.

How much can we learn about ourselves by studying behavior in other species? Since Darwin, this has been and still is a controversial and much-argued question in the biological and life sciences. The question began to receive a great deal of attention after the publication of E. O. Wilson's *Sociobiology* in 1975. Whereas this book dealt mainly with how social behaviors have evolved in many species across the animal kingdom, near the end of his book Wilson suggested that aspects of human social behavior may be genetically determined and may also have evolved according to the principles of natural selection. Thus, for biologists, the term *sociobiology* has come to mean the study of social behavior from a Darwinian, evolutionary, and adaptationist point of view. In the social sciences, however, the same approach applied to humans, and especially to the role intellect and consciousness may have played in human evolution, has recently acquired the label *evolutionary psychology* (e.g., see Buss 1994; Wright 1994).

Sociobiologists and evolutionary psychologists argue that the human mind and social behaviors evolved originally from biological processes and natural selection. Thus, they see as their task the identification of those psychological traits and tendencies that evolved to produce behaviors that were originally adaptive to human beings in some way. They are not ruling out the effects of learning, culture, and experience, nor are they advocating some simple form of genetic determinism that says all of our behaviors are somehow "caused" by genes. Rather, the goal is the one stated originally by Darwin and his followers in the 19th century: to understand human evolution and behavior within the context of evolutionary theory, as we understand the evolution and behavior of other animals.

This goal provoked controversy because many scientists and other thinkers strongly oppose the idea that human behavior could have been shaped by genetic forces and natural selection. Opposers prefer explanations that emphasize the role of culture, learning, and experience, the effects of which are assumed to operate according to principles other than those of evolutionary theory. Cultural evolution, for example, is often presumed not to take place at the individual level but at a group level. In some respects, the controversy is related to the scientists' background and education, with social scientists typically emphasizing the role of the culture and the environment and biologists and natural scientists stressing genetic inheritance and natural selection.

The controversy has many consequences for how the study of animals and humans is conducted. So, for example, if modern humans are just the same as any other animal species, this assumption tends to invite comparisons between humans and other animal species. It assumes we can understand ourselves better by studying other animals. On the other hand, if modern humans are uniquely a product of culture and learning experiences, comparisons with other animals become less relevant, if not totally irrelevant.

Durham (1979) actually attempted to achieve a synthesis of human cultural and biological evolution by arguing for the coevolution of both. Durham assumed that early human evolution was primarily organic evolution operating on the individual by means of the principle of natural selection, as described by Darwin. So those individuals that adapted and learned better were those that survived and reproduced more often. A culture, however, has the potential to increase not only the fitness of the individual but of the entire population within the culture. Thus, competition among cultures led to the survival of the more fit cultures, namely, those that best exploited their environments to their own advantage. However, Durham still emphasized that cultural fitness would depend on the reproductive success of individuals within the culture.

I will not attempt to resolve this ongoing controversy within the confines of this chapter. Rather, let us note that both groups of scientists agree that the evolution and behavior of early human ancestors *were* governed by genes and natural selection. Thus, while questions about the relative importance of genes and culture for modern humans remain controversial, it is meaningful to attempt to understand the evolution of early humans in terms of genetics, competition, and natural selection. It is highly likely that some physical characteristics and behaviors of modern humans represent the results of evolutionary processes that took place long ago, though such factors may be less relevant nowadays. In this chapter, we will examine some of the facts and ideas about human evolution that scientists find both fascinating and relevant to modern humans.

Human Evolution

Modern scientists believe that the common ancestor of apes and humans existed on the earth about 8 million years ago. Sometime after this period, chimpanzees and the hominids, including the ancestors of *Homo sapiens,* began to evolve from this common ancestor. Although we often associate chimps and gorillas with monkeys, apes differ from monkeys both physically and genetically more than they do from humans. It is now generally presumed that the ancestors of human beings arose originally in Africa.

The earliest fossils that have been accepted as hominids, members of our family Hominidae, are those classified in genus *Australopithecus* (the southern ape). The first A. skull was discovered by Raymond Dart in 1925. Much of the recent work on human fossils has been performed by the Leakey family (Louis, Mary, and their son Richard) and by Donald Johanson and his colleagues. As far as can be estimated, the oldest A. fossils come from about 4 million years ago.

Bipedal Walking

From the examination of A. fossils, scientists have concluded that these early hominids walked upright on the ground using two legs. How can one tell from a fossil that the individual walked on two legs? The answer

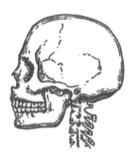

Human Neck
The human head is balanced
on the top of the backbone.

Gorilla Neck
The backbone of a gorilla meets
its head at an angle.

Figure 17.1 Skull comparisons reveal that the early
ancestors of human beings walked on two legs.

has to do with how the spinal column is attached to the skull. In apes, the
opening at the base of the skull for the spine is placed far back, indicating that the animal's head leaned forward as the animal walked on all
fours. In the hominids, on the other hand, the opening (called the **foramen magnum**) is near the center of the skull, indicating that the head is
balanced on top of the spine and the individual walked on two legs. Thus,
scientists can determine if the individual walked on two legs or four even
when only the fossil of the skull has survived (see Figure 17.1).

The examination of fossil footprints in rocks can also yield information about how animals moved around. Hay and Leakey (1982), for
example, examined fossil footprints in African rocks that were dated
from about 3 million years ago. The footprints were very similar to ours,
indicating these hominids walked upright.

Bipedal walking was the first big step, so to speak, toward creating
the new primate family Hominidae. Earlier in this century, theorists believed that walking evolved in order to free the hands to carry tools that
were being made by evolving larger brains. But fossil evidence has
shown that bipedalism occurred before there was any meaningful increase in brain size over earlier ancestors. So why did bipedalism evolve?
What advantage did it afford our ancestors?

Early in this century, the predominant theory was that bipedalism
evolved when human ancestors left the trees of the deep forest to live on
the grassy plains and savannas of Africa. But this theory does not clarify the causal factors that would make bipedalism advantageous. Currently, there are several theories to explain this phenomenon but no final conclusions on why bipedalism evolved in early hominids. For
example, Lovejoy (1981, 1988) proposed that walking allowed early hominid males to more easily catch high-energy food (meat) and to carry

the food back in their arms to females that remained with the young at a nest or campsite. In this way, the female could stay in one place, protect infants, and possibly have more of them. Thus, the origins of the nuclear family and more monogamous sexual relationships might be traced to the evolution of bipedal walking.

Another theory was proposed by Rodman and McHenry (1980). They showed that bipedalism provided early humans with a more energy-efficient means of locomotion relative to other apes such as chimpanzees, which travel on all fours. Bipedalism would have been advantageous when the African environment became dry, forcing early humans to travel more widely to obtain their main food source, fruit.

Bipedalism is fundamental for all the human history that follows (Leakey 1994). It not only came before the other new hominid traits that we identify as uniquely human but made many of these traits possible. For example, standing upright allows an individual to see objects farther away and to manipulate the environment and objects such as tools.

In 1962, Louis Leakey made an important discovery at Olduvai Gorge in Tanzania. He excavated the fossils of a species that he classified as one of the earliest known members of our genus, *Homo habilis* ("handy man"). Although controversy still exists about exactly how to classify these hominids, recent excavations have obtained more complete fossil human skeletons from about 2 million years ago. These fossils indicate that hominids at this time were small relative to modern humans, standing under four feet tall and weighing less than 50 pounds. Currently, most thinkers believe that *H. habilis* was one of our ancestors. They apparently used simple tools.

Many issues remain unsettled, and arguments continue about how many species of early hominids there were and which species may have been our ancestors. The shape and order of species in our own "family tree" prior to 2 million years ago has not been resolved at this point.

Larger Brain Size

Around 2 million years ago, there were at least six different hominid species on earth and probably more (Leakey 1994). *Homo erectus* was one of those species and is now presumed to have been one of our ancestors. All known hominid species prior to *H. erectus* were very apelike, with relatively small brains, faces that jutted forward, little neck, and no waist. *H. erectus* had a larger brain, a flatter face, smaller teeth, and a more athletic body. Hominid fossils from this period also indicate that there was greater sexual dimorphism than in modern humans. Males were about five feet tall and probably weighed twice as much as females, which averaged four feet in height.

H. erectus was the first of our ancestors to hunt other animals, to use fire, to make a variety of tools from animal bones and stone, to run like us, and probably the first to leave Africa (Leakey 1994). Most *H. erectus* fossils have actually been found in Europe and Asia rather than Africa. This human ancestor may also have been the first to use language, but language cannot be traced in the fossil record, so we don't really know. As early as 250,000 years ago, *H. erectus* probably used fire for warmth, cooking, and keeping predators away from campsites.

The earliest tools made by *Homo* species were small flakes about 1 inch long that were made by striking two stones together, one piece "flaking" off. Some have been dated as old as a half million years (see Figure 17.2). *H. erectus* made sharp flint tools by striking a larger piece of flint with a stone. Flint is a glasslike form of silicon dioxide; pieces of it can be very sharp. These stone flakes were a major evolutionary advancement, enabling *H. erectus* to gain access to new foods and resources by cutting meat, hides, wood, and soft plants (Leakey 1994). Later in their development, *H. erectus* made hand axes by attaching a hard stone to a handle.

Whereas the typical brain size for apes was about 450 cubic centimeters and for the australopithecines about 500, for *H. habilis* it was about 600–800 cubic centimeters and for *H. erectus* 850–1100, compared with an average size of about 1,400 cubic centimeters for modern humans. The fact that the brain of *H. erectus* was 50% larger than the brain of apes probably indicated the greater intelligence and adaptability of the *Homo* line.

Studies of the fossils and campsites of *H. erectus* that existed 400,000 years ago have led to the conclusion that these early humans were scav-

Figure 17.2   The earliest stone tools used by human ancestors were simply sharp flakes of stone used for cutting.

engers, hunters, and meateaters for many thousands of years, as are many human cultures today. These early humans probably learned a great deal about animals and their traits from observing and hunting animals, and they gradually evolved ways to communicate information to new members about where and what to hunt, how to pursue and kill animals, and how to protect themselves from predators.

During the last 300,000 years, the earth went through a series of ice ages during which cold and warm periods of climate alternated for spans as long as 10,000 to 20,000 years. These changes forced early human groups to find ways to adapt to living in colder climates. Among these groups was one of the earliest distinct subspecies of *Homo sapiens,* the Neanderthals (*H. sapiens neanderthalensis*), who began to populate Europe about 150,000 years ago. Although their name has often been associated with apelike brutishness and stupidity, all the evidence we have indicates that Neanderthals were as fully developed as other *Homo* lines, living in social groups, making clothing to withstand the cold, burying their dead, and using fire. Even though the Neanderthals are not believed to be our ancestors, they apparently existed side by side with our ancestors for many centuries until they mysteriously disappeared around 32,000 years ago (see Figure 17.3).

Schaller and Lowther (1969) suggested that group hunting and killing in humans may have been an essential element in the development of human social behavior. Group hunting can be effective only

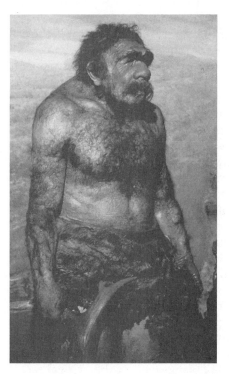

Figure 17.3 Though the Neanderthal humans differed from us in many anatomical details, if one walked among us today, he or she would probably not be particularly noticeable because of the great variability among modern humans.

through social cooperation, which might be necessary to decide where and what to hunt, to develop an encircling strategy (as in the chimpanzees described in Chapter 15), to race in relays as in hyenas, to bring down larger prey as with wild dogs, to protect the food from scavengers, and to bring the food back to the communal nest. Isaac (1978) suggested that hunting may have begun the sharing of food, leading eventually to language, social reciprocity, and the development of intelligence.

Homo Sapiens

How and why did modern humans arise? Most likely, our species evolved sometime between 150,000 years and 34,000 years ago. There are no fossils the same or similar to us prior to a half million years ago, but *Homo* fossils of 34,000 years ago are the same as we are. Diamond (1992) believes that human evolution began to take its great leap forward about 34,000 years ago because the evidence shows that, only after this time, humans began to domesticate animals and develop agriculture. The forging of metals and the invention of writing arose much more recently. The evidence for this "great leap" comes to us most clearly from fossils located in France and Spain, from which the humans identified as active at that time are called Cro-Magnons, named after the site in France where many fossils were found.

Cro-Magnon tools were new and more complex than anything found with earlier hominid fossils. We know that Cro-Magnon hunters of only 35,000 to 10,000 years ago used fire to herd animals such as mammoths and horses over cliffs or into canyons for slaughter. Other information indicates that many other early humans lived largely on open savannas and grasslands and gradually became generalized, opportunistic feeders, much like the savanna baboons discussed in Chapter 14. In addition, humans are relatively good long-distance runners, probably allowing them to chase some prey animals until the animals were exhausted.

Cro-Magnons invented new hunting weapons such as barbed harpoons and bows and arrows to catch larger prey such as deer, horses, pigs, and buffaloes. Finally, cutting tools had longer edges because they were cut from larger stones. Bones and antlers were also used as tools. Parts created separately were bound together, such as spear points set in shafts and ax heads attached to handles, creating more sophisticated weapons for larger prey. For smaller game, ropes and nets were constructed to snare animals such as rabbits. Similarly, ropes and fishhooks have been found in ancient sites in South Africa.

What was it about our ancestors that allowed them to survive and prosper while other varieties of *H. sapiens* did not? The explanation could not simply have been greater brain size: the Neanderthals actually had brains about 10% larger than ours! The details of how and why all this took place are unresolved and debatable, and there are many possibilities. One plausible theory involves the participation of verbal communication. Diamond (1992) suggests that the critical factor may have been the evolution of the biological factors underlying spoken complex language in our ancestors but in no other *Homo* species. Language would have afforded great advantages to early humans living in small groups and depending on hunting skills. A well-developed language would provide tribe members with the ability to communicate to each other very precise information about prey animals, their location, and how to hunt cooperatively. The possibility that language evolved in our ancestors but in no other *Homo* species, including the Neanderthals, may also help explain why early Cro-Magnons did not interact with the Neanderthals.

Culture

By 30,000 years ago, our species (*H. sapiens sapiens*) was the only surviving member of genus *Homo* and had spread from Africa to Europe, Asia, and Australia. Human settlements in the Americas took place more recently, at about 10,000 years ago, when Asian populations migrated across the Bering Strait.

The changes that have taken place during the past 35 centuries in how human beings live are due primarily to cultural evolution, not to any noticeable changes in human biology. In his book *The Runaway Brain,* Wills (1993) suggests that the biological evolution of modern humans was accelerated by the development of human cultures, which preserve knowledge and experience and pass them on to the next generation. As cultures became more complex, Wills argues, human brains grew larger to accommodate the greater need for individuals to encode and remember cultural information. In turn, greater brain capacity made it possible for humans to create even more complex cultures and technology, and, perhaps, eventually, the complexities of language—another way to encode and remember experiences. Thus, Wills has proposed the provocative idea that larger brains and more complex cultures stimulated the development of each other, accelerating the pace of evolutionary change through entire populations.

The human generalist capacity to be omnivorous—to eat either animals and/or plants—enabled our ancestors to travel far and wide to eventually occupy all of the continents except Antarctica. One of the unique accomplishments of our species around 12,000 years ago was the development of agriculture. This meant that small human groups had to stay in one place to plant, tend, and cultivate crops. This began the tendency for humans to settle down in larger communities and eventually develop cities.

Comparative Human Behavior

Humans versus Modern Apes

A newborn ape has a brain size of about 200 cubic centimeters, which is about half the size of its forthcoming adult brain. The young ape's brain grows to its adult size rapidly, in just a few years. On the other hand, the newborn human brain (about 385 cubic centimeters in volume) is much larger. Still, the developing human brain has a long journey ahead to reach its adult size of about 1,350 cubic centimeters on the average and sometimes as large as 1,600. As human ancestors gradually evolved larger brains, and as human infants started out at birth with larger brains and heads, human females had to evolve a wider and rounder pelvis and birth canal to permit the infant's head to safely survive the birthing process. Consequently, the birth of a newborn human infant is one of the longest and most difficult in nature.

The nurturing and care of this larger brain has meant that humans have a longer gestation period, develop more slowly, are weaned later, and reach sexual maturity later than other mammal species comparable in size. Human infants are helpless longer than other primate species and require much parental attention, protection, and care for many years just to survive, let alone prosper.

The fact is, human beings take longer to develop, stay more childlike for a longer period of time, and stay more youthful in maturity than any other species. Scientists call this phenomenon **neoteny.** (See Figure 17.4.) In evolution, we seem to have pushed our development off to later and later stages—thereby extending our period of learning as well as our life span. For our size, human beings have the longest life spans of any animal on Earth. Other animals our size typically live one-third to one-

Figure 17.4   The human adult resembles a young chimpanzee more than it resembles an adult chimpanzee.

half as long—including chimps and other large primates. This unusually extended pattern of childhood and maturation gives the individual time to absorb the experiences, language, and customs of the society into which the individual is born—to become acculturated.

Furthermore, most animals play only during their childhood and during development. Very few mammals continue to play throughout their lives: some monkeys, otters, dolphins, humans—but not many. The human brain is primed to learn all of its life, and consequently to play too. Even the great apes discussed in Chapter 15 play very little in adulthood, except for adults occasionally playing with young offspring.

Female Menopause

Men remain fertile long into their old age, and there are many instances of men in their eighties or even nineties still fathering children. Women, on the other hand, typically experience menopause sometime in their forties and can no longer bear children after that. This is very unlike the typical pattern for wild animals, in which fertility for the female usually continues until death. In light of the theory of evolution, this situation for females appears paradoxical since it would seem that women would maximize their reproductive potential by remaining fertile and continuing to bear children as long as possible. Diamond (1996) points out that in only one other species do the females live a large proportion of their lives after their fertility ends, namely, the short-finned pilot whale (*Globicephala macrorhynchus*).

Diamond (1996) explains that menopause begins to make some sense if we start with a different assumption: that the strategy of a human female making fewer babies could actually result—in the long run—in her making more! The modern theory of evolution specifies that animals will behave in ways that maximize their total, lifetime reproductive success, not simply the number of offspring born. It may be that, in the human evolutionary past, a woman could do more to maximize her genetic potential by devoting her later years to her existing offspring, potential grandchildren, and other relatives than by producing her own children. As we have seen, human children have an extraordinarily long period of development during which they require much care and attention. Therefore, it is important for the mother (or other caretakers) to see to the young's survival during this time. As the female ages, each successive birth she undergoes increases the risk of dying in childbirth, and each child she adds to those she is already caring for increases her burden of caretaking. If she does die during childbirth, all of the children she has had who are still with her are at risk.

For these reasons, Diamond (1996) concluded that, in our evolutionary past, an older mother who bore children probably risked more than the potential gain obtained from stopping to bear children in midlife. Natural selection may have favored those females who had children primarily when they were young and whose biology terminated their fertility many years before their lives ended. On the other hand, the fact that women in the distant past may not have lived much past menopause argues against this explanation.

Human Uniqueness

We can only make guesses about the psychological characteristics and behaviors of human ancestors, but, of course, we can say many things about modern humans. In other words, how unique *Homo sapiens* is relative to our predecessors can always be debated, but we can certainly describe our uniqueness relative to other living animals. Traditionally, scientists and philosophers alike have emphasized the uniqueness of the human brain and its capacity for intelligence, creativity, problem solving, and especially language. Others have added our capacity for artistic expression, morality, and technological innovation.

More recently, social scientists have been fascinated with human consciousness or self-awareness, and many stimulating and highly speculative books have been written about this topic in recent years (e.g., see Jaynes 1976; Dennett 1991; Penrose 1994). However, the topic is problematic because, since we do not understand very well the nature of human consciousness, it is difficult to make any precise comparisons with other species, other than global descriptions such as humans have more consciousness than other animals. Developments in this area probably await significant contributions from neurophysiologists and technological advances such as magnetic resonance imagery and other brain scans.

Sexual Selection in Humans

Over a hundred years ago, Darwin (1871) argued in *The Descent of Man* that sexual selection was at the heart of human evolution. Yet it has been only in the last 30 years that scientists have begun to consider seriously the principles of evolution in the development of human sex differences. In general, biologists assume that human sex differences evolved according to the same principles that evolved sex differences in other species, those summarized earlier in Chapter 10.

Obvious Physical Differences

Can you imagine how, in the dawn of human history, human sex differences in appearance might have developed? First, what are the obvious differences?

1. Males have thicker bones, bigger shoulders, more muscle, and lower voices than females.

2. Males are 5 to 12% larger, on the average, than females.
3. Males have beards and more body hair than females.
4. Females have larger breasts and hips than males.

As discussed in earlier chapters, polygyny is the most prevalent mating system in modern mammals. We also know that sexual dimorphism is related to the mating system in mammals: the more females a male can monopolize for reproduction, the larger the successful males are likely to be relative to females. We have already observed this in elephant seals, lions, and deer, for example. Polygyny leads to greater variance in reproductive success for males than for females (i.e., some males produce many offspring, some a few, others none).

The fact that human males are 5 to 12% larger than females may indicate that there is, or has been, some polygynous competition for females. Murdock (1967) determined that 708, or 83%, of 849 human cultures that he examined had polygyny at least occasionally, and many human cultures have harem polygyny in which successful males typically have two or more wives. In addition, Alexander, Hoagland, Howard, Noonan, and Sherman (1979) found that, in those societies where monogamy is practiced, males are actually less different physically from females than in societies in which there is polygyny.

Polygyny works for both males and females if there are plenty of resources provided by the successful male to the females he monopolizes. However, as mentioned earlier, human babies have very long early developmental periods relative to other primates. In early human evolution, it was likely that successful child rearing often required an investment in child care and cooperation from both parents. This situation would appear to encourage monogamy and reinforce the evolution of female traits, which would lead to male investment in monogamy.

Human females have evolved some distinct traits that do encourage male parental investment and devotion to offspring. Human females have a menstrual cycle but do not have an estrous cycle. Thus, human female sexuality is no longer strongly tied to their biology or period of menstruation. Human sexual interest and activity in females has been disconnected from physiology to some extent and is more a matter of culture and experience. So, in human females, the correct chemicals (hormones) in the bloodstream are necessary for sexual arousal and function but are not sufficient. In humans, sex is "all in the mind" or brain. Reproduction is still tied to the monthly cycle, but sexual interest and behavior are not. In baboons, on the other hand, sexual behavior is entirely under hormone control. Female baboons will not mate unless in heat, and males are only interested in females that are in heat.

These two facts taken together—constant sexual readiness and concealment of ovulation—mean that early human males had to copulate regularly with a female to be sure that she was fertilized by him. In addition, in order to be sure that he fathered her offspring, a male probably had to guard the female to prevent other males from impregnating her.

Some of the physical differences of men from women may have arisen out of this kind of competition among men for females and from the advantages that larger, stronger males had in guarding females. Other evidence also supports this conclusion. For one thing, human males have extramarital affairs more often than females, with more different partners, a fact consistent with polygyny (Chamie and Nsuly 1981). Men are also more likely than women to remarry, to have children by a second spouse, and to never marry at all (Chamie and Nsuly 1981). All of these facts support the conclusion that human male variability in reproduction success exceeds that of the female. Thus, it is possible to conclude that, in their evolutionary history, humans have been affected by those same sexual selection conditions that have created polygyny in other species.

Jealousy Theory

Whether human sex differences in behavior (not in morphology) are attributable to evolutionary processes is a much more debatable proposition. Traditional and cultural institutions across the world almost universally reinforce specific roles for males and females, and many of these roles may have arisen out of experience, learning, and culture rather than biological evolution.

But modern scientists are finding it useful to use evolutionary theory to try to account for some human social and sexual behaviors, especially those for which other theories appear to be inadequate or lacking. As an example, let's examine the case of jealousy—an emotion most of us know about, even if we don't want to admit personally that we've felt it.

Jealousy is experienced and reported in all known human cultures across the world and probably is an important cause of some social problems like spouse battering and homicide. So it's not a trivial emotion; it's potentially destructive and dangerous. Jealousy is a complex experience composed of cognitive (knowledge), emotional (feelings), and motivational aspects. It is activated by a perceived threat to a valued relationship, often a sexual relationship but not necessarily so (whether the threat is real or not). Evidence shows that such feelings of jealousy are often activated by cues interpreted as threats to the relationship. For example, these might be eye contact between an individual's partner and a rival, or perceived decreased sexual interest from a partner, or a partner's increased flirting with rivals. Ultimately, these feelings may lead to action designed to eliminate the threat and reassert the validity of the original relationship.

Studies have shown that jealousy is not the domain of one sex more than the other—both experience jealousy. But evidence does show that males and females tend to respond to different cues for jealousy. Buss, Larsen, Westen, and Semmelroth (1992) presented college students with the following question and choices of response:

> What would distress you more?
> A. Imagining your mate having sexual intercourse with someone else.
> B. Imagining your mate forming a deep emotional attachment to someone else.

When this question was presented to a large sample of male and female American adults, 85% of the women chose B while 60% of the men chose A.

Could the explanation for this difference be buried to some extent in our evolutionary past? What problem does a male have that a female does not? One problem the male had in the distant past is **paternity uncertainty** because fertilization of the female ovum is internal. In other words, unless the male is constantly accompanying the female or guarding her, he cannot be sure that her offspring is his. Buss (1994, 1995) has been a strong advocate for using our species' history of paternity uncertainty as an explanation for sex differences in modern humans about jealousy, and, according to him, paternity uncertainty was an adaptive problem for early men, leading them to behave in certain ways.

How would the female's reproductive investment differ from the male's? Women do not have uncertainty about their parenting because they carry the offspring with them, in their bodies, until birth. If her mate is with another woman, the female does not lose her offspring (if she's pregnant), but she may lose her partner's time, attention, commitment, protection, resources, and so on. So, what should be important to the female in terms of fitness and reproductive success is not so much her partner's sexual fidelity as her partner's availability and devotion, his deeper commitment to the relationship. The male, on the other hand, does not want to invest years of care and commitment to another male's offspring. To prevent this, he must make sure a female who could bear his offspring does not mate with other males.

Thus, according to this evolutionary theory, information that activates jealousy in men would be biased toward cues related to the sex act itself, whereas the information that activates jealousy for women would reflect cues to the loss of commitment and investment from the man. The potential of children not being one's own makes the male more vigilant about (and potentially reactive to) his mate's sexual behavior. On the other hand, the female may react more with jealousy about the potential commitment of the male partner to another female, diminishing his investment in her. These tendencies in human nature may be the inheritance of our evolutionary past, from a time before cultural, moral, and religious sanctions became more important.

There is further information that supports this theory. What about that 40% of males who selected choice B? When researchers looked into their backgrounds, it was found that the vast majority of these males had never had a committed sexual relationship. So, responding to this item (and the experience of jealousy) are probably also modified by experiences during development. To some extent, sexual jealousy arises out of sexual experiences (Buss et al. 1992).

Other facts are consistent with this theory. Cross-cultural examinations of human mating patterns provide additional data. For example, across many cultures, males have a greater desire than females for casual sex partners, males have more frequent sex fantasies, males engage in more switching of mating partners than females, and males are more likely than females to engage in promiscuous sex and to use prostitutes (Oliver and Hyde 1993; Buss 1994).

This evolutionary account of sex differences in jealousy is not the only theory of jealousy available, but it does illustrate how theoretical principles derived from evolutionary theory can be applied to human experiences. The history of psychology in its first hundred years is largely a history of psychology's obsession with mechanical and developmental causes of behavior. The evolutionary perspective on human behavior, which has been mostly ignored by psychologists until very recently, may offer some fresh ideas and a fertile ground for developing new theories and revising old ones.

Male Violence

Evolutionary theory has also invaded attempts to understand male violence, especially against women. For example, Wilson and Daly (1996) have pointed out that, when men kill their wives, most often such events are related to male feelings of jealousy and sexual proprietariness: the resentment of female infidelity and the woman's efforts to leave the marriage. This appears to be the prevalent pattern across many cultures. Wilson and Daly proposed that, in our evolutionary past, violence and threats by possessive males were successful in competing with and deterring sexual rivals and limiting female autonomy. The male risk of losing his mate to a rival and the risk of investing his parenting in offspring that were not his may have adapted males to resist the possibility of these events with violence.

Thus, threats and violence may still be a part of the living male genetic heritage because male ancestors who possessed these traits were more successful in passing on their genes to their male offspring. When some modern men are confronted with the appropriate cues that arouse their proprietary feelings about their wives—cues such as pressure from potential rivals and the attractiveness of the woman to others—these tendencies to react violently may emerge. Of course, in most modern societies, such extreme reactions do not work well because now females have more autonomy and control than in the past, and the legal sanctions embedded in our culture no longer accept violence as a solution. Even though such reactions are no longer adaptive, evolutionary theory may help to understand where such reactions come from, to some extent.

The same approach can be applied to violence against stepchildren. Daly and Wilson (1996) documented that a much larger proportion of children under five years of age are killed by stepfathers than are killed by biological fathers, and most of the victims of stepfathers were beaten to death. Although these events are appalling and reprehensible to us, they do make sense in the context of evolutionary theory. Evolutionary thinking tends to suggest that the affection and parental investment of stepparents toward stepchildren will be less than toward biological offspring. Stepparents are not invested genetically in children who are not their own.

Conclusions

In this chapter, I have attempted to avoid taking a strong, biologically deterministic view of human behavior because the relative importance of biological versus cultural influences on human behavior is not well understood. Similarly, many of the details of human evolution are missing or poorly understood. Though new fossil evidence and genetic studies will help to fill in some of these details, there will probably be some features of human evolution that will always be mysterious and debatable. The fossil record can provide only so much information, and inferences about early human behavior, language, and consciousness are difficult to place beyond the realm of speculation. Nevertheless, scientists will continue their search for our origins because few questions are more fundamental and profound than "Where do we come from?" and "How did we get here?"

Summary

The application of the theory of evolution to human social behavior is a relatively recent development in the biological and behavioral sciences. Although the importance of culture and learning for human development are not denied, evolutionary theorists try to determine the ways in which modern humans are still affected by their evolutionary past. Thus, understanding our own past—human evolution—may be as relevant to our behavior as understanding animal evolution is to behavior of animals.

Human evolution began about 8 million years ago when chimpanzees and early humans (hominids) diverged from a common ancestor. Bipedal walking is implicated in early human evolution but exactly why it evolved is not completely understood. Different theories, for example, emphasize the ability of freed hands to carry food or manipulate tools, or the energy efficiency of bipedal locomotion, or the visual advantages of standing upright.

The next step was larger brain size, as indicated by *Homo erectus,* an ancestor of modern humans that hunted other animals and used fire and tools. More recently, Neanderthal humans, a separate subspecies, coexisted with the ancestors of modern humans up to about 32,000 years ago. Modern humans evolved sometime after 150,000 years ago. At about 34,000 years ago humans began to engage in agriculture and the domestication of animals. Exactly what caused modern cultural evolution to begin is not precisely known, and, again, there are many theories. Language abilities unique to humans may have played a role, as well as growth in brain capacity.

Relative to other species, humans take longer to mature and stay more youthful in maturity. Human females are unusual in that their fertility typically ends in midlife, followed by many years of life afterward. This pattern may have evolved because of the advantages for offspring in having older parental figures supporting their survival.

Physical differences between human males and females suggest that polygynous mating systems, in which males compete for females, may have been prevalent sometime in the human past. The constant sexual readiness and concealment of ovulation in human females may have given reproductive advantages to larger, stronger males who could compete more effectively for females. The principles of evolutionary theory and sexual selection have aided scientists in understanding, for example, human sex differences in experiencing feelings of jealousy. In addition, the fact that, in most cultures, frustrated human males are more violent than frustrated females may be accounted for in part by evolutionary theories of sexual selection.

Glossary

adaptation (1) an attribute of the **phenotype** (physical or behavioral) that tends to enhance individual **fitness;** (2) the process that leads to traits and behaviors that are **adaptive**

adaptive tending to increase **fitness**

adaptive radiation the development of new species as one seed species expands its range into new environments favoring new traits

aggregation a group of animals of the same species that lives together for defensive purposes but without any organized social structure

agonistic behavior any behavior involving conflict with another individual but not including predator-prey interactions

allele for a given location on a **chromosome,** one of two or more slightly different molecular forms of a gene that code for different versions of the same trait

allopatric speciation speciation that is the consequence of geographic isolation of populations of one **species**

alpha in a **dominance hierarchy,** the animal to which all the hierarchy members are subordinate

altricial dependent and relatively helpless after birth, typically requiring extensive parenting in order to survive

altruism behavior of an individual that increases the **fitness** of others while decreasing the individual's own chances of reproductive success

anaclitic depression severe clinical depression experienced by primate infants that are separated from their primary caregiver to whom they have become attached

analogy a resemblance in function between two or more body structures that is due to **convergent evolution;** two such structures are said to be analogous

anecdotal method informal method for studying animal behavior; facts and observations are weaved together, enhanced, and embellished to tell a story that sounds plausible

anthropocentrism the assumption that human beings are the central fact of the universe around which all other phenomena revolve

anthropomorphism the attribution of human characteristics to animals

ape a primate of family Pongidae, comprising the great apes (bonobos, chimpanzees, gorillas, and orangutans), or family Hylobatidae, comprising the lesser apes (gibbons and siamangs)

aposematism (*see* **warning display**)

arthropod an invertebrate animal of phylum Arthropoda having a hard exoskeleton, specialized segments, and jointed appendages (e.g., insects, spiders, millipedes, and crabs)

artificial selection consistent changes in gene frequencies created by breeding organisms for a particular trait

asexual reproduction mode of reproduction by which an individual arises from a single parent and inherits only that parent's genes

assessment in animal behavior, the evaluation of the **fitness** of an individual by another member of the same species

Batesian mimicry   the physical resemblance of an edible animal (e.g., an insect) to an inedible one, so that predation (e.g., by birds) is discouraged

behavioral ecology   the study of how behavior contributes to the **adaptation** of animals to their environments

behaviorism   a movement in psychology founded by John B. Watson in 1913 emphasizing complete objectivity and explanations of behavior based primarily on learning and the environment

biogeography   the study of the geographical distribution of living things

blind   a lightly built structure designed to conceal observers from the observed

bottleneck effect   an extreme case of **genetic drift**; a dramatic decrease in population size leads to only a selection of surviving **alleles,** thus severely limiting genetic diversity in the survivors

bourgeois strategy   survival **strategy** in which an individual fights hard for a resource or **territory** that it owns but backs down if it intrudes into a new area and is challenged

brachiation   locomotion accomplished by swinging by the arms from one hold or branch to another, as in the gibbons

brood parasite   a species whose females (the parasite) lay their eggs in the nests of other individuals (the hosts) that ultimately raise the parasites' young

Bruce effect   in mice, abortion in a pregnant female elicited by the presence of an unfamiliar male

call   a short vocalization used by an animal to serve a specific communication function, such as an alarm

camouflage   an organism's form, color, or behavior that helps it blend in with its surroundings

cannibalism   predation on members of a species by the same species

carnivore   an animal that eats fresh meat

caste   a set of individuals in a group that are morphologically (but not necessarily genetically) different from other group members and are specialized in their behavior

chorus   a group of frogs, toads, or insects that emit **calls** to attract others

chromosome   strings of **DNA** and proteins lying in the nucleus of cells and containing **genes**

class   the taxonomic category of organisms that is below **phylum** and above **order**

clutch   a group of eggs laid at one time

codominance in genetics, a **phenotype** in which a pair of nonidentical **alleles** are both expressed (rather than one being **dominant**)

coevolution   the joint evolution of two or more species that interact closely during their lifetimes

communication   the production of information signals by one individual and their comprehension by another individual

comparative method   the attempt to understand evolutionary relationships among species by comparing their similarities and dissimilarities

comparative psychology   traditionally, the branch of psychology concerned with understanding animal behavior and, especially, differences in animal behavior

compass sense   an animal's awareness of direction, especially the direction in which it needs to travel

competitive exclusion   the selection of a preferred habitat by one **species** of animal that leads to competition with a similar species, resulting in one species' being driven out of the habitat

confusion effect   the decrease in predator effectiveness that occurs when a predator is confronted with swarms of prey rather than just a few

conspecific   a member of the same species

contact comfort   the need of newborn mammals, especially primates, for physical warmth and touch from others

convergent evolution   evolutionary change in which two or more unrelated species evolve similar traits because they experience (independently) similar selection pressures

Coolidge effect   the ability of some male mammals to copulate repeatedly with different females, whereas with one female the male rests between copulations

core area the part of an individual animal's **home range** that is most frequently occupied

cost-benefit analysis the analysis of the behavior of individuals in terms of the costs and benefits to the survival of the organism and its offspring

countershading the development of dark colors on parts of an animal that are exposed to the sun and of light colors on parts usually shaded

courtship display a **display** by one animal designed to attract members of the opposite sex for the purpose of mating

courtship ritual a series of mutual and interdependent behaviors performed by the male and female of a species before mating

critical period a time in an animal's life when particular experiences have a potent effect on development

crypsis (*see* **camouflage**)

dependent variable in an **experiment**, the factor that is measured in response to manipulation of the **independent variable**

dilution effect the increased safety from predators stemming from being a member of a large group as opposed to a smaller one

diploid having **chromosomes** consisting of two copies of each **gene**, one copy from each parent

display a stereotyped physical action used as a communication signal by individuals

disruptive coloration bold or contrasting markings on an animal's body that are designed to break up its outline and make it harder for predators to detect, as in the zebra

divergent evolution evolutionary change in which two or more similar species evolve different traits because they experience different selective pressures

DNA (deoxyribose nucleic acid) the chemical molecule of heredity; a complex molecular structure that can replicate itself and that directs the

synthesis of proteins in the bodies of all living things

dominance hierarchy a form of social organization in which some group members adopt a status subordinate to others

dominant in genetics, characterizing an **allele** whose **phenotype** is expressed when it is paired with a **recessive** allele

echolocation navigation by emitting high-energy sounds that bounce off objects in the environment and return as echoes to a hearing system; typical of bats, dolphins, and whales

ecological niche The physical and biological conditions under which the members of a **species** can live and reproduce

ecology the study of the interaction of organisms with their physical and chemical environments and with one another

estrus in mammals, the period of a female's sexual receptivity to males, usually cyclical and predictable

ethogram a detailed account of the behavior patterns of a species

ethology the branch of biology dealing with the study of animal behavior, especially behavior in its natural environment

eusociality social organization of animals characterized by cooperative care of the young, reproductive division of labor, sterile individuals working on behalf of individuals engaged in reproduction, and overlap of generations

evolution (1) a series of long-lasting changes in the genetic makeup of a population; (2) the general process by which population genes are changed and new species are formed

evolutionarily stable strategy (ESS) a characteristic of behavior that cannot be improved upon by some other characteristic in terms of its effect on **fitness**

experiment procedure for studying cause-and-effect relationships among variables; the effect of a manipulated variable (the **independent variable**) on another variable (the **dependent variable**) is assessed while other variables are held constant

family   the taxonomic category of organisms that is below **order** and above **genus**

female mimicry   reproductive **strategy** used sometimes by less dominant males; the males live with and mimic the females, escaping detection by dominant males and gaining mating opportunities with the females

field experiment   an **experiment** performed under natural conditions, outside the laboratory, with some loss of the control provided by the laboratory setting

fitness   the reproductive success of an individual relative to the average reproductive success in the population

fixed action pattern (FAP)   a largely instinctive response that is released or triggered by a well-defined stimulus and is performed in its entirety once it has begun

flagging behavior   behavior of one **species** designed to get the attention of another species; for example, the broken-wing display of a parent bird performed for a potential **predator** and designed to distract the predator away from the displayer's offspring

flehmen   a male response of lip curling and head raising after sniffing a female's urine, common in deer and antelopes

foraging   the activities of an animal that involve looking for and consuming its food supply

foramen magnum   the large opening in the base of the skull by which the spinal column is connected to the cranium

fossil   recognizable evidence of an organism that lived in the distant past; includes skeletons, shells, leaves, seeds, and tracks left in rocks

founder effect   genetic differences in an isolated population of animals due to the fact that the founder population (just by chance) contained **genes** different from those in other populations

founder population   a small group of organisms that become separated from a

larger group and whose **genes** constitute the **gene pool** of a new population

frequency-dependent selection   a form of **natural selection** in which the **fitness** of an individual depends on the frequency of its traits in the population; when the most frequent traits are preferred by **predators,** having less common traits may confer fitness advantages to the individual

gene   a unit of information about a heritable trait that can be passed on from a parent to offspring; each gene has a specific location on a **chromosome**

gene flow   the exchange of genes between different species or different populations of the same species

gene pool   the sum total of all **genotypes** in a **population**

genetic drift   a change in **allele** frequencies in a population over generations due only to chance events

genotype   the genetic constitution of an individual organism; it can refer to the constitution (**alleles**) of a single **gene** pair or the sum total of all an individual's genes

genus (pl. genera)   a classification category into which all **species** displaying certain phenotypic similarities and evolutionary relationships are grouped

habitat   the typical place (and its char-·acteristics) where an organism lives

habituation   a form of learning in which a response to a stimulus lessens in frequency or intensity because the stimulus is unimportant or inconsequential

haplodiploidal   referring to species in which male individuals are derived from **haploid** (unfertilized) eggs, whereas females arise from **diploid** (fertilized) eggs (e.g., most ants)

haploid   having **chromosomes,** each of which is unique, with no copies

herbivore   an animal that eats mainly plants

heritability (*H***)**   the proportion of variance in the **phenotypes** of population members that is attributable to genetic differences; when $H = 1.00$, all variability is due to **genes;** when $H = 0$, all variability is due to the environment

hermaphroditism   the coexistence of both male and female sex organs in the same individual

home range   the geographical area that an individual animal occupies and patrols

homology   a similarity between two or more body structures that is due to inheritance from a common ancestor; two such structures are said to be homologous

hormone   any substance secreted by an endocrine gland into the bloodstream or lymph that affects the physiological activity of other organs in the body

imprinting   a specialized form of learning that occurs early in life, at a specific time or **sensitive period,** which resists alteration later

inbreeding   the mating of genetic relatives with one another

inclusive fitness   the sum of an individual's personal reproductive success plus its effect on the reproductive success of its relatives other than direct descendants

independent variable   in an **experiment,** the factor that is manipulated to determine its effect on the **dependent variable**

industrial melanism   the development of dark pigmentation as **adaptive camouflage** to an environment darkened by human industrial activity

insight   a form of learning characterized by rapid and sudden acquisition of new, complex behaviors that solve a problem without any obvious trial and error preparation

instinct   a behavior that develops or emerges without the necessity for specific individual experiences (learning); see **fixed action pattern (FAP)**

instinctive drift   the tendency of innately organized behaviors in some species to reappear in behavior even when environmental influences may not favor such behaviors

instrumental conditioning   a form of learning in which a behavior occurs in frequency because it is followed by a reward; differs from **operant conditioning** in that the experimenter defines each opportunity for the subject to respond, whereas in operant conditioning the response can appear at any time

intersexual selection   a mate choice of one sex by the other

interspecific predation   the predation on one species by another species

intrasexual selection   differences in reproductive success among individuals of one sex due to their competition for mates

intraspecific predation   (*see* cannibalism)

ischial callosities   the hardened and hairless tissues on the rear ends of some primates such as baboons and chimpanzees

kin selection   (1) the propagation of specific genes because of the individual's contribution to the reproductive success of its relatives (*see* **inclusive fitness**); (2) the theory that helping and cooperation among genetically related animals can be explained by the gains in **fitness** obtained by individuals who do not themselves reproduce

kingdom   the highest level of taxonomic category of organisms (e.g., animal, plant, and bacteria kingdoms)

larva (pl. larvae)   in animals such as insects, a sexually immature but free-living stage between the embryo and the adult stages

latrine   a place where members of a **species** (e.g., the spotted hyena) defecate in common

learning   a long-lasting and (usually) **adaptive** change in an animal's behavior due to a specific experience or experiences

lek   a traditional site used by groups of male animals to display and attract females for breeding

lordosis   a copulatory position adopted by female four-legged animals

mammal a vertebrate animal of class Mammalia that has offspring nourished by milk produced by the mammary glands of the female

map sense an animal's awareness of its location

marking a physical trace that an animal leaves in its environment as a communication to other members of its species; scent marking is typical

marsupial a mammal of order Marsupialia, characterized by fetal development taking place mainly in an external pouch of skin on the mother (e.g., kangaroos, opossums, and koalas)

maturation the unfolding of an organism's genetic potential as it grows and develops

Mertensian mimicry the physical resemblance of a prey animal to something dangerous to a predator (e.g., eye spots on a moth's wings)

metacommunication a communication about communication (e.g., the play bow in dogs)

method of deprivation (see **method of isolation**)

method of isolation experimental method in which animals live for a period of time without social contacts or without other specific experiences; used to assess the relative importance of experiential and genetic factors on development or subsequent performance on tasks

migration the periodic traveling of members of a species from one environment to another, most commonly on a seasonal basis

mimicry the resemblance of one species (the mimic) to another (the model) in color, form, and/or behavior that provides the mimic some survival advantages

mixed strategy survival **strategy** of an animal in which two or more specific tactics may be used because, in general, the tactics are equally successful

mobbing a group attack on a formidable predator intended to drive it away

mollusk an animal of phylum Mollusca that contains invertebrate animals having a tissue fold draped around a soft body (e.g., snails, clams, squids, and octopuses)

monogamy mating system in which a male and female mate exclusively with one another during a breeding season

Morgan's canon the philosophical principle that, everything else being equal, the best explanation for animal behavior is the simplest explanation

morphology the physical form and structure of an organism

Mullerian mimicry the physical resemblance of two inedible species (usually insects) to one another, each taking advantage of the warning properties of the other

mutation a change in the base sequence of DNA or RNA in an individual organism

mutualism an interaction between two animals or two species that benefits both

natal dispersal the movement of a young animal from its birthplace to that of its first attempt at breeding

natural selection the evolutionary process in which the genes of those individuals that are more successful reproductively increase in frequency in the population

navigation using cues provided by the environment to travel in a specific direction to a specific location

neoteny the persistence of juvenile traits into adulthood

observational learning learning that occurs when one animal watches the activities of another (the model)

omnivore an animal that eats both animal and vegetable matter

operant conditioning a form of learning in which an animal produces specific behaviors in order to receive favorable consequences (reinforcements); the increase in the frequency of a response when it is followed by stimuli that are reinforcing

optimality theory the theory that the traits of organisms maximize benefits while minimizing costs

order the taxonomic category of organisms that is below **class** and above **family**

paleontology the study of forms of life that existed in earlier geologic times by means of examining their fossils

parental investment any parental behavior that increases the chances of offspring survival at the cost of the parent's ability to invest in other offspring

pasting the marking of one's **territory** by depositing chemical scents from special glands on vegetation as the individual inhabits the territory (as in spotted hyenas)

phenotype any attribute of an organism that is measurable or observable, other than its genetic material or **genotype**

phenotype matching situations in which the behavior of one individual toward another depends on how similar the individuals are to one another, whether in appearance, odor, or other phenotypic characteristic

pheromone a chemical produced and released by one individual that influences the behavior of another individual (the receiver)

philopatry the tendency of animals to remain at, return to, or rest at certain places

photoperiod the length of time the sun shines during the day

phylogeny the evolutionary history of a species

phylum the higher taxonomic category of organisms that is below **kingdom** and above **class**

piloting **navigation** by means of landmarks and other visual signs on earth or water

pod (1) a group of whales; (2) a school of fish in which the bodies of individuals actually touch

polyandry a mating system in which a female typically mates with more than one male during the breeding season, whereas the male mates with only one female

polygamy any multiple mating system—polyandry, polygyny, or polygynandry

polygeny a situation in which two or more **genes** affecting the same trait are located at different places on the **chromosomes**

polygynandry a mating system in which both males and females have multiple mates during the breeding season

polygyny a mating system in which the male mates with more than one female during the breeding season but the female mates with only one male

population a group of individuals of the same **species** that occupies a given area

precocial relatively independent and self-sufficient when young; precocial species are typically capable of locomotion and feeding themselves soon after birth

predation the killing and eating of some animals (prey) by other animals (predators)

predator an animal that eats other animals, its **prey**

preparedness a genetic predisposition to learn from specific experiences during development

prey an animal sought after and eaten by another animal, the **predator**

primary defense a defense against **predators** that is built into the **prey** animal's physical makeup or lifestyle and is present all the time (e.g., camouflage)

primate a member of the Primate order of mammals, which includes prosimians, tarsiers, lemurs, monkeys, apes, and humans

priming pheromone a chemical **signal** that alters the physiology of the receiver in a way that causes it to respond differently at a later time

prisoner's dilemma a two-person, decision-making game sometimes used as a model for exploring and explaining the evolution of cooperative behaviors among individuals

progressivism the assumption that evolutionary changes through time produce only improvements in organisms; a fallacy in modern evolutionary theory

promiscuity (*see* polygynandry)

prosimian an early member of the Primate order, comprising lemurs, lorises, tarsiers, and bush babies

protandrous hermaphroditism individual development that begins as male but becomes female later

protein   a complex organic compound consisting of one or more polypeptide chains, each made up of many amino acids; a building block of animal bodies

protogynous hermaphroditism
individual development that begins as female but becomes male later

proximate causes   any factors that direct or control behavior and occur immediately before the behavior

punishment   a form of learning in which an animal learns not to perform a certain behavior because that behavior is followed by painful or unpleasant events

purposivism   in evolution, the assumption that evolution proceeds toward a goal or purpose; a fallacy in modern evolutionary theory

recessive   in genetics, characterizing an allele whose phenotype is not expressed when it is paired with a dominant allele

reciprocity (reciprocal altruism)   an action by an animal (the donor) that helps another animal (the recipient) and that is to be repaid in the future by the recipient

recruitment   a process of communication in which a member or members of a society are directed to a place where work is required; most often applied to ant colonies

reinforcer   an event following a response that makes the same response more likely to occur again (as compared to no reinforcer)

releaser   a sign stimulus used in communication

releaser pheromone   a chemical signal that is quickly detected and causes an immediate response in the receiver

reproductive success   the number of surviving offspring of an individual

ritualization   the evolutionary process in which a signal behavior evolves from a movement that originally did not have a signal function

RNA (ribose nucleic acid)   a complex molecule in the nucleus of cells of organisms that translates DNA instructions into specific proteins

rutting   the seasonal sexual excitement of many species of deer, goats, and sheep

satellite   a less dominant male that associates with dominant males and, in so doing, increases its opportunities for mating with females; typical in frogs and toads

search image   the ability of a predator to more easily detect its prey after experiencing the prey

secondary defense   a defense against predators that occurs in a prey animal only when it is threatened by a predator (e.g., running away)

selective breeding   (see artificial selection)

selfish herd   the tendency for animals that live in groups to place themselves at the center of the group, using other individuals as shields against predators

sensitive period   a stage of life when a specific trait or behavior is most strongly influenced by particular experiences

serendipity   an accidental scientific discovery; often, the discovery of an important scientific principle while the scientist is looking for something else

sex-linked   with respect to an inherited trait, determined by a gene located on a sex chromosome

sexual conflict   the differences in behaviors that maximize fitness for males and females of a species

sexual dimorphism   differences in morphology and behavior between the male and the female of a species

sexual selection   a process of natural selection in which a trait is favored that gives the individual an advantage in reproductive success

shaping   a method of operant conditioning in which successive approximations to a desired response are reinforced until the desired response occurs

sign stimulus   any stimulus that reliably elicits a fixed action pattern (FAP)

signal   a behavior or product of behavior that is specialized for communicating information from one individual to another

society a group of individuals of one **species** that are organized to cooperate with one another through reciprocal communication

sociobiology the branch of biology that studies the evolution and adaptive significance of social behavior

song an elaborate vocal **signal** produced by an animal, usually to attract a mate or proclaim **territoriality**

speciation the processes of **evolution** by which a new **species** arises

species in animal classification, a population of genetically related animals that freely interbreed with one another under natural conditions

sperm competition competition between males of the same **species** to prevent each other's sperm from fertilizing a female's eggs

stotting the springing gait of certain gazelles and antelopes that occurs especially in the presence of **predators**

strain (*see* **subspecies**)

strategy a set of related traits and behaviors that solve a particular problem confronted by a living organism and that evolve due to the influence of **natural selection**

submissive display stereotyped behavior used by subordinate individuals of a **species** to indicate their acceptance of their dominance by another individual or individuals

subsong a simple **song** that is sung by some male birds during their development and that is an early stage leading to their final song

subspecies within one **species**, different population groups that occupy different geographical areas and typically differ only slightly in physical **morphology**

synchrony the regular occurrence of different events or behaviors of animals at the same time

taxonomy the system of classifying and naming organisms

teleology (*see* **purposivism**)

territoriality the tendency of an individual animal to occupy and defend a territory

territory a geographical area that one or more individuals defends against competitors

testosterone in male mammals, a major sex hormone that helps control male reproductive functions

tonic immobility the freezing behavior of certain **species** when suddenly confronted by a **predator**, characterized by muscle relaxation and temporary unconsciousness

tradition a particular behavior and/or functional site that is passed from one generation to another through **learning**

troop a group of **primates** such as baboons or other monkeys

ultimate causes in the study of animal behavior, the factors of **evolution, genes,** past experience, and development that affect an animal's current behavior

ungulate any four-footed, hoofed mammal

uniformitarianism the assumption that physical and biological processes that operated in the past are not different from those operating now

vestigial organ a body part of an organism that evolved with a specific function but no longer serves any specific function (e.g., the human appendix)

warning display the advertisement by an animal that it is dangerous and should be avoided (e.g., bright color or marking proclaiming danger)

zoology the branch of biology dealing with animals, especially their classification, anatomy, and physiology

References

Albert, D. J., Walsh, M. L., Gorzalka, B. B., Siemens, Y., & Louie, H. (1986). Testosterone removal in rats results in a decrease in social aggression and a loss of social dominance. *Physiology and Behavior, 36,* 401–407.

Alexander, R. D., Hoagland, J. L., Howard, R. D., Noonan, K. M., & Sherman, P. W. (1979). Sexual dimorphism and breeding systems in pinnipeds, ungulates, primates and humans. In N. A. Chagnon and W. Irons (Eds.), *Evolutionary biology and human social behavior: An anthropological perspective.* N. Scituate, MA: Duxbury.

Altmann, J. (1980). *Baboon mothers and infants.* Cambridge, MA: Harvard Univ. Press.

Axelrod, R., & Hamilton, W. D. (1981). The evolution of cooperation. *Science, 211,* 1390–1396.

Ayala, F. J. (1982). *Population and evolutionary genetics: A primer.* Menlo Park, CA: Benjamin/Cummings.

Ayala, F. J., & Campbell, C. A. (1974). Frequency-dependent selection. *Annual Review of Ecological Systems, 5,* 115–138.

Azrin, N. H., & Holz, W. C. (1966). Punishment. In W. K. Honig (Ed.), *Operant behavior: Areas of research and application.* New York: Appleton-Century-Crofts.

Badrian, A., & Badrian, N. (1984). Social organization of *Pan paniscus* in the Lomako Forest, Zaire. In R. Susman (Ed.), *The pygmy chimpanzee,* pp. 325–346. New York: Plenum.

Balda, R. P. (1980). Recovery of cached seeds by a captive *Nucifraga caryocatactes. Zeitschrift fur Tierpsychologie, 52,* 331–346.

Balda, R. P., & Kamil, A. C. (1989). A comparative study of cache recovery by three corvid species. *Animal Behaviour, 38,* 486–495.

Baptista, L. F., & Petrinovich, L. (1984). Social interaction, sensitive phases and the song template hypothesis in the white-crowned sparrow. *Animal Behaviour, 32,* 172–181.

Barlow, G. W. (1968). Ethological units of behavior. In D. Ingle (Ed.), *The central nervous system and fish behavior,* pp. 217–232. Chicago: Univ. of Chicago Press.

Beach, F. A. (1949). The snark was a boojum. In T. E. McGill (Ed.), *Readings in animal behavior.* New York: Holt, Rinehart & Winston.

Bednarz, J. C. (1988). Cooperative hunting in Harris hawks (*Parabuteo unicinctus*). *Science, 239,* 1525–1527.

Beecher, M. D. (1990). The evolution of parent-offspring recognition in swallows. In D. A. Dewsbury (Ed.), *Contemporary issues in comparative psychology,* pp. 360–380. Sunderland, MA: Sinauer Associates.

Bekoff, M. (1974a). Social play in coyotes, wolves and dogs. *Bioscience, 24,* 225–230.

Bekoff, M. (1974b). Social play and play-soliciting by infant canids. *American Zoologist, 14,* 323–340.

Bent, A. C. (1940). *Life histories of North American birds.* Washington, DC: United States Natural Museum.

Berman, C. M. (1980). Mother-infant rela-tionships among free-ranging rhesus monkeys on Cayo Santiago: A comparison with captive pairs. *Animal Behaviour, 28,* 860–873.

Bermant, G. (1976). Sexual behavior: Hard times with the Coolidge effect. In M. H. Siegel, & H. P. Ziegler (Eds.), *Psychological research: The inside story,* pp. 76–103. New York: Harper & Row.

Berven, K. A. (1981). Mate choice in the wood frog, *Rana sylvatica. Evolution, 35,* 707–722.

Bestiary. (1992). London: Folio Society.

Birch, H. C. (1945). The relation of previous experience to insightful problem-solving. *Journal of Comparative and Physiological Psychology, 38,* 367–383.

Birdsall, D. A., & Nash, D. (1973). Occurrence of successful multiple insemination of females in natural populations of deer mice (*Peromyscus maniculatus*). *Evolution, 27,* 106–110.

Birkhead, T. R. (1996). Mechanisms of sperm competition in birds. *American Scientist, 84,* 254–262.

Boesch, C. (1991). Teaching in wild chimpanzees. *Animal Behaviour, 41,* 530–532.

Boesch, C., & Boesch, H. (1989). Hunting behavior of wild chimpanzees in the Tai National Park. *American Journal of Physical Anthropology, 78,* 547–573.

Boesch-Achermann, H., & Boesch, C. (1993). Tool use in wild chimpanzees: New light from dark forests. *Current Directions in Psychological Science, 2,* 18–21.

Bolles, R. C. (1970). Species-specific defense reactions and avoidance learning. *Psychological Review, 77,* 32–48.

Bowlby, J. (1973). *Separation: Anxiety and anger.* New York: Basic Books.

Boycott, B. B. (1965). Learning in the octopus. *Scientific American, 212,* 42–50.

Bradbury, J. W. (1977). Lek mating behavior in the hammer-headed bat. *Zeitschrift fur Tierpsychologie, 45,* 225–255.

Breland, K., & Breland, M. (1961). The misbehavior of organisms. *American Psychologist, 16,* 661–664.

Breland, K., & Breland, M. (1966). *Animal behavior.* New York: Macmillan.

Brockelman, W. Y., & Schilling, D. (1984). Inheritance of stereotyped gibbon calls. *Nature, 312,* 634–636.

Brockmann, H. J. (1990). Mating behavior of horseshoe crabs, *Limulus polyphemus. Behaviour, 114,* 206–220.

Brodie, E. D., Jr. (1977). Hedgehogs use toad venom in their own defense. *Nature, 268,* 627–628.

Brown, C. H., & Waser, P. M. (1984). Hearing and communication in blue monkeys (*Cercopithecus mitis*). *Animal Behaviour 32,* 66–75.

Brown, J. L. (1964). The evolution of diversity in avian territorial systems. *Wilson Bulletin, 76,* 160–169.

Brownell, P. H. (1984). Prey detection by the sand scorpion. *Scientific American, 251(6),* 86–97.

Bruce, H. M. (1960). A block to pregnancy in the house mouse caused by the proximity of strange males. *Journal of Reproduction and Fertility, 1,* 96–103.

Budnitz, N., & Dainis, K. (1975). *Lemur catta:* Ecology and behavior. In I. Tattersall, & R. W. Sussman (Eds)., *Lemur biology,* pp. 219–235. New York: Plenum.

Burghardt, G. M. (1982). Comparison matters: Curiosity, bears, surplus energy and why reptiles don't play. *Behavioral and Brain Sciences, 5,* 159–160.

Burghardt, G. M. (1984). On the origins of play. In P. K. Smith (Ed.), *Play in animals and humans.* New York: Basil Blackwell.

Burke, T., Davies, N. B., Bruford, M. W., & Hatchwell, B. J. (1989). Parental care and mating behavior of polyandrous dunnocks *Prunella modularis* related to paternity by DNA fingerprinting. *Nature, 338,* 249–250.

Buskirk, R. E. (1981). Sociality in Arachnida. In H. R. Hermann (Ed.), *Social insects.* New York: Academic Press.

Buss, D. M. (1994). *The evolution of desire: Strategies of human mating.* New York: Basic Books.

Buss, D. M. (1995). Psychological sex differences: Origins through sexual selection. *American Psychologist, 50,* 164–168.

Buss, D. M., Larsen, R. J., Westen, D., & Semmelroth, J. (1992). Sex differences in jealousy: Evolution, physiology, and psychology. *Psychological Science, 3,* 251–255.

Butynski, T. M. (1982). Harem male replacement and infanticide in the blue monkey (*Cercopithecus mitis stuhlmanni*) in the Kibale Forest, Uganda. *American Journal of Primatology, 3,* 1–22.

Cade, W. H. (1981). Attentive male strategies: Genetic differences in crickets. *Science, 212,* 563–564.

Calhoun, J. B. (1962). Population density and social pathology. *Scientific American, 206,* 139–148.

Carlson, A. D., & Copeland, J. (1978). Behavioral plasticity in the flash communication system of fireflies. *American Scientist, 66,* 340–346.

Caro, T. M. (1986a). The functions of stotting: A review of the hypotheses. *Animal Behaviour, 34,* 649–662.

Caro, T. M. (1986b). The functions of stotting in Thomson's gazelles: Some tests of the predictions. *Animal Behaviour, 34,* 663–684.

Carr, A. (1967). Adaptive aspects of the scheduled travel of *Chelonia*. In R. M. Storm (Ed.), *Animal orientation and navigation*. Corvallis, OR: Oregon State Univ. Press.

Chamie, J., & Nsuly, S. (1981). Sex differences in remarriage and spouse selection. *Demography, 18,* 335–348.

Chance, M. R. A. (1960). Kohler's chimpanzees—how did they perform? *Man, 60,* 130–135.

Chivers, D. J. (Ed.). (1980). *Malayan forest primates*. New York: Plenum.

Clark, C. W. (1991). Moving with the herd. *Natural History, 100,* 38–42.

Clayton, F. L., & Hinde, R. A. (1968). Habituation and recovery of aggressive display in *Betta spendens*. *Behaviour, 30,* 96–106.

Clutton-Brock, T. H., & Albon, S. D. (1979). The roaring of red deer and the evolution of honest advertisement. *Behaviour, 69,* 145–170.

Clutton-Brock, T. H., Albon, S. H., & Guinness, F. W. (1989). Fitness costs of gestation and lactation in wild mammals. *Nature, 337,* 260–262.

Clutton-Brock, T. H., & Harvey, P. H. (1977). Primate ecology and social organization. *Journal Zoo. London, 183,* 1–39.

Coile, D. C., & Miller, N. E. (1984). How radical animal activists try to mislead humane people. *American Psychologist, 39,* 700–701.

Connor, R. C., & Peterson, D. M. (1994). *The lives of whales and dolphins*. New York: Henry Holt & Co.

Cook, L. M., Mani, G. S., & Varley, M. E. (1986). Postindustrial melanism in the peppered moth. *Science, 231,* 611–613.

Cooper, R., & Zubek, J. (1958). Effects of enriched and restricted early environments on the learning ability of bright and dull rats. *Canadian Journal of Psychology, 12,* 159–164.

Cox, C. R., & LeBoeuf, B. J. (1977). Female incitation of male competition: A mechanism in sexual selection. *American Naturalist, 111,* 317–335.

Crook, J. H., & Gartlan, J. S. (1966). Evolution of primate societies. *Nature, 210,* 1200–1203.

Cullen, E. (1957). Adaptations in the kittiwake to cliff nesting. *Ibis, 99,* 275–302.

Daly, M., & Wilson, J. I. (1996). Violence against stepchildren. *Current Directions in Psychological Science, 5,* 77–81.

Darwin, C. R. (1859). *The origin of species by natural selection*. London: John Murray.

Darwin, C. R. (1871). *The descent of man and selection in relation to sex*. London: John Murray.

Darwin, C. R. (1873). *On the expression of emotion in men and animals*. New York: D. Appleton.

Davies, N. B. (1978). Territorial defence in the speckled wood butterfly (*Pararge aegeria*): The resident always wins. *Animal Behaviour, 26,* 138–147.

Davies, N. B. (1983). Polyandry, cloaca-pecking and sperm competition in dunnocks. *Nature, 302,* 334–336.

Davies, N. B. (1985). Cooperation and conflict among dunnocks, *Prunella modularis*, in a variable mating system. *Animal Behaviour, 33,* 628–648.

Davies, N. B., & Brooke, M. de L. (1988). Cuckoo vs. reed warbler: Adaptations and counteradaptations. *Animal Behaviour, 36,* 262–284.

Davies, N. B., & Halliday, T. R. (1978). Deep croaks and fighting assessment in toads (*Bufo bufo*). *Nature, 274,* 683–685.

Davies, N. B., & Lundberg, A. (1984). Food distribution and a variable mating system in the dunnock, *Prunella modularis. Journal of Animal Ecology, 53,* 895–913.

Dawkins, M. (1971). Perceptual changes in chicks: Another look at the "search image" concept. *Animal Behaviour, 19,* 556–574.

Dawkins, R. (1989). *The selfish gene* (revised edition). Oxford: Oxford Univ. Press.

Dawkins, R., & Carlisle, T. R. (1976). Parental investment, mate desertion and a fallacy. *Nature, 262,* 131–133.

Dawkins, R., & Krebs, J. R. (1978). Animal signals: Information or manipulation? In J. R. Krebs, & N. B. Davies (Eds.), *Behavioural ecology—an evolutionary approach.* Sunderland, MA: Sinauer Associates.

Dawkins, R., & Krebs, J. R. (1979). Arms races between and within species. *Procedures of the Royal Society of London, 205,* 489–511.

Dennett, D. C. (1991). *Consciousness explained.* Boston: Little, Brown.

de Waal, F. B. M. (1989). *Peacemaking among primates.* Cambridge, MA: Harvard Univ. Press.

Dewsbury, D. A. (1978). *Comparative animal behavior.* New York: McGraw-Hill.

Dewsbury, D. A. (1988). The comparative psychology of monogamy. In D. W. Leger (Ed.), *Comparative perspectives in modern psychology: Nebraska Symposium on Motivation* (Vol. 35), pp. 1–50. Lincoln, NE: Univ. of Nebraska Press.

Dewsbury, D. A. (1990). Early interactions between animal psychologists and animal activists and the founding of the APA Committee on Precaution in Animal Experimentation. *American Psychologist, 45,* 315–327.

Diamond, J. (1992). *The third chimpanzee: The evolution and future of the human animal.* New York: HarperCollins.

Diamond, J. (1996). Why women change. *Discover, 17,* 130–137.

Dixson, A. F. (1981). *The natural history of the gorilla.* New York: Columbia Univ. Press.

Dobzhansky, T. (1955). *Evolution, genetics, and man.* New York: John Wiley.

Dodds, W. J., & Orlans, F. B. (Eds.). (1982). *Scientific perspectives on animal welfare.* New York: Academic Press.

Drickamer, L. C., & Stuart, J. (1984). Peromyscus: Snow tracking and possible cues for navigation. *Amer. Mid. Nat., 111,* 202–204.

Drickamer, L. C., & Vessey, S. H. (1992). *Animal behavior* (3rd ed.). Dubuque, IA: Wm. C. Brown.

Durham, W. H. (1979). Toward a co-evolutionary theory of human biology and culture. In N. A. Chagnon, & W. Irons (Eds.), *Evolutionary biology and human social behavior: An anthropological perspective.* N. Scituate, MA: Duxbury.

Earle, S. A. (1979). The gentle whale. *National Geographic, 155(1),* 2–17.

Edmunds, M. (1975). *Defence in animals.* New York: Longman.

Emlen, S. T. (1975). The stellar-orientation system of a migratory bird. *Scientific American, 233,* 102–111.

Emlen, S. T., & Oring, L. W. (1977). Ecology, sexual selection, and the evolution of mating systems. *Science, 197,* 215–233.

Epstein, R., Kirshuit, C. E., Lanza, R. P., & Rubin, L. C. (1984). "Insight" in the pigeon: Antecedents and determinants of an intelligent performance. *Nature, 308,* 61–62.

Erichsen, J. T., Krebs, J. R., & Houston, A. I. (1980). Optimal foraging and cryptic prey. *Journal of Animal Ecology, 49,* 271–276.

Erwin, T. L. (1983). Beetles and other insects of tropical rain forest canopies at Manaus, Brazil, sampled by insecticidal fogging. In S. L. Sutton, T. C. Whitmore, & A. C. Chadwick (Eds.), *Tropical rain forest: Ecology and management,* pp. 59–75. London: Blackwell.

Estes, W. K. (1944). An experimental study of punishment. *Psychological Monographs, 57* (Whole No. 263).

Evans, M. R., & Hatchwell, B. J. (1992). An experimental study of male adornment in the scarlet-tufted malachite sunbird: I. The pectoral tufts in territorial defense. *Behav. Ecol. Sociobiol., 29,* 413–419.

Fagen, R. (1981). *Animal play behavior.* New York: Oxford Univ. Press.

Faulkes, C. G., Abbott, D. H., & Mellnor, A. L. (1990). Investigation of genetic diversity in wild colonies of naked mole-rats (*Heterocephalus glaber*) by DNA fingerprinting. *Journal Zoo. London, 221,* 87–97.

Fenton, M. B., & Fullard, J. H. (1981). Moth hearing and the feeding strategies of bats. *American Scientist, 69,* 266–275.

Fischer, E. A. (1980). The relationship between mating system and simultaneous hermaphroditism in the coral reef fish, *Hypoplectus nigricans. Animal Behaviour, 28,* 620–633.

Fisher, A. C., Jr. (1979). Mysteries of bird migration. *National Geographic, 156(2),* 154–193.

Fisher, R. A. (1930). *The genetical theory of natural selection.* Oxford: Oxford Univ. Press.

Fitzgibbon, C. D. (1989). A cost to individuals with reduced vigilance in groups of Thomson's gazelles hunted by cheetahs. *Animal Behavior, 37,* 508–510.

Fontaine, R. P. (1994). Play as physical flexibility training in five ceboid primates. *Journal of Comparative Psychology, 108,* 203–212.

Ford, J. K. B. (1991). Family fugues. *Natural History, 100,* 68–76.

Foree, D. D., & LoLorde, V. M. (1973). Attention in the pigeon: The differential effects of food-getting vs. shock-avoidance procedures. *Journal of Comparative and Physiological Psychology, 85,* 551–558.

Fossey, D. (1983). *Gorillas in the mist.* Boston: Houghton Mifflin.

Franks, N. R. (1989). Army ants: A collective intelligence. *American Scientist, 77,* 138–145.

Fuller, J. L., & Wimer, R. E. (1973). Behavior genetics. In D. A. Dewsbury, and D. A. Rethlingshafer (Eds.), *Comparative psychology: A modern survey,* pp. 197–237. New York: McGraw-Hill.

Gallup, G. G., Jr. (1970). Chimpanzees: Self-recognition. *Science, 167,* 86–87.

Gallup, G. G., Jr. (1977). Self-recognition in primates: A comparative approach to the bidirectional properties of consciousness. *American Psychologist, 32,* 329–338.

Garcia, J., Hankins, W. G., & Rusiniak, K. W. (1974). Behavioral regulation of the milieu interne in man and rat. *Science, 185,* 824–831.

Gardner, B. T., & Gardner, R. A. (1969). Teaching sign language to a chimpanzee. *Science, 162,* 664–672.

Gardner, B. T., & Gardner, R. A. (1975). Early signs of language in child and chimpanzee. *Science, 187,* 752–753.

Gendron, R. P. (1986). Search for cryptic prey: Evidence for optimal search rates and the formation of search images in quail. *Animal Behaviour, 34,* 898–912.

Gill, F. B., & Wolf, L. L. (1975). Economics of feeding territoriality in the golden-winged sunbird. *Ecology, 56,* 333–345.

Giraldeau, L. A., & Kramer, D. L. (1982). The marginal value theorem: A quantitative test using load size variation in a central place forager, the eastern chipmunk, *Tamias striatus. Animal Behaviour, 30,* 1036–1042.

Glander, K. E. (1981). Feeding patterns in mantled howling monkeys. In A. C. Kamil, & T. D. Sargent (Eds.), *Foraging behavior: Ecological, ethological and psychological approaches.* New York: Garland Press.

Goldfarb, W. (1943). Infant rearing and problem behavior. *American Journal of Orthopsychiatry, 13,* 249–266.

Goldfarb, W. (1945). Effects of psychological deprivation in infancy and subsequent stimulation. *American Journal of Psychiatry, 102,* 18–33.

Goodall, J. (1971). *In the shadow of man.* Boston: Houghton Mifflin.

Goodall, J. (1986). *The chimpanzees of Gombe.* Cambridge, MA: Harvard Univ. Press.

Gottlieb, G. (1991). Experiential canalization of development: Results. *Developmental Psychology, 27,* 35–39.

Gould, S. J. (1994). The evolution of life on the earth. *Scientific American, 271(4),* 85–91.

Gould, S. J., & Eldredge, N. (1977). Punctuated equilibria: The tempo and mode of evolution reconsidered. *Paleobiology, 3,* 115–151.

Green, S. (1975). Dialects in Japanese monkeys. *Zeitschrift fur Tierpsychologie, 38,* 305–314.

Greene, E. (1987). Individuals in an osprey colony discriminate between high and low quality information. *Nature, 329,* 239–241.

Greenenough, W. T., & Green, E. J. (1981). Experience and the aging brain. In J. L. McGaugh, J. G. March, & S. B. Kiesler (Eds.), *Aging: Biology and Behavior.* New York: Academic Press.

Grier, J. W., & Burk, T. (1992). *Biology of animal behavior* (2nd ed.). St. Louis, MO: Mosby-Year Book.

Griffin, D. R. (1959). *Echoes of bats and men.* New York: Doubleday.

Griffin, D. R. (1981). *The question of animal awareness* (2nd ed.). New York: Rockefeller Univ. Press.

Gross, M. R. (1985). Disruptive selection for alternative life histories in salmon. *Nature, 313,* 47–48.

Gross, M. R., & Sargent, R. C. (1985). The evolution of male and female parental care in fishes. *American Zoologist, 25,* 807–822.

Gross, M. R., & Shine, R. (1981). Parental care and mode of fertilization in ectothermic vertebrates. *Evolution, 35,* 775–793.

Hall, C. S. (1934). Emotional behavior in the rat: 1. Defecation and urination as measures of individual differences in emotionality. *Journal of Comparative Psychology, 18,* 385–403.

Hamilton, W. D. (1964). The genetical evolution of social behavior. *Journal of Theoretical Biology, 7,* 1–52.

Hamilton, W. D. (1971). Geometry for the selfish herd. *Journal of Theoretical Biology, 31,* 295–311.

Hamilton, W. D., & Zuk, M. (1982). Heritable true fitness and bright birds: A role for parasites? *Science, 218,* 384–387.

Harlow, H. F. (1971). *Learning to love.* San Francisco: Albion.

Harlow, H. F., & Harlow, M. K. (1962). Social deprivation in monkeys. *Scientific American, 207,* 136–146.

Harlow, H. F., Harlow, M. K., & Suomi, S. J. (1971). From thought to therapy: Lessons from a primate laboratory. *American Scientist, 59,* 538–549.

Harlow, H. F., & Zimmerman, R. R. (1959). Affectional responses in the infant monkey. *Science, 130,* 421–432.

Hay, R. L., & Leakey, M. D. (1982). The fossil footprints of Laetoli. *Scientific American, 246,* 50–57.

Hayes, C. (1951). *The ape in our house.* New York: Harper.

Heinrich, B. (1989). *Ravens in winter.* New York: Summit Books.

Hess, E. H. (1973). *Imprinting.* New York: Van Nostrand.

Holldobler, B. (1977). Communication in social Hymenoptera. In T. A. Seboek (Ed.), *How animals communicate,* pp. 418–471. Bloomington, IN: Indiana Univ. Press.

Holldobler, B., & Wilson, E. O. (1994). *Journey to the ants.* Cambridge, MA: Harvard Univ. Press.

Hollis, K. L. (1984). The biological function of Pavlovian conditioning: The best defense is a good offense. *Journal of Experimental Psychology: Animal Behavior Processes, 10,* 413–425.

Hollis, K. L. (1990). The role of Pavlovian conditioning in territorial aggression and reproduction. In Dewsbury, D. A. (Ed.), *Contemporary issues in comparative psychology,* pp. 197–219. Sunderland, MA: Sinauer Associates.

Holmes, W. (1940). The colour changes and colour patterns of *Sepia officinalis. L. Proc. Zool. Soc. London, 110,* 17–35.

Holmes, W. G. (1991). Predator risk affects foraging behavior of pikas: Observational and experimental evidence. *Animal Behaviour, 42,* 111–119.

Holmes, W. G., & Sherman, P. W. (1982). The ontogeny of kin recognition in two species of ground squirrels. *American Zoologist, 22,* 491–517.

Holmes, W. G., & Sherman, P. W. (1983). Kin recognition in animals. *American Scientist, 71,* 46–55.

Honeycutt, R. L. (1992). Naked mole-rats. *American Scientist, 80,* 43–53.

Hopkins, C. D. (1974). Electric communication in fish. *American Scientist, 62,* 426–437.

Howard, R. D. (1978). The evolution of mating strategies in bullfrogs, *Rana catesbiana. Evolution, 2,* 850–871.

Hrdy, S. B. (1977). *The langurs of Abu: Female and male strategies of reproduction.* Cambridge, MA: Harvard Univ. Press.

Hrdy, S. B. (1979). Infanticide among animals: A review, classification, and examination of the reproductive strategies of females. *Ethology and Sociobiology, 1,* 13–40.

Hunt, G. R. (1996). Manufacture and use of hook-tools by New Caledonian crows. *Nature, 379,* 249–251.

Huntingford, F., & Turner, A. (1987). *Animal conflict.* London: Chapman & Hall.

Ims, R. A. (1987). Responses in spatial organization & behaviour to manipulations of the food source in the vole *Clethrionomys rufocanus. Journal of Animal Ecology, 56,* 585–596.

Isaac, G. (1978). The sharing hypothesis. *Scientific American, 238,* 90–106.

Itani, J. (1958). On the acquisition & propagation of a new food habit in the troop of Japanese monkeys at Takasakiyama. *Primates, 1,* 131–148.

Jarman, P. J. (1974). The social organisation of antelopes in relation to their ecology. *Behaviour, 48,* 215–267.

Jaynes, J. (1976). *The origins of consciousness in the breakdown of the bicameral mind.* Boston: Houghton Mifflin.

Jenni, D. A. (1974). Evolution of polyandry in birds. *American Zoology, 14,* 129–144.

Johnsgard, P. A. (1981). *Those of the gray winds: The sandhill cranes.* New York: St. Martin's Press.

Johnston, T. D., & Gottlieb, G. (1981). Visual preferences of imprinted ducklings are altered by the maternal call. *Journal of Comparative and Physiological Psychology, 95,* 663–675.

Kacelnik, A. (1984). Central place foraging in starlings (*Sturnus vulgaris*). I. Patch residence time. *Journal of Animal Ecology, 53,* 283–299.

Kalmijn, A. J. (1971). The electric sense of sharks and rays. *Journal of Experimental Biology, 55,* 371–383.

Kamil, A. C., & Clements, K. C. (1990). Learning, memory, and foraging behavior. In Dewsbury, D. A. (Ed.), *Contemporary issues in comparative psychology,* pp. 7–30. Sunderland, MA: Sinauer Associates.

Kano, T., & Mulavwa, M. (1984). Feeding ecology of the pygmy chimpanzees of Wamba. In Susman, R. (Ed.), *The pygmy chimpanzee,* pp. 233–274. New York: Plenum.

Kaufman, I. C., & Rosenblum, L. A. (1967). Depression in infant monkeys separated from their mothers. *Science, 155,* 1030–1031.

Kaufman, T. H. (1962). Ecology and social behavior of the coati, *Nasua nasica,* on Barro Colorado Island, Panama. *University of California Publications in Zoology, 60,* 95–222.

Kawai, M. (1965). Newly acquired precultural behavior of the natural troop of Japanese monkeys on Koshima Island. *Primates, 6,* 1–30.

Keeton, W. T. (1974). The orientation and navigational basis of homing in birds. *Advanced Studies of Behavior, 5,* 47–132.

Kenward, R. E. (1978). Hawks and doves: Factors affecting success and selection in goshawk attacks on wild pigeons. *Journal of Animal Ecology, 47,* 449–460.

Kessel, E. L. (1955). The mating activities of balloon flies. *Systematic Zoology, 4,* 97–104.

Kettlewell, H. B. D. (1965). Insect survival and selection for pattern. *Science, 148,* 1290–1296.

Kiltie, R. A. (1989). Wildfire and the evolution of dorsal melanism in fox squirrels, *Sciurus niger. Journal of Mammalogy, 70,* 726–739.

King, M. C., & Wilson, A. C. (1975). Evolution of two levels in humans and chimpanzees. *Science, 188,* 107–188.

Kingdon, J. S. (1980). The role of visual signals and face patterns in African forest monkeys (guenons) of the genus *Cercopithecus. Transactions of the Zoological Society of London, 34,* 425–475.

Kirchner, W. H., & Towne, W. F. (1994). The sensory basis of the honeybee's dance language. *Scientific American, 270* (June), 74–80.

Kleiman, D. G. (1977). Monogamy in mammals. *Quarterly Review of Biology, 52,* 39–69.

Klimley, A. P. (1995). Hammerhead city. *Natural History, 10,* 33–39.

Kohler, W. (1925). *The mentality of apes.* New York: Harcourt, Brace.

Kramer, D. L., & Weary, D. M. (1991). Exploration vs. exploitation: A field study of time allocation to environmental tracking by foraging chipmunks. *Animal Behaviour, 41,* 443–449.

Krebs, J. R. (1971). Territory and breeding density in the great tit, *Parus major. Ecology, 52,* 2–22.

Krebs, J. R., & Davies, N. B. (1993). *An introduction to behavioural ecology* (3rd ed.). Oxford: Blackwell Scientific Publications.

Kruuk, H. (1972a). *The spotted hyena: A study of predation and social behavior.* Chicago: Univ. of Chicago Press.

Kruuk, H. (1972b). Surplus killing by carnivores. *Journal of Zoology, 166,* 233–244.

Kuroda, S. (1984). Interactions over food among pygmy chimpanzees. In R. Susman (Ed.), *The pygmy chimpanzee,* pp. 301–324. New York: Plenum.

Lack, D. (1966). *Population studies of birds.* Oxford: Clarendon Press.

Lack, D. (1968). *Ecological adaptations for breeding in birds.* London: Methuen.

Larkin, T. S., & Keeton, W. T. (1976). Bar magnets mask the effect of normal magnetic disturbances on pigeon orientation. *Journal of Comparative Physiology, 110,* 227–231.

Leakey, R. (1994). *The origin of humankind.* New York: Basic Books.

LeBoeuf, B. J., & Reuter, J. (1988). Lifetime reproductive success in northern elephant seals. In T. H. Clutton-Brock (Ed.), *Reproductive success.* Chicago: Univ. of Chicago Press.

Lloyd, J. E. (1965). Aggressive mimicry in *Photuris:* Firefly *femmes fatales. Science, 149,* 653–654.

Lorenz, K. (1932). Betrachtungen uber das Erkennen der arteigenen Triebhandlungen der Vogel. *J. Ornithol., 80,* 50–98.

Lorenz, K. (1935). Der Kumpan in der Umwelt des Vogels. *Journal fur Ornithologie, 83,* 137–413. (Reprinted as "Companions as factors in the bird's environment" in K. Lorenz (1970), *Studies in animal and human behavior,* Vol. 1, Cambridge, MA: Harvard Univ. Press)

Lorenz, K. (1971). Comparative studies of the motor patterns of Anatinae. In K. Lorenz (Ed.), *Studies in animal and human behavior,* Vol. II. Cambridge, MA: Harvard Univ. Press.

Lorenz, K. (1981). *The foundations of ethnology.* New York: Simon & Schuster.

Lovejoy, C. O. (1981). The origin of man. *Science, 211,* 341–450.

Lovejoy, C. O. (1988). Evolution of human walking. *Scientific American, 259,* 118–125.

Lynch, C. B., & Hegmann, J. P. (1972). Genetic differences influencing behavioral temperature regulation in small mammals. I. Nesting by *Mus musculus. Behav. Gen., 2,* 43–54.

MacArthur, R. H. (1958). Population ecology of some warblers of northeastern coniferous forests. *Ecology, 39,* 599–619.

MacKinnon, J. (1974). The ecology and behaviour of wild orangutans, *Pongo pygmaeus. Animal Behaviour, 22,* 3–74.

Marler, P. (1970a). Birdsong and speech development: Could there be parallels? *American Scientist, 58,* 669–673.

Marler, P. (1970b). A comparative approach to vocal learning: Song development in white-crowned sparrows. *Journal of Comparative Physiological Psychology Monographs, 71,* 1–25.

Marler, P. (1973). A comparison of vocalization of red tailed monkeys and blue monkeys, *Cercopithecus ascanius* and *C. mitis,* in Uganda. *Zietschrift fur Tierpsychologie, 33,* 239–248.

Marler, P. (1985). Representational vocal signals in primates. In B. Holldobler, & M. Lindauer (Eds.), *Experimental behavioral ecology and sociobiology,* pp. 211–221. Sunderland, MA: Sinauer Associates.

Marler, P., & Mundinger, P. (1971). Vocal learning in birds. In H. Moltz (Ed.), *The ontogeny of vertebrate behavior.* New York: Academic Press.

Marler, P., & Peters, S. (1988). The role of song phonology and syntax in vocal learning preferences in the song sparrow, *Melospiza melodia. Ethology, 77,* 125–149.

Marler, P., & Tamura, M. (1964). Culturally transmitted patterns of vocal behavior in sparrows. *Science, 146,* 1486.

Mason, W. A., & Berkson, G. (1975). Effects of maternal mobility on the development of rocking and other behaviors in rhesus monkeys: A study with artificial mothers. *Developmental Psychobiology, 8,* 197–211.

May, M. (1991). Aerial defense tactics of flying insects. *American Scientist, 79,* 316–328.

Maynard Smith, J. (1974). The theory of games and the evolution of animal conflict. *Journal of Theoretical Biology, 47,* 209–221.

Maynard Smith, J. (1976). Evolution and the theory of games. *American Scientist, 64,* 41–45.

Maynard Smith, J. (1991). Theories of sexual selection. *Trends in Ecology and Evolution, 6,* 146–151.

Maynard Smith, J., & Price, G. R. (1973). The logic of animal conflict. *Nature, 246,* 15–18.

Maynard Smith, J., & Ridpath, M. G. (1972). Wife sharing in the Tasmanian native hen *Tribonyx mortierii:* A case of kin selection. *American Naturalist, 106,* 447–452.

McCosker, J. E. (1977). Flashlight fishes. *Scientific American, 236*(3), 106–114.

Mech, L. D. (1970). *The wolf: The ecology and behavior of an endangered species.* Garden City, NY: Natural History Press.

Menzel, E. W. (1971). Communication about the environment in a group of young chimpanzees. *Folia Primat., 15,* 220–232.

Menzel, E. W. (1978). Cognitive mapping in chimpanzees. In S. H. Hulse, H. F. Fowler, & W. K. Honig (Eds.), *Cognitive processes in animal behavior.* Hillsdale, NJ: Erlbaum.

Metzgar, L. H. (1967). An experimental comparison of screech owl predation on resident and transient white-footed mice (*Peromyscus leucopus*). *Journal of Mammalogy, 48,* 387–391.

Miles, H. L. (1983). Apes and language: The search for communicative competence. In J. de Luce & H. T. Wilder (Eds.), *Language in primates: Perspectives and implications,* pp. 43–61. New York: Springer.

Miller, N. E. (1985). The value of behavioral research on animals. *American Psychologist, 40,* 423–440.

Mineka, S., & Suomi, S. J. (1978). Social separation in monkeys. *Psychological Bulletin, 85,* 1376–1400.

Mock, D. W., Drummond, H., & Stinson, C. H. (1990). Avian siblicide. *American Scientist, 78,* 438–449.

Moehlman, P. D. (1979). Jackal helpers and pup survival. *Nature, 277,* 382–383.

Moehlman, P. D. (1987). Social organization in jackals. *American Scientist, 75,* 366–375.

Molnar, R. E. (1977). Analogies in the evolution of comb and display structures in ornithopods and ungulates. *Evolutionary Theory, 3,* 165–190.

Morgan, C. L. (1894). *An introduction to comparative psychology.* New York: Scribner.

Mortimer, M. A. E. (1963). Notes on the biology and behavior of the spotted-necked otter (*Lutra maculicollis*). *Puku, 1,* 192–206.

Moynihan, M. H., & Rodaniche, A. F. (1977). Communication, crypsis, and mimicry among cephalopods. In T. A. Sebeok (Ed.), *How animals communicate.* Bloomington, IN: Indiana Univ. Press.

Murdock, G. P. (1967). *Ethnographic atlas.* Pittsburgh, PA: Univ. of Pittsburgh Press.

Norris, K. S., & Mohl, B. (1983). Can odontecetes debilitate prey with sound? *American Naturalist, 122,* 85–104.

Norton-Griffiths, M. (1969). The organization, control and development of parental feeding in the oystercatcher (*Haemotopus ostralegus*). *Behaviour, 34,* 55–114.

Oliver, M. B., & Hyde, J. S. (1993). Gender differences in sexuality: A meta-analysis. *Psychological Bulletin, 114,* 29–51.

Olton, D. S., & Samuelson, R. J. (1976). Remembrances of places passed: Spatial memory in rats. *Journal of Experimental Psychology: Animal Behavior Processes, 2,* 96–116.

Orians, G. H. (1969). On the evaluation of mating systems in birds and mammals. *American Naturalist, 103,* 589–603.

Oring, L. W. (1981). Avian mating systems. In D. S. Farner, & J. R. King (Eds.), *Avian biology* (vol. 6). London: Academic Press.

Oring, L. W., & Lank, D. B. (1982). Sexual selection, arrival times, philopatry and site fidelity in the polyandrous spotted sandpiper. *Behavioral Ecology and Sociobiology, 10,* 185–191.

Owen-Smith, N. (1977). On territory in ungulates and an evolutionary model. *Quarterly Review of Biology, 52,* 1–38.

Packer, C. (1977). Reciprocal altruism in *Papio anubis. Nature, 265,* 441–443.

Packer, C. (1986). The ecology of sociality in felids. In D. I. Rebenstin, & R. W. Wrangham (Eds.), *Ecological aspects of social evolution.* Princeton, NJ: Princeton Univ. Press.

Parker, G. A. (1970). Sperm competition and its evolutionary consequences in the insects. *Biological Review, 45,* 525–568.

Patterson, F. G. (1978). The gestures of a gorilla: Language acquisition by another pongid. *Brain and Language, 12,* 72–97.

Payne, R. B. (1977). The ecology of brood parasitism in birds. *Annual Review of Ecological Systems, 8,* 1–28.

Penrose, R. (1994). *Shadows of the mind: A search for the missing science of consciousness.* New York: Oxford Univ. Press.

Pepperberg, I. M. (1990). Cognition in an African gray parrot (*Psittacus erithacus*): Further evidence for comprehension of categories and labels. *Journal of Comparative Psychology, 105,* 318–325.

Pfaffenberger, C. J., Fuller, J. L., Ginsberg, B. E., & Bielfelt, S. W. (1976). *Guide dogs for the blind: Their selection, development and training.* Amsterdam: Elsevier.

Plomin, R., DeFries, J. C., & McClearn, G. E. (1990). *Behavioral genetics: A primer* (2nd ed.). New York: W. H. Freeman.

Polis, G. A., Myers, C. A., & Hess, W. R. (1984). A survey of intraspecific predation within the class Mammalis. *Mammal Review, 14,* 187–198.

Poppleton, F. (1957). An elephant birth. *African Wild Life, 11,* 106–108.

Porter, R. H., Wynick, M., & Pankey, J. (1978). Sibling recognition in spiny mice (*Acomys cahirinus*). *Behavioral Ecology and Sociobiology, 3,* 61–68.

Premack, D. (1971). On the assessment of language competence in the chimpanzee. In A. M. Schrier & F. Stollnitz (Eds.), *Behavior of nonhuman primates* (Vol. 4), pp. 186–228. New York: Academic Press.

Provence, S., & Lipton, R. (1962). *Infants in institutions.* New York: International Universities Press.

Pyke, G. H., Pulliam, H. R., & Charnov, E. L. (1977). Optimal foraging: A selective review of theory and tests. *Quarterly Review of Biology, 52,* 137–154.

Randall, J. A. (1978). Behavioral mechanisms of habitat segregation between sympatric species of *Microtus*: Habitat preference and interspecific dominance. *Behavioral Ecology and Sociobiology, 3,* 187–202.

Reading, A. J. (1966). Effect of maternal environment on the behavior of inbred mice. *Journal of Comparative and Physiological Psychology, 62,* 437–440.

Reeve, H. K., Westneat, P. W., Noon, W. A., Sherman, P. W., & Aquadro, C. F. (1990). DNA "fingerprinting" reveals high levels of inbreeding in colonies of the eusocial naked mole-rat. *Proceedings of the National Academy of Science USA, 87,* 2496–2500.

Reichard, U. (1995). Extra-pair copulations in a monogamous gibbon (*Hylobates lar*). *Ethology, 100(2),* 99–112.

Ridley, M. (1978). Paternal care. *Animal Behaviour, 26,* 904–932.

Riechert, S. E. (1984). Games spiders play III: Cues underlying context-associated changes in agonistic behavior. *Animal Behaviour, 32,* 1–15.

Rodman, P. S., & McHenry, H. M. (1980). Bioenergetics of hominid bipedalism. *American Journal of Physical Anthropology, 52,* 103–106.

Roeder, K. D. (1967). *Nerve cells and insect behavior.* Cambridge, MA: Harvard Univ. Press.

Roff, M. (1974). Childhood antecedents of adult neuroses, severe bad conduct, and psychological health. In D. Ricks, A. Thomas, & M. Roff (Eds.), *Life history research in psychopathology* (Vol. 3). Minneapolis, MN: Univ. of Minnesota Press.

Rohwer, S., & Rohwer, F. C. (1978). Status signalling in Harris sparrows: Experiential deceptions achieved. *Animal Behaviour, 76,* 1012–1022.

Rollin, B. E. (1981). *Animal rights and human morality.* Buffalo, NY: Prometheus Books.

Romanes, G. J. (1882). *Animal intelligence.* London: Kegan, Paul, Trench.

Romanes, G. J. (1884). *Mental evolution in animals.* London: Kegan, Paul, Trench.

Rosenzweig, M. R. (1966). Environmental complexity, cerebral change, and behavior. *American Psychologist, 21,* 321–332.

Rottman, S. J., & Snowden, C. T. (1972). Demonstration and analysis of an alarm pheromone in mice. *Journal of Comparative and Physiological Psychology, 81,* 483–490.

Rudran, R. (1978). Socioecology of the blue monkey (*Cercopithecus mitis stuhlmanni*) of the Kibale Forest, Uganda. *Smithsonian Contributions to Zoology, 249,* 1–88.

Rumbaugh, D. M., Gill, T. V., & von Glasersfeld, E. C. (1973). Reading and sentence completion by a chimpanzee. *Science, 182,* 731–733.

Russell, R. J. (1993). *The lemurs' legacy: The evolution of power, sex, and love.* New York: C. P. Putnam's Sons.

Rutberg, A. T. (1983). The evolution of monogamy in primates. *Journal of Theoretical Biology, 104,* 93–112.

Rutberg, A. T. (1986). Dominance and its fitness consequences in American bison cows. *Behaviour, 96,* 62–91.

Ryan, M. J., & Tuttle, M. D. (1983). The ability of the frog eating bat to discriminate among normal and potentially poisonous frog species using acoustic cues. *Animal Behaviour, 31,* 827–833.

Sauer, E. G. F. (1957). Die Sternenorientierung nachtlich ziehender Grasmucken (*Sylava atricapilla, borin* und *curruca*). *Zeitschrift fur Tierpsychologie, 14,* 29–70.

Savage-Rumbaugh, E. S., Revcik, R. A., Rumbaugh, D. M., & Rubert, E. (1985). The capacity of animals to acquire language: Do species differences have anything to say to us? *Philosophical Transactions.* Royal Society of London, *B308,* 177–185.

Savage-Rumbaugh, E. S., Rumbaugh, D. M.. & Boysen, S. (1980). Do apes use language? *American Scientist, 68,* 49–61.

Schaller, G. (1972). *The Serengeti lion.* Chicago: Univ. of Chicago Press.

Schaller, G. B. (1963). *The mountain gorilla.* Chicago: Univ. of Chicago Press.

Schaller, G. B., & Lowther, G. (1969). The relevance of carnivore behavior to the study of early hominids. *Southwest Journal of Anthropology, 25,* 307–341.

Schiller, P. (1952). Innate constituents of complex responses in primates. *Psychological Review, 59,* 177–191.

Schmidt-Koenig, K., & Schlichte, H. J. (1972). Homing in pigeons with reduced vision. *Proc. Nat. Acad. Sci. USA, 69,* 2246–2247.

Schwartz, J. (1987). *The red ape: Orangutans and human origins.* Boston: Houghton Mifflin.

Schwegmeyer, P. L. (1988). Scramble-competition polygyny in an asocial animal: Male mobility and mating success. *American Naturalist, 131,* 885–892.

Scott, J. P., & Fuller, J. L. (1965). *Genetics and the social behavior of the dog.* Chicago: Univ. of Chicago Press.

Searle, L. V. (1949). The organization of hereditary maze-brightness and maze-dullness. *General Psychology Monographs, 39,* 279–335.

Seibt, U., & Wickler, W. (1987). Gerontophagy vs. cannibalism in social spiders *Stegodyphus mimosarum* Pavesi and *Stegodyphus dumicola* Pocock. *Animal Behaviour, 35,* 1903–1905.

Seligman, M. E. P. (1970). On the generality of the law of learning. *Psychological Review, 77,* 406–418.

Seyfarth, R. M., Cheney, D. L., & Marler, P. (1980). Monkey responses to three different alarm calls: Evidence of predator classification and semantic communication. *Science, 210,* 801–803.

Sherman, P. W. (1977). Nepotism and the evolution of alarm calls. *Science, 197,* 1246–1253.

Sherman, P. W., Jarvis, J. U. M., & Alexander, R. D. (Eds.). (1991). *The biology of the naked mole rat.* Trenton, NJ: Princeton Univ. Press.

Sherman, P. W., Jarvis, J. U. M., & Braude, S. H. (1992). Naked mole rats. *Scientific American, 267(2),* 72–78.

Shettleworth, S. J. (1983). Memory in food-hoarding birds. *Scientific American, 248,* 102–110.

Shettleworth, S. J. (1984). Learning and behavioral ecology. In Krebs, J. R., & Davies, N. B. (Eds.), *Behavioural ecology: An evolutionary approach,* pp. 179–194. Sunderland, MA: Sinauer Associates.

Skeels, H. (1966). Adult status of children with contrasting early life experiences. *Monographs of the Society for Research in Child Development, 31(3).*

Skinner, B. F. (1938). *Behavior of organisms: An experimental analysis.* New York: Appleton-Century-Crofts.

Skinner, B. F. (1953). *Science and human behavior.* New York: Macmillan.

Skinner, B. F. (1958). Reinforcement today. *American Psychologist, 13,* 94–99.

Slater, P. J. B. (1989). Bird song learning: Causes and consequences. *Ethology, Ecology and Evolution, 1,* 19–46.

Slatkin, M., & Maynard Smith, J. (1979). Models of coevolution. *Quarterly Review of Biology, 54,* 233–263.

Smith, W. J. (1984). *The behavior of communicating: An ethnological approach* (2nd ed.). Cambridge, MA: Harvard Univ. Press.

Smuts, B. (1983a). Dynamics of special relationships between adult male and female olive baboons. In R. Hinde (Ed.), *Primate social relationships: An integrated approach,* pp. 112–116. Oxford: Blackwell.

Smuts, B. (1983b). Special relationships between adult male and female olive baboons: Selective advantages. In R. Hinde (Ed.), *Primate social relationships: An integrated approach,* pp. 267–271. Oxford: Blackwell

Smuts, B. B., Cheney, D. L., Seyfarth, R. M. M., Wrangham, R. W., & Struhsaker, T. (1986). *Primate societies.* Chicago: Univ. of Chicago Press.

Snowdon, C. T. (1990). Mechanisms maintaining monogamy in monkeys. In D. A. Dewsbury (Ed.), *Contemporary issues in comparative psychology,* pp. 225–251. Sunderland, MA: Sinauer Associates.

Snyderman, M., & Rothman, S. (1987). Survey of expert opinion on intelligence and aptitude testing. *American Psychologist, 42,* 137–144.

Southern, W. E. (1972). Magnets disrupt the orientation of juvenile ring-billed gulls. *BioScience, 22,* 476–479.

Steele, B. F., & Pollock, C. P. (1968). A psychiatric study of parents who abuse infants and small children. In R. E. Helfer, & C. H. Kempe (Eds.), *The battered child,* pp. 103–147. Chicago: Univ. of Chicago Press.

Stephens, D. W. (1987). On economically tracking a variable environment. *Theoret. Pop. Biol., 32,* 15–25.

Stewart, B. S. (1996). Uncommon commuters. *Natural History, 105(2),* 59–63.

Stinson, C. H. (1979). On the selective advantage of fratricide in raptors. *Evolution, 33,* 1219–1225.

Strum, S. C. (1981). Baboons: Social strategies par excellence. *Wildlife News, 16,* 2–6.

Strum, S. C. (1987). *Almost human.* London: Elmtree Books.

Suomi, S. J., Harlow, H. F., & Novak, M. A. (1974). Reversal of social deficits produced by isolation rearing in monkeys. *Journal of Human Evolution, 3,* 527–534.

Tacha, T. C. (1988). Social organization of the sandhill cranes from midcontinental North America. *Wildlife Monograph, 99,* 1–37.

Terrace, H. S. (1979). *Nim.* New York: Knopf.

Terrace, H. S. (1982). Evidence for sign language in apes: What the ape signed or how well was the ape loved? *Contemporary Psychology, 27,* 67–68.

Thorndike, E. L. (1898). Animal intelligence: An experimental study of the association processes in animals. *Psychological Monographs, 2* (No. 8).

Tinbergen, N. (1951). *The study of instinct.* Oxford: Oxford Univ. Press.

Tinbergen, N. (1952). The curious behavior of the stickleback. *Scientific American, 187,* 22–26.

Tinbergen, N. (1953). *The herring-gull's world.* London: Collins.

Tinbergen, N. (1958). *Curious naturalists.* New York: Doubleday.

Tinbergen, N. (1963a). On aims and methods of ethology. *Zeitschrift fur Tierpsychologie, 20,* 410–433.

Tinbergen, N. (1963b). The shell menace. *Natural History, 72* (Aug.), 28–35.

Tolman, E. C. (1948). Cognitive maps in rats and man. *Psychological Review, 55,* 189–208.

Trivers, R. L. (1971). The evolution of reciprocal altruism. *Quarterly Review of Biology, 46,* 35–57.

Trivers, R. L. (1972). Parental investment and sexual selection. In B. Campbell (Ed.), *Sexual selection and the descent of man 1871–1971.* Chicago: Aldine.

Trivers, R. L. (1974). Parent-offspring conflict. *American Zoologist, 14,* 249–264.

Tryon, R. C. (1940). Studies in individual differences in maze ability VII: The specific components of maze ability and a general theory of psychological components. *Journal of Comparative and Physiological Psychology, 30,* 283–335.

Tsingalia, H. M., & Rowell, T. E. (1984). The behavior of adult blue monkeys. *Zeitschrift fur Tierpsychologie, 64,* 253–268.

Turner, E. R. A. (1964). Social feeding in birds. *Behaviour, 24,* 1–46.

Tyler, M. J., & Carter, D. B. (1981). Oral birth of the young of the gastric brooding frog *Rheobatrachus silus. Animal Behaviour, 29,* 280–282.

van Hooff, J. A. R. A. M. (1962). Facial expressions of the higher primates. *Sym-posium of the Zoological Society of London, 8,* 97–125.

van Lawick, H., & van Lawick-Goodall, J. (1970). *Innocent killers.* Boston: Houghton Mifflin.

von Frisch, K. (1967). *The dance language and orientation of bees.* Cambridge, MA: Harvard Univ. Press.

Waage, J. K. (1979). Dual functions of the damselfly penis: Sperm removal and transfer. *Science, 203,* 916–918.

Walcott, C., Gould, J. L., & Kirschvink, J. L. (1979). Pigeons have magnets. *Science, 205,* 1027–1029.

Weber, N. A. (1972). The attines: The fungus-cutting ants. *American Scientist, 60,* 448–456.

Weigmann, C. K. & Lamprecht, J. (1991). Intraspecific nest parasitism in bar-headed geese, *Anser indicus. Animal Behaviour, 41,* 677–688.

Weiner, J. (1994). *The beak of the finch: A story of evolution in our time.* New York: Alfred A. Knopf.

Weiss, B. A., & Schneirla, T. C. (1967). Intersituational transfer in the ant *Formica schaufussi* as tested in a two-phase single choice point maze. *Behaviour, 28,* 269–279.

Welty, J. C. (1962). *The life of birds.* Philadelphia, PA: Saunders.

Welty, J. C. (1975). *The life of birds* (2nd ed.). Philadelphia, PA: Saunders.

Whitfield, D. P. (1986). Plumage variability and territoriality in breeding turnstone, *Arenaria interpres:* Status signalling or individual recognition? *Animal Behaviour, 34,* 1471–1482.

Wiley, R. H. (1973). Territoriality and nonrandom mating in sage grouse, *Certrocerus urophasianus. Animal Behavior Monographs, 6,* 85–169.

Wilkinson, G. S. (1984). Reciprocal food sharing in the vampire bat. *Nature, 308,* 181–184.

Williams, G. C. (1975). *Sex and evolution.* Princeton, NJ: Princeton Univ. Press.

Wills, C. (1993). *The runaway brain: The evolution of human uniqueness.* New York: Basic Books.

Wilson, E. O. (1975). *Sociobiology: The new synthesis.* Cambridge, MA: Harvard Univ. Press.

Wilson, E. O. (1985). The sociogenesis of insect colonies. *Science, 228,* 1489–1495.

Wilson, E. O. (1992). *The diversity of life.* Cambridge, MA: Harvard Univ. Press.

Wilson, E. O., & Bossert, W. H. (1971). *A primer of population biology.* Sunderland, MA: Sinauer Associates.

Wilson, M. I., & Daly, M. (1996). Male sexual proprietariness and violence against wives. *Current Directions in Psychological Science, 5,* 2–7.

Wingfield, J. C. (1984). Environmental and endocrine control of reproduction in the song sparrow, *Melospiza medodia.* I. Temporal organization of the breeding cycle. *General Comparative Endocrinology, 56,* 406–416.

Wittenberger, J. F. (1981). *Animal social behavior.* Boston: Duxbury Press.

Wolcott, D. L., & Wolcott, T. G. (1984). Food quality and cannibalism in the red land crab *Gecareinus lateralis. Physiological Zoology, 57,* 318–324.

Woolfenden, G. E., & Fitzpatrick, J. W. (1984). *The Florida scrub jay.* Princeton, NJ: Princeton Univ. Press.

Wright, R. (1994). *The moral animal: The new science of evolutionary psychology.* New York: Pantheon.

Wylie, I. (1981). *The cuckoo.* London: Batsford.

Zach, R. (1979). Shell dropping: Decision making and optimal foraging in northwestern crows. *Behaviour, 68,* 106–117.

Zahavi, A. (1975). Mate selection—a selection for a handicap. *Journal of Theoretical Biology, 53,* 205–214.

Name Index

Subject Index

Credits

Photo Credits

This page constitutes an extension of the copyright page. We have made every effort to trace the ownership of all copyrighted material and to secure permission from copyright holders. In the event of any question arising as to the use of any material, we will be pleased to make the necessary corrections in future printings. Thanks are due to the following authors, publishers, and agents for permission to use the material indicated.

Chapter 1:   5 Figure 1.1 Corbis-Bettemann, **7** Figure 1.2 © Archive/Photo Researchers, **11** Figure 1.3 © Chris Huss/The Wildlife Collection, **12** Figure 1.4 © O. S. F./Animals Animals, **16** Figure 1.5a © George Holton/Photo Researchers, **16** Figure 1.5b © Oeter Weimann/Animals Animals, **20** Figure 1.7 © Mark Moffett/Minden Pictures

Chapter 2:   27 Figure 2.1 © Michael K. Nichols/National Geographic Image Collection, **33 (top left)** Figure 2.3a © Michael H. Francis/The Wildlife Collection, **(right)** Figure 2.3b © Martin Harvey/The Wildlife Collection, **(bottom left)** Figure 2.3c © HPH Photography/The Wildlife Collection, **36** Figure 2.4 © Stevan Stefanovic/Okapia/Photo Researchers, **39 (left)** Figure 2.5a © A. Rider/Photo Researchers, **(right)** Figure 2.5b © Charles Melton/The Wildlife Collection

Chapter 3:   50 (top left) Figure 3.1a © G. C. Kelley/Photo Researchers, **(top right)** Figure 3.1b © Martin Harvey/The Wildlife Collection, **(middle left)** Figure 3.1c © M. P. Kahl/Photo Researchers, **(middle right)** Figure 3.1d © Dean Lee/The Wildlife Collection, **(middle bottom left)** Figure 3.1e © Lynnwood M. Chase/Photo Researchers, **(middle bottom right)** Figure 3.1f © Tom McHugh/Photo Researchers, **(bottom**

left) Figure 3.1g © Maslowski/Photo Researchers, **(bottom right)** Figure 3.1h © Mitsuaki Iwago/Minden Pictures, **52** Figure 3.2a © J. H. Robinson/Photo Researchers, **54 (top left)** Figure 3.3a © Heather Angel, **(top right)** Figure 3.3b © Tim Davis/Photo Researchers, **(bottom left)** Figure 3.3c © David Cavagnaro, **(bottom right)** Figure 3.3d © T. De Roi/O. S. F./Animals Animals, **57** Figure 3.4 © A. W. Ambler/Photo Researchers, **62** Figure 3.5 © Richard Herrmann/The Wildlife Collection, **64** Figure 3.6 © Robert Maier/Animals Animals

Chapter 4:   77 (left) Figure 4.2a © Tom Vezo/The Wildlife Collection, **77 (right)** Figure 4.2b © Margot Conte/Animals Animals, **83 (left)** Figure 4.5a © Ralph A. Reinhold/ Animals Animals, **83 (right)** Figure 4.5b © Gerard Lacz/Peter Arnold, Inc.

Chapter 5:   92 Figure 5.1 © Johnny Johnson/Animals Animals **96** Figure 5.4 Courtesy of Animal Behavior Enterprises, Inc., **98** Figure 5.5 Superstock, **100** Figure 5.5 © W. V. Crich/Photo Researchers

Chapter 6:   113 Figure 6.1a © Biophoto Associates/Photo Researchers **115** Figure 6.2 © Michael Francis/The Wildlife Collection, **116**

391

Illustration Credits

TO THE OWNER OF THIS BOOK:

I hope that you have found *Introduction to Animal Behavior* useful. So that this book can be improved in a future edition, would you take the time to complete this sheet and return it? Thank you.

School and address: _____

Department: _____

Instructor's name: _____

1. What I like most about this book is: _____

_____

_____

2. What I like least about this book is: _____

_____

_____

3. My general reaction to this book is: _____

_____

4. The name of the course in which I used this book is: _____

_____

5. Were all of the chapters of the book assigned for you to read? _____

   If not, which ones weren't? _____

6. In the space below, or on a separate sheet of paper, please write specific suggestions for improving this book and anything else you'd care to share about your experience in using the book.

_____

_____

_____

_____

Optional:

Your name: _____ Date: _____

May Brooks/Cole quote you, either in promotion for *Introduction to Animal Behavior* or in future publishing ventures?

Yes: _____ No: _____

Sincerely,

Roland J. Siiter